Green Finance for Sustainable Global Growth

Sang-Bing Tsai
University of Electronic Science and Technology of China Zhongshan Institute, China & Civil Aviation University of China, China & WUYI University, China

Chung-Hua Shen
Shih-Chien University, Taiwan

Hua Song
Renmin University of China, China

Baozhuang Niu
South China University of Technology, China

A volume in the Advances in Environmental Engineering and Green Technologies (AEEGT) Book Series

IGI Global
DISSEMINATOR OF KNOWLEDGE

Published in the United States of America by
IGI Global
Business Science Reference (an imprint of IGI Global)
701 E. Chocolate Avenue
Hershey PA, USA 17033
Tel: 717-533-8845
Fax: 717-533-8661
E-mail: cust@igi-global.com
Web site: http://www.igi-global.com

Library of Congress Cataloging-in-Publication Data

Library of Congress Cataloging-in-Publication Data

Names: Tsai, Sang-Bing, 1973- editor. | Shen, Chung-Hua, editor. | Song, Hua, 1969- editor. | Niu, Baozhuang, editor.
Title: Green finance for sustainable global growth / Sang-Bing Tsai, Chung-Hua Shen, Hua Song, and Baozhuang Niu, editors.
Description: Hershey PA : Business Science Reference, [2019] | Includes bibliographical references.
Identifiers: LCCN 2018037401| ISBN 9781522578086 (hardcover) | ISBN 9781522578093 (ebook)
Subjects: LCSH: Sustainable development. | Finance--Environmental aspects. | Economic development--Environmental aspects.
Classification: LCC HC79.E5 G68984 2019 | DDC 332--dc23 LC record available at https://lccn.loc.gov/2018037401

This book is published in the IGI Global book series Advances in Environmental Engineering and Green Technologies (AEEGT) (ISSN: 2326-9162; eISSN: 2326-9170)

British Cataloguing in Publication Data
A Cataloguing in Publication record for this book is available from the British Library.

All work contributed to this book is new, previously-unpublished material.
The views expressed in this book are those of the authors, but not necessarily of the publisher.

For electronic access to this publication, please contact: eresources@igi-global.com.

Advances in Environmental Engineering and Green Technologies (AEEGT) Book Series

ISSN:2326-9162
EISSN:2326-9170

Editor-in-Chief: Sang-Bing Tsai, University of Electronic Science and Technology of China Zhongshan Institute, China & Ming-Lang Tseng, Lunghwa University of Science and Technology, Taiwan & Yuchi Wang, University of Electronic Science and Technology of China Zhongshan Institute, China

MISSION

Growing awareness and an increased focus on environmental issues such as climate change, energy use, and loss of non-renewable resources have brought about a greater need for research that provides potential solutions to these problems. Research in environmental science and engineering continues to play a vital role in uncovering new opportunities for a "green" future.

The **Advances in Environmental Engineering and Green Technologies (AEEGT)** book series is a mouthpiece for research in all aspects of environmental science, earth science, and green initiatives. This series supports the ongoing research in this field through publishing books that discuss topics within environmental engineering or that deal with the interdisciplinary field of green technologies.

COVERAGE

- Industrial Waste Management and Minimization
- Pollution Management
- Electric Vehicles
- Biofilters and Biofiltration
- Sustainable Communities
- Green Transportation
- Alternative Power Sources
- Waste Management
- Air Quality
- Policies Involving Green Technologies and Environmental Engineering

IGI Global is currently accepting manuscripts for publication within this series. To submit a proposal for a volume in this series, please contact our Acquisition Editors at Acquisitions@igi-global.com or visit: http://www.igi-global.com/publish/.

The Advances in Environmental Engineering and Green Technologies (AEEGT) Book Series (ISSN 2326-9162) is published by IGI Global, 701 E. Chocolate Avenue, Hershey, PA 17033-1240, USA, www.igi-global.com. This series is composed of titles available for purchase individually; each title is edited to be contextually exclusive from any other title within the series. For pricing and ordering information please visit http://www.igi-global.com/book-series/advances-environmental-engineering-green-technologies/73679. Postmaster: Send all address changes to above address.

Titles in this Series

For a list of additional titles in this series, please visit:
https://www.igi-global.com/book-series/advances-environmental-engineering-green-technologies/73679

Handbook of Research on the Adverse Effects of Pesticide Pollution in Aquatic Ecosystems
Khursheed Ahmad Wani (ITM University Gwalior, India) and Mamta (Jiwaji University, India)
Engineering Science Reference • ©2019 • 538pp • H/C (ISBN: 9781522561118) • US $295.00

Harnessing Marine Macroalgae for Industrial Purposes in an Australian Context Emerging ...
Göran Roos (Economic Development Board of South Australia, Australia) Anthony Cheshire (Balance Carbon Pty Ltd, Australia) Sasi Nayar (South Australian Aquatic Sciences Centre, Australia) Steven M. Clarke (South Australian Research and Development Institute, Australia) and Wei Zhang (Flinders University, Australia)
Engineering Science Reference • ©2019 • 291pp • H/C (ISBN: 9781522555773) • US $195.00

Advanced Methodologies and Technologies in Engineering and Environmental Science
Mehdi Khosrow-Pour, D.B.A. (Information Resources Management Association, USA)
Engineering Science Reference • ©2019 • 506pp • H/C (ISBN: 9781522573593) • US $295.00

Transitioning Island Nations Into Sustainable Energy Hubs Emerging Research and ...
Catalina Spataru (UCL Energy Institute, UK)
Engineering Science Reference • ©2019 • 172pp • H/C (ISBN: 9781522560029) • US $135.00

Recent Challenges and Advances in Geotechnical Earthquake Engineering
T.G. Sitharam (Indian Institute of Science, India) and J. S. Vinod (University of Wollongong, Australia)
Engineering Science Reference • ©2019 • 315pp • H/C (ISBN: 9781522569480) • US $195.00

Agrifood Economics and Sustainable Development in Contemporary Society
Gabriel Popescu (Bucharest Academy of Economic Studies, Romania)
Engineering Science Reference • ©2019 • 401pp • H/C (ISBN: 9781522557395) • US $195.00

For an entire list of titles in this series, please visit:
https://www.igi-global.com/book-series/advances-environmental-engineering-green-technologies/73679

IGI Global
DISSEMINATOR OF KNOWLEDGE

701 East Chocolate Avenue, Hershey, PA 17033, USA
Tel: 717-533-8845 x100 • Fax: 717-533-8661
E-Mail: cust@igi-global.com • www.igi-global.com

Table of Contents

Preface xv

Acknowledgment xvii

Chapter 1
A General Introduction and Overview of Supply Chain Finance 1
Haoran Yue, South China University of Technology, China
Jingwen Xu, South China University of Technology, China
Jingmai Wang, South China University of Technology, China
Dilang Wu, South China University of Technology, China
Baozhuang Niu, South China University of Technology, China

Chapter 2
Is Supply Chain Finance the Solution to the Financing Conundrum? 30
Baozhuang Niu, South China University of Technology, China
Zihao Mu, South China University of Technology, China
Youchu Zeng, Procter & Gamble, China

Chapter 3
Analysis of Sustainable Development Path for Green Finance: A Case Study of China 62
Hsu Chao Feng, University of Electronic Science and Technology of China Zhongshan Institute, China
Lee Bi Ru, University of Electronic Science and Technology of China Zhongshan Institute, China

Chapter 4
An Empirical Study of Green Finance Research Through Bibliometrics 84
Feng Hu, Guangdong University of Technology, China
Haibo Wei, Guangdong Water and Power Survey and Design Institute, China

Chapter 5
Social Capital Accounting: The Social Capital Protocol and the United Nations' Sustainable Development Goals 107
John P. Wilson, University of Sheffield, UK
Sonal Choudhary, University of Sheffield, UK

Chapter 6
Analysis of Internet Financial Planning Based on the Development in China and America 147
Chi Chien Zhu, Foshan University, China
Wen Yang, Shenzhen University, China

Chapter 7
Internet Financial Regulation and Law Analysis of China 173
Chi Chien Zhu, Foshan University, China
Jiye Hu, China University of Political Science and Law, China

Chapter 8
Chinese Internet Finance Credit Investigation Issue and Legal Countermeasures 193
Cheng-Yong Liu, Beijing Institute of Technology – Zhuhai, China
Cheng Chen, National Taiwan University, Taiwan

Chapter 9
The Role of Banks in Renewable Energy Finance: An Analysis of Turkey 219
Meryem Filiz Baştürk, Uludag University, Turkey

Chapter 10
Green Finance for Sustainable Global Growth: Costs and Benefits of Green Buildings Compared With Conventional Buildings 244
Elizabeth Motunrayo Ojo-Fafore, University of Johannesburg, South Africa
Clinton Aigbavboa, University of Johannesburg, South Africa
Wellington Thwala, University of Johannesburg, South Africa
Pretty Remaru, University of Johannesburg, South Africa

Chapter 11
An Analysis of Green Taxation in Turkey for Sustainable Growth 270
Erdal Eroğlu, Çanakkale Onsekiz Mart University, Turkey

Chapter 12
Nonlinear Effect of Financial Efficiency and Financial Competition on Heterogeneous Firm R&D: A Study on the Perspective of Sustainable Finance 297
Min Xiao Du, Yingkou Institute of Technology, China
Yu Wang, Dalian University of Technology, China
Yang Gao, Dalian University of Technology, China
Bei Bei Chen, Dalian University of Technology, China
Sang-Bing Tsai, University of Electronic Science and Technology of China Zhongshan Institute, China & Civil Aviation University of China, China & WUYI University, China

Chapter 13
The Use of Carbon Finance for Struggling With Climate Change 321
Filiz Konuk, Sakarya University, Turkey

Compilation of References 348

About the Contributors 390

Index 395

Detailed Table of Contents

Preface xv

Acknowledgment xvii

Chapter 1
A General Introduction and Overview of Supply Chain Finance 1
Haoran Yue, South China University of Technology, China
Jingwen Xu, South China University of Technology, China
Jingmai Wang, South China University of Technology, China
Dilang Wu, South China University of Technology, China
Baozhuang Niu, South China University of Technology, China

Supply chain finance (SCF) is a new finance service mode surrounding the core enterprises in the supply chain. Different from the traditional finance service, SCF focuses on the trading process rather than the bank credit. Depending on the large trading data and process gathered by core enterprises, SCF is able to effectively integrate the flows of information, logistics, and funds, which transforms the numerous risks of many single enterprises into the controllable risks of the entire supply chain. Therefore, SCF is capable of providing comprehensive finance service regardless of companies' size with the minimum risk level, especially for the small and medium-sized enterprises which have difficulties in receiving finance service from traditional finance institutions. The emergence of SCF has established an accessible channel to help small and medium-sized enterprises obtain effective finance service. In this chapter, the authors introduce the definition, features, structures, and other basic information of SCF. The authors then examine the different types of SCF.

Chapter 2
Is Supply Chain Finance the Solution to the Financing Conundrum? 30
Baozhuang Niu, South China University of Technology, China
Zihao Mu, South China University of Technology, China
Youchu Zeng, Procter & Gamble, China

Small and medium-sized enterprises are the major driving forces to boost China's economic growth. However, the transformation and upgrading of small and medium-sized enterprises are always subject to the scale of operation and other factors, which result in severe impediment to obtain loans or other finance service from traditional commercial banks. As the State Council reports, small and medium-sized enterprises' finance troubles were highlighted at the State Council's executive meeting and suggested China should enrich the fundraising channels for small and medium-sized enterprises. Based on the unique finance service features, supply chain finance has the potential of satisfying the large finance demand to become an effective fundraising and other finance service channel for small and medium-sized enterprises. Thus, it is vital to explore the operation process of supply chain finance in a deeper level.

Chapter 3
Analysis of Sustainable Development Path for Green Finance: A Case Study of China....62
Hsu Chao Feng, University of Electronic Science and Technology of China Zhongshan Institute, China
Lee Bi Ru, University of Electronic Science and Technology of China Zhongshan Institute, China

The development of green finance is a global trend in the current era. At present, developing the green finance has been included as an important national development project by the Chinese government. With the rapid economic growth, the priorities or trade-offs between the economic development and the natural environment have also aroused different contradictions and problems. With the improvement of people's quality of life, they start to pay more attention to the pollution of the surrounding environment. Therefore, the government should properly intervene and propose effective measures, and green finance is an excellent tool to reconcile social economy and environmental protection and transform the physical investment, thus guiding the social resources towards the environmental protection industry and reaching an optimal interests allocation among the market, society, and government. Consequently, in the face of such a situation, it is necessary to propose a series of models and paths that suit the needs of the Chinese society and promote sustainable development.

Chapter 4
An Empirical Study of Green Finance Research Through Bibliometrics....84
Feng Hu, Guangdong University of Technology, China
Haibo Wei, Guangdong Water and Power Survey and Design Institute, China

Green finance issues have triggered the increasing research enthusiasm of researchers. With the rapid growing of publications related to green finance, it is difficult for readers to deeply understand the intellectual structure, research hotspots, and trends. In addition, the dynamic nature of a research front poses challenges for the scientists, research policymakers, and many others to keep up with the rapid advances of the state of the art in science. Therefore, the authors conducted a bibliometric analysis from the Web of Science over the period of 1998–2017. Co-word analysis and co-citation analysis are employed to explore institution distribution, journal co-citation analysis, author co-citation analysis, document co-citation analysis, and keyword co-word analysis, particularly in high frequency items, intellectual turning points, burst points, and emerging trends. The results can be useful for institutions and researchers worldwide to understand the panorama of green finance research, find the potential research gaps, and focus on the future research trends.

Chapter 5
Social Capital Accounting: The Social Capital Protocol and the United Nations' Sustainable Development Goals 107
John P. Wilson, University of Sheffield, UK
Sonal Choudhary, University of Sheffield, UK

Sustainability accounting has become a mainstream practice for a large majority of S&P500 companies, and this reflects global society's increasing interest and concern around sustainability issues. In particular, the United Nations published its "Transforming Our World: The 2030 Agenda for Sustainable Development," and 193 countries signed up to achieving the 17 Sustainable Development Goals (SDGs) and 169 associated targets. The UN also called upon companies to help this process across their supply chains and developed a natural capital protocol for assessing and valuing environmental areas and a social capital protocol (SCP) for assessing and valuing human and societal capital such as skills, knowledge, wellbeing, shared values, and institutions. This chapter systematically investigates each of the 12 steps of the social capital protocol and identifies a range of benefits and substantial challenges which companies will face if they wish to account for their social impact across the supply chain.

Chapter 6
Analysis of Internet Financial Planning Based on the Development in China and America 147
Chi Chien Zhu, Foshan University, China
Wen Yang, Shenzhen University, China

Based on an analysis of China residents' financial needs and the main risks of internet financial planning, taking internet financial planning as a breakthrough point, the chapter compares the current situation and development experience of internet finance between developed countries and China from Chinese investors' perspective to analyze the tendency of internet finance development in China. This chapter finds the scale of China residents' financial planning remains to be enlarged. It finds that the gradual improvement of the supervision, the survival of the fittest of financial platform, the development of robot-adviser, and other financial innovations show the optimistic outlook of internet financial planning in China. This study shows theoretical value and practical significance to analyze the future of internet financial planning model and financial product selection in China.

Chapter 7
Internet Financial Regulation and Law Analysis of China 173
Chi Chien Zhu, Foshan University, China
Jiye Hu, China University of Political Science and Law, China

In recent years, internet finance has developed rapidly in China; however, the inherent characteristics of the internet have magnified the high-risk nature of the financial industry. Consequently, this leads to the complication of risk types, the acceleration of risk propagation, and the increase of interconnection of risk system, and these issues pose a serious challenge to regulation. Including the improvement of internet finance laws and regulations, the establishment of a multi-level internet financial supervision system, and the increase of the internet financial security system, the most effective risk prevention measures can be supplemented by administrative means carried out to resolve the stock risk through the nationwide internet financial rectification. At present, the traditional financial business mode is mainly under the control of the current financial law. This kind of law is rarely related to internet finance. Even if it is involved slightly, it is due to the early formulation time and needs to be revised.

Chapter 8
Chinese Internet Finance Credit Investigation Issue and Legal Countermeasures 193
Cheng-Yong Liu, Beijing Institute of Technology – Zhuhai, China
Cheng Chen, National Taiwan University, Taiwan

In recent years there has been a phenomenon of "Thirst for Credit Investigation Information" within China's internet finance industry. To compensate for the new credit investigation demands that traditional measures of credit investigation lack, big data credit investigation has been widely recognized as a viable solution. Big data credit investigation however poses greater risks to the rights and interests of the information subject. In order to solve the existing problems associated with the data credit investigation industry, the author advocates that special laws and regulations be revised or formulated on the basis of balancing the rights and interests of the information subject with those of public interests. In the future, the combination of big data credit investigation system with blockchain technology may effectively solve the problems that are harmful to the rights and interests of the information subject, such as information-isolated island and information security.

Chapter 9
The Role of Banks in Renewable Energy Finance: An Analysis of Turkey 219
Meryem Filiz Baştürk, Uludag University, Turkey

In today's world, global warming and environmental problems resulting from fossil waste have directed economies' attention to renewable energy. Renewable energy has become quite important to developing countries, in particular those that depend on foreign energy sources and confront continuously increasing energy demand since they need renewable energy to be able to achieve their goal of sustainable growth and do this without destructing the environment and by reducing their foreign dependency. Higher costs of renewable energy investment when compared to traditional energy investment affect the investment made in this field, though. The fundamental problem in renewable energy investment is how to finance it as it is not economically rational to invest in sectors with high costs. This chapter explores the role of banks in financing renewable energy by focusing on Turkey.

Chapter 10
Green Finance for Sustainable Global Growth: Costs and Benefits of Green Buildings Compared With Conventional Buildings 244
Elizabeth Motunrayo Ojo-Fafore, University of Johannesburg, South Africa
Clinton Aigbavboa, University of Johannesburg, South Africa
Wellington Thwala, University of Johannesburg, South Africa
Pretty Remaru, University of Johannesburg, South Africa

Green buildings have become one of the most famous and fastest growing construction concepts. As the world is becoming environmentally viable, all investors and contractual workers will need to know the figures of green financing and if the dangers of contributing are justified regardless of the arrival sum. This chapter aims to compare green building and conventional building using the cost differences and economy impact to ascertain the benefits of green building over the conventional building of green building. Data was collected through questionnaire survey from 50 construction professionals. The result of this chapter shows that green buildings are more expensive than conventional buildings; however, the benefits accrue from green building makes green building cheaper in the long run.

Chapter 11
An Analysis of Green Taxation in Turkey for Sustainable Growth 270
Erdal Eroğlu, Çanakkale Onsekiz Mart University, Turkey

Ecological problems such as global warming, climate change, and loss of biodiversity are at the top of governments' agendas as negative externalities like fewer water sources, food and energy shortage, drought, desertification, and migration have recently been deeply felt by societies. Environmentally related taxes are one of the most important instruments of fiscal policy used to internalize "negative externalities" to prevent environmental pollution and to ensure sustainable growth. This type of tax represents the ideal principle that "the polluter pays." Most of the European and OECD countries today have revised their tax systems to stop environmental destruction and have begun to implement environmental taxation. The purpose of this chapter is to carry out an analysis of green taxation in Turkey for sustainable growth. In this regard, this study aims to analyze green taxation practices and regulations within the scope of a sustainable economy in Turkey and offer solutions by considering the practices in various countries with effective green taxation policies.

Chapter 12
Nonlinear Effect of Financial Efficiency and Financial Competition on Heterogeneous Firm R&D: A Study on the Perspective of Sustainable Finance 297
Min Xiao Du, Yingkou Institute of Technology, China
Yu Wang, Dalian University of Technology, China
Yang Gao, Dalian University of Technology, China
Bei Bei Chen, Dalian University of Technology, China
Sang-Bing Tsai, University of Electronic Science and Technology of China Zhongshan Institute, China & Civil Aviation University of China, China & WUYI University, China

Green finance focuses on the coherence and sustainability of finance. This chapter studies the influence of financial scale, financial efficiency, and financial competition on enterprise R&D investment, which includes the different side effects of financial quantity and quality, and to some extent reflects the coherence and sustainability of financial development. The authors use manufacturing company data, regional financial quantity, and quality indicators from 2005 to 2007. The results reveal that (1) less developed area enterprises, or low- and medium-technology enterprises, a large amount of financial quantity expansion cannot support the R&D activities of high innovation efficiency, and (2) financial efficiency and financial competition have a nonlinear effect on firm R&D. Low financial efficiency leads to a lack of efficient firm R&D financial development. The results of the chapter reveal a crucial approach to improve the effect of financial inefficiency on firm R&D by changing from merely expanding financial quantity to improving quality instead.

Chapter 13
The Use of Carbon Finance for Struggling With Climate Change 321
Filiz Konuk, Sakarya University, Turkey

The developments in science and technology have brought a lot of problems with them. The most important of these is climate change, which appears at the global level. The effect of climate change, which comes first as an environmental problem, cannot be ignored. Management, which has had serious income and economic losses because of weather conditions, has taken several precautions in order to reduce climate change risks. One of these is weather derivations. Weather derivations are a safety type that makes the determined payments if there are defined weather events. However, the most commonly used are weather option agreements, weather swap agreements, and weather future agreements. In the chapter, climate change and the weather derivations that are a means that managements use to avoid climate change risks will be explained.

Compilation of References 348

About the Contributors 390

Index 395

Preface

Green finance refers to the fundamental policies implemented by financial authorities that are oriented towards environmental protection. In green finance, the potential environmental effects of investment and financing decisions are considered. Potential returns, risks, and costs associated with the environment are acknowledged in daily financial businesses, and ecological protection and pollution treatments are stressed in financial operations. Such guidance of socioeconomic resources can promote the sustainable development of society.

Green finance encompasses two dimensions. One dimension refers to the approaches adopted by the financial industry to promote environmental, economic, and social sustainability, which involve guiding capital flow to the development of resource-saving technology and ecological protection industries. As a result, enterprises are motivated to emphasize environmental protection and promote green consumption behavior among consumers. The other dimension concerns the sustainability of the financial industry itself; in other words, the industry must maintain sustainability and prevent opportunistic behavior that focuses on achieving short-term benefits.

Unlike conventional finance, green finance compellingly emphasizes the environmental benefits for human society. Efficient environmental protection and resource use are considered target outcomes of green finance activities, which aim to reinforce a focus on maintaining ecological balance among all economic entities. Green finance requires coordinated development among financial activities, environmental protection, and ecological balance to achieve a sustainable economic society.

The target audiences of this book are professionals, researchers, students, and professors working in fields such as green finance, internet finance, and sustainable finance, and the topic is primarily the use of new theories, technologies, methods, and techniques.

This book contains the following 13 chapters:

Chapter 1: A General Introduction and Overview of Supply-Chain Finance
Chapter 2: Is Supply-Chain Finance the Solution to the Financing Conundrum?
Chapter 3: Analysis of a Sustainable Development Path for Green Finance – A Case Study of China
Chapter 4: An Empirical Study of Green-Finance Research Through Bibliometrics
Chapter 5: Social Capital Accounting: The Social Capital Protocol and the United Nations' Sustainable Development Goals
Chapter 6: Analysis of Internet Financial Planning Based on the Development in China and America
Chapter 7: Internet Financial Regulation and Law Analysis of China
Chapter 8: Chinese Internet Finance Credit Investigation Issue and Legal Countermeasures
Chapter 9: Role of Banks in Renewable-Energy Finance – Analysis of Turkey
Chapter 10: Green Finance for Sustainable Global Growth – Costs and Benefits of Green Buildings Compared With Conventional Buildings
Chapter 11: An Analysis of Green Taxation in Turkey for Sustainable Growth
Chapter 12: Nonlinear Effect of Financial Efficiency and Financial Competition on Heterogeneous Firm R&D – A Study on the Perspective of Sustainable Finance
Chapter 13: The Use of Carbon Finance in the Fight Against Climate Change

Acknowledgements are made to IGI Global for professional assistance in the publication of this book and the authors of all the chapters for their contributions.

Sang-Bing Tsai
University of Electronic Science and Technology of China Zhongshan Institute, China & Civil Aviation University of China, China & WUYI University, China
2018.10.22

Acknowledgment

We acknowledge IGI Global for their professional assistance in the publication of this book, as well as all the chapter authors for their contributions to this book. These editors were supported by University of Electronic Science and Technology of China Zhongshan Institute, China & Civil Aviation University of China, China & Environment and Sustainable Development Center of China Civil Aviation University, China & WUYI University, China & Capital University of Economics and Business, China & China Academy of Corporate Governance, Nankai University, China & Shih-Chien University, Taiwan & Nanjin Audit University, China & Renmin University of China, China & South China University of Technology, China.

Chapter 1
A General Introduction and Overview of Supply Chain Finance

Haoran Yue
South China University of Technology, China

Jingmai Wang
South China University of Technology, China

Jingwen Xu
South China University of Technology, China

Dilang Wu
South China University of Technology, China

Baozhuang Niu
South China University of Technology, China

ABSTRACT

Supply chain finance (SCF) is a new finance service mode surrounding the core enterprises in the supply chain. Different from the traditional finance service, SCF focuses on the trading process rather than the bank credit. Depending on the large trading data and process gathered by core enterprises, SCF is able to effectively integrate the flows of information, logistics, and funds, which transforms the numerous risks of many single enterprises into the controllable risks of the entire supply chain. Therefore, SCF is capable of providing comprehensive finance service regardless of companies' size with the minimum risk level, especially for the small and medium-sized enterprises which have difficulties in receiving finance service from traditional finance institutions. The emergence of SCF has established an accessible channel to help small and medium-sized enterprises obtain effective finance service. In this chapter, the authors introduce the definition, features, structures, and other basic information of SCF. The authors then examine the different types of SCF.

DOI: 10.4018/978-1-5225-7808-6.ch001

INTRODUCTION

In October 2017, the General Office of the State Council issued the *Guiding Opinions on Actively Promoting Innovation and Application of Supply Chains*, encouraging core enterprises to establish supply chain financial service platforms, develop online account receivable financing and other supply chain financial models, emphasizing SCF to serve the real economy. SCF relies on real estate industry and trading process to develop credit services for small and medium-sized enterprises (SMEs), which transforms asset mortgage control into trade operation monitoring. Since its naissance, SCF has become an important tool to promote the healthy development of China's real estate industry and eased the financing difficulties of the real economy.

According to the data from the National Bureau of Statistics, by the end of July 2018, the balance of account receivable of China's industrial enterprises was 13.9 trillion yuan, an increase of 11.5% compared to the same period in 2017. Meanwhile, the proportion of account receivable in current assets also increased to 25.2%. Correspondingly, in the first half of 2018, the increment of aggregate financing was 9.1 trillion yuan. Among them, RMB loans to the real economy accounted for 96.3% of the social financing scale in the same period, an increase of 22.5% year-on-year. According to another set of data, overdue payments continued to increase. The proportion of companies who experienced overdue payments over 120 days increased from 19% in 2016 to 26% in 2017, and those who experienced excessive long-term overdue payments (over 180 days) increased from 35% in 2016 to 47% in 2017. The large amount of account receivable that cannot be put into production operations have brought heavy pressure for the survival of SMEs.

In February 2018, China's first *Social Financing Cost Index* was released, showing that the average costs of China's social financing were 7.6% (not including various types of handling charge, etc.). While SMEs' financing costs were generally higher than 10%. Judging from the situation in China, SMEs are generally lack of self-owned funds (Chen and Hu, 2011), moreover, their business volume is far lower than the threshold of the securities market in China. To satisfy the daily business turnover, SMEs have to turn to commercial bank loans and other traditional financial services for raising funds. Nevertheless, traditional financial services are reluctant to lend because SMEs are usually lack of assets, guarantees and mortgages. The inherent contradictions between the asset and the fund side make it difficult for the SMEs to obtain finance service through traditional financial channels.

SMEs in the industrial chain not only face large quantities of account receivable that cannot be put into production and operation, but also encounter long-term difficulties in financing. Traditional financial services regard companies and businesses as isolated entities, resulting in inefficient and expensive financial services. Chen and Hu (2011) consider SCF as an innovative financing solution. In contrast to traditional financial services, SCF concentrates on the transaction process, which effectively integrates the flows of logistics, information, business and capital, the financial services is under a trust-based, limited-constrained partnership.

Based on industrial features, SCF focuses on the core supply chain parties or core data holders, providing comprehensive finance service for the whole supply chain relevant enterprises depending on trading process. The biggest features of SCF include: self-liquidating, achieving the value transferring of asymmetric time requirements, credits, effective risk control and balanced bargaining power. The self-liquidating of SCF refers to the fees (interest) and risks generated by financial service can be covered by future revenues from supply chain trade. SMEs do not have perfect credit data and lack standard mortgages, but they have stable cash flow in stable supply chain trade. Thus, to an appreciable extent, SCF relies on the use of loan which is called supply chain circulation guarantee to ensure the risk of SCF is controllable.

SCF thrives around the world in tackling financing difficulties for SMEs. The international banking giants have adopted a series of financial innovations and business operations. As Demica (2014) reported, the annual growth rate of international SCF reached 30-40 percent from 2011 to 2013, and the growth rate will not fall below 10 percent before 2020. 80% of large banks believe that SCF products are very important for the differentiated competition of commercial banking business. The world's 50 largest banks have chosen to provide companies with SCF services. In 2001, the National Development Bank of Mexico (Nafin) developed the Productivity Chain Plan: providing online and offline factoring services to small and medium-sized suppliers. This was a successful example of reverse factoring financing in the supply chain. In 2005, JP Morgan Chase acquired Vastera, a logistics company, to form a new logistics team in Asia to provide financial services for the supply chain and distribution chain. The action was considered as a marriage between physical and financial supply chain. Meanwhile, the Standard Chartered Bank set credit value to the relationship between suppliers and buyers with its own model, which provided SCF services to companies and their suppliers without traditional guarantees.

Banks in China have also taken corresponding measures. In 1999, Shenzhen Development Bank began to set foot in the cargo credit business. By 2005, it had successively signed strategic cooperation agreements with SINOTRANS, CMST and COSCO, which officially opened the prelude to China's SCF activities. In the same year, China Merchants Bank (CMB) declared SMEs as the focus of its business transformation. It used SCF as a breakthrough to change business processes and tried out at 9 branches. In 2006, Shanghai Pudong Development Bank (SPDB) launched the SCF Solution along with six sub-projects. In July 2014, Ping An Bank (PAB) officially launched Orange e with the positioning of building an integrated service platform for online supply chain. So far Ping An Bank has formed strategic partnerships with 12 enterprise groups including Haier, Dongfang Electronic Payment, Kingdee Software, etc, realizing the expansion of supply chain finance from line to surface. Recently, Industrial and Commercial Bank of China (ICBC) and six central enterprises such as COFCO, CRRC, China Power Construction and State Grid had established a central enterprise SCF alliance in September 2017. The "Chief Finance Officer", a business magazine in China, has stated in its 2012 China Supply Chain Financing Demand Report that more and more SMEs which had been unable to pass the rating auditing and obtain credit support in terms of their financial statements have now turned to the SCF approach (Liu et al., 2015). Almost all banks have carried out SCF business. The development prospects of SCF are broad for banking industry to innovate financial products and increase profit sources.

In addition to helping solve the financing problems of SMEs, there are three great significant factors in the development of SCF below.

The integrated management of logistics, information and capital flows requires the development of SCF. At present, many domestic companies are incapable of coordinating the flows of logistics, information, and capital, the operation of material and capital flow is inefficient. As a result, the companies fail to receive the goods after the payment of funds, or the funds are not recovered after the sales of goods. Wuttke et al., (2013b) argue that capital flow could be aligned with the product and information flows in the supply chain through SCF, ultimately improving capital flow management. SCF shows an advantage because its services (such as material bank or financing warehouse) not only provide integrated financial business for the entire supply chain, but also can be applied to achieve effective payment and collection solutions.

The development of SCF is the need of banks and other financial institutions to ease the pressure of competition. In recent years, the rapid growth of the capital market has led more large and high-quality companies to adopt low-cost means such as equity, bonds and asset securitization to obtain funds. Furthermore, financial disintermediation causes a decrease in the growth rate of commercial bank lending, the proportion of bank loans in total corporate financing also decreases. Consequently, banks suffer from the significantly negative impacts that interest spreads of deposit and loan. What's worse, the arrival of foreign banks brought fierce competition. By carrying out SCF services, banks are able to effectively supervise the operation of platform, realize the visible and controllable business processes, close the loop between capital and logistics operations, thus effectively prevent capital security through the margin account. In addition, it is also possible to monitor the security of circulating assets through 3rd Party Logistics (3PL) supervision.

The development of SCF is demanded by companies to make the most promising way of profit. In the international market, whether it is a large-scale manufacturing enterprise that is the core enterprise of the supply chain, a large-scale logistics enterprise that undertakes the overall logistics business of the supply chain, or a financial enterprise that charges the supply chain capital flow service, the similarity is they are all active participants in the SCF activities. In China, Alibaba and JD Finance have also taken advantage of their own e-commerce platforms to enter the SCF market earlier and cumulated high quality asset-end resources. SCF has become one of the most important revenue sources for super large companies.

This chapter first introduces traditional financial services and analyzes the problems existing in traditional financial services. Based on this, the author proposes SCF as a solution, and examine the different types of SCF.

BACKGROUND

Over the past few decades, more and more companies have realized the importance of supply chain management and recognized the distinctive competitive advantages that a well-managed supply chain can bring to the company. In academia, numerous articles have been published to examine the methods of managing supply chain. As the concept of supply chain management becomes more and more sophisticated, companies gradually become experts at managing the physical flow of their supply chain. The logistics efficiencies, the trade flows efficiencies and the information flow efficiency have been improved significantly. On the contrary, the cash flow, which was supposed to be the supporting process of the supply chain operation, has become the bottleneck that restricts the development of supply chain now. While the integration of material and information flows within the supply chain has been discussed and tested in practice, the flow of financial resources is increasingly taking center stage of attention (Hofmann, 2005). Supply Chain Finance (SCF) has played an increasingly important role in practices and attracted growing attention from academia and industry.

There are several reasons promoting the appearance and development of SCF.

1. The financing demand of small and medium-sized enterprises (SMEs). Small and medium-sized enterprises are important parts of the supply chain. However, many SMEs are trapped in financial shortage, their development and further influence the operation of supply chain are restricted. Until now, bank credit remains the main financing channel for SMEs. Due to SMEs' poor credit, incomplete financial regulation, weak risk resistance capacity and absence of collateral security, major banks are reluctant to lend to SME, as the cost is high but the profit is low. Therefore, a new financing mode is required to solve the mismatch between financial supply and demand, SCF is proven to be the best way to solve this problem.

2. Integrated management of logistic, information business and funds. At present, many domestic companies failed to effectively integrate the flows of logistics, information and capital, which make the supply chain operation poorly efficient. As a result, the companies are unable to receive the goods after payment of funds, or the funds are not recovered after the sales of goods. SCF services (such as material bank or financing warehouse) can not only provide integrated services for the entire supply chain, but also be applied to effective payments and collection solutions.
3. Banks and other financial institutions are in need of mitigating stress and transition. The development of SCF is the need of banks and other financial institutions to ease the pressure of competition. In recent years, the rapid growth of the capital market has led more large and high-quality companies to adopt low-cost means such as equity, bonds and asset securitization to obtain funds. Furthermore, financial disintermediation causes a decrease in the growth rate of commercial bank lending, the proportion of bank loans in total corporate financing also decreases. Consequently, banks suffer from the significantly negative impacts that interest spreads of deposit and loan. What's worse, the arrival of foreign banks brought fierce competition. By carrying out SCF services, banks are able to effectively supervise the operation of platform, realize the visible and controllable business processes, close the loop between capital and logistics operations, thus effectively prevent capital security through the margin account.

The financial flow almost participates in every link of the supply chain operations. Investigating the flow of financial side of supply chain helps understand the financing that provides financial supports to the supply chain operations, and gives the supply chain parties deeper comprehension about supply chain operations. As more and more researches focus on the topic of SCF, the research questions become more diverse, and several literature reviews on the themes of SCF have been published (Liu et al., 2015; Gelsomino et al., 2016; Xu et al., 2018; Bals, 2018). Specifically, Liu et al. (2015) conduct a systematic literature review of 151 Chinese SCF articles, providing valuable insights in similarities as well as differences between SCF programs and research in China compared to western economies. Using rigorous bibliometric and visualisation tools, Xu et al. (2018) identify four research clusters. Gelsomino et al. (2016) conduct a comprehensive work. They establish that there are two main streams of SCF research: the research that focuses on the supply chain perspective and the research that focuses on the finance perspective. The supply chain-oriented perspective focuses on the role of collaboration amongst supply chain members. This perspective extends the boundaries of SCF beyond simple financial solutions. It takes inventory, supply chain processes, and even collaborative solutions into consideration for fixed asset financing, such as pay-on-production schemes. While the finance-oriented perspective mainly highlights the financial aspects and considers the SCF approach as a set of financial solutions, which is often provided by financial institutions (Camerinelli, 2009).

From the supply chain-oriented perspective, Timme et al. (2000) are deemed to be one of the forerunners to propose the definition of SCF. They believe SCF is an approach aiming to improve the supply chain efficiency. It is meant to improve payment terms, reduce costs and accelerate cash flows. Collaborations between the financial side and the operating side require an encompassing approach. It should not be an isolated concept, instead, it is an aspect of a more integrated system or program to map the gaps between SCM operating performance and financial performance. Pfohl and Gomm (2009) point out that, in order to increase the value of all participating companies, SCF acts as the inter-company optimization of financing as well as the integration of financing processes with customers, suppliers, and service providers. Chen and Hu (2011) define SCF as an innovative financing solution that bridges the bank and capital-constrained firms in the supply chain, SCF creates value for supply chain with capital constraints by reducing the mismatch risk of supply and demand in the financial flow. Hofmann (2005) proposes a representative definition. He argues that, located at the intersection of logistics, supply chain management, collaboration, and finance, SCF is an approach for two or more organizations in a supply chain, including external service providers, to jointly create value through means of planning, steering, and controlling the flow of financial resources on an inter-organizational level. SCF aims to optimize financial flows at an inter-organizational level through solutions implemented by financial institutions or the core enterprises in the supply chain. Wuttke et al., (2013b) think the objective of SCF is to align financial flows with product and information flows within the supply chain, ultimately the improvement of cash-flow management. SCF can bring new opportunities for obtaining loans (especially for "weak" supply chain players), reduce working capital within the supply chain and lower debt costs through the cooperation of enterprises.

From the finance-oriented perspective, William Atkinson (2008) thinks that SCF can be seen as the combination of services and technology solutions, which connects supply side, demand side and the finance institution together. More and Basu (2013) define SCF as managing, planning, controlling all the transaction activities and processes related to the flow of cash among supply chain stakeholders in order to improve their working capital. Lamoureux and Evans (2011) regard SCF solutions as a combination of technology solutions and financial services that closely connected with global value chain anchors, suppliers, financial institutions and frequently, technology service providers. They are designed to improve the effectiveness of financial supply chains by preventing detrimental cost shifting and by improving the visibility, availability, delivery, and cost of cash for all global value chain participants.

Several papers take surveys about the development of SCF in market and provide some successful existing SCF initiatives (Templar et al., 212; Wuttke et al., 2013; Caniato et al., 2016; Li and Chen 2018; Song et al., 2018). John Mathis and Cavinato (2010) put eyes on the global supply chain financial management and investigate the financial supply chain strategies of Zara and Toyota. They demonstrate that collaboration between the finance and supply chain functions is paramount for an effective financial supply chain management strategy. Templar et al. (2012) collect empirical evidence from different industries to analyze motivations, strategies, enablers, and inhibitors of different SCF applications. They also point out the current level of immaturity of SCF practices in business, and the existing gap between SCF theory and practice, which seem to be decreasing. Using the information derived from eight case studies based on 40 interviews, Wuttke et al. (2013a) identify patterns among these cases. Five testable propositions are derived explaining antecedents, contingencies, financial supply chain management (FSCM) practices, and performance effects of FSCM, thus providing a holistic framework of FSCM. Caniato et al. (2016) analyze 14 cases of the application of SCF solutions among Italian companies, and find that different factors lead to the adoption of different SCF solutions. Recently, Tunca and Zhu (2018) conduct a detailed introduction about the supplier finance intermediation service of china's biggest B2B retailer JD. To explore the role of SCF in third-party logistics, Li and Chen (2018) conduct interviews with five Chinese TPL firms chosen as representatives of diverse TPL firm types. They find that the roles of SCF vary in firms with different orientations.

There are several kinds of methods that researchers adopt to investigate SCF. The first stream focuses on the firms' operational decisions considering financial constraint. Lai et al. (2009) examines the impact of financial constraints and investigates the supply chain efficiency under preorder mode, consignment mode or the combination two mode. Assuming the retailer is the Stackelberg leader and has full bargaining power, they show that in the presence of financial constraint, the supplier will sell part of the inventory to the retailer through preorder, which shares the inventory risk in the supply chain, they find the combination mode is the most efficient mode for the supply chain. Tang et al. (2018) build a model consisting of three parties (manufacturer, supplier with finance constraint and bank) to investigate the impact of financing shame on parties' performance. They find that if the supplier is severely financially constrained, the manufacturer's information advantage makes buyer direct financing (BDF) the preferred financing scheme when contracting with an efficient supplier. Considering contract choice, Kouvelis and Zhao (2016) examine the coordination of a capital-constrained supply chain under three kinds of contracts (e.g., revenue-sharing, buyback, and quantity discount) with bankruptcy costs.

The second stream focuses on channel coordination under SCF. In this respect, the solution that most commonly addressed is trade credit. Extant literature extensively analyzing the benefit of trade credit. Schwartz (1974) argue that trade credit may substitute for access to traditional capital markets, allowing suppliers to share their low-cost financing with their buyers who are more financially constrained. Other advantages of trade credit include mitigating buyers' opportunistic behavior (Burkart and Ellingsen 2004, Chod 2016). Jing and Seidmann (2014) also proposed that trade credit is more effective than bank credit in mitigating double marginalization when production costs are relatively low. Peura et al. (2017) shows that when the firms are financially constrained, trade credit softens horizontal price competition. There are also some researches discussing the firm's operational decisions under trade credit. Recently, Li et al. (2018) conduct a game-theoretic framework to model the suppliers credit term decision. Their results show that either a short or a long credit term can be sub-optimal for the supplier in profitability. Several studies have analyzed optimal inventory policies with the presence of trade credit. Gupta and Wang (2009) present a discrete time model of the retailer's operations with random demand. They show that the base-stock inventory control policy continues to be optimal strategy no matter what the value of credit terms are. Luo and Shang (2013) characterize a firm's inventory policy under payment default. Most recently, Giri and Sharma (2017) develop an integrated inventory model with a partial delay in payments for both the supplier and retailer, albeit without deterioration and shortages. Tiwari et al (2018) conduct an inventory model for deteriorating items under a two-level partial trade credit.

The third stream focuses on risk analysis and management under SCF. Adopting results from option pricing theory, Birge (2000) shows that the financial risk can be incorporated into planning models by adjusting capacity and resource levels. Xu and Birge (2005) demonstrate that facing the bankruptcy risk due to the demand uncertainty, a newsvendor-like firm will reduce inventory investment under capital constraint. Babich et al. (2007) examine how the correlation between competing suppliers' disruption risks influences their pricing decisions. Incorporating a supplier with bankruptcy risk, Babich (2010) uses a dynamic, stochastic, periodic-review model to examine the manufacturer's joint capacity reservation and financial subsidy decisions to minimize risk level. Recently, Moretto et al (2018) investigate whether financial and vendor ratings can be integrated into a supply chain credit rating model that jointly considers financial indicators of the supplier and its operational evaluation provided by buyers. They also show the benefits and challenges of such a model for all the stakeholders involved.

MAIN FOCUS OF THE CHAPTER

The main focus of proposing this chapter is to give an outline introduction about SCF, hoping to help the SMEs aware of the new fund raising channel when they have trouble in acquiring traditional financing service. The authors first introduce the definition of SCF. Next, the main feature and structure of SCF are presented. In the last, three kinds of financing products are recommended.

1. Definition

SCF is based on industrial features, concentrating on the core supply chain parties or core data holders, the objective is to provide comprehensive finance service for the whole supply chain relevant enterprises depending on trading process. SCF achieves the value transferring of asymmetric time requirements, credits, risk control abilities and bargaining powers. The biggest feature of SCF is self-liquidating.

2. Features of SCF

There are four main features of SCF: Self-liquidating repayment, closure of operation, risk control and specific use of credit extension. Specifically, self-liquidating repayment means, the sales revenue is used to pay the loan first, the design of product is based on credit extension's asset supporting, such as factoring.

Closure of operation means full control of the flows of funds, logistics and other factors in the enterprise's operation. Risk control requires with monitoring the whole operation process after lending of bank. Specific use of credit extension means that after lending, every account of the enterprise must correspond to the specified trading background, besides, the amount, time and trading object must be matched.

3. The Structure of SCF System

Because of the sophisticated involvement of interest parties, SCF becomes a closed financial ecosystem with clear boundaries. The authors character the structure of SCF system in the following figure. The SCF system can be divided into three parts: The participant, the environment and the SCF product. The participants in SCF system include the enterprises who need financial service or support, the banks who provide lending service, the supportive entities such as 3PL that help the bank monitor the logistics of lenders' logistics and the core enterprises who trade with the financially constrained enterprises (Liu et al., 2015). The SCF environment include the technology and the institution that support or supervise the operation of SCF system.

Figure 1. The structure of SCF system

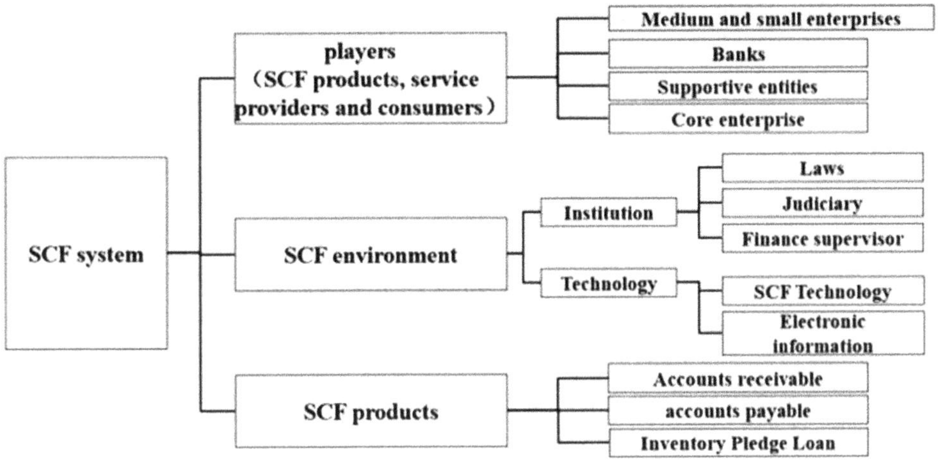

4. SCF Products

The circulating fund of a SME in the supply chain is mainly occupied by account receivable, advance payment and inventory (Song, 2015). Taking the risk control and solutions into consideration, the financing institutions divide the SCF products into account receivable financing, advance payment financing and inventory financing in accordance with the assurance measures. The following part will offer a detailed introduction about these three financing products.

4.1 Account Receivable Financing

Account receivable financing is a type of asset-financing arrangement in which a company uses its receivables, i.e., outstanding invoices or money owed by customers, as collateral in a financing agreement. The company receives an amount that is equal to the reduced value of the receivables pledged. This type of financing helps the un-bankable companies free up capital that is stuck with unpaid debts and obtain business funding instantly. When a business leverages its account receivables to boost its cash flow, it doesn't have to worry about the repayment schedules. Instead of focusing on collecting bills, it only needs to pay attention on other core aspects of its business.

The factoring company focuses on the credit of the company's client, not their own credit. As long as the company that looking to sell their invoices are doing business with solid and creditworthy clients, account receivable financing is a feasible option. Startups, private businesses and other financially constrained companies benefit greatly from this way.

There are usually several means of account receivable financing: Factoring, reverse factoring, and pledging.

Factoring

Factoring is a type of supplier financing in which firms independently sell their reliable receipts (such as receivables) at a discount (interest with service fee) to a financier, the factor, and receive immediate cash (Klapper, 2006; Soufani, 2002; Xu et al., 2018). Although factoring provides operation funds financing, it is not equal to loan, because there is no debt repaying or debt increasing in balance sheet.

Taking the domestic factoring as an example. Domestic factoring refers to the receivables formed within the domestic buyer and domestic seller's trade. On this basis, banks provide receivables account management, financing and collection for the providers. Banks also take the risk of bad debts. Domestic factoring is a comprehensive financial service.

Although factoring presents a number of diverse advantages, it sometimes carries negative connotations. In particular, companies typically cost more when financing through factoring than through traditional lenders such as banks. Consequently, businesses who turn to factoring companies are sometimes perceived to have poor credit. Factoring companies take several elements into account when determining how much to offer a company in exchange for its account receivables. In most cases, account receivables owed by large companies or corporations are more valuable than invoices owed by small companies or individuals. Similarly, new invoices are more valuable than old invoices. Generally, the easier the factoring company feels a bill is to collect, the more valuable it is, and the harder a bill is to collect, the less it is worth. However, analysts in the industry claim these misgivings are not

Figure 2. The pattern of factoring

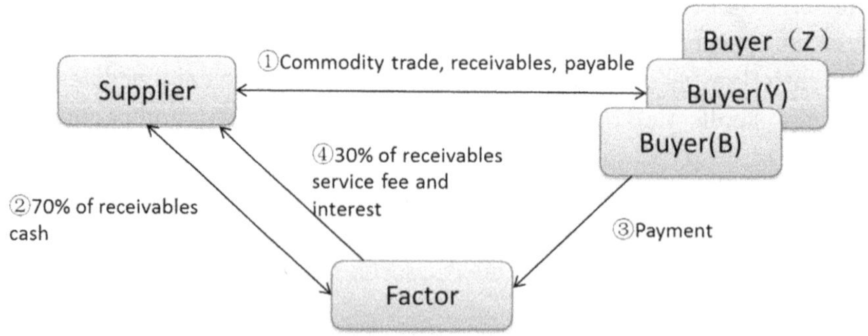

found in reality, and they state successful companies often use account receivables financing as needed.

Reverse Factoring

Reverse factoring is a financial arrangement in which a corporation facilitates early payment of its trade credit obligations to suppliers (van der Vliet et al., 2015; Tanrisever et al., 2012; Xu et al., 2018). A study initiated by the Bank of England concludes that reverse factoring offers significant opportunities to rejuvenate lending to SME firms (Association of Corporate Treasurers, 2010). Reverse factoring is offered for those buyers with high-credit receivables' object. Thus, the bank will only need to evaluate the risk of buyer's credit to deploy reverse factoring. The recycled flow of fund is direct from buyer.

In reverse factoring, supplier lacks credit but the buyer is highly credited. The risk of credit and loan comes from high-credit clients breaking the contract. With reverse factoring, creditor can achieve "Factoring without right of recourse".

Pledging

Pledging refers to the financing method through which an enterprise obtains funds from banks, financial credit companies and other financial institutions with the creditor's rights of account receivable as collateral. If the buyer refuses to pay or is incapable of paying, the financing institution shall have the right of recourse to demand repayment from the supplier after financing to the supplier.

After making detailed introduction about different models of account receivable financing, the authors are going to point out the associated costs that deserve to be paid attention to:

Figure 3. The pattern of reverse factoring

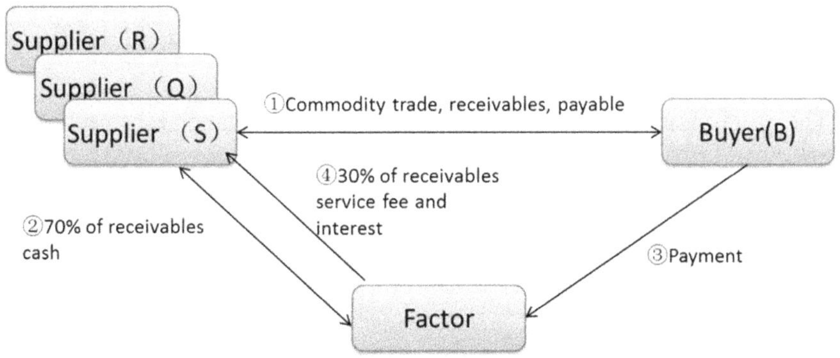

Figure 4. The pattern of pledging

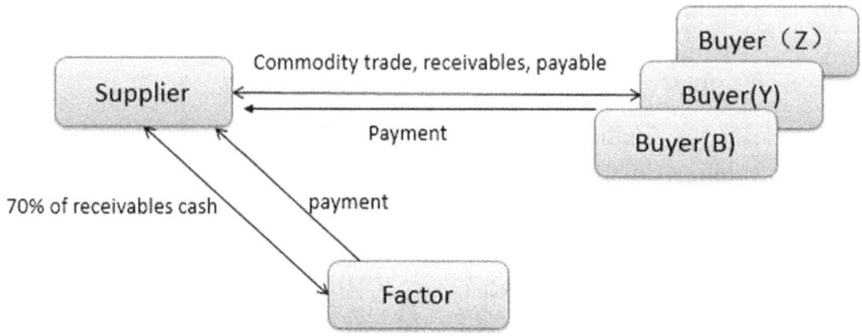

1. **Opportunity Cost:** Credit sale means that the enterprise cannot collect the payment in time, which can be used for other investment and gain profits, thus generating opportunity cost.
2. **Overhead Expenses:** Customer credit investigation fee, account record and storage fee, collection of information and other expenses constitute the overhead fee.
3. **Bad Debt Costs:** The biggest risk is the loss caused by bad debt that grows in proportion to its size.

Although financing by account receivables may have quite a few risks, however, it is still an indispensable financing tool for SMEs especially when a core party plays a dominant role in the supply chain. Here the authors have to emphasize the advantages account receivable financing possesses in a comprehensive manner:

- Enterprises can obtain funds without increasing their liabilities, and invest the funds to accelerate their development.
- It is a way of high flexibility because a large number of purchase invoices can be directly and automatically converted into funds when the turnover increases.
- With account receivables as collateral and good customer credit, the SMEs are able to obtain loans at relatively low interest rates.
- The professional credit audit services provided by financial institutions is less costly and more efficient.
- In order to obtain funds, the company has to improve their management ranging from finance, accounting to marketing and human resource, which motivates the company to strengthen management and make scientific decisions.

4.2 Advance Payment Financing

The core enterprise in a supply chain usually requests the downstream SMEs to pay for the commodity in advance, but the goods are not delivered on time, which results in cash shortage for downstream companies. Taking into account that the downstream companies actually have the ownership of the commodity, the financial institutions will be willing to lend to SMEs as long as the core party promises to obey the buy-back rule. Such a financing method is called advance payment financing. Advance payment financing can be understood as future inventory financing, the guarantee basis is the power of delivery under the advance payment, or after the power is realized, the on-road inventory or actual inventory. In the following part, the authors will introduce two modes of advance payment financing.

Receipt First, Money After Pledge

In reality, the inventory level of hot sale products is usually low, so the fund demand of an enterprise is aggregating in the field of advance payment.

For clients, the period of pledge covers the manufacturing arrangement and on-road time, and the goods can be transferred into inventory financing after delivery. This financing mode has more impacts on mitigating the stress of fund demand than inventory financing. Secondly, client can acquire discount on large procurement under the support from banks, the probability of locking the procurement price also exists.

For banks, they can use the extension of trade chain to exploit the business resources of upstream. Besides, seller's buy-back clause makes it easy to control risk when the client breaks the contract.

Figure 5. The pattern of receipt first, money after pledge

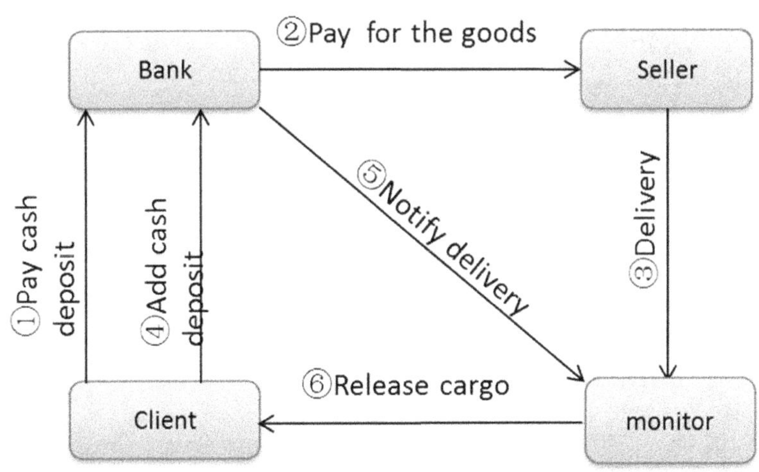

However, there are some risks such as the on-road inventory risk. Moreover, the company should focus more on investigating the upstream capacity of delivery, refund, contract and the transfer process after delivery.

Confirming Storage Pledge

This kind of advance payment financing is suitable for the following situations. First, client is in need of large procurement discount and one-off payment, but the supplier is unable to achieve one-off delivery. Second, the client pays in the slack season to provide the circulating fund that upstream needs, then acquires a discount price in return. Then client picks up goods in busy season in batches. Third, both client and upstream supplier are in geographically different places with banks, the banks lack effective supervision on on-road logistics and after delivery process.

For client, it gets the discount price. "Pay in slack season, sell in busy season" is good for locking price. Besides, goods is directly managed by upstream, then the supervision cost is saved. For seller, it can acquire large advance payment to mitigate the stress of circulating funds, locking in future sales and decreasing the uncertainty.

For banks, combining the two variables (logistics supervision and sellers) simplifies the difficulty of risk control. Banks introduce the refund responsibility of lacking delivery to solve the problem of collateral realization. Besides, it is beneficial for banks to exploit the abundant upstream resources.

From the above figure, one can see that under the advance payment financing, the downstream financing enterprises need to offer deposit to banks and the core party provides guarantee for them, thus the fund stress can be relieved by monitoring

Figure 6. The pattern of confirming storage pledge

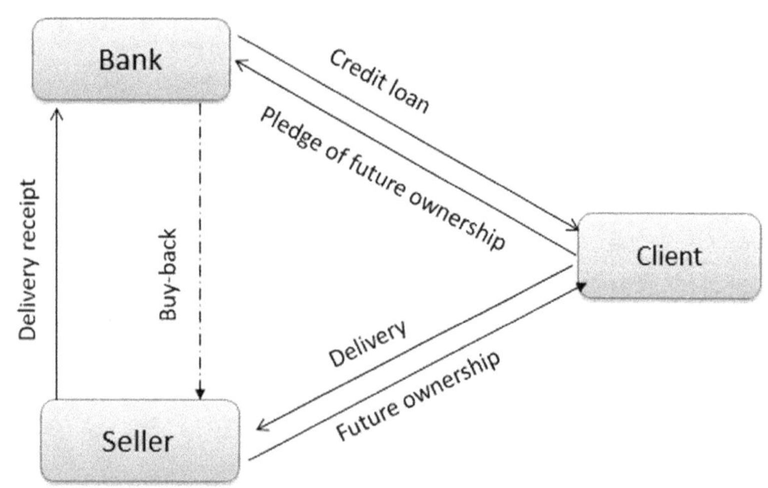

the goods pick-up in batches. At the same time, distributors can obtain preferential price when purchase in batches. Advance payment financing is an efficient tool for the SMEs to relieve capital shortage when they serve for the core party in the supply chain.

4.3 Inventory Financing

When a company needs to finance, it is common that the company has no account receivables or credit guarantee by other parties in the supply chain but only the inventory. In this case, inventory financing is a good choice for those companies in fund shortage. Inventory financing is a kind of financing mode that the company can take inventory as pledge and obtain funds from financial institutions after the inventory is evaluated and assessed by professional 3PL (Hofmann, E. 2009; Caniato et al,., 2016; Song et al., 2016). Three patterns of inventory financing will be elucidated in the following passage.

Static Pledge and Credit

Static pledge is suitable for the situation in which the inventory is the only proper collateral. The client's mode is purchasing in bulks, selling in times. Relatively, this financing mode has strict standards on clients, which is proper for trade-type clients.

For client, it can vitalize the funds which is overstock on inventory and expand the scale of operation. For bank, the cash ability of inventory collateral is relatively strong, as well as the derivative effect. Inventory financing only permits to ransom the products with cash deposit instead of trading goods for goods.

Figure 7. The pattern of static pledge and credit

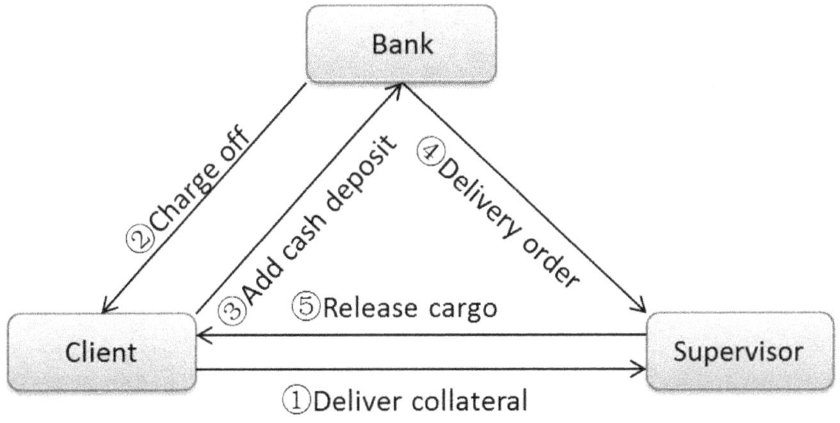

In this kind of inventory financing way, there are some key points needed to pay attention to, such as the property right and the price fluctuation of collateral. Additionally, the market size and the mobility of collateral are also of great importance.

Dynamic Pledge and Credit

Dynamic pledge and credit is suitable for stable inventory or single kind of product, whose value is easy to evaluate. Besides, it is suitable for frequent turnover which is difficult to use static pledge. It is proper for manufacturing clients.

For client, it can trade products for products, so the pledge only influences the operation slightly. Especially for the stable inventory, it is beneficial to vitalize the inventory under rational conditions. For bank, the cash deposit in dynamic pledge is less than static pledge, thus the cost of operation becomes less as well.

Those key points the authors pointed out in static pledge also deserve to be emphasized in dynamic pledge. Furthermore, it is imperative to prevent the mixture of dead stock when trading and adjusting the minimum inventory line according to price fluctuation.

Standard Warehouse Receipt Pledge

Standard warehouse refers to self-owned or third-party-owned standard warehouse as collateral. Standard warehouse receipt is a physical delivery certificate issued by the designated delivery warehouse of the futures exchange in accordance with the procedures prescribed by the exchange.

Figure 8. The pattern of dynamic pledge and credit

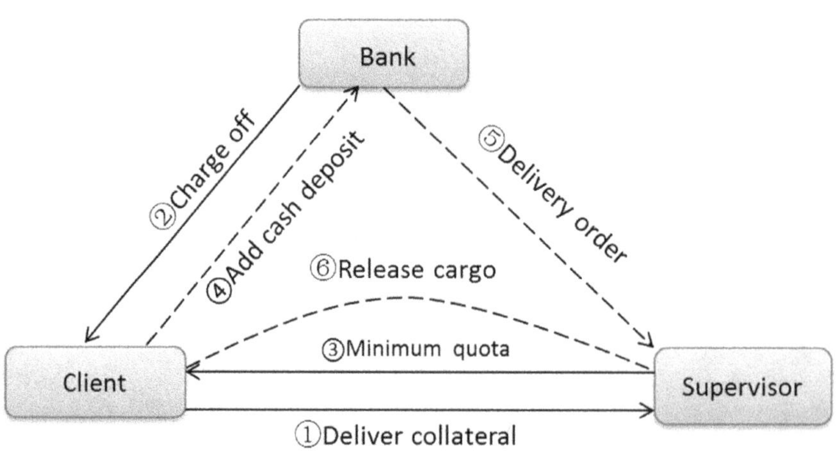

Standard warehouse receipt pledge is suitable for the clients who purchase or sell through futures exchange market, or hedge to avoid risks through futures exchange market.

On the one hand, for client, standard warehouse receipt has simple procedure and lower costs. On the other hands, for bank, both the costs and risks are low due to the high mobility of standard warehouse receipt. It is beneficial for banks to dispose the collaterals when the client breaks the contract.

Figure 9 depicts a typical pattern of standard warehouse receipt pledge. However, under the situation when the client needs to be provided with standard receipt to gain the pledge, banks will deliver the receipt to futures exchange, empowering it to participate in goods transaction. Then the money of transaction is used to repay the pledge first by the futures agents.

There are four risk key points here:

1. Prevent clients from using funds to operate opportunist activities.
2. Focus on different futures exchanges' procedure requirements.
3. Design effective dropping price compensation mechanism.
4. Know how to retrieve collaterals in advance.

In general, account receivable financing, advance payment financing and inventory financing presented above are three typical financing modes in SCF, which are applicable to financing activities under different conditions. However, even the three financing modes are major business modes in SCF, one can combine them to form a portfolio financing scheme aiming at diverse problems faced by core party, upstream suppliers or downstream sellers.

Figure 9. The pattern of standard warehouse receipt pledge

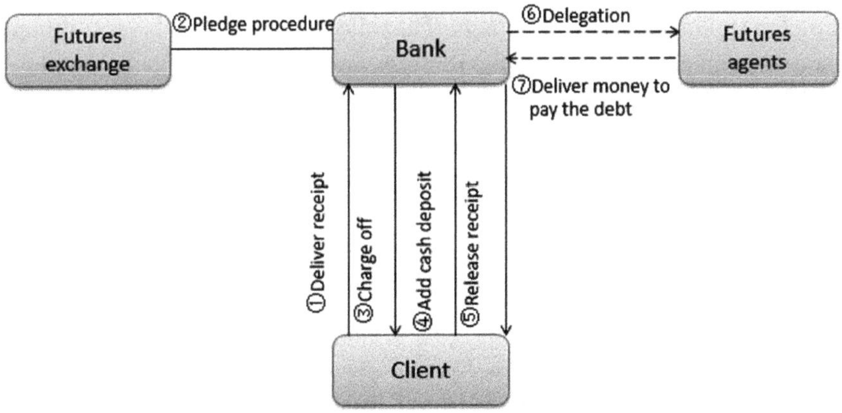

5. SCF Strategies for SMEs

In the former part, the authors have introduced three kinds of SCF product, including account receivable products, advance payment products, and inventory products. Depending on the structure of supply chain, different kinds of SMEs may adopt different SCF products. For example, if a firm is the supplier of the core enterprise, it may be suitable to adopt accounts receivable financing. If the firm is a supplier of the core enterprise, advance payment financing may be a better way. Except the relationship between the SMEs and the core enterprise, the authors think SMEs should take some measures to get better access to SCF and turn it into actual use.

First, establish good cooperation relationship with the core enterprise. SCF is highly dependent on the core enterprises, it takes the credit of the core enterprise as assurance to provide finance service. As a result, though SCF can help improve the operation of supply chain, it brings the core enterprise some risks and costs to participate the supply chain finance. Therefore, some enterprise may be unlikely to help the SMEs. To dispel the worry of the core enterprise, SMEs should built good cooperation relationship with the core enterprise, to make sure the fully use of SCF and improve the competitiveness of the supply chain.

Second, increase the investment in electronic equipment, and improve the informatization level. Supply chain finance and the Internet are increasingly integrated, the operation data has become an essential factor of credit rating and risk control for the SCF providers. Therefore, the digitization and informatization in firm's operation process can not only help enhance the management capacity of the firm, but also improve its financing ability.

FUTURE DEVELOPMENT

The future development of SCF is discussed in this section. In the long term, SCF will inevitably gain deeper development. The following three trends are summarized: First, the survival possibility of SMEs is increasingly dependent on the supply chain. For the bank in the interest rate market and financial disintermediation background, it's required to control risk by deep insight in the supply chain. Second, SCF covers traditional credit services, trade financing, and electronic financial instruments which has integrated features. Compared to traditional bank credit services, the risk control of SCF is relatively advanced and has advantages for adapting to the market environment. Third, the development of supply chain is rapid and irreversible, accordingly the demand for core enterprises to enhance the value of the entire supply chain will increase. This provides a broader space for the development of SCF.

First of all, industrial integration based on internet platform is intensified. Klapper (2006) finds that via the Internet, more commercial banks and SMEs are allowed to participate in the electronic platform, which reduces time and labor costs and improves security. Seeing from the trend of development of supply chain management in China, Liu et al. (2017) point out that the traditional supply chain is gradually transformed into the coordinated and integrated supply chain. The initial stage of SCF development is promoted by banks based on account receivable, movable property, and advance payment. The foundation for risk management is the upstream and downstream transaction of core enterprises, while banks serve as financing parties do not participate in supply chain operations. In the second stage, the promoters of SCF are no longer traditional commercial banks, but are core enterprises in the industry. They directly participate in the supply chain operation process on the basis of logistics, information, business and capital flows by cooperating with financial institutions to provide financing services. With the gradual maturation and development of supply chain services in the second stage, the basis for SCF will gradually evolve from a "chain" to a "net" type. The virtual electronic supply chain based on the Internet platform uses high-speed communications to allow all SMEs in the virtual industrial cluster to join the network platform at a low cost or even without cost. Any enterprise cooperates with other participants will make synchronous development and production, to realize efficient distribution and precise services to meet the decentralized and dynamic needs of customers. Therefore, the virtual electronic supply chain has achieved a high degree of integration of all stakeholders, serving as a binding platform for numerous sub-platforms and sub-ecologies.

Second, industry as an ecological begin to combine with the financial ecology. It means that industrial supply chain promotes the innovation and development of financial ecology, in turn, finance further promote the growth of the industrial supply chain ecology. SCF is an effective way to optimize corporate financing structure and cash flow based on the supply chain. On the one hand, taking the cash conversion cycle into consideration, Grosse-Ruyken et al. (2011) shows that efficient and effective SCF realizes the acceleration of industrial cash flow and shortened cash flow cycle. On the other hand, SCF can also achieve financial value-added and stable development. Therefore, to develop SCF, not only does it need innovation in the industry, but it also requires innovation in the finance. In a nutshell, cooperation between financial institutions of different sizes and the establishment of collaborative mechanisms is essential. At present, there are various types of financial institutions in China. Taking the banking system as an example. There are national commercial banks, provincial-level commercial banks, foreign-funded commercial banks, regional commercial banks, rural commercial banks, private financial institutions and internet banks which have different positions, channels, and advantages. If they can fully cooperate based on their respective advantages, the cash flow of the entire supply chain network is optimized, the cash flow is not only accelerated but also created.

Then, financial technology becomes the leading force in promoting SCF. The role of internet in the past was only an aid to the development and management of financial activities, but it matters now. Due to the diversity of the supply chain's main entities and the heterogeneity of activities, there is no standard, securely signed electronic bills and electronic warehouse receipts, which impedes the smooth management of business processes. Similarly, without a good cloud platform and cloud computing, the virtual electronics supply chain cannot be realized. In order to truly grasp the supply chain operation rules and effectively understand the behavior of each participating entity, it is necessary to establish and develop big data. For the uniqueness and authenticity of the match between capital and assets, it is conducive to use blockchain technology and internet of Things or other technology. This help SCF in achieving distributed accounting, fund management, and smart contracts, with the aid of these technology, the one-to-one correspondence relationship between capital and assets is connected. Obviously, without the support of financial technology, SCF will encounter a huge bottleneck.

Another core element of the long-term development of SCF is risk control. The essence of finance is risk valuation and credit. If these two points are ignored, a huge financial crisis will occur. Therefore, the warning and management of risks is at the top priority of SCF. In general, risk control needs to start from the following aspects: supply chain structure management, process management, and element management. Structure management refers to the ability to design and construct a supply chain operation and service system effectively and reasonably, so that the role of each main entity is clear. Therefore, the responsibilities and rights are also clearly defined. At the same time, SCF can close the loop between capital and logistics operations, realizing self-liquidating. Process management refers to the clear flow of the entire business and financial activities, realizing the vertical management. To achieve a risk-control structure, the ability to design and provide risk mitigation measures in collaboration with various financial institutions matters. Element management is the ability to obtain financial products and other business information data in a high efficient way. Only by the means of information-oriented construction can the supply chain build a credit system through reputational assets under the premise of comprehensive control of the creditworthiness of each entity.

In the end, collaborative specialization will become the theme of future SCF. The successful implementation of SCF requires the full communication and collaboration of various forms of organization in the ecosystem. Hofmann and Kotzab (2010) study how a collaborative approach to cash-to-cash management leads to optimal solutions. Along the same line of reasoning, by the analysis of the Motorola financial supply chain management strategy, Blackman et al. (2013) highlight how the introduction of a collaborative approach to managing the financial flows within the supply chain generates cost savings for all of the companies involved. Apart from upstream and downstream companies in the supply chain and related business participants, these entities also include three crucial types of organizations. Firstly, platform service providers, an entity undertakes to collect, aggregate, and integrate structured and other non-structured data that occur in supply chain operations. Second, risk managers, who is in charge of analyzing and customizing financial products based on information and data provided by platform service providers to serve specific products. Finally, the liquidity providers, the entity that provides liquidity, and also the ultimate risk bearer. These three types of organizations play different roles and jointly promote the development of SCF. Therefore, it is necessary for these three types of institutions to fully explore and develop their respective capabilities to maximize the differentiated services. The high specialization leads to positive synergy.

CONCLUSION

In this chapter, the authors introduce definition, features, structures and products of SCF. Unlike traditional financial services that focus on companies and businesses in isolation, SCF focuses on the transaction process, which has become a powerful tool to solve the financing difficulties of SMEs. For banks and other financial institutions, SCF is an important way to achieve differentiated competition and open the SME markets. By using high-value-added services to bind core enterprises and customer clusters, the efficiency of the entire supply chain is improved. In turn, core enterprises can also be viewed as funding providers to provide funds for supply chain members, especially SMEs, to meet the needs of industrial transformation and upgrading, realizing the value of their long-term accumulated industry expertise and resources through SCF.

The authors then examine the different types of SCF. The essence of SCF is to help companies activate liquid assets, namely, account receivable, advance payment and inventory. Therefore, products are usually divided into three categories: account receivable products, advance payment products, and inventory products. Account receivable products help upstream companies convert account receivable into cash or notes payable. Advance payment products help downstream companies expand single purchases, increase purchasing capacity, and convert cash assets that should have been paid into short-term loans or notes payable. Inventory products are more straightforward, using the company's stock as a guarantee, in exchange for more liquid cash assets. It is similar to the advance payment products since it involves the control of cargo rights and the management of logistics supervision companies.

In the end, the trends of SCF are also mentioned. In the future, an innovative SCF model that combines internet and financial product with the core of "transaction credit pledge" will be the mainstream. This is the best way to prompt finance serving the real economy in current stage. Under the new model, having acquired full-chain, multidimensional, and cross-validated historical transaction data, the banks can use financial technology such as big data, blockchain, and cloud computing to retrospective and assess credit data. By using it as pledged assets of SMEs, it's easier for the banks to execute credit rating and lending, so as to get rid of the rigid guarantees of core enterprises, and expand innovative supply chain financial services as well. Its core is the construction of transaction credit for SMEs. Unlike traditional corporate credit, transaction credits of SMEs are based on historical transaction data, which requires three-dimensional and multidimensional data covering all aspects of production, operations, sales, finance, taxation, customs, and lending. Since the transaction credit data segregation is scattered among the government, enterprises, and banks, lacking an integrated sharing mechanism or corresponding personnel makes the construction still lack top-level design and planning. Only by effectively solving the above problems and improving the credit construction of SMEs, can authorities break through the bottleneck of the current SCF model and achieve the leaping development.

ACKNOWLEDGMENT

The authors are grateful to the editors and the reviewers for their helpful comments. Baozhuang Niu is the corresponding author. This work was supported by NSFC Excellent Young Scientists Fund (No. 71822202); NSFC (No. 71571194); and Chang Jiang Scholars Program (Niu Baozhuang 2017).

REFERENCES

Association of Corporate Treasurers. (2010). *Supply chain finance: Report of the supply chain finance working group.* Technical Report, ACT.

Atkinson, W. (2008). Supply chain finance: The next big opportunity. *Supply Chain Management Review*, *12*(3), 57–60.

Babich, V. (2010). Independence of capacity ordering and financial subsidies to risky suppliers. *Manufacturing & Service Operations Management: M & SOM*, *12*(4), 583–607. doi:10.1287/msom.1090.0284

Bals, C. (2018). Toward a Supply Chain Finance (SCF) Ecosystem–Proposing a Framework and Agenda for Future Research. *Journal of Purchasing and Supply Management*. doi:10.1016/j.pursup.2018.07.005

Birge, J. R. (2000). Option methods for incorporating risk into linear capacity planning models. *Manufacturing & Service Operations Management: M & SOM*, *2*(1), 19–31. doi:10.1287/msom.2.1.19.23269

Blackman, I. D., Holland, C. P., & Westcott, T. (2013). Motorola's global financial supply chain strategy. *Supply Chain Management*, *18*(2), 132–147. doi:10.1108/13598541311318782

Burkart, M., & Ellingsen, T. (2004). In-kind finance: A theory of trade credit. *The American Economic Review*, *94*(3), 569–590. doi:10.1257/0002828041464579

Caniato, F., Gelsomino, L. M., Perego, A., & Ronchi, S. (2016). Does finance solve the supply chain financing problem? *Supply Chain Management*, *21*(5), 534–549. doi:10.1108/SCM-11-2015-0436

Chen, X., & Hu, C. (2011). The value of supply chain finance. In *Supply Chain Management-Applications and Simulations*. InTech. doi:10.5772/19208

Chod, J. (2016). Inventory, risk shifting, and trade credit. *Management Science*, *63*(10), 3207–3225. doi:10.1287/mnsc.2016.2515

D'Avanzo, R., Lewinski, H. V., & Wassenhove, L. N. V. (2003). The link between supply chain and financial performance. *Supply Chain Management Review*, *7*(6), 40–47.

Demica. (2014). *A study on the growth of supply chain finance, as evidenced by SCF dedicated job titles at top European bank*. Demica.

Forward-Looking Industry Research Institute. (2015). *Report of market prospective and investment strategy planning on China supply chain finance industry (2015-2020)*. Author.

Gelsomino, L. M., de Boer, R., Steeman, M., & Perego, A. (2018). An optimisation strategy for concurrent Supply Chain Finance schemes. *Journal of Purchasing and Supply Management*. doi:10.1016/j.pursup.2018.07.004

Gelsomino, L. M., Mangiaracina, R., Perego, A., & Tumino, A. (2016). Supply chain finance: A literature review. *International Journal of Physical Distribution & Logistics Management*, *46*(4), 348–366. doi:10.1108/IJPDLM-08-2014-0173

Giri, B. C., & Sharma, S. (2017). Optimising an integrated production–inventory system under cash discount and retailer partial trade credit policy. *International Journal of Systems Science: Operations & Logistics*, 1-20.

Grosse-Ruyken, P. T., Wagner, S. M., & Jonke, R. (2011). What is the right cash conversion cycle for your supply chain. *International Journal of Services and Operations Management*, *10*(1), 13–29. doi:10.1504/IJSOM.2011.041987

Gupta, D., & Wang, L. (2009). A stochastic inventory model with trade credit. *Manufacturing & Service Operations Management: M & SOM*, *11*(1), 4–18. doi:10.1287/msom.1070.0191

Hofmann, E. (2005). Supply chain finance: some conceptual insights. *Beiträge Zu Beschaffung Und Logistik*, 203-214.

Hofmann, E. (2009). Inventory financing in supply chains: A logistics service provider-approach. *International Journal of Physical Distribution & Logistics Management*, *39*(9), 716–740. doi:10.1108/09600030911008175

Hofmann, E., & Kotzab, H. (2010). A supply chain-oriented approach of working capital management. *Journal of Business Logistics*, *31*(2), 305–330. doi:10.1002/j.2158-1592.2010.tb00154.x

Jing, B., & Seidmann, A. (2014). Finance sourcing in a supply chain. *Decision Support Systems*, *58*(1), 15–20. doi:10.1016/j.dss.2013.01.013

Klapper, L. (2005). *The role of factoring for financing small and medium enterprises*. The World Bank. doi:10.1596/1813-9450-3593

Klapper, L. F. (2006). The role of factoring for financing small and medium enterprises. *Journal of Banking & Finance*, *30*(11), 3111–3130. doi:10.1016/j.jbankfin.2006.05.001

Kouvelis, P., & Zhao, W. (2016). Supply chain contract design under financial constraints and bankruptcy costs. *Management Science*, *62*(8), 2341–2357. doi:10.1287/mnsc.2015.2248

Lai, G., Debo, L. G., & Sycara, K. (2009). Sharing inventory risk in supply chain: The implication of financial constraint. *Omega*, *37*(4), 811–825. doi:10.1016/j.omega.2008.06.003

Lamoureux, J. F., & Evans, T. A. (2011). *Supply chain finance: a new means to support the competitiveness and resilience of global value chains*. Working Paper. No. 2179944. Social Science Research Network.

Lee, Y. W., & Stowe, J. D. (1993). Product risk, asymmetric information, and trade credit. *Journal of Financial and Quantitative Analysis*, *28*(2), 285–300. doi:10.2307/2331291

Li, H., Mai, L., Zhang, W., & Tian, X. (2018). Optimizing the Credit Term Decisions in Supply Chain Finance. *Journal of Purchasing and Supply Management*. doi:10.1016/j.pursup.2018.07.006

Li, S., & Chen, X. (2018). The role of supply chain finance in third-party logistics industry: a case study from China. *International Journal of Logistics Research and Applications*, 1-18.

Liu, W. H., Bai, E., Liu, L. W., & Wei, W. Y. (2017). A Framework of Sustainable Service Supply Chain Management: A Literature Review and Research Agenda. *Sustainability*, *9*(3), 421. doi:10.3390u9030421

Liu, X., Zhou, L., & Wu, Y. C. (2015). Supply chain finance in china: Business innovation and theory development. *Sustainability*, *7*(11), 14689–14709. doi:10.3390u71114689

Luo, W., & Shang, K. (2013). *Managing inventory for entrepreneurial firms with trade credit and payment defaults.* Working paper, IESE Business School.

More, D., & Basu, P. (2013). Challenges of supply chain finance: A detailed study and a hierarchical model based on the experiences of an Indian firm. *Business Process Management Journal*, *19*(4), 624–647. doi:10.1108/BPMJ-09-2012-0093

Moretto, A., Grassi, L., Caniato, F., Giorgino, M., & Ronchi, S. (2018). Supply chain finance: From traditional to supply chain credit rating. *Journal of Purchasing and Supply Management*. doi:10.1016/j.pursup.2018.06.004

Petersen, M. A., & Rajan, R. G. (1997). Trade credit: Theories and evidence. *Review of Financial Studies*, *10*(3), 661–691. doi:10.1093/rfs/10.3.661

Peura, H., Yang, S. A., & Lai, G. (2017). Trade credit in competition: A horizontal benefit. *Manufacturing & Service Operations Management: M & SOM*, *19*(2), 263–289. doi:10.1287/msom.2016.0608

Pfohl, H. C., & Gomm, M. (2009). Supply chain finance: optimizing financial flows in supply chains. *Logistics Research*, *1*(3-4), 149-161.

Song, H. (2015). *Supply chain finance*. China Renmin University Press. (in Chinese)

Song, H., Yu, K., & Lu, Q. (2018). Financial service providers and banks' role in helping SMEs to access finance. *International Journal of Physical Distribution & Logistics Management*, *48*(1), 69–92. doi:10.1108/IJPDLM-11-2016-0315

Song, Z., Huang, H., Ran, W., & Liu, S. (2016). A Study on the Pricing Model for 3PL of Inventory Financing. *Discrete Dynamics in Nature and Society*.

Soufani, K. (2002). On the determinants of factoring as a financing choice: Evidence from the UK. *Journal of Economics and Business*, *54*(2), 239–252. doi:10.1016/S0148-6195(01)00064-9

Tang, C. S., Yang, S. A., & Wu, J. (2018). Sourcing from suppliers with financial constraints and performance risk. *Manufacturing & Service Operations Management: M & SOM*, *20*(1), 70–84. doi:10.1287/msom.2017.0638

Tanrisever, F., Cetinay, H., Reindorp, M., & Fransoo, J. (2012). Value of reverse factoring in multi-stage supply chains. *SSRN*, *2183991*, 28.

Templar, S., Cosse, M., Camerinelli, E., & Findlay, C. (2012). *An investigation into current supply chain finance practices in business: a case study approach.* Unpublished paper.

Timme, S. G., & Williams-Timme, C. (2000). The financial-SCM Connection. *Supply Chain Management Review*, *4*(2), 33–40.

Tiwari, S., Cárdenas-Barrón, L. E., Goh, M., & Shaikh, A. A. (2018). Joint pricing and inventory model for deteriorating items with expiration dates and partial backlogging under two-level partial trade credits in supply chain. *International Journal of Production Economics*, *200*, 16–36. doi:10.1016/j.ijpe.2018.03.006

Tunca, T. I., & Zhu, W. (2017). Buyer intermediation in supplier finance. *Management Science*, mnsc.2017.2863. doi:10.1287/mnsc.2017.2863

Van der Vliet, K., Reindorp, M. J., & Fransoo, J. C. (2015). The price of reverse factoring: Financing rates vs. payment delays. *European Journal of Operational Research*, *242*(3), 842–853. doi:10.1016/j.ejor.2014.10.052

Wuttke, D. A., Blome, C., Foerstl, K., & Henke, M. (2013). Managing the innovation adoption of supply chain finance—Empirical evidence from six European case studies. *Journal of Business Logistics*, *34*(2), 148–166. doi:10.1111/jbl.12016

Wuttke, D. A., Blome, C., & Henke, M. (2013). Focusing the financial flow of supply chains: An empirical investigation of financial supply chain management. *International Journal of Production Economics*, *145*(2), 773–789. doi:10.1016/j.ijpe.2013.05.031

Xu, X., & Birge, J. R. (2004). *Joint production and financing decisions: Modeling and analysis*. Ssrn Electronic Journal.

Xu, X., Chen, X., Jia, F., Brown, S., Gong, Y., & Xu, Y. (2018). Supply chain finance: A systematic literature review and bibliometric analysis. *International Journal of Production Economics*, *204*, 160–173. doi:10.1016/j.ijpe.2018.08.003

Yao, Y., & Dresner, M. (2008). The inventory value of information sharing, continuous replenishment, and vendor-managed inventory. *Transportation Research Part E, Logistics and Transportation Review*, *44*(3), 361–378. doi:10.1016/j.tre.2006.12.001

KEY TERMS AND DEFINITIONS

Account Receivables Financing: A type of asset-financing arrangement in which a company uses its receivables as collateral in a financing agreement.

Advance Payment Financing: A financing mode in which the buyer takes the prepaid account of his accrued income as the security deposit and borrows money from the bank and other financial capitals.

Core Enterprises: The enterprises that master the key technology, the most important part of the supply chain.

Factoring: A type of supplier financing in which firms independently sell their reliable receipts at a discount to a financier and receive immediate cash.

Inventory Financing: A kind of financing mode that the company can take inventory as pledge and obtain funds from financial institutions after the inventory is evaluated and assessed by professional 3PL.

Supply Chain Finance: A financing model that is based on industrial features, concentrating on the core supply chain parties or core data holders.

Trade Credit: A deferred payment terms offered by a seller to a buyer to encourage sales, a crucial part of supply chain finance.

Chapter 2
Is Supply Chain Finance the Solution to the Financing Conundrum?

Baozhuang Niu
South China University of Technology, China

Zihao Mu
South China University of Technology, China

Youchu Zeng
Procter & Gamble, China

ABSTRACT

Small and medium-sized enterprises are the major driving forces to boost China's economic growth. However, the transformation and upgrading of small and medium-sized enterprises are always subject to the scale of operation and other factors, which result in severe impediment to obtain loans or other finance service from traditional commercial banks. As the State Council reports, small and medium-sized enterprises' finance troubles were highlighted at the State Council's executive meeting and suggested China should enrich the fundraising channels for small and medium-sized enterprises. Based on the unique finance service features, supply chain finance has the potential of satisfying the large finance demand to become an effective fundraising and other finance service channel for small and medium-sized enterprises. Thus, it is vital to explore the operation process of supply chain finance in a deeper level.

DOI: 10.4018/978-1-5225-7808-6.ch002

INTRODUCTION

Due to the constraints of small scale of operation, lacking in collateral and other reasons, the small and medium-sized enterprises often have difficulties in obtaining financing from traditional commercial banks. Compared to the traditional financial service, supply chain finance is effective in settling this conundrum for small and medium-sized enterprises, instead of focusing on a single enterprise's operation scale or fixed assets, supply chain finance emphasizes on the operation process and the status of supply chain core enterprises. Liu et al. (2015) indicate that the scale of financing provided by supply chain finance has reached 5.75 billion yuan with 20% annual growth rate in 2011. The emergence of online retail giants further facilitates the combination of supply chain finance and e-commerce platforms, many online retail giants have entered the supply chain finance market and made substantial success. Taking online retail giant JD.COM as an example, JD Finance successfully raised 6.65 billion yuan from investors in January 2016. Then JD.COM continued to speed up the deployment of finance services: In June 2017, JD.COM decided to push for better development of finance business by separating JD Finance from the company. Different from the traditional commercial banks, the large trading data accumulation enables the online retail giants to occupy the core position in supply chain, which is beneficial to eliminate the information asymmetry, evaluate the risks and increase the finance service efficiency. In this chapter, the authors take the Chinese online retail giant JD.COM as an example to investigate the differences between supply chain finance and traditional finance service, the authors then use a quantitative method to discuss the optimal interest rates under different situations for the online retail enterprises which are also the finance service providers in the supply chain.

As China's economy transformed into the "new normal" phase, the small and medium-sized enterprises are also in need of transformation and upgrade. Premier Li proposed the "Made in China 2025" plan in 2015, which indicates China's determination in promoting the industry upgrade in manufacturing. However, when facing the opportunity of upgrade, financing difficulty has become a longstanding problem for small and medium-sized enterprises. The following statistics illustrate this problem, according to the MSME (Micro, Small and Medium Enterprises) Finance Report, in 2017, 65 million or 40% of formal micro, small and medium-sized enterprises have the unmet financing needs in developing countries, the MSME finance gap in developing countries is estimated to be $ 5.2 trillion, 1.4 times the current level of MSME lending. In China, the financing situation for small and medium-sized enterprises is also not optimistic, more than 43% of small and medium-sized enterprises has encountered the financing gap. In other words, traditional financing institutions like banks can only meet 57% of the financing needs of small and medium-sized enterprises (SME Finance Forum, 2017). There are a wide variety of reasons for banks to reject the loan application from small and medium-sized enterprises, such as high risk credits, high interest rate and collateral shortage, most of which are on account of the complexity of traditional banks' finance service procedure.

The conditions of applying for loans from traditional banks are high standards, the credit ratings for small and medium-sized enterprise are relatively low because of the small scale of operating or low market share, which makes the lending hard to access. Besides, the information asymmetry between banks and enterprises increases the difficulty for banks to evaluate the genuine financial condition and repayment ability of enterprises. From the enterprises' perspective, the lack of fixed assets also makes the enterprises reluctant to apply the loans from banks, providing a certain amount of fixed assets as collaterals is a huge obstacle. Small and medium enterprises comprise 97% of all firms, accounting for 80% of urban employment, and for 60% of total GDP (OECD, 2016). Yet a recent report indicates that 62% of China's small and medium-sized enterprises have no lending relationships with banks (State Council, 2016). The report also points out that the banks are more willingly to provide to large enterprises like state-owned enterprises than the small enterprises because the latter will increase the workloads for banks. Consequently, the low efficiency of small and medium-sized enterprises financing through traditional banks is predictable, which severely impedes the development for small and medium-sized enterprises, furthermore, the economic growth. In addition, the harsh financing situation for small and medium-sized enterprises is not improving, China's credit crackdown has affected smaller businesses hardest, small businesses are particularly vulnerable, many of those small businesses are struggling for loans from banks (New York Times, 2018).

The superior features of supply chain finance shows a considerable potential to solve the financing conundrum for small and medium-sized enterprises. Different from the traditional finance service, supply chain finance is led by the core enterprises instead of the banks. Under this mode, the supply chain finance service is able to cover the whole supply chain parties, especially the small and medium-sized enterprises which are the vulnerable groups when facing banks. Moreover, supply chain finance is operating based on the authentic trading process, which can be regarded as an integration of fund, information and logistics flows, the frequent and authentic exchange of trading data forms a strong correlation connecting the upstream and downstream of supply chain enterprises. Thus, compared to the traditional finance service, supply chain finance establishes a whole information-transparent chain and effectively alleviates the asymmetry problem. Supply chain finance achieves the financing in trading process through various financial products, it is a more accessible and target-focused financing mode process than traditional finance service.

Depending on the large trading data and funds of core enterprises, the financial cost and risk are minimized while the efficiency of finance service is increased. All the above excellent characteristics manifest the vast development prospect of supply chain finance: The global supply chain finance market is $46.5 billion worldwide with a growth of 30% per year, Asia is the youngest supply chain finance market, the whole market is expected to see the largest growth of up to 50% per year in the world (PYMNTS.com, 2015). Furthermore, Chinese government becomes a driving force for developing supply chain finance. Various state policies and proposals are issued to support the supply chain finance development, most notably the concept of modern supply chain finance proposed by 19th CPC National Congress, which takes China's supply chain finance development to a new level. In china, major areas have already been laid out concerning the supply chain; rural areas, an integrated, smart and green supply chain, financing services for the supply chain, and its global perspectives (China Daily, 2017). Supply chain finance is a strong response to China's call for supply-side structural reform and finance service innovation.

The stability and efficiency of supply chain finance is largely dependent on the core enterprises. Core enterprises refer to these which possess the key resources and have significant impact on the downstream and upstream, one of the most important features of core enterprises is the ability to integrate the fund, information and logistics flows of the whole chain, which can help improve the core competitiveness of the supply chain. As e-commerce continues to prosper in China, the online giants like Alibaba and JD.COM are able to occupy the core position in supply chain with large possession of trading data and funds. The combination of supply chain finance and online retailer is a prevalent practice as small and medium-sized enterprises' fundraising channel. As the forerunner in China's online-retailer-led supply chain finance, JD.COM has started its second loan service for small and medium-sized enterprises in October 2017. In a bid to support the enterprises that cannot obtain financing from banks, JD.COM launched a new service aimed at credit and payment for small and medium-sized enterprises through its e-commerce finance unit (Caixin Global, 2017). JD.COM already issued about 250 billion yuan to approximately 100 thousand small and medium-sized enterprises. At the 48th annual meeting of the World Economic Forum (WEF) in Davos, Switzerland. Liu Qiangdong, the founder and CEO of JD.COM, made the following comment about online-retailer-led supply chain finance mode, "to help optimize risk control system, reduce the rate of bad debts, by reducing the rate of bad debts, then create value."(Waonews, 2018)

JD Finance will play an important role in JD.COM's green growth plan. JD.COM regards JD Finance as a great addition to the green finance development, JD.COM believes the operations of JD Finance assist to "drive long-term sustainable growth across our established and emerging business areas" (JD.COM, 2017). JD Finance is becoming a channel to promote green finance growth, several projects that aimed at green finance are launched. For instance, in order to address the financial problems in remote and poor areas, JD Finance has been cooperating with China UnionPay to execute the credit rating and loans of rural areas project. JD Finance also believes that the spinoff from JD.COM makes it capable of operating the separate payment business and applying for certain financial licenses, which significantly facilitates the deployment of finance services in rural areas. JD.COM knows that, only when the finance services gap between urban and rural areas narrows, can the goal of sustainable finance growth be achieved. The case of JD.COM demonstrates developing supply chain finance is a good way to realize green and sustainable finance growth.

The above industrial evidences indicate the thriving growth of online-retailer-led supply chain finance in China. Online retailers own abundant supply chain resources including trading data, funds, information and logistics, the possession and integration of such resources make online retailers become eligible finance service providers. Different from traditional finance services, online-retailer-led supply chain finance is offered based on authentic trading data possessed by the online retailers, thus, the finance providers (i.e., online retailers) are capable to eliminate the information asymmetry and lower the bad debts risk, the finance service model is established aimed at the small and medium-sized enterprises, which can be regarded as an effective complementary service to fill the gap of traditional finance.

In this chapter, the authors develop a stylized model to examine the popular supply chain finance mode in the tide of China's current financial reform, i.e., the online-retailer-led supply chain finance. Taking the leading Chinese online retail giant JD.COM as an example, the authors first show that in the structure of monopoly supply chain, JD.COM, as the finance service provider, can achieve maximum profit with interest rate adjustment. For the finance service receiver, the downstream retailer which sells through JD.COM's platform, it is also able to get maximum profit by ordering specific quantity. In other words, the online-retailer-led supply chain finance mode forms a win-win situation for both the finance provider and receiver.

The authors then analyze the optimal quantity decision under the push and pull supply chain with the existence of financial factors. The result shows that in the structure of online-retailer-led supply chain finance, the demand uncertainty accounts for the quantity decision differential under push and pull supply chain for downstream retailer. The retailer is suggested to be aware of its selling strategy when determining the quantity size.

The authors find that because of the impact of interest rate, the order quantity of retailer is less than normal supply chain. This order quantity reduction effect can be explained as follows: The retailer has to consider about the future repayment when ordering, which makes retailer adopt a conservative strategy and ordering a smaller quantity from supplier. According to Choi and Chiu (2012), one of the key measurement indexes for sustainability is the quantity of order. Because when retailer is facing demand uncertainty, a smaller order quantity means a less possibility of products remaining unsold, which further means less waste. That is to say, the sustainable growth can be improved because of the emergence of online-retailer-led supply chain finance which reduces the supply chain order quantity.

This chapter aims to present a brief introduction of the currently prevalent supply chain finance in China, especially when the supply chain finance is led by the online retail giants, which is a wide practice in China's e-commerce industry. To grasp this thriving trend of supply chain finance, the authors give a brief introduction of the supply chain finance mode led by the Chinese leading online retail giant JD.COM, through which the authors want to provide a deeper understanding of this new type supply chain finance mode. Besides, in order to get a deeper understanding of online-retailer-led supply chain finance, the authors develop a stylized model incorporating finance factors, through which the operational decisions and outcomes under different scenarios are discussed. The authors try to find the optimal decisions and strategies in the context of supply chain finance. At last, it is in line with the authors' wish that the results analyzed from this chapter, in some way can be helpful to the enterprises, especially the small and medium-sized one, in obtaining the financing service from other channels rather than only the commercial banks. Providing the small and medium-sized enterprises with some supply chain finance suggestion is the final object of this chapter.

The chapter is organized as follows. In the "BACKGROUND", the authors provide a literature review of related studies. In the "MAIN FOCUS OF THE CHAPTER" section, the authors illustrate the purposes of this chapter, the authors also present a brief introduction of JD.COM's finance development, which is the focused supply chain finance mode in this chapter. In the "Problems & Model Setting, Notations, Assumptions" section, the authors propose the basic model setting and analyze the preferred interest rate for JD.COM as well as the optimal quantity decision for downstream retailer. In this section, the authors examine and solve the problems in a quantitative way. The "CONCLUSION" section concludes the main findings. The "FUTURE RESEARCH DIRECTIONS" section discusses some future research possibilities related to this topic.

BACKGROUND

This work is closely related to the firm's operational decisions with financial constraints. In recent years, this stream of literature has received much attention due to the development of supply chain finance. Buzacott and Zhang (2004) first incorporate the asset-based financing into a firm's production decision, they argue that many traditional supply chain models related to firm's production, inventory or other operational procedures have ignored the firm's financial states, which may lead to infeasible practices in reality. Similar with the authors' model setting, Xu and Birge (2004) develop models to illustrate the impact of financial constraints on firm's production decisions, the interactions of firm's production and financial decisions are regarded as an important tradeoff of debts' taxes benefits and financial distress costs. Caldentey and Haugh (2006) believe the fact that there are some frictions when firm operates in the market, one of the most significant frictions is financial constraints or distress, thus, they investigate the problem of dynamically hedging to explore a risk-averse firm's optimal operating policy and trading strategy with the presence of financial issues. Boyabath and Toktay (2011) consider a monopolist firm's optimal technology decisions who faces the financial constraints and is able to alleviate the constraints by getting loans from a creditor, they analyze both the technology types (flexible or dedicated) and capacity level with demand uncertainty, which forms the optimal strategic management in an imperfect capital markets. Alan and Gaur (2015) establish a single-period newsvendor model which contains a finance-constrained firm and a bank to study the firm's optimal capital allocation decisions (between a new business and external capital market) to maximize its expected profits, the firm can get financial support from bank based on its assets, they find the collateral value of the firm is a function of bank's belief regarding the firm's demand distribution, which differs from the conventional wisdom that the bank uses the simple rules of thumb to evaluate the collateral value. Yang and Birge (2009) develop a stylized model incorporating financial distress factor to show how the trade credit increases supply chain efficiency by acting as a risk-sharing mechanism. Lai et al. (2009) also investigate the efficiency issue regarding the financial constraint, they argue that although extant literature has examined the supply chain efficiency level with many operational factors, the impact of financial constraint is neglected. In contrast, they prove the combination of preorder and consignment is the most efficient sourcing strategy if the firm encounters financial constraint. Kouvelis and Zhao (2010) develop a model consisting of a retailer, a supplier and a bank, similarly, the retailer faces the problem of financial constraints. They derive the optimal operational decisions for both the downstream (order quantity) and upstream (wholesale price) parties. Kouvelis and Zhao (2012) use the *supplier early payment discount scheme* as framework to discuss the optimal trade credit contract, the work is innovative because they assume both the supplier and retailer are financially constrained. Craig and Raman (2013) develop an effective mathematical model to analyze the downstream retailer's store liquidation problem, in order to acquire some suggestions when retailer choosing financial strategy. In contrast to the aforementioned studies, this work examine the creative mode of online-retailer-led supply chain finance, which is rarely investigated in the extant literature. To be specific, structurally, instead of adding a bank or creditor who operates outside the supply chain system, the authors attempt to solve the financial problem for small and medium-sized enterprises with the inner strength of supply chain system, i.e., to explore the possibility of online retailer being the finance service provider, and derive different insights from the previous studies.

The literature on bankruptcy is also related to this work. Baird and Picker (1991) consider a supply chain incorporating several creditors and a firm who faces the risk of bankruptcy, they believe the risk of bankruptcy is the bridge to construct the negotiations between the firm and creditor. Similarly, Bebchuk and Chang (1992) develop a game-theoretical model to describe the bankruptcy negotiation process, they derive some expected outcomes of the negotiation. Considering a more complex setting, Kordana and Posner (1999) illustrate different bankruptcy rules, it is worth noting that their work complements the literature on bankruptcy negotiation by extending the negotiation process to multiple creditors with imperfect information. Wilner (2000) sets a three-period sequential decision model, in which the firm encounters the risk of bankruptcy, the optimal pricing, lending, renegotiation strategies are derived. Broadie et al. (2007) discuss the scenario where a debt-risky firm applies for liquidation and reorganization, they show how the optimal negotiation outcomes vary under liquidation and reorganization. Yang et al. (2015) compare the market competition intensity and supply chain relationship in the context of bankruptcy risk, they explicitly examine each supply chain party's reaction both under liquidation and reorganization scenarios, three effects are derived (predation, bail-out and abetment) that alter each party's decision incentive. There are both similarities in and differences between the above literature and our work: The purpose is similar, i.e., we all try to build the supply chain models with consideration of bankruptcy risk. However, the above studies focus on the bankruptcy negotiation process, they emphasize on the negotiation outcomes under different bankruptcy rules (e.g., liquidation and reorganization). While this work puts less attention on the bankruptcy rules and concentrates on the optimal decisions under different supply chain structures (push and pull), the authors incorporate both the bankruptcy risk and finance factors, which is not discussed in the above studies. Therefore, this work contributes to the literature from different perspective compared to the previous studies.

There has been a growing number of studies on selling to a newsvendor retailer with the short-term financing. Lariviere and Porteus (2001) investigate a scenario where the manufacture sells to a retailer who faces the newsvendor problem, they show the manufacturer's profit and wholesale quantity are increasing in market size under certain conditions, while the wholesale price depends on the market variability, Özer et al. (2007) present a strategic analysis of a newsvendor retailer, they propose a "dual purchase" contract, through which a strict Pareto improvement is achieved for supply chain. However, neither of these studies considers the factors of bankruptcy or financial constraints when analyzing the newsvendor problem, which are discussed in this work. Dada and Hu (2008) set a Stackelberg model incorporating a bank and a capital constrained newsvendor retailer, they analyze the inventory procurement problem for the retailer and find if the borrowing cost is not too high, the retailer will borrow funds in order to maintain procurement, but the amount of funds can only satisfy a procurement quantity that less than the channel optimality. Consequently, the bank will charge an interest rate that is decreasing in the newsvendor's equity. Li et al. (2005) consider a multi-period newsvendor problem to analyze the optimal inventory level, they find the optimal inventory level is subject to the type of firm, which is either dividend-maximizing or profit-maximizing. In the setting of non-competitive loan prices, Gupta (2008) demonstrates a comparison of supplier and bank financing for a newsvendor. This work can be regarded as a complementary part for Gupta (2008)'s study because the authors expand the financing model to both the push and pull supply chain scenarios, which is not studied in Gupta (2008)'s work. Among the typical literature on newsvendor problem, the majority concentrates on the operational decisions (e.g., ordering time, inventory level, etc.) of each player. Although previous studies have provided a wide range of solutions to improve the profitability or supply chain coordination in a newsvendor supply chain. The authors' work differs from theirs by analyzing the role of supply chain finance in supply chain operation, namely, the authors add the modern finance factor into the traditional newsvendor problem, which is helpful to acquire a clearer comprehension about how the newsvendor problem will change if supply chain finance is considered.

The last related literature is that on analysis of order time. Cachon (2004) divides the order time along with the order price into two kinds: *before* the season, and *during* the selling season. He further investigates the supply chain efficiency under different order time (push, pull and the single wholesale price contracts) and surprisingly finds the efficiency is higher under the single wholesale price contract. Iyer and Bergen (1997) analyze the QR (Quick Response) supply chain in the fashion apparel industry, in which the impact of forecasting update on order time is examined. Similarly, Donohue (2000) discusses the pricing schemes and optimal contracts under different ordering stages in a fashion supply chain, note that the timings of order varies with production modes as well as the wholesale price. Ferguson et al. (2005) investigate the impact of order commitment time on the profit distribution between upstream and downstream, with the consideration of demand uncertainty, interestingly, they find the demand information update is not always in favor of the manufacturer and supplier. Focusing on the timing decisions of the upstream supplier, Taylor (2006) study the order time decisions for downstream retailer when the market demand is uncertain. Generally, it is beneficial for retailer make an early order time decision because the upstream manufacturer is unable to charge a high wholesale price. However, the result is reversed when the retailer has more accurate information about the market demand. Nevertheless, none of the above papers consider the possibility of adding financial factors into ordering time game, and the impact of supply chain finance parameters on both the upstream and downstream decisions. While this work analyze the variance with different order timing scenarios.

MAIN FOCUS OF THE CHAPTER

For the traditional supply chain finance, banks have to do sufficient pre-loan investigation in risk control before releasing the lending, which includes but not limited to the trade background of both sides, the stability of trade, the market value and liquidity of collaterals. Besides, even though the individual risk evaluation of the loan enterprise is not the most important part, the banks still need to take it as an evaluation reference for the entire loan risk level. Therefore, in order to maintain the loan risks in a controllable range, banks are required to spend lots of manpower and material resources in the pre-loan investigation. Such pre-loan investigation always includes complex evaluation procedures, which further causes high costs for bank loans. The costs are finally borne by loan applicants, i.e., the loan applicants have to bear a high interest rate when repay the loans.

As a giant e-commerce platform, JD.COM has natural advantages in supply chain finance. First, the platform is able to steadily accumulate large amount of trading data, which enables JD.COM to see the monthly income, operation state and credit level of each single seller enterprise with relatively low costs. In other words, JD.COM analyzes the trade background and other risk variables from the large trading data. Through big data analysis or other analysis tools, JD.COM can precisely evaluate the true loan demand of the seller, which further lower the loan risk level and the costs of information discrimination.

In addition, JD.COM has developed its own payment license and tool, the seller can only retrieve his total income through such payment tool. Using this means of payment, JD.COM assures the seller's income is the prior source of repayment. Besides, JD.COM is able to effectively control seller's fund flow and reduce the rate of bad loans.

Given the above superior features of supply chain finance, in this chapter, the authors focus on the prevalent phenomenon that the online retailer serves as both platform and finance service provider in China's present supply chain finance practice. JD.COM, who is one of the most successful supply chain finance forerunners in China, serving as a great example for the researchers to investigate the distinguished online-retailer-led supply chain finance mode. The authors concentrate on modelling the structure of the supply chain finance, through which the strategic ordering, financial and other supply chain decisions can be derived. Hopefully, to a certain degree, the findings have the potential to be helpful in understanding the essence of online-retailer-led supply chain finance mode.

A Brief Introduction of JD.COM's Supply Chain Finance Business

JD.COM is one of the earliest forerunners in developing the online-retailer-led supply chain finance in China's e-commerce industry. Through a long period of financing practice, JD.COM has developed a variety of financing services suitable for different kinds of enterprises. In this section, the authors present a brief introduction about JD.COM's supply chain finance business.

Stage 1: Cooperation With Banks

In the initial stage, due to capital shortage, JD.COM is incapable of providing financing service through its own fund. Thus, JD.COM chose to cooperate with banks. With the abundant fund support of banks, JD.COM steadily developed its supply chain finance business in the initial stage.

Depending on the high credit level and large trading data, JD.COM could help the upstream suppliers obtain loans and financing from the banks. JD.COM adopted a relatively conservative strategy that the supply chain finance business is only open to its self-operated business suppliers. This is because JD.COM has a stricter supplier management standards for its self-operated products, namely, JD.COM has more information about these self-operated business suppliers, which can help JD.COM reduce the finance risks.

Specifically, in the initial stage, JD.COM provides the supply chain finance including order financing, warehouse receipt financing and accounts receivable financing.

Stage 2: Release Loans With Self-Owned Funds

As the revenue continues to rise, JD.COM gradually becomes capable of possessing vast capital and fund. JD.COM begins to construct the foundation of the self-support supply chain finance business. JD.COM deployed the self-support supply chain finance business "JingBaobei" in the end of 2013. In the "JingBaobei" business, JD.COM acts as both the supply chain core enterprise and bank. In this stage, the service target is still the self-operated business supplier whose credit level is relatively high.

Stage 3: Open Finance Service to the Third-Party Sellers

Either the "JD.COM+bank" supply chain finance mode in the initial stage or the self-support "JingBaoBei" supply chain finance mode in the second stage, the service targets are all JD.COM's self-operated suppliers. Along with the increasing experience and funds in developing supply chain finance, JD.COM began to provide the third-party sellers with the financing services in the end of 2014, which has a broader scope of service.

Problems and Model Setting, Notations, Assumptions

The rigorous criteria of bank loan prevent small and medium-sized enterprises from obtaining financing. In contrast, one of the important reasons that supply chain finance prevails is the relatively less stringent criteria for loans, such criteria like receivables, receipts and even inventory are easier to meet compared to traditional banks. The prosperity of e-commerce gives core position to the online retailers in supply chain, which enables them to possess natural advantages in operating supply chain finance and further solving the financing problems for small and medium-sized enterprises. To address this problem, in this section, the authors consider a standard vertical supply chain model consisting of a supplier, a retailer and JD.COM to explore the operation of supply chain finance. The supplier is well funded that it does not have to apply for loans from commercial banks or JD.COM. On the contrary, the retailer is facing the problem of insufficient funds. JD.COM plays two roles in the supply chain: 1) JD.COM acts as the e-commerce service provider who provides platform for the retailer. JD.COM charges a certain percentage fee according to the retailer's sales revenue as the platform fee. 2) JD.COM also acts as the finance service provider like banks. JD.COM has the access to the trading data and other key information of retailers, such ability enables JD.COM to fully evaluate the retailer's credit rating. Thus, JD.COM is capable of satisfying the financing demand of the retailer. For analytical tractability, the authors assume that there is no default risks, the retailer repays the capital with interest to JD.COM.

The demand of selling season is stochastic, the authors assume the demand distribution function and probability density function to be $F(x)$ and $f(x)$, respectively. Assume $F(x)$ is strictly increasing in x and $F(0) = 0$, the demand distribution function satisfies the IGFR (Increasing Generalized Failure Rate) condition. Besides, the products will only be manufactured once before the selling season starts.

Supply chain can be divided into two extreme forms, i.e., the push and pull supply chain. In the pull supply chain, supplier determines its production capacity Q_1 before the selling season. Retailer will not place the order until the beginning of selling season eliminates demand uncertainty. That's to say, retailer determines the order quantity when the selling season starts and the demand is truly realized, the order quantity is not more than the supplier's production capacity. Thus, the supplier takes the risks in the pull supply chain. In contrast, in the push supply chain, retailer determines the order quantity Q_2 and places order before the selling season, the supplier also manufactures and delivers the products to retailer before the selling season. Retailer takes all the risks brought by demand uncertainty, including the product shortage induced by overlarge demand or the product waste induced by too little demand.

From the above illustration, one can see that, in the push supply chain, the whole supply chain operations are driven by the manufacturing behavior of supplier, the retailer is in the relatively passive position. Given this situation, the wholesale price is determined by supplier. Whereas in the pull supply chain, demand becomes the driver of supply chain operations. Retailer will not place any order until demand uncertainty is eliminated. Therefore, the supplier is often in the passive position in the bargaining, and the retailer has the right to determine wholesale price.

Above all, the sequences of events in push and pull supply chain are presented in the following table:

The authors' work considers the optimal decisions for all parties as JD.COM acts as both the platform and finance service providers. The notations of the model are as follows.

According to the newsvendor model, the expected sales

$$S(Q) = E\{\min[Q, D]\} = Q - \int_0^Q F(x)dx\,.$$

Furthermore, there exists $\bar{F}(x) = 1 - F(x)$ and the inequalities $c < w < p$ and $p \geq w(1 + r)$ hold. The retail and wholesale prices satisfy the above assumptions in reality.

Table 1. Sequence of events

Time	Push Supply Chain	Pull Supply Chain
1	JD.COM determines loan rate r	JD.COM determines loan rate r
2	Supplier determines wholesale price w	Retailer determines wholesale price w
3	Retailer determines order quantity Q_2	Supplier determines production capacity Q_1

Table 2. Notations in basic model

Notations	Meaning	Notations	Meaning
c	Production cost	Q_1	Supplier's production capacity (pull)
w	Wholesale price	Q_2	Retailer's order quantity (push)
p	Retail price	$f(x)$	Demand probability density function
r	Interest rate	$F(x)$	Demand distribution function
r_f	Risk-free interest rate	Π_s	Supplier's profit
B	Retailer's own capital	Π_r	Retailer's profit
D	Actual (Realized) demand	Π_j	JD.COM's profit
α	Ratio of JD.COM's platform fee	$S(Q)$	Retailer's expected sales

Given retailer's expected sales, production cost and supplier's production capacity, the supplier's objective profit function can be expressed as: $\Pi_s(w,Q) = wS(Q) - cQ$.

The profit function is strictly concave and has a unique maximizer. To maximize profit, supplier's production capacity should satisfy the following equation:

$$\bar{F}(Q) = \frac{c}{w} \tag{1}$$

The one-to-one correspondence between Q and w, w is therefore:

$$w(Q) = \frac{c}{\bar{F}(Q)} \tag{2}$$

The retailer's expected profit function before paying the platform fee to JD.COM is:

$$\bar{\Pi}_r(w,Q,r) = pS(Q) - [wS(Q) - B](1+r) \tag{3}$$

Thus, after paying JD.COM the platform fee, the actual profit of retailer is:

$$\Pi_r(w,Q,r) = (1-\alpha)\{pS(Q) - [wS(Q) - B](1+r)\} \tag{4}$$

By substituting the optimal w into retailer's profit function, the authors have the retailer's profit function subject to Q and r :

$$\Pi_r(Q,r) = (1-\alpha)\{p[\frac{p-(1+r)c}{p} - F(Q)]j(Q)\}, \tag{5}$$

where $j(Q) = \dfrac{S(Q)}{\bar{F}(Q)}$.

The profit of JD.COM consists of two parts: the interest received and the platform fee from the retailer, which can be expressed as:

$$\Pi_j(w,Q,r) = [wS(Q) - B](1+r) + \alpha\,\Pi_r(Q) \tag{6}$$

Upon substitution, the authors also have JD.COM's profit function subject to Q and r:

$$\Pi_j(Q,r) = [cj(Q) - B](1+r) + \alpha j(Q)\{p[\frac{p-(1+r)c}{p} - F(Q)] + Br_f\} \tag{7}$$

Proposition 1. When JD.COM is in a perfect competition market, there exists a unique Q^* which maximizes $\Pi_r(Q^*)$.

If JD.COM is in a perfect competition market as a financial institution and acts as a risk neutral investor. Then JD.COM's profit from offering the loan is equal to the risk-free profit. Therefore, JD.COM will set the loan interest rate $r = r_f$. JD.COM's profit function is:

$$\Pi_j(Q,r_f) = [cj(Q) - B](1+r_f) + \alpha\{pj(Q)[\frac{p-(1+r_f)c}{p} - F(Q)] + Br_f\} \tag{8}$$

The retailer's actual profit function is:

$$\Pi_r(Q,r_f) = (1-\alpha)\{pj(Q)[\frac{p-(1+r_f)c}{p} - F(Q)] + Br_f\} \tag{9}$$

Derive the first-order condition of the profit function:

$$\Pi_r'(Q) = (1-\alpha)p\{\frac{p-(1+r_f)c}{p} - [F(Q) + j(Q)h(Q)(1 - \frac{p-(1+r_f)c}{p})]\}, \tag{10}$$

where $h(Q) = \dfrac{f(Q)}{\bar{F}(Q)}$

Derive the second-order condition:

$$\Pi_r''(Q) = -p(1-\alpha)\{f(Q) + \frac{(1+r_f)c}{p}[j(Q)h(Q)]'\} \tag{11}$$

The demand distribution function $F(Q)$ satisfies the IFR (Increasing Failure Rate) condition, Cachon (2004) proves that when $F(Q)$ satisfies IFR condition, there exists $[j(Q)h(Q)]' > 0$. Besides, from $f(Q) > 0$, one can get $\Pi_r''(Q) < 0$, $\Pi_r(Q)$ is a concave function with respect to Q. Then there is $Q^* = \arg\max \Pi_r(Q)$ which maximizes $\Pi_r(Q^*)$. In the meantime, JD.COM's and supplier's profit function are $\Pi_j(Q^*)$ and $\Pi_s(Q^*)$, respectively.

Proposition 2. When JD.COM is the monopolist in the market, $B = 0$ and the demand distribution satisfies $[h^2(Q) + h'(Q)]' > 0$, there exists (Q^*, r^*) which maximizes $\Pi_r(Q^*, r^*)$ and $\Pi_j(Q^*, r^*)$.

From Equation (10), the first-order condition of retailer's profit function with respect to Q is derived:

$$\frac{\partial \Pi_r}{\partial Q} = (1-\alpha)p\{\frac{p-(1+r)c}{p} - [F(Q) + j(Q)h(Q)(1 - \frac{p-(1+r)c}{p})]\} \tag{12}$$

From Proposition 1, $\dfrac{\partial \Pi_r}{\partial Q} = 0$ has a unique solution, $\Pi_r(Q, r)$ is a concave function with respect to Q. Thus, when $\Pi_r(Q)$ is maximized, Q satisfies:

$$\bar{F}(Q) = \frac{c}{p}[1 + j(Q)h(Q)](1 + r) \tag{13}$$

Because of the one-to-one correspondence, r can be denoted by Q:

$$r(Q) = \frac{p\bar{F}(Q)}{c[1 + j(Q)h(Q)]} - 1 \tag{14}$$

Substitute Equation (14) into JD.COM's profit function $\prod_j (Q, r)$:

$$\prod_j (Q, r(Q)) = \frac{pS(Q)}{1 + j(Q)h(Q)} + \alpha \bar{\prod}_r (Q, r(Q)) \tag{15}$$

Derive the first-order condition, there is:

$$\prod_j'(Q) = p\frac{\bar{F}(Q)[1 + j(Q)h(Q)] - S(Q)[j(Q)h(Q)]'}{[1 + j(Q)h(Q)]^2} + \alpha \bar{\prod}_r'(Q, r(Q)) \tag{16}$$

From Equation (13), there is:
$\frac{\partial \prod_r (Q, r(Q))}{\partial Q} = 0$,i.e., $\bar{\prod}_r'(Q, r(Q)) = 0$.

Therefore, the first-order condition of JD.COM's profit function can be simplified as:

$$\prod_j'(Q) = p\frac{\bar{F}(Q)\{1 + j(Q)h(Q) - j(Q)[j(Q)h(Q)]'\}}{[1 + j(Q)h(Q)]^2} \tag{17}$$

The following equation holds:

$$[j(Q)h(Q)]' = j'(Q)h(Q) + j(Q)h'(Q) = [1 + j(Q)h(Q)]h(Q) + j(Q)h'(Q)$$

Thus, Equation (17) can be further simplified as:

$$\prod_j'(Q) = p\frac{\bar{F}(Q)[1 - j^2(Q)h^2(Q) - j^2(Q)h'(Q)]}{[1 + j(Q)h(Q)]^2} \tag{18}$$

There exist $\bar{F}(0) = 1$, $j(0) = 0$ and $h(0) = 0$, thus, $\Pi'_j(0) = p * \bar{F}(0) = p > 0$.

At the same time, the demand distribution function $F(Q)$ satisfies the IFR, there exists $h'(Q) > 0$. From the aforementioned condition $[j(Q)h(Q)]' > 0$, the inequality $[j^2(Q)h^2(Q)] > 0$ can be derived. Obviously, there is $[j^2(+\infty)h^2(+\infty) = +\infty]$, hence, there exists $\Pi'_j(+\infty) < 0$. From the zero point theorem, there exists a root for the numerator part of Equation (18) $A(Q) = 1 - j^2(Q)h^2(Q) - j^2(Q)h'(Q)$ in $Q \in (0, +\infty)$.

Based on the assumption

$$[h^2(Q) + h'(Q)]' > 0, A(Q) = 1 - j^2(Q)[h^2(Q) + h'(Q)]$$

is a strictly decreasing function. Therefore, there exists a unique $Q^* > 0$ to make $\Pi'_j(Q^*) = 0$. Also, when $Q < Q^*$, $\Pi'_j(Q^*) > 0$, when $Q > Q^*$, $\Pi'_j(Q^*) < 0$. Q^* is the unique maximizer of $\Pi_j(Q^*, r(Q^*))$. JD.COM will choose the interest rate $r(Q^*)$ to maximize the profit, $r(Q^*)$ satisfies:

$$r(Q^*) = \frac{p\bar{F}(Q^*)}{c[1 + j(Q^*)h(Q^*)]} - 1 \tag{19}$$

Optimal Decisions Under Uniform Distribution in Pull and Push Supply Chain System

Mathematically, the uniform distribution satisfies the assumption that $[h^2(Q) + h'(Q)]' > 0$. Based on the assumptions of Proposition 2, the authors take uniform distribution as an example to compare how the optimal decisions vary in push and pull supply chain system.

In this section, the demand Q is uniformly distributed on $[0, b]$. The notations are as follows.

1. Pull Supply Chain System

From the previous section, the first-order condition of JD.COM's profit is:

$$\Pi'_j(Q_1) = p\frac{\bar{F}(Q_1)[1 - j^2(Q_1)h^2(Q_1) - j^2(Q_1)h'(Q_1)]}{[1 + j(Q_1)h(Q_1)]^2} \tag{20}$$

Table 3. Notations under uniform distribution

Notations	Expressions
$F(Q)$	$\frac{Q}{b}$
$f(Q)$	$\frac{1}{b}$
$S(Q)$	$Q-\frac{Q^2}{2b}$
$j(Q)$	$\frac{bQ-\frac{1}{2}Q^2}{b-Q}$
$h(Q)$	$\frac{1}{b-Q}$
$\bar{F}(Q)$	$\frac{b-Q}{b}$

Substitute the expressions in Table 3 into Equation (20) to make it equal to 0, there is:

$$Q_1^* = (1-\sqrt{\frac{2\sqrt{2}-2}{2}})b \tag{21}$$

In the pull supply chain system, the sequence of events is as follows:

1. JD.COM determines the loan interest rate $r(Q_1^*)$,
2. Retailer determines the wholesale price $w(Q_1^*)$,
3. Supplier determines the production capacity Q_1^*.

2. Push Supply Chain System

In push supply chain system, the retailer may face the situation that the order quantity exceeds the actual demand. Consequently, the retailer's sales profit fails to repay the capital with interest, i.e., the retailer bankrupts. Thus, it is necessary to classify the retailer's sales depending on the relative sizes of order quantity and demand.

1. When the demand size is smaller than order quantity, i.e., $D<Q_2$.
   a. When $pD<wQ_2(1+r)$, the sales profit fails to repay the capital with interest, the retailer bankrupts, the revenue equals to 0. There exists $D<z$, where $z = \frac{wQ_2(1+r)}{p}$.
   b. When $pD\geq wQ_2(1+r)$, the sales profit is larger than the sum of capital and interest, the retailer has positive revenue $pD-wQ_2(1+r)$. There exists $D\geq z$.
2. When the demand size is larger than order quantity, i.e., $D>Q_2$.
   a. $p\geq w(1+r)$, then the inequality $pQ_2\geq wQ_2(1+r)$ holds, the sales profit is able to cover the expense of capital and interest. The retailer's revenue equals to:

$pQ_2-wQ_2(1+r)$.

Before paying the platform fee, the retailer's expected profit is:

$$\bar{\Pi}_r(w, Q_2, r) = \int_z^{Q_2} [pD - wQ_2(1+r)]f(D)dD + \int_{Q_2}^{+\infty} [pQ_2 - wQ_2(1+r)]f(D)dD \tag{22}$$

After paying the platform fee, the retailer's expected profit is:

$$\Pi_r(w, Q_2, r) = (1-\alpha)[\int_z^{Q_2} pDf(D)dD + pQ_2\bar{F}(Q_2) - pz\bar{F}(z)] \tag{23}$$

Derive the first-order condition with respect to Q_2:

$$\frac{\partial \Pi_r}{\partial Q_2} = (1-\alpha)[p\bar{F}(Q_2) - w(1+r)\bar{F}(z)] \tag{24}$$

The demand is uniformly distributed, therefore the above equation can be simplified as:

$$\frac{\partial \Pi_r}{\partial Q_2} = (1-\alpha)[b - \frac{w(1+r)+p}{p}Q_2]\frac{p-w(1+r)}{b} \tag{25}$$

Based on the assumptions, there exists $\frac{p - w(1+r)}{b} > 0$. Therefore, Equation (25) is the strictly decreasing function with respect to Q_2 and $\Pi_r'(0) = (1-\alpha)[p - w(1+r)] > 0$. Thus, there exists a unique Q_2^* which makes $\Pi_r'(Q_2^*) = 0$. When $Q > Q_2^*$, there exists $\Pi_r'(Q_2) < 0$, when $Q < Q_2^*$, there exists $\Pi_r'(Q_2) > 0$. That's to say, there exists a unique Q_2^* which maximizes $\Pi_r(w, Q_2^*, r)$.

There is a one-to-one correspondence between Q_2 and w, so when $\Pi_r'(Q_2) = 0$, the following equation about Q_2 and w holds:

$$w(Q_2) = \frac{p(b - Q_2)}{1+r} \tag{26}$$

The profit function for supplier is:

$$\Pi_s(w, Q_2) = (w - c)Q_2 \tag{27}$$

Substitute Equation (26) into (27):

$$\Pi_s(Q_2) = \frac{1}{1+r}\{-pQ_2^2 + [pb - c(1+r)]Q_2\} \tag{28}$$

Derive the first-order condition:

$$\Pi_s'(Q_2) = \frac{1}{1+r}[-2pQ_2 + pb - c(1+r)] \tag{29}$$

When $\Pi_s'(Q_2) = 0$, i.e., when the following equation exists, the supplier's maximum profit is realized:

$$Q_2^* = \frac{pb - c(1+r)}{2p} \tag{30}$$

There exists $Q_2<b$ in the above equation, which can be divided into two cases:

From the assumptions, there exist $p>w(1+r)>c(1+r)$ and $b>1$, then the inequality $\frac{pb - c(1+r)}{2p} \geq 0$ holds. Thus, there exists a threshold $Q_2^* \in [0, b]$ that makes the following relationship: When $Q_2^* < Q \leq b$, $\Pi_s'(Q_2) < 0$, and when $0 \leq Q \leq Q_2^*$, $\Pi_s'(Q_2) \geq 0$. Therefore, when $Q = Q_2^*$, the supplier gets maximum profit, the following equation about r and Q_2 holds:

$$r(Q_2) = \frac{pb - 2pQ_2}{c} - 1 \tag{31}$$

Substitute Equation (31) into (26):

$$w(Q_2) = \frac{c(b - Q_2)}{b - 2Q_2} \tag{32}$$

Now the authors discuss JD.COM's profit:

1. When demand size is smaller than order quantity, i.e., $D<Q_2$
   a. When $pD<wQ_2(1+r)$, the retailer fails to repay the capital with interest and bankrupts. JD.COM's gets all of retailer's sales profit as its own profit:

$$\Pi_j(w, Q_2, r) = pD \tag{33}$$

   b. When $pD \geq wQ_2(1+r)$, the retailer's sales profit is larger than the sum of capital and interest. JD.COM's profit equals to the capital with interest and platform fee:

$$\Pi_j(w, Q_2, r) = wQ_2(1 + r) + \alpha[pD - wQ_2(1 + r)] \tag{34}$$

2. When the demand size is larger than order quantity, i.e., $D>Q_2$
   a. The sales profit is able to cover the expense of capital and interest, thus, JD.COM's profit is:

$$\Pi_j(w, Q_2, r) = wQ_2(1 + r) + \alpha[pQ_2 - wQ_2(1 + r)] \tag{35}$$

Above all, JD.COM's expected profit $\Pi_j(w, Q_2, r)$ is:

$$\int_0^z pDf(D)dD + \int_z^{Q_2} \{wQ_2(1+r) + \alpha[pD - wQ_2(1+r)]\} f(D)dD + \int_{Q_2}^{+\infty} \{wQ_2(1+r) + \alpha[pQ_2 - wQ_2(1+r)]\} f(D)dD \tag{36}$$

Simplify Equation (36):

$$\Pi_j(w(Q_2), Q_2, r(Q_2)) = \int_0^z pDf(D)dD + \int_z^{+\infty} pzf(D)dD + \alpha\,\bar{\Pi}_r \tag{37}$$

Derive the first-order condition with respect to Q_2:

$$\Pi_j'(Q_2) = pzz'f(z) + pz'\int_z^{+\infty} f(D)dD - pzz'f(z) + \alpha\,\bar{\Pi}_r'(r(Q), w(Q_2), Q_2) \tag{38}$$

There exists the equation $\bar{\Pi}_r'(r(Q_2), w(Q_2), Q_2) = 0$, the above equation can be simplified as:

$$\Pi_j'(Q_2) = pz'\bar{F}(z) \tag{39}$$

Substitute Equation (31) and (32) into z:

$$z = \frac{wQ_2(1+r)}{p} = (b - Q_2)Q_2 \tag{40}$$

Simplify Equation (37) as:

$$\Pi_j'(Q_2) = pQ_2(b - 2Q_2)\bar{F}(z) \tag{41}$$

$r(Q_2) = \frac{p(b-2Q_2)}{c} - 1 > 0$, so $(b\text{-}2Q_2)>0$, then $\Pi_j'(Q_2) > 0$. Namely, JD.COM's profit function is a decreasing function with respect to Q_2, JD.COM will choose the interest rate $r = r(Q_{2\max})$ to maximize the profit.

When JD.COM provides the finance service, the interest rate will not be lower than the market risk-free rate r_f. From Equation (31), there is:

$$Q_2 \leq \frac{1}{2}[b - \frac{c}{p}(1 + r_f)] \tag{42}$$

Let $Q_2^* = \frac{1}{2}[b - \frac{c}{p}(1 + r_f)]$, then $r(Q_2^*) = r_f$. The sequence of events is as follows:

1. JD.COM determines the risk-free interest rate r_f,
2. Supplier determines the wholesale price equals to:

$$w(Q_2^*) = \frac{c(b - Q_2^*)}{b - 2Q_2^*} \tag{43}$$

3. Retailer determines the order quantity Q_2^*.

SOLUTIONS AND RECOMMENDATIONS

The above analysis has presented supply chain finance as a viable finance service channel to help the small and medium-sized enterprises with fund shortage. The authors also have some recommendations for both parties involving in this process.

For online retailer, the finance service provider. Depending on the vast trading data possession, online retailer is usually at the core position in supply chain. Therefore, it is easy for online retailer to adjust the relations among different supply chain parties. Although there exist various types of online retailer (e.g., B2B, B2C, C2C), the authors recommend online retailers to keep on gathering trading data, because that is the key reason why online retailer plays the core role in the whole supply chain operations. Relying on the authentic trading data, constructing an integrated credit system is a chief objective, through which the financing risks can be appropriately controlled. Online retailer should be aware that providing the finance service has the potential to form a win-win situation if the interest rate is set properly. However, online retailer should also note that becoming a supply chain finance provider requires significant capital and funds, it is irrational to make the transition into the finance service provider regardless of the actual situation. Thus, the authors recommend online retailer to determine the service scope according to own conditions, sometimes, seeking cooperation opportunity with banks is not a bad choice at all.

For downstream retailer or other small and medium-sized enterprises. As the weak sides in the traditional finance, in order to maintain the operation, they are suggested to know the rising supply chain finance is an effective way to solve their financing conundrum. However, the small and medium-sized enterprises should understand there also exist many financial risks in supply chain finance. For example, as the above analysis shows, demand uncertainty can be a critical risk to their future repayment. Facing the unrealized demand and other uncertain factors, the authors recommend small and medium-sized enterprises to do comprehensive self-evaluation of financing risks before applying. Although the relatively low criteria of supply chain finance definitely facilitates the applicants with efficient finance service, it should be carefully evaluated to avoid abusing for both demand and supply sides.

For traditional banks, although offering finance services to small and medium-size enterprises is not as profitable as serving the large enterprises. The authors recommend banks to attach more importance of the cooperation with online retailers. Banks, especially commercial banks, are supposed to notice they are no longer the only finance services institutions. With the foreseeable growth of supply chain finance, more online retailers are predicted to enter the field of finance services field. The finance market of small and medium-sized enterprises will become a main battleground for banks and online retailers to promote finance services profitability and sustainability. Banks should not regard themselves as the monopolist in providing finance services, as the incumbent, banks are likely to face the intense competition brought by the newly entrant online retailers. The head-to-head contend for small and medium-sized enterprises resources is not beneficial to develop the sustainable supply chain finance. On the contrary, the authors recommend banks to carefully evaluate the value of cooperating with online retailers in collaboratively offering finance services to small and medium-sized enterprises. The efficient supply chain finance services require both the support of sufficient funding and the full evaluation of data. Despite the large sums of funding holding, banks do not have the access to the authentic trading data of supply chain operations, which is exactly the key advantage of online retailers. Cooperation with online retailers endows banks with complementary advantages, through which banks and online retailers will provide small and medium-sized enterprise with more efficient supply chain finance services. Furthermore, the sustainability of supply chain finance is also increasing in the efficiency, because an efficient supply chain finance means less consumption of resources, which is in accordance with the principle of green and sustain finance.

The essence of supply chain finance is credit financing, rating the credit with inner supply chain transactions. In the traditional way of supply chain finance, financial institutions rely on the accumulated data from third-party logistics and storage services providers to acquire the receivables or inventory information, in a bid to evaluate the credit level of finance service applicant enterprises. In the modern way of online-retailer-led supply chain finance, online retail giants like JD.COM have become the reliable finance service providers due to the large trading data possession. Depending on the prosperous momentum of supply chain finance, the layout of JD.COM's supply chain finance is capable of covering consumer finance, crowd funding and wealth management. JD Finance has served over 5 hundred thousand enterprises by 2017. Such successful finance practice for online retailer is closely related to the trading data controlling, online retailers are ought to realize that internet their key resources lie in the trading data and supply chain core position occupation, rather than the advantageous bargaining power or sufficient capital. In the authors' opinion, developing online-retailer-led supply chain finance is in favor of promoting green and sustainable finance. Because when the supply chain finance involves many small and medium-enterprises, who have great difficulties in obtaining finance services from traditional banks, their businesses are also hard to conduct due to lack of funding and the transaction process will meet with much friction. As a result, the normal operations of the whole supply chain are hard to maintain and the supply chain will encounter the risk of collapse. Therefore, the authors recommend online retailers to put due attention in developing supply chain finance. Since a sustainable supply chain is largely depending on the normal operations of every involved enterprise. Developing online-retailer-led supply chain finance is not only constructing a new profit channel for online retailer, but also a vital way to help small and medium-size enterprises with financing and make a more sustainable supply chain.

CONCLUSION

From industrial observation, supplier determines the production capacity in pull supply chain. Typical example is the supply chain management of Dell, as the upstream PC components supplier, Dell first gathers the information about the downstream component demand then determines the production capacity accordingly for pull production. The evidences of supplier determines production capacity can also be found in extant literature. For instance, Cachon (2004) indicates that in pull supply chain, because retailer does not prebook order, therefore, supplier is the one to choose the production capacity. Furthermore, due to the constraint of one-time production, retailer can only order the quantity that is not more than supplier's production capacity. In the above case of this chapter, supplier determines the production capacity as:

$$Q_1^* = (1 - \sqrt{\frac{2\sqrt{2}-2}{2}})b \approx 0.356b$$

Contrarily, the retailer determines the optimal order quantity in push supply chain, which is:

$$Q_2^* = \frac{1}{2}[b - \frac{c}{p}(1 + r_f)] \approx 0.5b$$

There is $Q_1^* < Q_2^*$. In other words, the quantity level in pull supply chain is smaller than that in push supply chain. This occurs because in pull supply chain, the retailer will not determine the order quantity until the demand uncertainty is eliminated, retailer does not need to consider ordering additional quantity in case of demand augment (because demand uncertainty is eliminated). Therefore, supplier knows if the production capacity level is set too high, it is likely that retailer only orders a percent of the total production capacity, the rest will be wasted. This is the reason why supplier determines a relatively lower production capacity in pull supply chain, compared to the order quantity in push supply chain. However, in push supply chain, retailer has to place order when the actual demand is not realized, as a result, the retailer must take the demand fluctuation into account and order more than that in the pull supply chain, in anticipation of the possible demand augment. Therefore, the optimal quantity level is larger in push supply chain.

Besides, also note that when finance factor is incorporated in the push supply chain, the optimal order quantity for retailer is decreasing in the interest rate r ($Q_2^* = \frac{1}{2}[b - \frac{c}{p}(1 + r_f)]$), which means the existence of supply chain finance makes retailer less aggressive when ordering. It is easy to understand because retailer has to worry about the future repayment when he places the order, interest rate is now serving as a constraint that prevents retailer from over-ordering. Choi and Chiu (2012) indicate sustainability is closely related to the order quantity, because a smaller order quantity also shows a smaller possibility of wasting surplus products. Therefore, it can be concluded the online-retailer-led supply chain finance helps reduce the order quantity and promote sustain growth.

Since its birth, online-retailer-led supply chain finance has been growing rapidly due to many superior attributes like less stringent loan conditions. However, the development of online-retailer-led supply chain finance is still in the initial stage with many problems. In order to make a more efficient financing channel for small and medium-sized enterprises, more upgrade and amendment are required. Currently, the main fund support of online-retailer-led financing comes from banks and the self-owned funds. There are strict restraints in banks' loan service which is difficult to satisfy the large financing demand of online retailer. Thus, developing the new fund-raising channel is at the top of priority for online retailers.

FUTURE RESEARCH DIRECTIONS

This work can be extended to various directions. First, the authors' main focus in this paper is the supply chain finance decision analysis under single-period situation, although it is sufficiently essential to cope with the questions the authors interest in, a multi-period model is worth considering to see how the outcomes change in different periods. Second, the authors assume that JD.COM is the monopolist finance service provider in the market, it is reasonable to argue that the retailer should have alternative finance support institutions, that's to say, adding other online retailers who also provide finance services like JD.COM is an interesting research direction, which can be regarded as a complementary extension to this paper. Last but not least, JD.COM also provides supply chain finance services to agricultural retailer and supplier, for which green growth is an important assessment index. Although this work focuses on the supply chain finance mode for commodity retailer, it is advisable to analyze how supply chain finance exerts influence on agricultural supply chain. Adding the factors of agricultural products (e.g., guarantee period, output uncertainty), then exploring whether supply chain finance leads to better green growth for agriculture is of great significance.

REFERENCES

Alan, Y., & Gaur, V. (2015). *Operational investment and capital structure under asset-based lending*. Johnson School Research Paper Series, Cornell University.

Baird, D. G., & Picker, R. C. (1991). A simple noncooperative bargaining model of corporate reorganizations. *The Journal of Legal Studies*, *20*(2), 311–349. doi:10.1086/467889

Bebchuk, L. A., & Chang, H. F. (1992). Bargaining and the division of value in corporate reorganization. *Journal of Law Economics and Organization*, *8*(2), 253–279.

Boyabath, O., & Toktay, L. B. (2011). Optimal control and hedging of operations in the presence of financial markets. *Management Science*, *57*(12), 2163–2179.

Broadie, M., Chernov, M., & Sundaresan, S. (2007). Optimal debt and equity values in the presence of Chapter 7 and Chapter 11. *The Journal of Finance*, *62*(3), 1341–1377. doi:10.1111/j.1540-6261.2007.01238.x

Buzacott, J. A., & Zhang, R. Q. (2004). Inventory Management with Asset-Based Financing. *Management Science*, *50*(9), 1274–1292. doi:10.1287/mnsc.1040.0278

Cachon, G. (2004). The allocation of inventory risk in a supply chain: Push, pull, and advance-purchase discount contracts. *Management Science*, *50*(2), 222–238. doi:10.1287/mnsc.1030.0190

Caixin Global. (2017). *Quick Take: JD.com Finance Unit Launches Microlending in Chongqing*. Retrieved October 19, 2017, from https://www.caixinglobal.com/

Caldentey, R., & Haugh, M. B. (2006). Optimal control and hedging of operations in the presence of financial markets. *Mathematics of Operations Research*, *31*(2), 285–304. doi:10.1287/moor.1050.0179

China Daily. (2017). *Supply chain in focus with new approach*. Retrieved October 27, 2017, from http://www.chinadaily.com.cn/

Choi, T. M., & Chiu, C. H. (2012). Mean-downside-risk and mean-variance newsvendor models: Implications for sustainable fashion retailing. *International Journal of Production Economics*, *135*(2), 552–560. doi:10.1016/j.ijpe.2010.10.004

Craig, N., & Raman, A. (2013). *Improving store liquidation*. Harvard Business School.

Dada, M., & Hu, Q. J. (2008). Financing newsvendor inventory. *Operations Research Letters*, *36*(5), 569–573. doi:10.1016/j.orl.2008.06.004

Donohue, K. (2000). Efficient supply contracts for fashion goods with forecast updating and two production modes. *Management Science*, *46*(11), 1397–1411. doi:10.1287/mnsc.46.11.1397.12088

Ferguson, M., DeCroix, G., & Zipkin, P. (2005). Commitment decisions with partial information updating. *Naval Research Logistics*, *52*(8), 780–795. doi:10.1002/nav.20119

Gupta, D. (2008). *Technical note: Financing the newsvendor*. University of Minnesota.

Iyer, A., & Bergen, M. (1997). Quick response in manufacturer–retailer channels. *Management Science*, *43*(4), 559–570. doi:10.1287/mnsc.43.4.559

JD.com. (2017). *JD.com Announces Fourth Quarter and Full Year 2016 Results*. Retrieved March 2, 2017, from http://corporate.jd.com/

Kordana, K. A., & Posner, E. A. (1999). A positive theory of Chapter 11. NYU Law Review, 74(1), 161-178.

Kouvelis, P., & Zhao, W. (2010). The newsvendor problem and price-only contract when bankruptcy costs exist. *Production and Operations Management*, *20*(6), 921–946. doi:10.1111/j.1937-5956.2010.01211.x

Kouvelis, P., & Zhao, W. (2012). Financing the newsvendor: Supplier vs. bank, and the structure of optimal trade credit contracts. *Operations Research*, *60*(3), 566–580. doi:10.1287/opre.1120.1040

Lai, G., Debo, L. G., & Sycara, K. (2009). Sharing inventory risk in supply chain: The implication of financial constraint. *Omega*, *37*(4), 811–825. doi:10.1016/j.omega.2008.06.003

Lariviere, M. A., & Porteus, E. L. (2001). Selling to the newsvendor: An analysis of price-only contracts. *Manufacturing & Service Operations Management: M & SOM*, *3*(4), 293–305. doi:10.1287/msom.3.4.293.9971

Li, L., Shubik, M., & Sobel, M. J. (2005). *Control of dividends, capital subscriptions, and physical inventories*. Yale School of Management.

Liu, X. H., Zhou, L. G., & Wu, Y. C. J. (2015). Supply Chain Finance in China: Business Innovation and Theory Development. *Sustainability*, *7*(11), 14689–14709. doi:10.3390u71114689

New York Times. (2018). *As China Curbs Borrowing, Growth Shows Signs of Faltering*. Retrieved June 14, 2018, from https://www.nytimes.com/

OECD. (2016). *Financing SMEs and Entrepreneurs 2016 (Report)*. Retrieved 2016, from https://www.oecd-ilibrary.org/

Özer, O., Uncu, O., & Wei, W. (2007). Selling to the "newsvendor" with a forecast update: Analysis of a dual purchase contract. *European Journal of Operational Research*, *182*(3), 1150–1176. doi:10.1016/j.ejor.2006.09.057

PYMNTS.com. (2015). *Supply Chain Finance Market Growing Worldwide*. Retrieved April 8, 2015, from https://www.pymnts.com/news/2015/supply-chain-finance-market-growing-worldwide/

SME Finance Forum. (2017). *MSME finance gap (Report)*. Retrieved 2017, from https://www.smefinanceforum.org/

State Council of the People's Republic of China. (2016). *Made in China 2025*. Retrieved August 29, 2016, from http://english.gov.cn/2016special/madeinchina2025/

State Council of the People's Republic of China. (2017). *19th National Congress of the Communist Party of China*. Retrieved October 28, 2017, from http://english.gov.cn/19thcpccongress/

Taylor, T. (2006). Sale timing in a supply chain: When to sell to the retailer? *Manufacturing & Service Operations Management: M & SOM*, *8*(1), 23–42. doi:10.1287/msom.1050.0089

Waonews. (2018). *Davos Liu Qiangdong dialogue: the orientation of financial support of science and technology of Internet antitrust*. Retrieved January 24, 2018, from https://www.waonews.com/

Wilner, B. S. (2000). The exploitation of relationships in financial distress: The case of trade credit. *The Journal of Finance*, *55*(1), 153–178. doi:10.1111/0022-1082.00203

Xu, X., & Birge, J. R. (2004). *Joint production and financing decisions: Modeling and analysis*. Northwestern University.

Yang, S. A., & Birge, J. R. (2009). *How inventory is (should be) financed: Trade credit in supply chains with demand uncertainty and costs of financial distress*. London Business School.

Yang, S. A., Birge, J. R., & Parker, R. P. (2015). The Supply Chain Effects of Bankruptcy. *Management Science*, *61*(10), 2320–2338. doi:10.1287/mnsc.2014.2079

KEY TERMS AND DEFINITIONS

Core Enterprise: A core enterprise refers to the enterprises who possess key resources, information, or data in supply chain. Core enterprise can easily exert influence on upstream and downstream partners.

Newsvendor Retailer: A retailer who faces uncertain demand that follows certain distributions. Retailer determines the optimal order quantity via forecast.

Online Retailer: A retailer who provides e-commerce platform for other small retailers. Online retailer supports those small retailers with centralized services and management.

Pull Supply Chain: A custom-centric supply chain, which is depending on the realized demand to pull the manufacturing, production, and other supply chain processes.

Push Supply Chain: A manufacturing-centric supply chain, which is dependent on the manufacturing, production, and other supply chain processes to stimulate the demand.

Small and Medium-Sized Enterprise: An enterprise whose business scale is small with little capital and fixed assets. Such enterprise has difficulty in obtaining financing from traditional banks.

Supply Chain Finance: A prevalent and fast-growing form of financing for small and medium-sized enterprises due to its high efficiency in raising funds. It is often provided by supply chain core enterprises.

Chapter 3
Analysis of Sustainable Development Path for Green Finance:
A Case Study of China

Hsu Chao Feng
University of Electronic Science and Technology of China Zhongshan Institute, China

Lee Bi Ru
University of Electronic Science and Technology of China Zhongshan Institute, China

ABSTRACT

The development of green finance is a global trend in the current era. At present, developing the green finance has been included as an important national development project by the Chinese government. With the rapid economic growth, the priorities or trade-offs between the economic development and the natural environment have also aroused different contradictions and problems. With the improvement of people's quality of life, they start to pay more attention to the pollution of the surrounding environment. Therefore, the government should properly intervene and propose effective measures, and green finance is an excellent tool to reconcile social economy and environmental protection and transform the physical investment, thus guiding the social resources towards the environmental protection industry and reaching an optimal interests allocation among the market, society, and government. Consequently, in the face of such a situation, it is necessary to propose a series of models and paths that suit the needs of the Chinese society and promote sustainable development.

DOI: 10.4018/978-1-5225-7808-6.ch003

INTRODUCTION

With the economic development trend of China, the economic growth rate has gradually slowed down, and the economic structure is facing adjustment and industrial transformation and upgrading, which will become the only way to achieve sustainable development. Green finance is especially important and poses a significant impact on the economic structural adjustment and industrial structural optimization, Ma, et al. (2016) In 2005, Industrial Bank was the first to launch the green finance business, and became the first "Equator banks" in China in 2008; in March 2016, the "13th Five-Year Plan" promulgated by the National People's Congress clearly proposed to "build green financial system, develop green credit and bonds, and set up green development funds"; in August 2016, the People's Bank of China and other associations jointly issued Guiding Opinions on Building Green Financial System to further define China's policy framework of developing green finance. Therefore, it can be seen that the establishment of a green financial system has risen to a national strategy.

Green finance is a new concept in financial theories and financial practices, and also called environmental financing or sustainable finance in the existing literature. Green finance is a special financial activity or development strategy that requires the financial industry to carry out financial innovation business from a macro perspective based on the principle of environmental protection and sustainable development, achieve the coordinated development of the environment and economy, and promote the sustainable development of the financial industry. The evaluation of the green finance from a micro perspective generally starts from financial institutions to check the green operation and management service capabilities of the financial industry. The development of green finance is evaluated through the development of green financial business in the financial institutions, corporate green financial policies and information disclosure, etc.

Based on the analysis of relevant foreign literature, the main viewpoint of foreign scholars is to use green finance as a means of capital financing, such as green credit and bonds. For example, Wang (2010) believed that green finance refers to a financial business in which direct and indirect financing and ecological insurance are used in order to rationally utilize energy, natural resources, and protect ecological environment services, thus achieving energy saving, emission reduction, and consumption decline. It promotes the adjustment to and optimization of industrial structure and achieves the perpetual coordinated development of economic society and ecological environment.

In the 19th National People's Congress, the development of green finance rose to a national strategy. On the one hand, the development of green finance is in line with the global green transformation trend. On the other hand, green finance is the hub between the financial industry and the environmental industry. Against the supply-side background, developing green finance is conducive to eliminating the backwardness and overcapacity, and promoting the upgrading of industrial structure. In addition, the development of green finance can promote more rational and effective allocation of financial resources, and incline these resources towards environmental protection, which is in line with the global development trend and enhances the overall social capability to withstand economic risks.

Li Tu and Xin Chang proposed that green finance integrates social responsibility, environmental protection, and traditional financial competitiveness systems, and enhances the capability of commercial banks to identify environmental risks and development opportunities, which strengthens the enterprise competitiveness to a certain extent and provides a guarantee for the long-term enterprise development. With the continuous deepening of the sustainable development, the development of green finance cannot only effectively alleviate the problem of energy shortage, but also contribute to the upgrading of Chinese economic industry, thus greatly improving the international competitiveness of China.

Currently, environmental pollution, climate change, and energy security have attracted much attention and restricted the sustainable growth of the Chinese economy. It will be difficult to sustain the previous economic growth model at the expense of resource consumption and high environmental costs in the future. In the 18th National People's Congress, for the first time, "Beautiful China" was regarded as a grand goal of ecological civilization construction; the Fifth Plenary Session of the 18th CPC proposed the five development concepts, including innovation, coordination, green, openness, and sharing, and thus green development was risen to a national strategy. It was pointed out in the report of the 19th National People's Congress that the modernization for the Chinese people is a harmonious coexistence of human beings and nature.

It is necessary to create more material wealth and spiritual wealth to meet people's growing needs for a better life and to provide more quality ecological products to meet people's growing needs for the beautiful ecological environment. Additionally, it was deployed in the report to promote the green development, focus on solving urgent environmental problems, increase the protection of ecosystems and reform the ecological environment supervision system. Financial institutions should fully consider the impact of environmental factors in investment and financing decision-making, and invest more funds in environmental protection, energy conservation and emission reduction, resource regeneration and other programs through a series of institutional arrangements and product innovations, while reducing the investment in high-pollution and high-energy consumption enterprises in order to promote the sustainable economic development and green ecological civilization.

RELATIONSHIP BETWEEN GREEN FINANCE AND SUSTAINABLE DEVELOPMENT

Green finance represents a new trend and direction for future financial development and emerges as an innovation and reform in the financial field. It is of great significance to carry out green finance for the purpose of promoting industrial transformation and upgrading, driving the sustainable development of the regional economy, and accelerating the social progress. Various financial policies may be employed to support and guide the development of green finance. These policies may present different characteristics in different financial industries. For example, in the banking industry, the green credit is promoted mainly through credit policies and regulatory policies; in the securities industry, the green bond market is developed mainly through investment policies and the information disclosure of listed companies to guide the stock listing and trading activities. In the insurance industry, the development of green insurance is mainly guided by strengthening the environmental risk control of enterprises.

Since the industrial revolution, developed countries and industrialized countries have experienced rapid economic growth and improved the living standards, which was accompanied by serious environmental problems, Institute of Development Studies, SWUFE. (2015) Under the traditional development model, economic growth is at the expense of huge resource consumption, and neglecting the control of pollutant missions has made the resource utilization issue increasingly prominent, worsened the environmental pollution and deteriorated the ecological environment, which has brought massive challenges to the human living environment. The World Environment and Development Committee put forward the concept of sustainable development and advocates the protection of the ecological environment abreast with economic growth, which has become a common claim of all countries in the world.

Finance is the core of the modern economy. With the rapid development of sustainability concept and modern finance, the two have been integrated into multiple aspects and promote mutual development. Sustainable development requires strong financial support while the healthy financial development depends on the sustainable economic growth. Finance is based on sustainable economic development while sustainable development lays the foundation for the long-term prosperity of the financial industry. The financial sector implements green finance, regards environmental protection as inseparable of financial business operations, promotes the coordinated development of environmental protection and economy, and cooperates with the sustainable development strategies of countries around the world, which is the future development trend of the financial industry.

The proposal and practice of green finance concept is an important trend of modern financial development and an important embodiment of socially responsible investment. It is an extension of traditional finance, and the commanding height of financial innovation, financial development and financial competition in the 21st century. As an important part of modern economy, finance plays an important role in promoting the green growth of the economy and serves as a powerful guarantee for promoting sustainable economic development and considering the coordinated progress of the economy, society, and environment.

DEVELOPMENT STATUS OF GREEN FINANCE AT HOME AND ABROAD

Overview of International Green Finance

In general, the international experience in green financial systems is fragmented and developing. The central banks, financial regulators and capital market developers have only recently raised their concerns about the environment. Despite this, some progress has been made in the international development of green finance. For example, in Brazil, the central bank put forward new demands on the banking environment and social risks through long-term national dialogue on sustainable development; in Europe, the traditional disclosure of sustainable information is shifting to key issue of inciting long-term capital for sustainable economic recovery; in the United States, there are extensively linked business activities, economic risks, new social contractual relationships between government and workers on long-term development of climate changes, which require the routine disclosure of capital market on sustainable economic risk factors.

Development of Green Finance in Foreign Countries

In both developed and developing countries, the concept of green finance is spreading more widely around the world. There are many developing countries such as Bangladesh, Brazil, South Africa, India, which focus on green finance. Moreover, some developed countries are also paying attention to green finance. At the international level, in January 2014, the United Nations Environment Programme established a working group on designing sustainable financial system and exploring the policies to promote a close integration of the financial system with sustainable development in order to transform the financial system. In July of the same year, the World Bank released the "Environmental and Social Framework: Setting Standards for Sustainable Development" report, trying to build framework, requirements, standards, and processes for green financial development. Furthermore, more and more countries have begun to incorporate green finance into their policy system. With the promotion of the green finance concept, many countries have taken action to promote green finance in recent years.

For example, the central bank of Brazil announced a new regulatory measure April 2014, requiring commercial banks to develop the strategic action and governance framework for environmental management and social risk management and regard it as the core element of overall risk management, State Council Development Research Center Green China Financial System Research Group (2016). Meanwhile, the EU requires large listed companies to disclose the implementation of environmental and social policies; 80% of foreign aid projects by the US Ministry of Finance have developed green requirements; the regulatory guidelines promulgated by South Africa in 2011 require the companies to disclose their financial and sustainability capabilities.

Development of Green Finance in China

The development of green finance in China can be traced back to the reform and opening up in the 1980s. Especially in recent years, Yancheng Rural Financial Association Research Group (2016) great achievements have been made in China's green finance regarding the legal and policy environment, scale and market organization. Financial practice represented by large-scale green credit has also been at the forefront of the world.

First, under the governmental impetus, China's green financial regulatory system has been gradually established, At the beginning of the 21st century, the environmental protection ideas of Chinese government began to convert from the administrative means to the comprehensive legal, economic, financial and technological means in order to solve the environmental problems. From the 11th Five-year Period, the green financial policy system was initially established. The 12th Five-Year Plan unified the planning of environmental economic policies, including green finance, for the first time. The Third Plenary Session of the 18th CPC proposed to accelerate the construction of ecological civilization system, which has created a higher and more authoritative environmental economic policy space for the development of China's green finance.

At present, the green financial policy system of China mainly includes policies directly related to green finance and supporting policies related to tax prices and infrastructure construction. Overall, the basic framework of green financial policy system of China has been initially shaped, which has played a key role in the initiation and development of the green financial market in China.

After the rise of green finance in China, what concerns people the most is the development of green credit business because banks are the focus of the Chinese financial system. Green credit is credit policy introduced by the Ministry of Environmental Protection jointly with the People's Bank of China and the China Banking Regulatory Commission in order to curb high-energy consumption and high-pollution industries and solve the environmental issues. However, due to the lack of complete evaluation standards and enforcement regulations, the effect so far has been limited. The major understanding of the banking industry on green credit is that it contributes to the fulfillment of corporate social responsibility, social contributions, and reputation enhancement rather than a new growth point in credit risk and business development. The environmental assessment thresholds of loan projects are low, and only whether the loan project is equipped with an environmental impact assessment report and whether there are environmental violations are reviewed. In addition, the control measures mainly focus on the introduction of loans to suppress "two highs and one excess" (high emissions, high pollution, and excess capacity).

The China Banking Regulatory Commission issued the "Green Credit Guideline", which defines the scope of green credit, environmental and social risks more clearly. It not only covers social issues such as pollution and safety but also includes climate change for the first time. In the meanwhile, the Green Credit Guideline provides clearer guidance on the implementation of green credit from top to bottom within the banking industry and makes it fairly restrictive through incentives and accountability mechanisms. The Ministry of Environmental Protection also joined the China Insurance Regulatory Commission and the China Banking Regulatory Commission to successively launch the green insurance and green securities policies, all of which are based on solving environmental pollution. They have made some positive attempts in the field of green finance, and are gradually enriching the green financial products in China.

PROBLEMS OR CHALLENGES IN THE DEVELOPMENT OF GREEN FINANCE IN CHINA

Although great achievements have been made in the development of green finance in China, green finance still faces certain difficulties in meeting the above needs of green development and green economy. As the development of green industry is widely characteristic of huge initial investment, long return period, uncertain cash return and high risk, which affects the enthusiasm of financial institutions to participate, there are a series of problems in the development process of green finance, which is mainly driven by government policy.

Problems in the Development of Green Finance in China

A. Small Green Finance Volume, Lack of Scale Economy and Inadequate Implementation

Since 2008, the People's Bank of China, the China Banking Regulatory Commission, the China Insurance Regulatory Commission and the China Securities Regulatory Commission have promulgated and implemented a series of green financial policies. However, in general, the funds actually used for green development are still relatively insufficient, and the implementation is inadequate. Taking green credit as an example, the total loan for Industrial and Commercial Bank of China in 2012 was RMB 8803.7 billion, and the loan invested in green development was RMB 593.4 billion. Therefore, the proportion of green credit was 6.74%. The total loan of China Construction Bank was RMB 7512.3 billion, and the loan invested in green development was RMB 239.6 billion. Therefore, the proportion of green credit is 3.18%. In general, the innovation of green financial products is insufficient, and the market is still not perfect.

Since China launched green finance, although the financial industry has successively promoted financial innovation products that support green development, the gap between China and foreign leaders regarding green development is still obvious. The industrial understanding of green finance is that it is almost equivalent to green credit, which is to reduce the loan credit to high-pollution, high-energy consumption, and high-emissions enterprises. In addition, the industrial understanding of other green finance products, such as green securities, green insurance, and carbon finance products, is inadequate. The majority supports the energy conservation and emission reduction policies in the form, and the development of green financial markets needs to be improved.

B. Insufficient Profit Incentive and Single Mode of Green Finance

There are certain contradictions between the green development commonweal and the profitability of the financial industry. The essence of green development is to achieve sustainable development between economy and ecology, resources and environment. It presents strong commonweal while the financial industry is to make profits, which is the foundation of financial development. Green finance is an investment with high risk and low return. Therefore, there are potential contradictions between the two. Taking carbon finance as an example, the commercial banks provide bank loans to key energy conservation and emission reduction projects, issue short-term financing bills, medium-term notes and other green financing support, and launch financing services through innovative methods, such as account receivables mortgages, expected return mortgages, and equity pledges.

However, as there is no mandatory management of carbon emission reduction in China (no emission rights), the emission reduction demand is limited, and the carbon financial products promoted by the commercial banks have not yet achieved sustainable profitability. Besides, derivatives, such as carbon futures and carbon options, are almost blank. Single profit model of carbon finance, insufficient green financial system design, incomplete policies and regulations, and lack of green financial legal system make the practice of green financial policy measures lacking in pertinence and operability, which cannot meet the actual needs. At present, there is no system design on the national and legal level.

Instead, only the People's Bank of China, the China Banking Regulatory Commission, the China Insurance Regulatory Commission and the China Securities Regulatory Commission as well as the Ministry of Environmental Protection have enacted some departmental rules and regulations. Therefore, during the industrial structural transformation from high carbon to low carbon, the operating costs of transforming enterprises will increase significantly, which affects profitability. In the meanwhile, the financial subsidies, tax relieves and financial preferential policies have not been effectively promoted, affecting the enthusiasm of financial institutions to carry out green financial business.

C. Incomplete Information Disclosure of Green Finance

Information asymmetry leads to greater green financial risks, lower benefits, and incomplete information disclosure and sharing mechanism. In addition, the mandatory corporate environmental information disclosure system has not yet been established, and the environmental protection departments have not yet established effective environmental assessment standards. The information released through relevant channels is opaque, scarce and ineffective. The existing bank credit information system can only provide the environmental information on a limited number of enterprises.

As most non-listed companies are not within the scope of enterprises and programs that are not under the national monitoring, it is difficult to obtain their environmental protection information. Many enterprises conceal or falsely report their own environmental protection information to shirk environmental responsibility. This information asymmetry increases the risks of green finance, such as policy risk, credit risk, and technical risk. These risks will directly endanger the security and profitability of financial assets.

There is no effective communication mechanism between the government and financial institutions, and among the government industry sectors, the environmental management sectors and the financial regulatory sectors. In addition, the information disclosed by the banks on green credit is not consistent or clear, resulting in a lack of data comparability. The disclosure of important information on major pollutant emissions, control measures and effects of the listed companies is limited. If the externalities of environmental problems cannot be scientifically assessed, the positive environmental benefits generated by green schemes often fail to bring matching economic benefits.

D. Lacking Top-Level Strategic Development Design and Insufficient Legal Supervision of Green Finance

So far, China lacks a unified and clear concept and framework for green finance. Policy makers and participating institutions have different understandings of the concept of green finance. In addition, although China has defined the national strategy for green sustainable development, there is a lack of a top-level design and specific implementation support of the green financial strategy, and the cross-sectoral coordination mechanism is still not perfect, which makes the strategy difficult to be implemented fully and effectively in the formulation of financial policies. Besides, the law and the supervision system for green finance are not perfect, the responsibility belongings are not clear, the operability is not high, and the implementation is not in place. China has enacted laws, regulations, standards and normative documents on environmental protection, and has formed a relatively complete environmental protection policy system.

However, there are considerable institutional and functional repetitions among existing laws, and the relevant government departments have unclear rights and responsibilities. As a result, the relevant regulations in the specific implementation process have been weakened, the implementation and supervision are insufficient, which objectively reduces the standards of environmental protection, and makes it difficult to form strong external constraints on the behaviors that damage the environment.

Challenges in the Implementation of Green Finance in China

In March 2011, the "12th Five-Year Plan for National Economic and Social Development of the People's Republic of China" was issued, which clearly proposed to deepen the reform of the financial system, Green Finance Research Group of Industrial and Commercial Bank of China. (2017). The development of green finance in China takes a late start, and mainly involves green credit, green insurance, and green securities. The main development methods are green credit implemented by banks and green insurance implemented by insurance companies. In terms of green credit, Chinese commercial banks and overseas financial institutions cooperate in carbon financial business relying on the "Kyoto Protocol" and "Clean Development Mechanism". For example, Industrial Bank first joined the "Equator Principles", and cooperated with the International Finance Corporation (IFC) in 2006 to provide a loan of RMB 2.4 billion for energy conservation and emission reduction projects in China.

In 2012, the China Banking Regulatory Commission issued the "Green Credit Guideline", which sets clear requirements for banking financial institutions to effectively implement green credit and vigorously promote energy conservation, emission reduction, and environmental protection. With the increasing environmental pollution, the sustainable financial development has been deeply rooted in the hearts of the people. The status of green credit in the banks has also been continuously enhanced. In terms of green insurance, in 2007, the State Environmental Protection Administration issued the "Guiding Opinions on Environmental Pollution Liability Insurance Work".

In 2008, Ping An launched Environmental Pollution Liability Insurance. In case of pollution accidents, the enterprises bear compensation liability for the damage caused to a third party according to law. In terms of green securities, in 2008, the State Environmental Protection Administration issued the "Guiding Opinions on Strengthening the Environmental Protection Supervision of Listed Companies", making active exploration in regulating the investment of socially-raised funds, curbing the over-expanding of high-energy consumption, high-pollution and high-emission enterprises, and promoting the listed companies to fulfill environmental and social responsibilities.

ANALYSIS OF DEVELOPMENT DIRECTION AND PATH FOR GREEN FINANCE

Future Development Direction for Green Finance

The future development direction of green finance is to improve the policy support system for green finance, Yang, et al. (2015) guide the financial institutions to accelerate the green financial product innovation and the investors to adjust the investment that meets the needs of green development. In essence, green finance refers to a series of institutional arrangements, including loans, funds, bonds, stocks and insurance, etc., to guide social funds to support green industries such as environmental protection, energy conservation and clean energy under the guidance and encouragement by policies.

From the perspective of economic principles, green finance forms a new financial development paradigm through financial policy and product service innovations, visualizes the hidden return of green waters and mountains and the hidden cost of pollution, and reconstructs the price formation mechanism of funds. The economic value of natural resources and carbon-intensive investments is reduced through policy and market signals to change the behavioral preferences of financial entities. In terms of operation, the current support for rural finance and small and micro enterprises should be compared, and green financial policy support systems should be established and improved. In addition, the coordination and cooperation among taxation policy, monetary policy, credit policy and industrial policy should be promoted, and the incentive and constraint mechanisms for financial institutions to develop green financial business should be strengthened.

The green financial contents are integrated into banking supervision policies while the sustainable development is regarded as an important part of financial risk management, Wang, et al. (2016) Starting from the national conditions of China, following measures can be taken: (1) Do not include the eligible green credits in the deposit-to-loan ratio assessment indicator; (2) Introduce the environmental stress testing system, develop the standards, evaluation systems and methods for environmental stress testing on different financial asset portfolios; (3) Establish a preferential position for green assets in mortgage guarantees; (4) Establish more convenient securitization pipeline for green credit, promote the coordination between the securities market supervision policy and the development of green finance, and increase the efforts in the development of green bond market.

At present, the market-oriented financing pipeline in the green investment practices of China is mainly commercial loans. Compared with the actual needs of green investment and financing, the sustainability of the single financing structure is relatively low while the fund sources of green investment in China mainly depend on bank loans. It is not that the willingness of the investment entities to choose bank loans is stronger, but there are institutional restrictions of other financing channels. In response to the above problems, the regulatory policies of the future securities market should focus on three aspects: (1) Actively build the green bond market; (2) Establish the mandatory disclosure mechanism for environmental information of listed companies and bond issuers; (3) Promote the green investor network, and improve the investor social responsibility system.

Reference to the Experience of Green Finance in Foreign Countries

We analyze the experience of two typical green financial developed countries, namely the United States and the United Kingdom, People's Bank of China Hangzhou Center Branch Office Research Group (2011).

The United Kingdom: Give full play to the role of the government and strengthen policy guidance and supervision.

The United Kingdom continues to strengthen its legislation on green finance. In 2009, it launched the "Low Carbon Transformation Plan" and the "Renewable Energy Strategy". In 2012, the first policy green investment bank in the United Kingdom was put into operation. The bank is wholly owned by the UK government and aims to encourage more social capital to invest in green environmental protection projects. In order to ensure the operational sustainability, green investment bank selects the target industries based on the resource endowments in the United Kingdom, and establishes the offshore wind power generation, energy efficiency financing and biomass energy as the three priority investment areas.

The 2014 annual report of the bank shows that it has invested more than 50% of the green projects in the United Kingdom, making a direct investment of GBP 723 million, and driving a private investment of GBP 1.748 billion. The investment leverage ratio reaches 2.42, which effectively guides the private investment. Meanwhile, the United Kingdom focuses on the regulation of environmental risks in the financial industry. In 2000, the investment in pensions must consider the social and environmental issues. In 2015, the Bank of England Prudential Regulation Authority conducted the first assessment on the impact of climate change on the insurance industry in the United Kingdom, and promoted the healthy development of the financial industry.

The United States: The market mechanism is dominant and government supplements by incentive measures.

The United States adheres to market orientation in the development of green finance, emphasizes the role of resource allocation in capital markets and carbon trading markets, and vigorously develops green funds, green bonds, green indices, and carbon finance, etc. The United States is one of the first countries in the world to implement a greenhouse gas emissions trading system. The Chicago Climate Exchange is the first trading platform in the world to participate in greenhouse gas emissions trading under legal restrictions. The United States Regional Greenhouse Gas Emission Reduction Legislation Proposal under the platform is the first cross-regional market-oriented carbon-trading framework in the United States.

On this basis, the United States has continuously introduced new carbon financial derivatives that are innovated from the carbon emission allowances and certified carbon emission reductions. After the financial crisis, the United States began to implement the "green new policy" and increased the governmental financial investment and tax reduction in low-carbon industry. About USD 58 billion in the economic stimulus plan is invested in environmental protection and energy fields. In order to strengthen the use of government funds, the Connecticut Green Bank, the New York State Green Bank, and the New Jersey Energy Resilience Bank were successively established. These banks are funded by the government, but conduct independent commercial operations.

Analysis of Development Path for Green Finance

The development experience of green finance in developed countries provides the following ideas for improving the green financial mechanism, Yi, et al (2014).

First, the strong support of the government is the premise and guarantee for the development of green finance. Although the United States and other Western countries have promoted the market economy mechanism in the development of green finance, the government still plays a supporting role. On the contrary, the administrative color of Asian countries is more obvious.

In recent years, more and more countries have realized that there are market failures and government failures in green finance practices. Therefore, the two models show signs of gradual integration, and the role of the government has been re-examined. It is generally agreed that the government should be committed to creating an excellent market development environment, stimulate and guide the market willingness. On the one hand, it guides all parties to carry out green investment by formulating development plans and legal regulations at the national level. On the other hand, the loan interest, financial subsidies, tax relieves and other policies on green projects are adopted to encourage the development of green finance and play a propeller role.

Second, policy green banks serve as an important tool for the government to guide private green investment. At present, the United Kingdom has established green banks at the national level, while several states in the United States have established state-level green banks. These green banks are all funded by the government and maintain high independence under government supervision. Green banks not only provide long-term and stable financial support for green projects, but also partially solve the market failure of green project financing, and can generate information spillover effects on the entire financial market, increase investor confidence, and leverage the investment of social capital. For China, pilot green banks can be established on both national and provincial levels as policy financial institutions that achieve the governmental green policy objectives, make full use of their expertise, economies of scale and risk control in green investment, and drive social capital investment in green industry.

Third, the market-oriented operation is the key to the sustainable development of green finance. The development of green financial products in developed countries is more autonomous, and the government has less administrative intervention in financial institutions, but focuses on the use of market operations to promote the implementation of green investment strategies. Therefore, the implementation means of green finance is more comprehensive, and the products are more diverse. The long-term mechanism framework for green financial development is cored on the market operation mechanism. Under the governmental guidance and the social impetus, diversified market entities, such as policy financial institutions, commercial financial institutions, and intermediary service agencies, are promoted to effectively provide innovative financial products, including green credit, green bonds, green funds, green insurance and carbon finance.

SUGGESTIONS AND COUNTERMEASURES

With the rapid economic growth, the resource consumption and environmental pollution in China are becoming increasingly serious, which not only poses a huge threat to the sustainable economic development, but leads to immeasurable loss of life and property, Li, (2017) In this case, developing green economy has already become an inevitable strategic direction for China. In developing countries such as China, as long as the use of petrochemical energy resources and the energy consumption per unit can be reduced, the investment belongs to the category of green finance. Emerging market countries have incorporated the environmental risk factors into banking supervision rules, which has been widely recognized by the international community.

On the other hand, the excessive administrative intervention by the governments of developing countries has also been questioned. People realize that green finance promoted by administrative forces is flawed. The government should only play the role of coach, motivate the enterprises, guide the market, make more efforts in creating excellent policy environment, give full play to the role of the market and avoid excessive direct intervention.

We Propose the Following Four Suggestions on the Development of Green Finance in China

1. Improve the Construction of Government and Relevant Institutions

The participation of central and local government funds and the reform of related systems are required. A green banking system should be established to give full play to the professional capabilities, scale benefits and risk control advantages of green banks in green credit and investment. Besides, China Ecological Development Bank should be established at the national level, initiated by the government but not requiring the form of holding, which can achieve the oath effect on the whole society and the capital market, fully demonstrate the determination of the Chinese government to control environmental pollution and develop green economy, enhance the confidence of private funds in future policies and the risk appetite for green projects and contribute to guide more resources into the green industry.

Taking the United Kingdom Green Bank as an example, the investment funds of the bank only account for about 10% of the total green investment of the United Kingdom Green in recent years, but it has participated in and guided 50% of the total green investment projects in the United Kingdom, actively piloted the green banks held by private capital at the local level, promoted the commercial banks, and set up ecological finance divisions, etc. Green banks can conduct debt financing through the issuance of green bonds and central bank refinancing.

2. Set Up Professional Investment Platform for Green Industry

The fund sources are an important supplement to green credit. The PPP model, the development of green industry funds, and the use of limited government funds to encourage private capital equity investment, the support policies to encourage single PPP projects are applicable to PPP model based industrial funds. In addition, the organizational form and the governmental participation form of the green industry funds should be reasonably set, and the effective exit mechanism should be constructed. It is recommended that the state and local governments issue relevant support policies for the green industry funds.

In addition, the state and local governments should actively cooperate with relevant domestic educational institutions and environmental protection departments to create professional talents, innovate the green financial products and business models, and strengthen the innovations in green financial derivatives. Besides, institutionalized green financial derivatives market and green financial intermediary service market should be established, and the carbon trading market should be gradually developed.

Furthermore, various carbon financial derivatives, such as carbon forwards, carbon futures, carbon options, etc., should be innovated to build the carbon financial product system in China.

3. Encourage the Active Participation in the International Investment Activities of Green Finance

Foreign investment and development institutions, such as the Asian Infrastructure Investment Bank and the BRICS Bank, should join in the Equator Principles or establish high standards in accordance with the Equator Principles, set up environmental risk management system under the requirements not lower than those of the World Bank and the Asian Development Bank, fully disclose the environmental information, vigorously promote the external green investments and maintain the image of a responsible big country. The government organization departments should lead by example and require the invested enterprises and projects to fully consider the requirements of energy conservation and emission reduction in the procurement and construction process, and achieve environmentally friendly procurement.

4. Improve the Laws and Regulations for Green Finance

The green finance top-level design at the national level should be completed. Green finance is the concrete embodiment of ecological civilization construction in the financial field. In order to ensure the healthy and sustainable development of green finance, it is necessary to conduct top-level design at the national strategic level. It is suggested that the construction of legal and regulatory system supporting the green finance requires the cooperation and promotion of legislative authorities, relevant ministries and financial institutions. The legal security system should be formulated and improved as soon as possible, including the basic legal system of green finance, the implementation system of green financial business and the green financial supervision system.

In terms of policy support, relevant government departments may formulate a series of supporting policies and measures according to macro policies and sustainable development principles, provide an excellent external environment for green finance, form a positive incentive mechanism, guide all parties involved to actively participate in green finance and stimulate the market potential and vitality, such as tax relieves, financial subsidies, risk compensation, and credit guarantees. In terms of supervision, the financial supervisory authority and relevant competent departments should strengthen the implementation of existing restrictive and binding policies, unify and improve the green financial regulatory indicator system, strengthen off-site supervision and on-site inspections, and promote financial institutions to actively carry out green finance. In addition, they should clarify the responsibilities of environmental polluters, set up enhanced incentive and restraint mechanisms when they can accurately distinguish between environmentally illegal enterprises and environmentally friendly enterprises.

Specific Measures for the Long-Term and Effective Mechanism of Green Finance

The construction of a long-term and effective green finance mechanism requires rational positioning and coordination among the government, the market and the society. The specific measures are as follows (Ma, 2015):

1. Policy Guarantee Mechanism on the Macro Level

The policy guarantee mechanism is mainly the system construction and policy design of relevant government departments. In the early development stage of green finance, the government should strengthen the coordination and cooperation of the legal system, business system, taxation policy, regulatory policy and information communication mechanism, etc., form effective incentive and restraint mechanism, and create an excellent development environment for green finance. When promoting the construction of the green financial system, they should consider the national conditions, learn from foreign advanced experience, and strengthen the top-level design and overall planning from the national strategic level.

The green financial system includes the basic legal system, the business standard system, the business implementation system, the implementation standards and operation regulations of green financial supervision system. The implementation and supervision efforts should be increased, and standardized and fair market order should be constructed for the green market. According to the study, the governmental investment in green industry can drive 5-15 times of social investment, which presents strong leverage effect.

It is necessary to rationalize the relationship between the government and the market, innovate the financial investment mechanism, and change the governmental universal subsidy policy, convert the financial funds from green financial supply to incentives for market-oriented green financial supply, and ensure the efficiency and fairness of the use of financial funds by market means. The supervision evaluation system should be improved, and the supervision should be strengthened from local government, financial institutions, and enterprises. Besides, green performance evaluation should be conducted, and the guiding, incentive and constraint role of supervision evaluation system should be developed. Financial supervision departments, financial institutions and intermediary service agencies must establish a sound cross-sectoral coordination mechanism and build a bridge between the government and the market in order to promote information exchange among different departments.

2. Market Operation Mechanism on the Medium Level

The role of green finance in supporting green industries should be developed, and a sound green financial market is indispensable. In this respect, the green financial organization system should be improved. On the other hand, green financial product tools should be innovated to form a green financial market structure with diversified participants and financial products. Besides, the green financial organization system should be perfected:

(a) Expand the green financial market participants, encourage the existing banks for further greening, adjust the business operations in accordance with the Equator Principles and mobilize the enthusiasm of non-bank financial institutions, such as securities companies, insurance companies and fund companies; (b) Establish a green development bank, refer to the international experience, initiate a specialized green development bank by the national, provincial and municipal governments through the diversified capital approach of state-level banks in the United States, which consists of financial funds, sewage charges, and social capital; (c) Cultivate green financial intermediation service agencies, encourage the existing intermediary service agencies to implement the concept of green finance, and actively participate in green financial operations; accelerate the cultivation and development of professional intermediary service agencies, including green credit rating agencies, green financial product certification agencies, green asset assessment agencies, green financial information service agencies and environmental risk assessment agencies in order to provide technical support for green project financing; (d) Strengthen the construction of green financial talent team, formulate special green financial talent development strategies in relevant institutions which involve in the development of green finance, increase the combination of internal training and external introduction, actively cooperate with professional organizations, and carry out professional training on existing employees.

3. Conceptual Cultivation Mechanism on the Micro Level

The policy support mechanism at the macro level and the market operation mechanism at the medium level are the external guarantees for the long-term and effective mechanism of green finance. The key to make green finance participants spontaneously pay attention to environmental protection and to practice social responsibility is to convert the concept., Zhu, et al. (2015) The concept is the leader of action. Establishing a good green development concept will directly affect the financial behaviors of the participants. The relationship between environmental protection and economic development should be organized, and the green governance concept considering both economic development and environmental protection should be advocated.

Besides, ecological protection responsibility investigation system and environmental damage liability lifelong investigation system should be implemented by establishing a rigid performance evaluation system that reflects resource consumption, environmental damage and ecological benefits, and the local governments should be urged to promote green development. In the meanwhile, local governments should integrate green environmental protection concept into urbanization construction, vigorously promote the green transformation of urbanization, create a green and low-carbon livable city, and effectively serve the long-term interests of the people. Green financial values should be cultivated in financial institutions.

The financial institutions should fully realize that developing green finance is an inherent requirement of the development of the financial industry, and that actively carrying out green finance is not only important for expanding market share, improving environmental risk management capabilities, and enhancing long-term competitiveness, but also helps to establish a good social image and advocates the green consumption concept of residents. In March 2016, the National Development and Reform Commission and other 10 departments issued the "Guiding Opinions on Promoting Green Consumption", actively advocating the green consumption model, and fully exerting the leading role of green consumption, promoting the front-end industry upgrading and forcing the supply-side reform through the end green consumption. In addition, the publicity and education on green consumption should be improved, and the green low-carbon concept should be integrated into families, schools and social education, thus creating good social public opinion for the development of green finance, and promoting the greening of residents' lifestyles.

CONCLUSION

China is the most promising carbon emission reduction market and the largest CDM project supplier in the world, providing 150 million to 225 million tons of CO2 approved emission reduction credits per year. High labor costs and low energy conservation potential cost the advanced economies much higher to complete the emission reduction task than that of China. Therefore, the development prospect of green financial market in China is very broad. For China, green finance is the extension and development of traditional finance, and should be a modern financial system that follows the requirements and rules of market economy, orients towards the construction of ecological civilization through the means of developing various financial derivatives for the purpose of promoting sustainable development.

For both the environmental protection and the long-term corporate development, the implementation of green finance plays a vital role in determining whether China can achieve sustainable development. In the next few years, the concept of green finance and the sustainability concept will complement each other and jointly promote the development of the global economy and the environmental protection a. In the future, we should not only continue to improve the theoretical research and operational mechanism of green finance, but also confirm the technical operation and management norms of financial institutions for the development of green finance and keep promoting the research on green finance.

REFERENCES

Ba, S. S., Yang, C. P., & Yao, S. D. (2018). Review on the green financial research progress in China. *Journal of Financial Development Research*, 3-9.

Green Finance Research Group of Industrial and Commercial Bank of China. (2017). Research on the construction of green strategic system in commercial banks. *Financial Forum*, (1), 3-16.

Institute of Development Studies SWUFE. (2015). Environmental and Economic Policy Research Center Research Group of the Ministry of Environmental Protection. Green finance and sustainable development. *Financial Forum*, (10), 30-40.

Li, H. H. (2017). Analysis of profitability and commonweal relationships of green finance. *Financial Forum*, (5), 3-11.

Ma, C. (2015). Construction of green financial system in China. *Financial Forum*, (5), 18-27.

Ma, C. (2016). Development and prospect of green finance in China. *Comparative Economic and Social Systems*, (6), 26-32.

People's Bank of China Hangzhou Center Branch Office Research Group. (2011). Green finance: International experience, enlightenment and countermeasures. *Monetary Review*, 20-25.

State Council Development Research Center Green China Financial System Research Group. (2016). Logic and framework for development of green finance in China. *Financial Forum*, (2), 17-28.

Wang, H. H., & Liu, N. (2016). Exploration on the long-term sustainable development mechanism of green finance in China. *Taipei Economic Inquiry*, (4), 99-105.

Yancheng Rural Financial Association Research Group. (2016). Research on the development path of green finance in commercial banks. *Modern Finance*, (6), 46-48.

Yang, F., Shao, C. F., & Chu, M. T. (2015). Analysis of opportunities, challenges and countermeasures for the development of green finance in China. *Ecological Economics*, *31*(11), 85–87.

Yi, C. P., Chiang, C., & Peng, Y. (2014). Development status and optimization path of green finance-A case study in Hubei. *Journal of Huazhong Agricultural University*, (4), 112-117.

Zhu, Q., & Zhang, Q. (2015). Evaluating practices and drivers of corporate social responsibility: The Chinese context. *Journal of Cleaner Production*, *100*, 315–324. doi:10.1016/j.jclepro.2015.03.053

Chapter 4
An Empirical Study of Green Finance Research Through Bibliometrics

Feng Hu
Guangdong University of Technology, China

Haibo Wei
Guangdong Water and Power Survey and Design Institute, China

ABSTRACT

Green finance issues have triggered the increasing research enthusiasm of researchers. With the rapid growing of publications related to green finance, it is difficult for readers to deeply understand the intellectual structure, research hotspots, and trends. In addition, the dynamic nature of a research front poses challenges for the scientists, research policymakers, and many others to keep up with the rapid advances of the state of the art in science. Therefore, the authors conducted a bibliometric analysis from the Web of Science over the period of 1998–2017. Co-word analysis and co-citation analysis are employed to explore institution distribution, journal co-citation analysis, author co-citation analysis, document co-citation analysis, and keyword co-word analysis, particularly in high frequency items, intellectual turning points, burst points, and emerging trends. The results can be useful for institutions and researchers worldwide to understand the panorama of green finance research, find the potential research gaps, and focus on the future research trends.

DOI: 10.4018/978-1-5225-7808-6.ch004

1. INTRODUCTION

With rapid population growth and substantial increases in energy consumption, the ecological health of the world is being seriously challenged, and green growth has become a development trend in the world economy. The transformation from a resource-consuming economy to a resource-conserving and environmentally friendly economy has become the main objective and practical route of economic reform in major economies. Against the background of low carbon green growth, green finance, as a new financial pattern to integrate environmental protection with economic profits, emphasizing "green" and "finance" (Yao Wang and Qiang Zhi, 2016), has come into being and is becoming a key point for the development of many countries. Its goal is sustainable development.

Green finance refers to taking environmental protection as a basic policy, integrating environmental assessments into processes, considering potential environmental impacts in daily investment and financing decisions, and blending the potential returns, risks and costs related to environmental conditions into the daily business of banks. It focuses on the interests of the environment and guides economic subjects to pay attention to the balance of natural ecology through their own activities. It emphasizes the coordinated development of financial activities, environmental protection and ecological balance, and hopes to realize the sustainable development of economies and society. Therefore, green finance issues have attracted increasing research attention. Recent work includes studies on standardizing sustainable development of development banks (AU Gallagher and KP Yuan F, 2017), low carbon finance (Sudmant, A., Colenbrander, S., Gouldson, A., and Chilundika, N, 2017), green credit (Guan, R., Zheng, HT, Hu, J., Fang, Q., and Ren, RE, 2017), green investments (Maggioni, D., Santangelo, GD, 2017), etc. However, green finance is a complex issue and involves multi-disciplinary knowledge. It is difficult for a new researcher to understand the current research situation and identify the research gaps.

In this paper, the authors performed an empirical study of green finance through bibliometrics. Bibliometrics uses qualitative and statistical analysis to describe patterns in publications in a given field (Meen Chul Kim, Yoo Kyung Jeong, and Min Song, 2014). It can reveal some interesting features of academic and social communities, uncover cohesive collaboration among researchers and invisible communities, and represent the intellectual structure and hotspots of a knowledge domain (Newman, M. E. J., 2001). It is convenient for new or would-be green finance researchers to discover the current discipline distribution, research hotspots, influential institutions, scientists, journals, and to describe the co-occurrence relationships. This study performed a visual bibliometric analysis of green finance, and provides guidance concerning the current research status, hotspots and intellectual structure of the green finance knowledge domain.

2. METHODOLOGY

2.1. Data Sources

Commonly used data sources for bibliometrics are Web of Science (WoS), Scopus, Google Scholar (GS), and PubMed (Chaomei Chen, 2017). Each data source has its own advantages and drawbacks (Lokman I. Meho, Kiduk Yang, 2007). Compared with Scopus, GS, and PubMed, WoS has more detailed citation data to meet the citation analysis demands of different users. Moreover, WoS provides access to the most reliable, integrated, multidisciplinary research connected through linked content citation metrics from multiple sources within a single interface. The authors therefore selected WoS as the data collection platform. Furthermore, compared with monographs, conference proceedings, and personal blogs or web pages, academic journals tend to be more direct, consistent and important channels for scientists to publish, spread, accumulate, comment on and assume the lead in a specific scientific research field (Feng Hu, Wei Liu, Sang-Bing Tsai, Junbin Gao, Ning Bin, and Quan Chen, 2018). The authors therefore targeted the journal articles on WoS.

Our main task was to find green finance research articles. On March 20th 2018, the authors began the initial query on the term TS = (green finance) on WoS. The search results were limited by language (English) and literature type (Article). The authors found 358 articles. Nevertheless, some articles with semantically different terms and expressions but with the same meaning or with a subset of green finance were not retrieved by the query. These terms include “green financing”, “green credit”, “green securities”, “green investment”, “ecological finance”, “carbon finance”, “low carbon finance”, etc., and they needed to be added to the research filters. Eventually the authors obtained 6644 appropriate journal articles. The bibliographic records were downloaded, including titles, authors, institutions, keywords, references, etc.

2.2. Research Methods

Bibliometric analysis has been widely applied in many scientific fields (Chaomei Chen, 2017; Feng Hu, Wei Liu, Sang-Bing Tsai, Junbin Gao, Ning Bin, and Quan Chen, 2018; Nobre, G.C., Tavares, E, 2017; Gu, D., Li, J., Li, X., Liang, C, 2017; Zhigao Liu, Yimei Yin, Weidong Liu, and Dunford Michael, 2015). It integrates the technologies and methods of mathematics, statistics, information science, philology, and other disciplines to analyze the distribution regularities, intellectual base, research front, and evolution paths (Lokman I. Meho, Kiduk Yang, 2007). With the development of information technologies, many representative software tools, such as Citespace, IN-SPIRE, VantagePoint, CoPalRed, Leydesdorff's Software, Bibexcel, Sci2 Tool, VOSViewer, Network Workbench Tool, SciMAT, et al. (Feng Hu, Wei Liu, Sang-Bing Tsai, Junbin Gao, Ning Bin, and Quan Chen, 2018), can be exploited to facilitate the information visualization and scientific mapping of knowledge domains. In this survey, the authors used Citespace. Citespace was developed by professor Chaomei Chen at Drexel University (USA). It is a Java-based information visualization and scientific mapping software package, and it is freely available at http://cluster.cis.drexel.edu/~cchen/citespace/. Its main functions include co-word network analysis of keywords and subject categories, and co-citation network analysis of authors, documents, institutions and journals. More importantly, Citespace facilitates the identification of the chronological patterns of a specific knowledge domain, including research hotspots, intellectual turning points, and citation bursts.

Some distinctive bibliometric methods provided by Citespace have been employed to analyze the intellectual structure, research front and trends in green finance, including keyword co-word analysis (Callon, M., Courtial, J.P., Turner, W.A., and Bauin, S., 1983), document co-citation analysis (DCA) (Chaomei Chen, 2006; Small, H., 1973), author co-citation analysis (ACA) (Chaomei Chen, 1999; White, H.D., McCain, and K.W., 1998) and many other variations (Chaomei Chen, 2017). Among them, both co-word analysis and co-citation analysis are derived from co-occurrence analysis, which is based on the assumption that they are related to some degree when two items appear in the same context, and is used to measure the frequency of co-occurrence of pairs of keywords or noun phrases and other terms in the same document (Zhigao Liu, Yimei Yin, Weidong Liu, and Dunford Michael, 2015). Keyword co-word analysis is usually used in content analysis based on the assumption that keywords reflect the core content of a certain research literature (He, 1999). It focuses on the words or noun phrases, and terms from the title, abstract, author keywords, and keywords plus, and tends to explore research hotspots and changes in research themes in a knowledge domain by measuring the frequency of pairs of keywords occurring in the documents of a specific research field. Co-citation analysis is employed to detect the relationships among scholars, journals and the intellectual structure of a specific research field. This method assumes that if two items (documents, or authors and journals, etc.) are both cited by a third one, then they are related in some way, even though they don't directly cite each other (Braam et al. 1991a, b; Small 1973). The co-citation frequency is defined as the frequency of two items being cited simultaneously. The larger the frequency, the stronger their relationship (Zhigao Liu, Yimei Yin, Weidong Liu, and Dunford Michael, 2015).

In this paper, the authors performed a bibliometric analysis of green finance. The 20-year time interval between 1998 and 2017 was sliced into 10 2-year segments, which started with 1998-1999 and ended with 2016-2017. The authors selected the most cited or occurring items from each slice to build co-occurrence networks. Moreover, the Pathfinder algorithm was used to simplify the networks and highlight some important structural characteristics (Lokman I. Meho, Kiduk Yang, 2007).

The rest of this paper is organized as follows: In section 3, the authors present the bibliometric analysis and results, including the visualization of the intellectual structure, in particular the intellectual turning points, citation bursts, knowledge base and research fronts. In section 4, the authors present a discussion and conclusions.

3. ANALYSIS AND RESULTS

3.1. Discipline Distribution

Commonly, the discipline distribution of a given research field can detect the involved disciplines and reveal interdisciplinarity, discipline integration and their respective roles. In the WoS database, according to the subject area of each journal, all articles in a journal are usually distributed to one or more subject categories. A subject category co-occurrence network makes it possible to identify the involved disciplines and the intersection and the co-occurrence relationship of multiple disciplines in the intellectual development of a given research field.

Figure 1 shows the disciplines involved in the green finance research field between 1998 and 2017. This merged disciplines network consists of the 50 most commonly occurring subject categories from each slice after 97 iterations. Each node represents a subject category involved in green finance research. The size of each node is proportional to the frequency of a subject category. Each line between two nodes represents the relationship between two subject categories, and the width of the line indicates the link strength.

As shown in Figure 1, this co-occurrence network consists of 99 nodes and 401 links, indicating that 99 major disciplines are involved in green finance research. The most common subject category is Environmental Sciences with a frequency of 1173, followed by Energy and Fuels (931), Environmental Studies (911), Economics (800), and Green Sustainable Science Technology (561). Other subject categories with a co-occurrence frequency of less than 500 but more than 200 include Agriculture (470), Computer Science (420), Environmental Engineering (382), Management (307), Ecology (277), and Engineering Civil (248). In addition, although water resources (191), Operations Research and Management Science (184), etc, are relatively smaller, they are marked for references. As the different colors of each

Figure 1. Disciplines involved in green finance

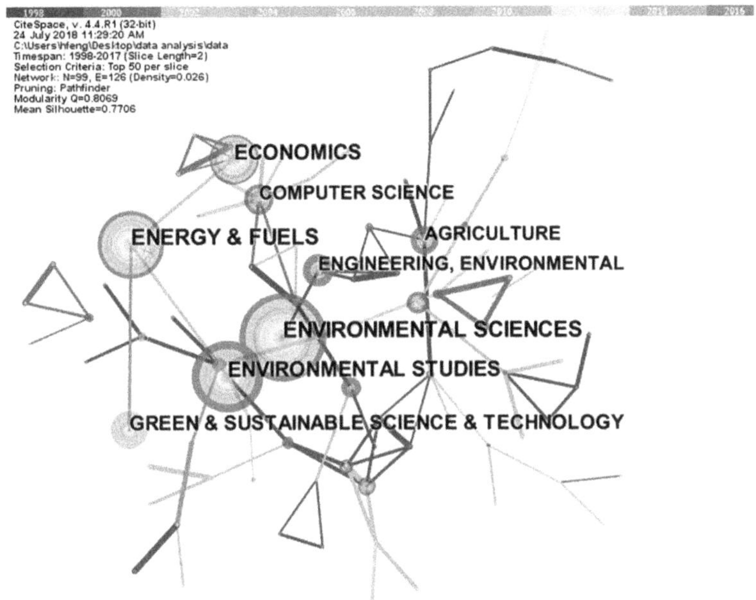

node show, between 1998 and 2017, the earlier research outcomes in green finance were published initially in the fields of Environmental Sciences (1998), Energy Fuels (1998), Environmental Studies (1998), Economics (1998), Green Sustainable Science Technology (1998), Environmental Engineering (1998), then Operations Research and Management Science (2000) and Management (2006). This reveals the chronological sequence of interdisciplinarity in green finance research.

It is worth noting that the Environmental Sciences category, with purple outer tree rings, is not only a landmark node with the highest co-occurrence frequency, but also has a higher betweenness centrality (0.44), which indicates that it is significant to the whole network. It links with Environmental Engineering with a strong link strength (0.53). The Environmental Engineering category, with purple outer tree rings, has the highest betweenness centrality (0.77), and the Environmental Studies category, with purple outer tree rings, has a betweenness centrality of 0.69. These three categories are extraordinary candidates for significant knowledge contributions to green finance research.

3.2. Institution Distribution

Institution distribution can identify the core research centres and scientific research collaboration in a given research field. Figure 2 shows a merged institutions co-occurrence network of green finance research between 1998 and 2017. This merged co-occurrence network consists of the 50 most commonly occurring institutions from each slice. Each node represents an institution contributing to green finance research. The size of each node is proportional to the number of publications by an institution (Chaomei Chen, 2006). Each line between two institution nodes represents the research collaboration relationship, and the width of the line indicates the scientific research collaboration strength (M. Navonil, B. Nik, J.E.T. Simon, and S. Stelios, 2013).

As shown in Figure 2, this institutions co-occurrence network consists of 336 nodes and 295 links, indicating 336 institutions contributing to the development of green finance research. Chinese Acad Sci has the highest frequency (125), followed by Univ Calif Berkeley (65), and Wageningen Univ (59). Other institutions with frequencies less than 50 but more than 30 include Univ Cambridge, Michigan State Univ, Univ British Columbia, Univ Queensland, Univ Oxford, Cornell Univ, Columbia Univ, Univ Teknol Malaysia, and Stanford Univ. Table 1 lists the academic groups and institutions with a frequency (the number of published journal articles) of more than 30. These twelve institutions are central to the green finance research field.

The modularity of the network is 0.8612, which means the specialties are clearly defined in terms of co-occurrence clusters. However, this network has a lower mean silhouette score of 0.1432 because of the numerous small clusters. This reveals that,

Figure 2. Institutions collaboration network

Table 1. Institutions with frequency more than 30

No.	Institution	Frequency	Burst	Centrality
1	Chinese Acad Sci	125		0.02
2	Univ Calif Berkeley	65		0.04
3	Wageningen Univ	59	3.54	0.02
4	Univ Cambridge	49		0.01
5	Michigan State Univ	49		0
6	Univ British Columbia	49	3.08	0
7	Univ Queensland	47		0
8	Univ Oxford	44	3.61	0.05
9	Cornell Univ	41	3.52	0.01
10	Columbia Univ	38		0.04
11	Univ Teknol Malaysia	31	3.22	0
12	Stanford Univ	30		0.15

although there is a wide scientific research collaboration between some institutions with higher co-occurrence frequencies, more institutions with lower co-occurrence frequencies are isolated and distributed. For example, the biggest node, Chinese Acad Sci, with the most publications (125) has wider research collaborations with Beijing Normal Univ, Harbin Inst Univ, Jilin Univ, and Chongqing Univ in China, but these research collaborations are not international, and are limited within China. Moreover, Chinese Acad Sci has a very low betweenness centrality score (0.02). However, compared to Chinese Acad Sci, Stanford Univ with 30 articles has the highest betweenness centrality score (0.15).

A node with red inner tree rings indicates that the number of articles published by these institutions changed dramatically over a certain period. The size of the node's red inner tree rings represents the strength of its burst property. According to the burst analysis in Table 1, there are five institutions with strong citation bursts. Among them, Univ Oxford has the strongest burst (3.61) between 2012 and 2015, followed by Wageningen Univ (3.54) between 2010 and 2012, and Cornell Univ (3.52) between 2012 and 2017. These institutions made great contributions to green finance research during certain periods.

3.3. Journal Co-Citation Analysis

As mentioned above, subject category co-occurrence analysis was performed based on the classification of all journals, including 6644 articles, while journal co-citation analysis (JCA) was conducted based on the cited journals, including 136,803 cited articles (references). Journal co-citation analyses were employed to identify the frequently cited journals and their co-occurrence relationships. These cited journals jointly compose the intellectual base of a given research field.

Figure 3 shows the merged co-citation network of highly cited journals between 1998 and 2017. This network was constructed of the 50 most cited references from each slice after 642 iterations. It contains 214 nodes and 737 links, indicating that 214 journals have contributed to the intellectual base development of green finance research. Table 2 lists the top 10 co-citation journals. The journal with the most co-citation articles is Energy Policy (4712), followed by Science (2209), Renewable and Sustainable Energy Reviews (1777), Ecological Economics (1679), and Journal of Cleaner Production (1590). Other journals with fewer than 15000 but more than 800 co-citation articles include Proceedings of the National Academy of Sciences of the United States of America, Nature, Energy, Energy Economics, and World Development. These top 10 co-citation journals are the main publication channels of cited articles. Moreover, the most common categories of the top 10 co-citation journals are Economics, Environmental Sciences, and Energy and Fuels. This result coincides with the macro-level analysis of subject categories (see section "Discipline distribution").

As shown in Figure 3, the nodes with purple outer tree rings indicate these co-cited journals have high betweenness centrality, and so act as bridges in the development of a scientific field linking research in different time periods. Ecological Economics Journal has the highest betweenness centrality (0.72), followed by Energy Policy (0.37), Energy (0.37), and Energy Economics (0.36). However, it is not the case that a journal with high frequency absolutely has a strong betweenness centrality score. As listed in Table 2, the high-frequency journals, including Science, Renewable & Sustainable Energy Reviews, Journal of Cleaner Production, and Nature, have a very weak betweenness centrality. Only those high-frequency journals with high betweenness centrality, such as Ecological Economics, Energy Policy, Energy, and Energy Economics, can be regarded as the pivotal journals in the green finance field.

3.4. Author Co-Citation Analysis

Author co-citation analysis (ACA) focuses on the authors who published the co-cited articles. It is critical to understand the academic communication, scientific research collaboration, and intellectual base diffusion in a specific research domain (Chaomei Chen, 2006). The relationships between co-cited authors can be identified by the co-occurrence frequencies of articles published by different authors.

Table 2. Top 10 most co-citation journals

Journal	Frequency	Centrality	Year	IF	Categories
Energy Policy	4712	0.37	2000	4.039	Economics; Energy & Fuels; Environmental Sciences; Environmental Studies
Science	2209	0	1998	41.058	Multidisciplinary Sciences
renewable & sustainable energy reviews	1777	0	2008	9.184	Green and Sustainable Science and Technology; Energy & Fuels
Ecological Economics	1679	0.72	2002	3.895	Environmental Sciences & Ecology; Business & Economics
Journal of Cleaner Production	1590	0	2008	5.651	Green and Sustainable Science and Technology; Environmental Engineering; Environmental Sciences
Proceedings of the National Academy of Sciences of the United States of America	1453	0.17	1998	9.504	Multidisciplinary Sciences
Nature	1426	0	1998	41.577	Multidisciplinary Sciences
Energy	875	0.37	2001	4.968	Thermodynamics; Energy & Fuels
Energy Economics	833	0.36	2008	3.91	Economics
World Development	803	0.05	2003	3.166	Economics; Planning & Development

Source: The Web of Science and Journal Citation Reports 2017; *IF* impact factor in 2017

Figure 4 shows the author co-citation network in the green finance research field between 1998 and 2017. The authors co-citation network consists of the 50 most cited authors from each slice. It consists of 336 nodes and 736 links, indicating that 336 authors contributed to the intellectual base development of green finance research. Each line between two nodes represents a co-citation relationship. The modularity of this network is 0.9147, which means the specialties are clearly defined in terms of co-citation clusters. However, this network has a relatively lower mean silhouette score of 0.3287 because of the numerous small clusters. Therefore, the authors of this paper only focus on the major clusters.

As shown in Figure 4, the authors with the most co-citation articles are mostly organizations, including the World Bank (683), Food and Agriculture Organization (FAO, the United Nations, 556), European Commission (EC, 355), Organisation for Economic Co-operation and Development (OECD, 308), International Energy

Figure 3. Journal co-citation network

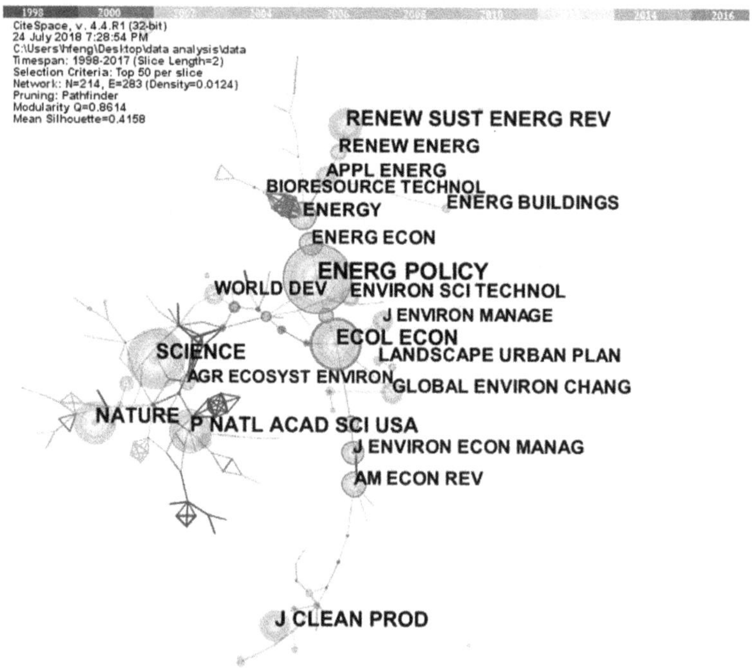

Agency (IEA, 284), etc. This result reveals that international energy and economic policies have had a profound impact on green finance research. In addition, Table 3 lists the 10 most co-cited pioneers. Among them, Porter ME, who is well known for his theories on economics, business strategy, and social causes and especially well-known for three generic competitive strategies (overall cost leadership, differentiation, and focus) and five forces analysis framework of competitiveness, ranks first, followed by Rockstrom J (170), Falkenmark M (155), Hoekstra A Y (145), Lal R (117), Zhu QH (113), and Sueyoshi T (110).

The nodes with purple outer tree rings indicate these co-cited authors have high betweenness centrality and act as the bridges in the development of a scientific field linking research in different time periods. As shown in Figure 4, the World Bank has the highest betweenness centrality (0.40), followed by European Commission (0.17), and the Organisation for Economic Co-operation and Development (0.17). Integrating the co-citation frequency and betweenness centrality score, the World Bank is identified as a leading authority on green finance research. Similarly, Rockstrom J (0.16) and Falkenmark M (0.16) are detected as well-known pioneers in the green finance research field, followed by Porter ME (0.11).

In addition, nodes with red inner tree rings indicate that the co-citation frequency of authors increased dramatically within a certain period. These authors perhaps profoundly influenced the future development of green finance research. According to the burst analysis, 88 cited authors have strong citation bursts. Among them, the most remarkable case is IEA, with the strongest citation burst of 15.06 between 2004 and 2009, followed by OECD (14.81) between 2002 and 2011, and EC (13.6) between 2003 and 2011. These authors or organizations perhaps have become new pioneers with profound future effects on the development of green finance research or it may simply reflect the rapid take-up of their ideas.

Table 3. The profile of the top 10 most co-cited pioneers

Author	Institution	Main Research Directions	Frequency	Betweenness Centrality	Burst	Year
Porter ME	Harvard Business School, Boston, USA	Competition, Strategy, Economic Development	215	0.11		2006
Rockstrom J	Stockholm University and the Stockholm Resilience Centre	Global Sustainability and Water Resources	170	0.16	6.18	1999
Falkenmark M	Stockholm University and the Stockholm Resilience Centre	Green Water, Ecohydrology, Hydrosolidarity and Water resilience	155	0.16	7.15	1999
Hoekstra AY	University of Twente	Water, Environment, Economics & Sustainability	145	0.02		2010
Lal R	Carbon Management and Sequestration Center, FAES/ OARDC, The Ohio State University, School of Natural Resources, Columbus, OH, USA	Environmental quality and sustainability; Food security; Climate change and soil carbon; Soil degradation and restoration	117	0.05	8.56	2004
Zhu QH	Shanghai Jiao Tong University, China	Green Supply Chain Management, Corporate Social Responsibility and Remanufacturing Management	113	0.01		2012
Sueyoshi T	New Mexico Institute of Mining and Technology	Data envelopment analysis; Economics; Operations management; Microeconomics Environmental impact assessment	110	0		2014
Harvey D	Graduate Center of the City University of New York	Geography, social theory, political economy	106	0.02		2008
Liu JG	School of Nature Conservation, Beijing Forestry University	Hydrology and water resources; Ecological services and management; Water and food security; Wetland conservation and management	103	0.01	8.24	2009
Jaffe AB	Brandeis University	Industrial organization; technological change and innovation; law and economics; environmental economics	97	0.17	4.5	2008

Source: Personal home page and Google scholar

Figure 4. Author co-citation network

3.5. Document Co-Citation Analysis

A specific knowledge domain can be conceptualized as a time-variant mapping from its research front to its intellectual base (knowledge base) (Chaomei Chen, 2006). The intellectual base is what is cited (reference documents) by the research fronts. Reference documents involve the previous research contents and the intellectual structure, and can reveal the citation trails of the research front. Therefore, document co-citation network analysis is helpful for later researchers to study the intellectual base structure, the dynamic nature of a research front, and paradigm developments of a specific research field (Persson, O., 1994).

The document co-citation network consists of the 50 most cited references from each slice. Figure 5 shows the salient merged network structure of co-citation reference documents with global pruning by the Pathfinder algorithm. This merged network contains 211,667 references. It consists of 433 nodes and 891 links. Each node represents a cited reference, and is depicted with a series of citation tree rings across multiple time slices. The size of each node is proportional to the co-citation frequency of the associated references (Chaomei Chen, 2006). Each line between two nodes represents the co-citation relationship, and the width of a line represents the strength of the co-citation relationship.

As shown in Figure 5, the most cited work in the green finance research field, with the biggest node, is the article "Food security: the challenge of feeding 9 billion people" (2010), published in Science by Godfray HCJ. This article outlines the major lines of research in food security and the challenge of feeding 9 billion people. This article suggested a multifaceted and linked global strategy was needed to ensure sustainable and equitable food security, and different components of this proposal were explored. The second node is the article "Solutions for a cultivated planet" (2011), published in Nature by Jonathan A. Foley. This article proposed some solutions for a cultivated planet, including halting agricultural expansion, closing 'yield gaps' on underperforming lands, increasing cropping efficiency, shifting diets and reducing waste. These strategies could double food production while greatly reducing the environmental impacts of agriculture. Following these two are articles by Tilman D (2011), Stern NH (2007), and Rockstrom J (2009).

A node with red inner tree rings has a significant citation burst in a given time period. The size of each red inner tree ring represents the burst strength. According to the citation burst analysis, there are 102 references with strong citation bursts. Table 4 lists the top 20 references with the strongest citation bursts between 1998 and 2017, which reveal the major milestones in green finance research. References with strong values in the Strength column tend to be significant milestones for green finance research. For example, the first milestone article is titled "Optical color image encryption by wavelength multiplexing and lensless Fresnel transform holograms" (2006), published by Linfei Chen and Daomu Zhao of Zhejiang University, China. The next milestone is titled "Solutions for a cultivated planet" (2011), published

Figure 5. Document co-citation network

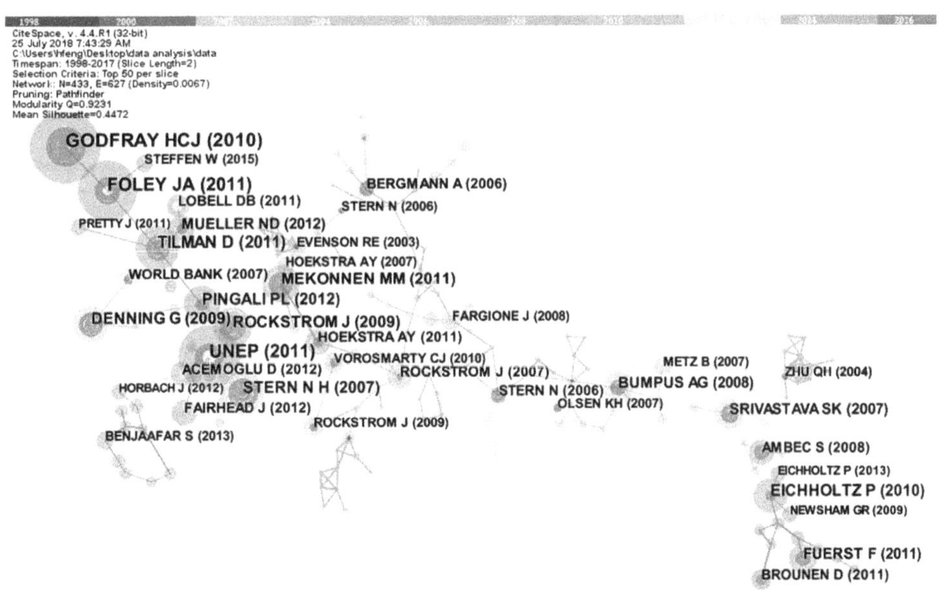

Table 4. Top 20 references with strongest citation bursts

References	Year	Strength	Begin	End	1998 - 2017
CHEN LF, 2006, OPT EXPRESS, V14, P8552, DOI	2006	7.8312	2012	2014	
FOLEY JA, 2011, NATURE, V478, P337, DOI	2011	7.764	2014	2017	
UNEP, 2011, GREEN EC PATHW SUST, V, P	2011	7.6212	2015	2017	
PINGALI PL, 2012, P NATL ACAD SCI USA, V109, P12302, DOI	2012	7.3789	2014	2017	
EICHHOLTZ P, 2010, AM ECON REV, V100, P2492, DOI	2010	7.3071	2015	2017	
AMBEC S, 2008, ACAD MANAGE PERSPECT, V23, P45, DOI	2008	7.2909	2014	2017	
STERN N H, 2007, EC CLIMATE CHANGE ST, V, P	2007	7.2489	2010	2014	
WORLD BANK, 2007, WORLD DEV REP 2008 A, V, P	2007	7.0117	2010	2013	
GODFRAY HCJ, 2010, SCIENCE, V327, P812, DOI	2010	6.9571	2013	2017	
METZ B, 2007, CLIMATE CHANGE 2007, V, P	2007	6.7678	2014	2015	
STERN N, 2006, STERN REV EC CLIMATE, V, P	2006	6.549	2008	2012	
JOSHI M, 2007, OPT COMMUN, V279, P35, DOI	2007	6.4296	2012	2014	
TILMAN D, 2011, P NATL ACAD SCI USA, V108, P20260, DOI	2011	6.1609	2013	2017	
DENNING G, 2009, PLOS BIOL, V7, P2, DOI	2009	5.8676	2010	2015	
MORENO J, 2003, ECOL LETT, V6, P803, DOI	2003	5.8201	2006	2011	
EVENSON RE, 2003, SCIENCE, V300, P758, DOI	2003	5.8201	2006	2011	
SEARCHINGER T, 2008, SCIENCE, V319, P1238, DOI	2008	5.7073	2010	2011	
FUERST F, 2011, REAL ESTATE ECON, V39, P45, DOI	2011	5.6552	2014	2017	
ROCKSTROM J, 2009, NATURE, V461, P472, DOI	2009	5.5122	2013	2017	
SRIVASTAVA SK, 2007, INT J MANAG REV, V9, P53, DOI	2007	5.4287	2011	2015	

by Jonathan A. Foley in Nature. The third milestone is titled "Green Revolution: Impacts, limits, and the path ahead" (2012), published by Prabhu L. Pingali in Proceedings of the National Academy of Sciences of the United States of America (PNAS). Other major milestones include articles on financial performance (Ambec Stefan and Lanoie Paul, 2008), green building (Piet Eichholtz, 2010), food security (Stern NH, 2007), and sustainable agriculture (Tilman D, 2011). These documents may have become new intellectual turning point documents with profound future effects on the development of green finance research or just simply reflect the rapid take-up of green finance ideas.

3.6. Keyword Co-Word Analysis

Commonly cited keywords reveal the core content of an article. Keyword co-word analysis can identify research hotspots and monitor research fronts of a knowledge domain (Callon, M., Courtial, J., and Laville, F., 1991). In this part, an exclusion list and an alias list in Citespace were used to deal with the general words, synonymy, and polysemy. For example, "Sustainable Development" and "Sustainability" were integrated and merged into one keyword "Sustainability". Table 5 lists the high-frequency keywords.

Based on these high-frequency keywords, a high-frequency keyword co-word network was constructed, as shown in Figure 6. This co-word network presents the keywords with a frequency of more than 30 and the relationships among them. Each node represents a keyword. The size of each node is proportional to the keyword frequency. The modularity of the network is 0.8138, which means the specialties are clearly defined in terms of co-occurrence clusters. However, this network has a mean silhouette score of 0.352 because of the numerous small clusters. This reveals that green finance is discussed in many scientific fields, and some keywords are isolated and distributed.

It is not surprising that the main research words, like green, finance, carbon, and investment, have higher co-occurrence frequencies. These words should be omitted because they are included in search terms. Some words and terms, such as climate change, energy and renewable energy, security, food security, environment, agriculture, etc., suggest a higher research focus on these areas. Besides these high-frequency words, some relevant keywords indicate the current emerging research hotspots, such as sustainability, policy, management, performance, carbon emissions, efficiency, corporate social responsibility, and so on.

In addition, a high-frequency keyword, "China", can be identified as an interesting finding in green finance research. "China" appeared in 2006 and became a high-frequency keyword with a frequency of 225, indicating that the development of

Table 5. Top 50 high frequency keywords

No.	Keywords	Frequency	No.	Keywords	Frequency	No.	Keywords	Frequency
1	sustainability	519	18	security	156	35	perspective	88
2	climate change	445	19	market	155	36	city	84
3	policy	391	20	growth	155	37	power	77
4	management	361	21	conservation	150	38	industry	74
5	system	300	22	agriculture	143	39	africa	73
6	renewable energy	278	23	biodiversity	143	40	finance	71
7	food security	262	24	emission	126	41	corporate social responsibility	71
8	model	259	25	innovation	125	42	optimization	69
9	impact	252	26	energy efficiency	121	43	risk	66
10	performance	233	27	governance	113	44	productivity	58
11	energy	231	28	developing country	113	45	india	50
12	china	225	29	ecosystem service	110	46	bioma	49
13	green	222	30	green economy	109	47	resource	49
14	investment	207	31	green building	100	48	carbon	48
15	green revolution	178	32	consumption	98	49	challenge	48
16	technology	163	33	strategy	97	50	mitigation	46
17	environment	160	34	efficiency	95			

China's green finance has attracted worldwide attention since 2006. By 2016, China's green bond market had become the largest in the world.

The nodes with purple outer tree rings, like management (0.25), agriculture (0.25), green revolution (0.22), security (0.20), etc., indicate these keywords have high betweenness centrality. They act as bridges in the development of this scientific field linking research in different time periods. These keywords will perhaps become new intellectual turning points or research directions with profound future effects on the development of green finance research or just simply reflect the rapid take-up of green finance ideas.

4. DISCUSSIONS AND CONCLUSION

In this paper the authors have presented a visual analysis of green finance through bibliometrics based on Web of Science. The main findings of this study are as follows:

Figure 6. Keyword co-word network

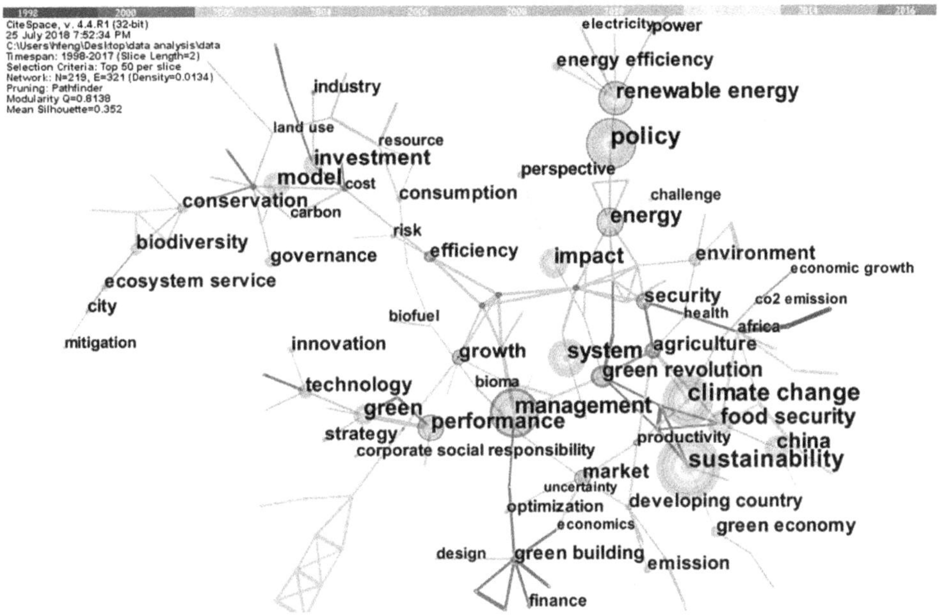

1. The outstanding contributive disciplines to the development of green finance research are Environmental Sciences, followed by Energy Fuels, Environmental Studies, Economics, and Green Sustainable Science Technology.
2. The current core institutions in green finance research are Chinese Acad Sci, Univ Calif Berkeley, Wageningen Univ, Univ Cambridge, Michigan State Univ, Univ British Columbia, Univ Queensland, Univ Oxford, Cornell Univ, Columbia Univ, Univ Teknol Malaysia, and Stanford Univ.
3. The pivotal journals in the green finance research field are Energy Policy, Science Renewable & Sustainable Energy Reviews, Ecological Economics, Journal of Cleaner Production, Proceedings of the National Academy of Sciences of the United States of America, Nature, Energy, Energy Economics, and World Development.
4. Author co-citation analyses identified some well-known organizations and prolific authors contributing to the development of green finance research. The organizations include World Bank, Food and Agriculture Organization (FAO, the United Nations), European Commission (EC), Organisation for Economic Co-operation and Development (OECD), International Energy Agency (IEA), etc. The pioneers include Porter ME, Rockstrom J, Falkenmark M, Hoekstra AY, Lal R, Zhu QH, Sueyoshi T, Harvey D, Liu JG, and Jaffe AB.

5. Document co-citation analyses identified the intellectual base and its network structure. The work with most co-citation is from Godfray HCJ (2010), followed by Jonathan A. Foley (2011), Tilman D (2011), Stern NH (2007), and Rockstrom J (2009). The high citation burst milestone works include those from Linfei Chen (2006), Jonathan A. Foley (2011), Prabhu L. Pingali (2012), Ambec Stefan (2008), Piet Eichholtz (2010), Stern NH (2007), and Tilman D (2011).
6. Keyword co-word analysis identified some research areas, such as climate change, energy and renewable energy, security, food security, environment, agriculture, etc., and some research focuses, such as sustainability, policy, management, performance, carbon emissions, efficiency, and corporate social responsibility, as particularly popular. It also indicated that China is often researched in relation to green finance.

The authors tried to vividly present the landscape of green finance research through bibliometrics. Co-word analysis and co-citation analysis were applied to detect discipline distribution, institution distribution, important journals, pioneer authors, milestone documents, and current research hotspots in green finance. Therefore, this study will help researchers understand the current research panorama. It will also be helpful for improving and upgrading research, development and application of green finance in the future. Moreover, it is a systematic review of green finance, and provides a reliable quantitative survey.

However, there are still some limitations of the bibliometric analysis. First, the analysis was restricted by the publications. It highlighted the Anglo-American journals, authors, and articles because of the limitations of the database (WoS), language type (English) and document type (journal articles). Second, it is very difficult to exactly identify all different co-citation authors because of naming conventions and hundreds of thousands of references. Finally, the analysis was also limited due to the current technologies and methods of visualization and scientific mapping. However, these limitations are common phenomena in social science research, and relate weakly to endogenous growth and knowledge paradigm shifts.

In the future, the authors intend to explore how and why the patterns and features identified vary over time. Furthermore, the authors are going to explore whether the intellectual structure detected is statistically correlated with the results reported in this paper. In addition, the authors will identify the evolution paths of green finance research. The authors are looking forward to conducting a similar analysis with other methods beyond the landscape of bibliometrics. The authors believe that coming research methods and instruments will be increasingly powerful and accessible.

ACKNOWLEDGMENT

This paper has been supported by Humanity and Social Science Youth Foundation of Ministry of Education, China (grant number 14YJC870008), Philosophy and Social Science Foundation of Guangdong Province during the "12th Five-Year Plan" (grant number GD13YTS01), Public Welfare and Ability Construction Special Foundation of Science and Technology Plan, Guangdong Province (grant number 2016A070705052), and Philosophy and Social Science Foundation of Guangzhou City during the "13th Five-Year Plan" (grant number 2017GZYB98) and Zhongshan City Science and Technology Bureau Project (grant number 2017B1015).

REFERENCES

Braam, R. R., Moed, H. F., & van Raan, A. F. J. (1991a). Mapping of science by combined co-citation and word analysis, I. Structural aspects. *Journal of the American Society for Information Science*, *422*(4), 233–251. doi:10.1002/(SICI)1097-4571(199105)42:4<233::AID-ASI1>3.0.CO;2-I

Braam, R. R., Moed, H. F., & van Raan, A. F. J. (1991b). Mapping of science by combined co-citation and word analysis, II: Dynamical aspects. *Journal of the American Society for Information Science*, *422*(4), 252–264. doi:10.1002/(SICI)1097-4571(199105)42:4<252::AID-ASI2>3.0.CO;2-G

Callon, M., Courtial, J., & Laville, F. (1991). Co-word analysis as a tool for describing the network of interactions between basic and technological research-The case of polymer chemistry. *Scientometrics*, *22*(1), 155–205. doi:10.1007/BF02019280

Callon, M., Courtial, J., & Laville, F. (1991). Co-word analysis as a tool for describing the network of interactions between basic and technological research-The case of polymer chemistry. *Scientometrics*, *22*(1), 155–205. doi:10.1007/BF02019280

Callon, M., Courtial, J. P., Turner, W. A., & Bauin, S. (1983). From translations to problematic networks – an introduction to co-word analysis. *Social Science Information Sur Les Sciences Sociales*, *22*(2), 191–235. doi:10.1177/053901883022002003

Chen, C. (1999). Visualising semantic spaces and author co-citation networks in digital libraries. *Information Processing & Management*, *35*(2), 401–420. doi:10.1016/S0306-4573(98)00068-5

Chen, C. (2006). CiteSpace II: Detecting and Visualizing Emerging Trends and Transient Patterns in Scientific Literature. *Journal of the American Society for Information Science and Technology*, *57*(3), 359–377. doi:10.1002/asi.20317

Chen, C. (2017). Science Mapping: A Systematic Review of the Literature. *Journal of Data and Information Science*, *2*(2), 1–40. doi:10.1515/jdis-2017-0006

Chen, L., & Zhao, D. (2006). Optical color image encryption by wavelength multiplexing and lensless Fresnel transform holograms. *Optics Express*, *14*(19), 8552–8560. doi:10.1364/OE.14.008552 PMID:19529234

Eichholtz, P., Kok, N., & Quigley, J. M. (2010). Doing Well by Doing Good? Green Office Buildings. *The American Economic Review*, *100*(5), 2492–2509. doi:10.1257/aer.100.5.2492

Foley, J. A., Ramankutty, N., Brauman, K. A., Cassidy, E. S., Gerber, J. S., Johnston, M., ... Zaks, D. P. M. (2011). Solutions for a cultivated planet. *Nature*, *478*(7369), 337–342. doi:10.1038/nature10452 PMID:21993620

Gallagher, A. U., & Yuan, F. (2017). Standardizing Sustainable Development: A Comparison of Development Banks in the Americas. *Journal of Environment & Development*, *26*(3), 243–271. doi:10.1177/1070496517720711

Gu, D., Li, J., Li, X., & Liang, C. (2017). Visualizing the knowledge structure and evolution of big data research in healthcare informatics. *International Journal of Medical Informatics*, *98*, 22–32. doi:10.1016/j.ijmedinf.2016.11.006 PMID:28034409

Guan, R., Zheng, H. T., Hu, J., Fang, Q., & Ren, R. E. (2017). The Higher Carbon Intensity of Loans, the Higher Non-Performing Loan Ratio: The Case of China. *Sustainability*, *9*(4), 667. doi:10.3390u9040667

He, Q. (1999). Knowledge discovery through co-word analysis. *Library Trends*, *48*(1), 133–159.

Hu, F., Liu, W., Tsai, S.-B., Gao, J., Bin, N., & Chen, Q. (2018). An Empirical Study on Visualizing the Intellectual Structure and Hotspots of Big Data Research from a Sustainable Perspective. *Sustainability*, *10*(3), 667. doi:10.3390u10030667

Kim, M. C., Jeong, Y. K., & Song, M. (2014). Investigating the integrated landscape of the intellectual topology of bibliometrics. *Scientometrics*, *101*(1), 309–335. doi:10.100711192-014-1417-1

Liu, Z., Yin, Y., Liu, W., & Michael, D. (2015). Visualizing the intellectual structure and evolution of innovation systems research: A bibliometric analysis. *Scientometrics*, *103*(1), 135–158. doi:10.100711192-014-1517-y

Maggioni, D., & Santangelo, G. D. (2017). Local Environmental Non-Profit Organizations and the Green Investment Strategies of Family Firms. *Ecological Economics*, *138*, 126–138. doi:10.1016/j.ecolecon.2017.03.026

Meho, L. I., & Yang, K. (2007). Impact of data sources on citation counts and rankings of LIS faculty: Web of science versus Scopus and Google scholar. *Journal of the American Society for Information Science and Technology*, *58*(13), 2105–2125. doi:10.1002/asi.20677

Navonil, M., Nik, B., Simon, J. E. T., & Stelios, S. (2013). Exploring the e-science knowledgebase through co-citation analysis. *Procedia Computer Science*, *19*, 586–593. doi:10.1016/j.procs.2013.06.078

Newman, M. E. J. (2001). The Structure of Scientific Collaboration Networks. *Proceedings of the National Academy of Sciences of the United States of America*, *98*(2), 404–409. doi:10.1073/pnas.98.2.404 PMID:11149952

Nishizawa, T. (2011). Changes in Development Finance in Asia: Trends, Challenges, and Policy Implications. *Asian Economic Policy Review*, *6*(2), 225–244. doi:10.1111/j.1748-3131.2011.01199.x

Nobre, G. C., & Tavares, E. (2017). Scientific literature analysis on big data and internet of things applications on circular economy: A bibliometric study. *Scientometrics*, *111*(1), 463–492. doi:10.100711192-017-2281-6

Persson, O. (1994). The intellectual base and research fronts of JASIS 1986–1990. *Journal of the American Society for Information Science*, *45*(1), 31–38. doi:10.1002/(SICI)1097-4571(199401)45:1<31::AID-ASI4>3.0.CO;2-G

Pingali, P. L. (2012). Green Revolution: Impacts, limits, and the path ahead. *Proceedings of the National Academy of Sciences of the United States of America*, *109*(31), 12302–12308. doi:10.1073/pnas.0912953109 PMID:22826253

Rockstrom, J., Steffen, W., Noone, K., Persson, A., Chapin, F. S., Lambin, E. F., ... Foley, J. A. (2009). A safe operating space for humanity. *Nature*, *461*(7263), 472–475. doi:10.1038/461472a PMID:19779433

Small, H. (1973). Co-citation in the scientific literature: A new measure of the relationship between two documents. *Journal of the American Society for Information Science*, *24*(4), 265–269. doi:10.1002/asi.4630240406

Small, H. (1973). Co-citation in the scientific literature: A new measure of the relationship between two documents. *Journal of the American Society for Information Science*, *24*(4), 265–269. doi:10.1002/asi.4630240406

Stefan, A., & Paul, L. (2008). Does It Pay to Be Green? A Systematic Overview. *The Academy of Management Perspectives*, *22*(4), 45–62. doi:10.5465/amp.2008.35590353

Stern, N. H. (2007). *The economics of climate change: the Stern Review*. Cambridge, UK: Cambridge University. doi:10.1017/CBO9780511817434

Sudmant, A., Colenbrander, S., Gouldson, A., & Chilundika, N. (2017). Private opportunities, public benefits? The scope for private finance to deliver low-carbon transport systems in Kigali, Rwanda. *Urban Climate*, *20*, 59–74. doi:10.1016/j.uclim.2017.02.011

Tilman, D., Balzer, C., Hill, J., & Befort, B. L. (2011). Global food demand and the sustainable intensification of agriculture. *Proceedings of the National Academy of Sciences of the United States of America*, *108*(50), 20260–20264. doi:10.1073/pnas.1116437108 PMID:22106295

Wang, Y., & Zhi, Q. (2016). The role of green finance in environmental protection: Two aspects of market mechanism and policies. *Proceedings of Applied Energy Symposium and Forum: Low-Carbon Cities and Urban Energy Systems (CUE)*, 104, 311-316. 10.1016/j.egypro.2016.12.053

White, H. D., & McCain, K. W. (1998). Visualizing a discipline: An author co-citation analysis of information science 1972–1995. *Journal of the American Society for Information Science*, *49*(4), 327–356.

Chapter 5
Social Capital Accounting:
The Social Capital Protocol and the United Nations' Sustainable Development Goals

John P. Wilson
University of Sheffield, UK

Sonal Choudhary
University of Sheffield, UK

ABSTRACT

Sustainability accounting has become a mainstream practice for a large majority of S&P500 companies, and this reflects global society's increasing interest and concern around sustainability issues. In particular, the United Nations published its "Transforming Our World: The 2030 Agenda for Sustainable Development," and 193 countries signed up to achieving the 17 Sustainable Development Goals (SDGs) and 169 associated targets. The UN also called upon companies to help this process across their supply chains and developed a natural capital protocol for assessing and valuing environmental areas and a social capital protocol (SCP) for assessing and valuing human and societal capital such as skills, knowledge, wellbeing, shared values, and institutions. This chapter systematically investigates each of the 12 steps of the social capital protocol and identifies a range of benefits and substantial challenges which companies will face if they wish to account for their social impact across the supply chain.

DOI: 10.4018/978-1-5225-7808-6.ch005

INTRODUCTION

Businesses must reconnect company success with social progress. Shared value is not social responsibility, philanthropy, or even sustainability, but a new way to achieve economic success. It is not on the margin of what companies do but at the center. (Porter and Kramer, 2011: 64)

In recent times sustainability has moved from being a peripheral 'green' issue to a mainstream one (Cochran, 2007) and, by 2015, 81% of S&P500 companies published a sustainability or corporate responsibility report (Governance and Accountability Institute, 2016). 2015 was also a significant year because it was the final year of the United Nations' Millennium Development Goals (MDGs) which were designed to improve the lives of the world's poorest people. Furthermore, on 25th September 2015, the United Nations (UN) (2015b) built on the progress achieved by the MDGs and published '*Transforming our world: the 2030 Agenda for Sustainable Development*' and committed all 193 signatory countries to achieving the 17 Sustainable Development Goals (SDGs) and 169 associated targets beginning 1 January 2016, with the aim of reaching them by 2030. These much wider goals were designed to: "end poverty, protect the planet and ensure prosperity for all as part of a new sustainable development agenda" (UN, 2018).

This green agenda acknowledged that humans could only survive and prosper if the world's resources on which they were dependent also survived. The UN (2015b: 4). stated:

We envisage a world in which every country enjoys sustained, inclusive and sustainable economic growth and decent work for all. A world in which consumption and production patterns and use of all natural resources – from air to land, from rivers, lakes and aquifers to oceans and seas – are sustainable.

To help achieve the MDGs, the UN had relied primarily on the support of governments and NGOs; however, with the SDGs it was evident that a broader coalition was needed to attain sustainability. The ambitious nature of the SDGs prompted the UN (2015b: parag. 67) to call on the support of businesses of all sizes: "to apply their creativity and innovation to solving sustainable development challenges;" and, to achieve these:

It is therefore recommended that your company considers the entire value chain – from the supply base and inbound logistics, across production and operations, to the distribution, use and end-of-life of products – as the starting point for assessing impact and defining priorities. (Global Reporting Index (GRI), United Nations

Global Compact (UNGC), and World Business Council for Sustainable Development (WBCSD), 2015: 12).

To achieve sustainability it is essential that it is measured and reported upon, and Bebbington, et al (2014: 4) described how: "sustainability accounting and accountability have the potential to be tools in the management, planning, control and accountability of organizations for their social and environmental impacts." The majority of research into sustainability and the supply chain adopts an instrumental logic which places economic interests above environmental and social ones (Gao & Bansal, 2013; Garriga & Melé, 2004). In particular, the focus is on how benefits can accrue to the supply chain by responding to environmental and social concerns rather than asking how a supply chain might become sustainable (Montabon et al, 2016). Companies which wish to operate sustainably need to consider the entire supply chain (Hutchins & Sutherland, 2008) and much of the research into sustainability in supply chains has focused on environmental sustainability (Wilhelm et al., 2015) with many companies adopting international certification e.g. ISO 14001 (2017); evaluating their carbon footprint; and implementing regulations and standardization (Klassen and Vereecke, 2012). Yet, social sustainability management is still at an initial stage, struggling how to understand, define and plan for social sustainability (Hutchins & Sutherland, 2008; Klassen and Vereecke, 2012; Seuring and Müller, 2008; WBCSD, 2017a). Furthermore, the majority of research from 2002 – 2014 into sustainable supply chain management did not consider the social dimension (Walker et al, 2014).

Three areas of economic, environmental and social sustainability (Elkington, 1997) were identified as a broad framework to consider the SDGs across the value / supply chain. Measurement of economic performance has generally agreed accounting standards e.g. International Accounting Standards Board (2018) and there are also frameworks for the consideration of environmental factors e.g. ISO 14000: Environmental Management (ISO 2017); however, the social impact of organisations on the supply chain has received much less consideration (WBCSD, 2017a; Seuring and Müller, 2008) and has greater degrees of ambiguity and complexity.

In response to these challenges the *Social Capital Protocol* was published: "to mainstream the measurement of social impacts for business" (WBCSD, 2017a: 4) and support companies across the supply chain to identify, measure, and value their social capital. The publication of the Social Capital Protocol in 2017 means that organisations have had limited time to absorb its implications, advantages and disadvantages. In addition, the Social Capital Protocol describes itself as a technical document which "will not be accessible to everyone" and it provides the guidance required to employ experts (WBCSD, 2017a: 7). Furthermore, not all organisations, particularly SMEs, may have the resources or insights to implement it.

It is with these considerations in mind that it is timely to critically examine the Social Capital Protocol's use as a business tool and illustrative social accounting framework for organisations working towards being socially responsible and responding to the UN's SDGs. In doing so we will consider the following objectives:

- Examine the triple bottom line and sustainability.
- Define social capital
- Examine the benefits of corporate social responsibility
- Critically examine the 12 steps of the Social Capital Protocol.
- Draw conclusions about the practicality and application of the Social Capital Protocol to address some of the core social capital sustainability issues.

BACKGROUND

The Triple Bottom Line and Sustainability

Concerns about sustainability have a long history e.g. Thomas Malthus (1798/1982) expressed unease about the ability of a growing nation to sustain itself in his seminal work: *An Essay on the Principle of Population*; and Meadows et al. (1972) in *Limits to Growth* also voiced apprehension about unconstrained human consumption. A foundation for the SDGs emerged at the 1972 Stockholm Conference on the Human Environment (UN, 1972: 1) which provided a list of "common principles to inspire and guide the peoples of the world in the preservation and enhancement of the human environment." Later, the World Commission for Environment and Development defined sustainable development as: "Development that meets the needs of the present without compromising the ability of future generations to meet their own needs." (Bruntland Report, 1987: 2.1).

In 1994, Elkington (1997) devised the term the "triple bottom line" which represents the three integrated areas of sustainability: social, environmental and economic or 'people, planet, profit' (Figure 1). This triple bottom line structure has since been adopted by numerous organisations including the United Nations (2015b: 3) which explained that: "We are committed to achieving sustainable development in its three dimensions – economic, social and environmental – in a balanced and integrated manner." The extent to which organisations apply the triple bottom line may vary substantially; for example, Colbert and Kurucz (2007) identified three corporate sustainability strategies: balanced operational; integrated operational; and, integrated strategic which illustrate increasingly deeper levels of integration and commitment.

Figure 1. The triple bottom line (Elkington, 1997)

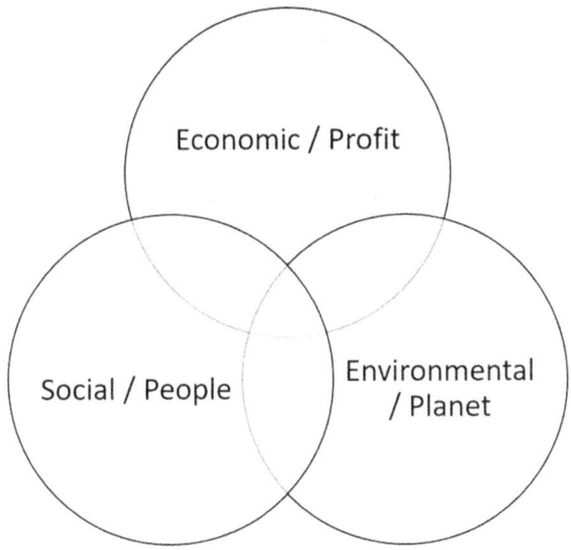

Building upon these, and other, arguments for sustainability the UN developed its eight Millennium Development Goals (MDGs) (UN, 2000) which addressed: poverty and hunger; universal primary education; gender equality; child mortality; maternal health; combating diseases including malaria and HIV; environmental sustainability and a global partnership for development.

Amid the Great Financial Crisis of 2008 there was a growing dissatisfaction with the narrow economic consideration of measures of Gross Domestic Product prompting President Nicolas Sarkozy of France to invite Nobel prize-winning economists Joseph Stiglitz and Amartya Sen together with French economist Jean Paul Fitoussi and others (Stiglitz, Sen and Fitoussi, 2009) to identify the limitations of GDP as a reliable indicator of economic, environmental and social sustainability. As an illustration they noted that traffic jams increase GDP but also add to air pollution thus decreasing quality of life. Stiglitz et al (2009: 12) emphasised the need to: "shift emphasis from measuring economic production to measuring people's wellbeing." Dimensions of well-being included: material living standards; health; education; personal activities including work; political voice and governance; social connections and relationships; present and future environment; and economic and physical insecurity.

In 2009, a seminal article by Rockström et al (2009) was published which identified nine planetary boundaries within which humanity might live sustainably. They noted that the relative stability of the Holocene era had been replaced by greater environmental uncertainty in the Anthropocene era which began with the Industrial

Revolution. They argued that human intervention had led to three planetary boundaries being transgressed: climate change, rate of biodiversity loss; and global nitrogen cycle changes. Significantly, it was identified that this ecological destruction could negate advances in social development (UNDP, 2013) and that global supply chains had contributed to this degradation (Matthews et al, 2016). Importantly, however, these same supply chains could also provide a positive environmental contribution and be a "locus for much of the change towards sustainability" (Mohrman & Worley, 2010: 291). The Oxfam 'Doughnut' (Raworth, 2012) built on the work of Rockström et al (2009) and constructed a model which described social and planetary boundaries for development.

The operational period for the MDGs ended in 2015 and they were superseded by the United Nations' Resolution (United Nations, 2015b) which committed all 194 signatory nations to address the sustainability challenges beginning 1 January 2016 with the aim of achieving them by 2030. 17 Sustainable Development Goals (SDGs) involving economic, environmental and social considerations were described: (1) No Poverty. (2) Zero Hunger. (3) Good Health and Well-being. (4) Quality Education. (5) Gender Equality. (6) Clean Water and Sanitation. (7) Affordable and Clean Energy. (8) Decent Work and Economic Growth. (9) Industry, Innovation and Infrastructure. (10) Reduced Inequalities. (11) Sustainable Cities and Communities. (12) Responsible Consumption and Production. (13) Climate Action. (14) Life Below Water. (15) Life on Land. (16) Peace, Justice and Strong Institutions. (17) Partnerships for the Goals. Furthermore, associated with the SDGs were 169 targets and an initial 230 indicators (United Nations Statistical Commission, 2017).

Social Capital

To function effectively, companies use three sets of 'capitals' - financial, natural and social and through their business activities these capitals are converted into outputs e.g. products and workers' skills which can enhance long-term viability. In these processes companies can have positive and negative impacts on people and society. The WBCSD (2017b: 30) stated that: "The global understanding of what creates value is changing and with it, so are the ways of measuring, communicating, and managing value. Financial value, void of social and environmental externalities, is no longer enough to assess the health of the economy or of a business." It is social capital which we examine here in more detail.

One of the earliest explorations and descriptions of the importance of the term 'social capital' was by Hanifan (1916) who explored the benefits to people and communities of grouping together in a USA rural school context rather than attempting to get by in isolation. He (1916: 130) stated that: "In community building as in business organization and expansion there must be an accumulation of [social] capital before constructive work can be done."

Another detailed examination of social capital' was undertaken by Bourdieu (1985: 248) who defined it as: "the aggregate of the actual or potential resources which are linked to possession of a durable network of more or less institutionalized relationships of mutual acquaintance or recognition." It would appear to consist of four main groupings: personal relationships; social network support, civic engagement; and, trust and cooperative norms (OECD, 2001). It is also the: "glue that holds societies together" (Serageldin 1996: 196). Significantly, where these exist in substantial amounts communities appear to benefit and tend to have higher economic growth; improved health; reduced crime figures; and, higher educational achievement (Halpern 2009). Given these benefits it is important to identify and place a value on the various dimensions of social capital; however, this has proved difficult and challenging with the result that there has been little detailed consideration of the measurement of social capital across the supply chain. It is for this reason that the Social Capital Protocol (WBCSD, 2017a) was developed and which we will investigate below.

Social Sustainability and Corporate Social Responsibility

The issue of sustainability and CSR has been a contentious one (Ehrenfeld, 2008) and among the early discussants in a *Harvard Law Review* debate was Berle (1931: 1049) who argued that: "All powers granted to a corporation or to the management of a corporation, or to any group within a corporation, whether derived from statute or charter or both, are necessarily and at all times exercisable only for the rateable benefit of all shareholders as their interest appears." A year later, this position was challenged by Dodd (1932: 1153) who asked: "For whom are corporate managers' trustees?" In responding to his own question he maintained: "There is in fact a growing feeling not only that business has responsibilities to the community but that our corporate managers who control business should voluntarily and without waiting for legal compulsion manage it in such a way as to fulfil those responsibilities." The following year, Berle (1954: 169) recanted on his arguments from two decades previously and conceded that: "[t]he argument has been settled (at least for the time being) squarely in favour of Professor Dodd's contention."

Another early discussion about corporate social responsibility (CSR) was Bowen's (1953) seminal book: *Social Responsibilities of the Businessman* and, since then, the area has grown from a peripheral 'green' consideration to a mainstream one (Cochran, 2007). The attractiveness of CSR was summed up by Votaw (1973: 11):

The term is a brilliant one; it means something, but not always the same thing, to everybody. To some it conveys the idea of legal responsibility or liability; to others it means socially responsible behaviour in an ethical sense; to still others, the meaning transmitted is that of "responsible for", in a causal mode; many simply equate it with a charitable contribution.

These various interpretations of CSR have been represented in Carroll's (1991) pyramid below which illustrates the four levels of responsibility.

To achieve more clarity, there have been numerous attempts to provide a generally agreed definition of CSR but this has proved relatively unsuccessful because of the changing beliefs and attitudes regarding the relationship between business and society (Hill et al, 2003). Also, this lack of a general consensus may be due, in part, to the different operational characteristics and contexts of organisations including: locations, profitability, products, resources, size, societal impacts etc. (Carroll and Buchholtz, 2000; Joyner and Payne, 2002). In spite of these challenges one broad definition stated that: "the social responsibility of business encompasses the economic, legal, ethical and discretionary expectations that society has of organizations at a given point in time" (Carroll, 1979, p. 500).

The problem with this definition, and other definitions, are their abstract nature, imprecision and inability to pin down what is a social issue (Barnett, 2007; Clarkson, 1995). This position was cogently summed up by Clarkson (1995: 96):

Figure 2. Carroll's (1991) pyramid of corporate social responsibility (adapted)

The fundamental problem was, and remains, that no definition of social responsiveness provides a framework for the systematic collection, organization, and analysis of corporate data. The term social responsiveness carries no clear meaning for managers, students, or academic researchers and scholars. Consequently, much time, energy, and paper have been consumed in attempts to explain the term. But it remains an [p. 97] elusive construct, lacking both logic and rigor, which limits seriously its usefulness for empirical research.

This imprecision was noted by the neo-classical economist Milton Friedman (1970) who observed that: "The discussions of the 'social responsibilities of business' are notable for their analytical looseness and lack of rigor." He argued that: "The social responsibility of business is to increase its profits" which can be summarised as, 'the business of business is business.' Friedman's arguments represent, perhaps, a high-water mark for corporate isolationism but the debate about boundaries and responsibilities has yet to be resolved as will be discussed below, particularly in relation to the Social Capital Protocol.

Another consideration is the extent to which one company should attempt to resolve "social misery" (Margolis & Walsh, 2003); what about other companies operating in the community and the same supply chain? What about the responsibilities of governments to care for and protect their citizens, isn't that what corporate taxation is for? Furthermore, despite the best efforts of scholarly researchers there is still a "lingering murkiness of the business case" between CSR and financial performance (Barnett, 2007: 794). And, summarising the arguments of CSR critics, Barnett (2007:795) wrote: "Devoting corporate resources to social welfare is tantamount to an involuntary redistribution of wealth, from shareholders.... to others in society who have no rightful claim."

Many sustainability issues are voluntary (Andersen and Skjoett-Larsen, 2009) and dependent upon a company's "ambition" (WBCSD, 2017a) yet there is increasing support for CSR. Among the main reasons for this are a number of benefits and drivers:

- Building Trust – Provides stakeholders with transparent information about non-financial performance (GRI 2017b; GRI, UNGC, WBCSD, 2015).
- Improved Processes and Systems – costs can be reduced by measuring and reducing energy consumption, material usage and waste (GRI 2017b; GRI, UNGC, WBCSD, 2015). Kolk (2003) suggested that this impact had more relevance to environmental factors than social ones.
- Progressing Vision and Strategy – Encourages companies to develop wider vision by incorporating sustainability in vision and strategies (GRI 2017b).

- Reducing Compliance Costs – Systematic measurement of sustainability performance data enhances regulatory compliance and avoid penalties (GRI 2017b).
- Competitive Advantage – Can drive innovation and leading companies can attract more investment, identify new markets, business opportunities etc. (GRI 2017b; GRI, UNGC, WBCSD, 2015; PwC, 2015).
- Common Language and Shared Purpose – The SDGs describe a common framework which drives action and provides clear language to stakeholders etc. (GRI, UNGC, WBCSD, 2015).
- Stabilizing societies and markets – Businesses can only be successful where societies are not failing (GRI, UNGC, WBCSD, 2015).
- License to Operate – Companies can "evidence and maintain their license to operate" (PwC, 2015: 6).
- Maintain customer loyalty (Setthasakko, 2007);
- Legislation (Pullman et al., 2009);
- Reduction of risk and reputational damage (Sajjad et al., 2015; Forsman-Hugg et al., 2013);
- Personal values of top management (Sajjad et al., 2015; Zhang et al., 2014).

In spite of arguments in favour of shareholder pre-eminence it would appear that most companies accept that they have a social responsibility (Governance and Accountability Institute, 2016) and the question has moved from "whether" to "how" to integrate the triple bottom line of people, planet and profit (Elkington, 1997) into management decisions (Epstein and Buhovac, 2014: 19). Next, we consider 'how' the impact on people can be assessed.

Tools and Frameworks for Examining Social Sustainability

In this section we examine some of the core tools and frameworks used for measuring social sustainability in business operations and their supply chain.

Social Impact Assessment

Social impact assessment has been defined as the process of: "analysing, monitoring and managing the intended and unintended economic and social consequences, both positive and negative, of business intervention and any social change process invoked by those interventions" (Vanclay, 2003: 1). One early accounting method for social impact assessment was the Social Return on Investment which began in 1997 and was based on cost-benefit analysis. Later, in 2000, the Global Reporting Initiative (GRI) published its first G1 guidelines which it described as "the first global framework for comprehensive sustainability reporting" (Global Reporting Initiative, 2017a). These guidelines which enable organisations to report on their social, environmental and economic impacts are now in their fourth iteration (GRI4) and, in October 2016, GRI issued the first global standards for sustainability reporting which were developed by the Global Sustainability Standards Board (2017).

Since these early developments, the number of social impact assessment tools has proliferated and the Foundation Centre (2017) has identified more than 150 tools, methods and best practices in its *Tools and Resources for Assessing Social Impact* database. These resources are founded on different assumptions, focus on different audiences and consider different categories of impact. Moreover, the majority of the tools have been designed for use by foundations, international development organisations and social investors with the result that businesses find it challenging to select and effectively employ the tools and resources (WBCSD, 2015). Furthermore, companies found it very difficult to choose from the multitude of tools and frameworks and integrate them into strategic decision-making which resulted in an undervaluation and, therefore, an under-investment in social resources. The overall effect of these factors is that there is "little consensus" (WBCSD, 2017a: 3) about which approaches to use and there is competition for uptake by the numerous providers of the tools. The outcome of all these issues is that "credibility and comparability suffer" (WBCSD, 2017c).

Three broad methodologies for social impact assessment were identified by Olsen and Galimidi (2008: 14): ratings systems, assessment systems and management systems. In an examination of 20 different tools, Florman et al (2016) identified a number of strengths: increasing usability, inclusiveness, value demonstration and enhancement; and concurrent weaknesses: resource intensive, subjective, inaccessible, and insufficiently transparent. Furthermore, "Most past and current SIA [social impact assessment] work appears to have been produced in a theoretical vacuum" (Taylor et al, 2003: 13).

Notwithstanding the challenges surrounding indicators, a number of key benefits have been identified by the UN Commission on Sustainable Development (Gouzee et al., 1995) which stated that sustainability indicators should address the following four areas:

- "alert decision-makers to priority issues,
- guide policy formulation,
- simplify and improve communication,
- foster a common understand of key trends"

The Social Capital Protocol is a framework for identifying, assessing and valuing social capital; and, "to be useful in practice, a model or framework must be applicable to the conditions that it is attempting to describe, analyze, or predict" (Clarkson, 1995: 94). To assess the extent to which the Protocol is useful it will be examined using a seven-stage process for developing sustainability indicators (Tahir and Darton, 2010; Darton, 2015):

1. Clear definition of what is to be assessed (the system boundary) and why.
2. The nature of the sustainable outcome (economic, environmental, societal) must be defined.
3. Coverage of key aspects is necessary.
4. Quantitative data are required, not qualitative judgements.
5. Duplication and needless complexity should be avoided.
6. Excluded - Only operational targets and indicators to be used
7. Composite weighted indicators used.

Tahir and Darton's seven stage process will be revisited in the conclusions to assess the applicability and accuracy of the Social Capital Protocol. In the following sections we will explore the development of the Social Capital Protocol.

The SDG Compass

To support the achievement of the SDGs the *SDG Compass* (GRI, UNGC, WBCSD, 2015) drew upon the United Nations (2011) *Guiding Principles on Business and Human Rights* and the 'protect, respect, remedy' framework as a baseline expectation for all companies to observe. Importantly, the activities of a business enterprise: "…and its 'business relationships' are understood to include relationships with business partners, entities in its value chain, and any other non-State or State entity directly linked to its business operations, products or services" (United Nations, 2011: 15). Essentially, the SDG Compass had five stages: (1) describing the SDGs and the business case for becoming involved; (2) defining priorities by mapping the value chain and selecting indicators; (3) defining the scope of goals and selecting KPIs; (4) integrating the sustainability goals across the business; (5) reporting and communicating performance.

The SDG Compass is also complemented by an 'SDG Industry Matrix' developed by the UNGC and KPMG (2016: 5) which was designed to "inspire and inform greater private sector action" for different industries. It described a number of opportunities for business and the societies in which they operate and among the opportunities it described: "Investing in supply chains which are ethical, inclusive, resource-efficient and resilient." The SDG website lists an inventory of 834 business indicators drawn from recognised sources (e.g. GRI, SASB, ILO, OECD and CDP) which are mapped against the SDGs and their targets (GRI, UNGC and WBCSD,

2017b). Both the SDG Compass and the SDG Industry Matrix complement the Social Capital Protocol which will now be discussed.

THE SOCIAL CAPITAL PROTOCOL

Acknowledging the inherent inconsistencies and confusion caused by the variety of social impact assessment tools, the WBCSD (2015: 5) issued a call for collaboration in measuring social impacts. Following two years of consultation the WBCSD (2017a) published its *Social Capital Protocol* to: "harmonize the currently fragmented landscape" (WBCSD: 2017d) and provide a consistent and standardized approach for businesses which would eventually mainstream social impact assessment. Social capital encompasses human capital (skills, knowledge and wellbeing) and societal capital (relationships, shared values, institutions) (Figure 3). These capital resources need to be developed to ensure society is resilient and cohesive thereby supporting businesses.

Social capital impact was defined as: "the extent to which a company's actions or decisions contribute positively or negatively to a change in the welfare, capabilities, relationships or livelihoods of people living in society" (WBCSD, 2017a: 8). Positive impacts provide benefits to a society while negative impacts impose costs and it was acknowledged that, for some companies, these remain 'externalities' and do not have internal relevance. The Protocol is intended to identify, measure and value the social capital dependencies which the business depends upon to create value e.g. human and social resources and relationships (WBCSD, 2017b).

Social capital may also be created between the buyers and suppliers in the supply chain which enables them to access and leverage resources which are found in the relationships as well as encouraging cooperation and reducing conflict (Autry and Griffis, 2008; Cousins et al, 2006; Krause et al, 2007; Lawson et al, 2008; Min et al, 2008). Three dimensions of social capital have been identified (Nahapiet and Ghoshal, 1998): cognitive social capital – shared meaning and vision; relational social capital – the friendships, obligations, respect and trust built by the various parties; and, structural social capital – the network of connections which allow access to valuable knowledge. These three dimensions would appear to correspond with the three areas described by the WBCSD (2017a).

The Protocol builds upon the work of many organisations including Accounting for Sustainability, Global Reporting Initiative (GRI), International Integrated Reporting Council (IIRC), and the Sustainability Accounting Standards Board (SASB); however, the focus of these organisations' tools is mainly on external reporting. In contrast, the Protocol is intended to provide information that enables decision-makers to increase social capital for the business and society (WBCSD, 2017b).

Figure 3. Social capital (adapted from WBCSD, April 2017a)

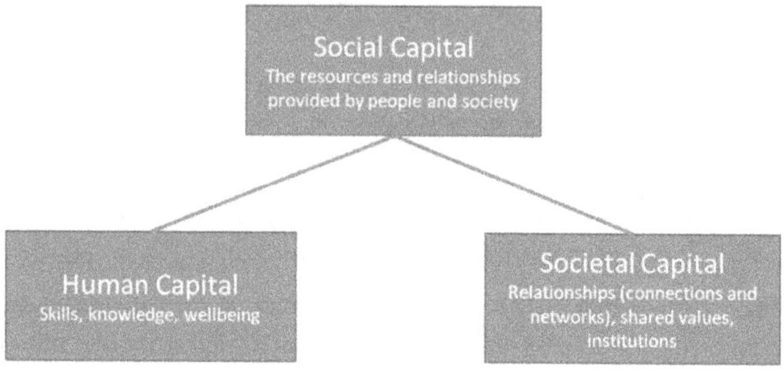

The Social Capital Protocol is based on the same concepts and principles as the Natural Capital Protocol (Natural Capital Coalition, 2016) and both are intended to lead to integrated reporting of people, planet and profit. The Natural Capital Protocol was designed to measure impacts on the natural environment and; therefore, it was revised to apply to the variety of contexts and the different maturity levels of social capital accounting. There are four stages of the social capital protocol: frame; scope; measure and value; apply and integrate which consist of twelve steps (Figure 4). Its purpose is to provide a consist process to guide companies and a framework to eventually harmonize and standardise approaches.

Having described the nature of the Social Capital Protocol, we will now critically examine each of the twelve steps to assess their benefits and how practical they are to achieve.

Stage 1: Frame – Identifying and Prioritizing the Social Capital Issues Relevant to the Business

Stage 1 encourages companies to develop an understanding of the importance of social capital and how its measurement and valuation can inform and assist communication, decision making and strategy.

Step 1: Relevant Social Capital Issues Mapped Across the Value Chain

To begin the task of undertaking a social capital audit, companies were recommended to identify their own 'social capital issues' which were most relevant to them (WBCSD, 2017a) e.g. ones they had already recognised or, alternatively, had identified through the use of frameworks. Among the frameworks suggested were ones which could provide baseline considerations e.g.: UN Universal Declaration of Human

Figure 4. The four stages of the social capital protocol (WBCSD, 2017a, with permission)

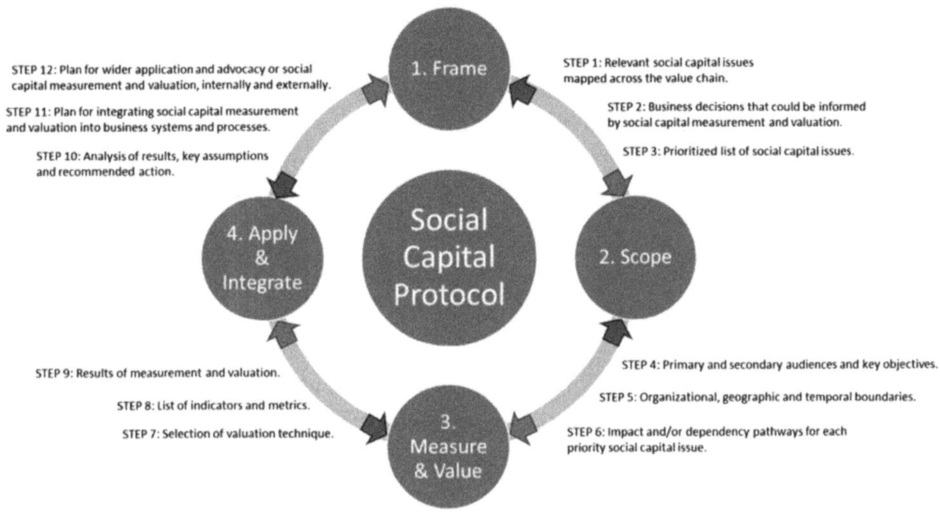

Rights (1948); UN Guiding Principles for Business and Human Rights (2011); UN Guiding Principles Reporting Framework (2015c) and ILO's (1998) Declaration on Fundamental Principles and Rights at Work (which identifies 32 internationally recognized human rights), and the ILO's (2017) Tripartite Declaration of Principles Concerning Multinational Enterprises and Social Policy. There are also more than 150 other frameworks identified by the Foundation Centre (2017) e.g. GRI.

Having identified social capital issues, companies are then encouraged to "map and rank the relevance of the issues across the value chain" (WBCSD, 2017a:15). For example, social issues in the forest products value chain for surrounding communities were: access to education, energy, healthcare, infrastructure, water and sanitation; and economic development. For employees both direct and indirect: decent jobs; fair wages; gender equality; health and safety; human rights; road safety; and training and skills development. And, for consumers: consumer awareness training; and, product safety (WBCSD, 2017b:10).

When social capital issues have been mapped they should be prioritized which can be achieved by assessing: the severity of impact; the possibility of the company impacting on the issue; the potential for remediation of negative impacts; and, the enhancement of positive impacts etc.

To demonstrate the mapping process, the Social Capital Protocol located five SDGs along the value chain to demonstrate the process; however, although this may have been a simplified model, in reality the majority of the SDGs can be applied to each of the stages in the supply chain. Significantly, only 1% of the companies surveyed by PricewaterhouseCoopers (2015) stated that they intend to assess the impact of all 17 SDGs, while 44% said they planned to assess themselves against all or some of the SDGs which they considered relevant.

Undertaking this mapping and ranking procedure would be a substantial task for businesses with only a small number of suppliers and products, for larger organisations this could become almost unmanageable. For example, a case study of BASF (WBCSD, 2017a: 19) revealed that it procured more than 30,000 different raw materials, and there were greater than 75,000 tier one suppliers.

Step 2: Business Decisions That Could Be Informed By Social Capital Measurement and Valuation

Step 2 addresses how the social impacts and dependencies identified in Step 1 relate to the making of business decisions. It is suggested that these social factors should be mapped against five business value drivers i.e.: obtain or maintain license to operate; improve the business enabling environment; optimize human resource management; strengthen value chains; and, fuel product and service growth and innovation. For example, negative impacts on local communities might be mitigated, or new health product lines developed for low-income consumers

A case study about Shell describes how a community feedback mechanism at all major operations allows them to receive and resolve matters quickly. This is easier said than done; in the delta region of Nigeria there have been numerous issues surrounding the local Ogoni community, oil spillages, and the effect on farming and fishing (Boele et al, 2001). Not all of this is the fault of Shell since many of the spillages are due to local people tapping into pipelines, however, some of Shells financial contributions to communities do not reach them because of corruption (Ikelegbe, 2005).

Although many companies communicate their virtues of corporate social responsibility and sustainability their strategic business interests are often the main priority (Banerjee, 2008). Moreover, not only has capitalism often successfully adopted the language of sustainability (Fernando, 2003) companies may also "cherry pick the SDGs" in order assist the growth of their businesses (PricewaterhouseCoopers, 2015: 12). This pragmatic approach to business may not necessarily be detrimental if it produces scalable solutions which benefit society (PricewaterhouseCoopers, 2015: 12). This view accords with Porter and Kramer's (2011) proposal of shared value in which companies enhance their competitiveness at the same time as advancing the economic and social conditions of communities where they operate.

Step 3: Prioritise Social Capital Issues

It was recommended that companies prioritise issues which have a substantial impact on their ability to add value for themselves and key stakeholders over the short, medium and long term. This can be achieved with a materiality assessment (Calabrese et al, 2016) involving a consideration of 'relevant' social capital issues and their 'significance' to the company and stakeholders. This would then allow companies to determine which social capital issues to focus upon.

For companies which are just beginning the process it was suggested that they might focus on just one pragmatic starting point dependent on the resources available. This approach may lead to cherry-picking i.e. choosing those indicators which are easy to identify and which may be favourably viewed by stakeholders (Guthrie and Farneti, 2008). It is an approach; however, which is practical and which allows lessons learned from initial experiences to be scaled up and applied more widely. It would appear that few, if any, companies are intending to assess all the SDGs across all of the supply chain (PricewaterhouseCoopers, 2015).

Stage 2: Scope – Audiences, Boundaries, and Social Capital Pathways

This Stage is predominantly concerned with identifying a practical scope and suitable boundaries in order that social capital priority areas identified in Stage 1 can be measured and valued.

Step 4: Primary and Secondary Audiences and Key Objectives

Step 4 involves identifying the internal and/or external audience and the objectives which are to be measured and valued. The internal audience can include representatives from across the company, executives to employees and contractors. The external audience might include shareholders, NGOs, community, customers etc. Feedback from these audiences about social capital issues identified in Stage 1 can then be used to inform business decisions.

Among the challenges which might be faced in a consultation process with external stakeholders are: selecting appropriate stakeholders; weighting their views and other evidence; and the extent to which their views should impact on business decisions etc. (Barnett, 2007; Spitzeck, and Hansen, 2010). Another concern, articulated by Clarkson (1995), lies with identifying the level of analysis and the extent to which a consideration of society extends beyond a company.

Another factor is how the "sustained, inclusive and sustainable economic growth [which is] essential for prosperity" (United Nations, 2015b) is compatible with environmental sustainability (Elkins, 2000), an issue which is considered to be "the key economic question" (Goldin and Winters, 1995: 2). The European Commission (2012: 9) even noted that sustainable consumption might be considered by some to be a "reversal of progress towards greater quality of life." The interactions of social, environmental and economic factors need to be integrated into decision making but which should take preference? (Hutchins & Sutherland, (2008). Markman and Krause (2016) suggest that environmental considerations should come first, then social and finally economic.

Step 5: Organizational, Geographic, and Temporal Boundaries

Identifying boundaries is necessary for practical and conceptual reasons because they enable clarity and focus as well as the effective use of resources. Organisational boundaries include: value chain, corporate, project, site and product. Geographical boundaries are: global, regional, national, and local. Temporal boundaries include the time period of past, present or future impacts and dependencies; plus, the duration which could be a snapshot, months or even years.

In order to determine the extent of the boundaries, companies were advised to consider: stakeholder and audience interest; the effectiveness of addressing high priority social capital issues; company ambition level and resources; data availability; objectives and scope of impacts. Companies can begin by considering just one aspect on the value chain such as women's professional advancement in a Bangladeshi supplier factory. When the methodology is fully functional it can be extended to other suppliers.

It is important here to draw attention to the inclusion of "company ambition level" (WBCSD 2017a: 38) and 'resources' because these can vary significantly and are not tied to any clear specifications. What is the level of ambition for a company – alleviating all global poverty? Furthermore, conducting a comprehensive assessment of a product portfolio across the whole supply chain can be an almost impossible task; in the case of BASF 60,000 product applications would need to be mapped and, thus BASF conducted Step 5 on a case by case basis.

Another concern is that sustainability reporting is voluntary with no statutory regulation and there is limited independent assurance. Moreover, collecting and aggregating economic, environmental and social data across geographical locations, different operations, different sectors, across long supply chains can be very costly and subject to cost-benefit analysis (Jones et al, 2016).

Also, the temporal and spatial scales of sustainability indicators are often ambiguous thereby creating challenging limitations to measurement and research (Rahdari and Rostamy, 2015). For example, assessing the impact of company activity might change from having a positive impact in the short term to becoming negative in the long term. For example, the effect of DDT spraying in reducing mosquitos and the consequent reduction in malaria was later found to be injurious to humans and the environment (Pedercini et al, 2011).

A major challenge facing enlightened companies can be the internal cost associated with sustainability practices and the fact that financial returns may accrue over the medium and longer terms rather than the short term. Unilever recently had to fight off a hostile bid from 3G, owners of Kraft Heinz, who wanted to introduce extensive cost-cutting and increase short-term profits. Significantly, in a previous takeover bid for Cadbury, Kraft had promised not to close a factory but within a few weeks of the takeover they had announced plans to close Cadbury's Somerdale factory and move production to Poland. Prior to this, the Takeover Panel had accepted Kraft's statement that the UK would be a "net beneficiary in terms of jobs" and that it would be "in a position to continue to operate the Somerdale factory" (The Guardian, 2010).

Following 3G's bid withdrawal, Unilever CEO Paul Polman introduced some cost cutting and the sale of some brands. He said,

I have to find a balance between not giving up on our long-term sustainable compounding model, and satisfying increasingly a group of shareholders who want to see at any time the short-term return. That's a fine balance, I don't deny it. (Daily Telegraph, 2017)

For companies to independently implement deep and extensive sustainability practices can place them at risk of takeover or being uncompetitive and going out of business. Essentially, firms have four main strategies in how they might incorporate social responsiveness i.e.: reactive, defensive, accommodative, and proactive each of which comes with differing costs (Carroll, 1979; Wartick and Cochran, 1985). For sustainability to be successful a level playing field is needed in which all competing firms play by the same rules and this is not something which one company or those in a supply chain can achieve. There needs to be legislation which is enforced at both national and international levels rather than companies operating in a piecemeal fashion.

Step 6: Impact and/or Dependency Pathways for Each Priority Social Capital Issue

All businesses impact upon and are dependent on social capital and both positive and negative social impacts may result from the operations of the company e.g. economic growth; enterprise development and entrepreneurship; job creation; rural development; wages and benefits; women's empowerment etc. Secondly, there are social dependencies, the factors which affect the ability of the company to operate e.g.: diversity, engaged workforce, infrastructure; rule of law; skilled talent pipeline; worker health and wellbeing etc.

Impact and dependency pathways provide a logical framework which illustrate e.g. financial costs to a business or, perhaps, a social capital dependency. The impact pathway can have five or more stages involving a consideration of inputs, activities, outputs, outcomes, and impacts which may clarify causal effects in the chain (WBCSD, 2017a).

Exploring social sustainability impacts along the supply chain or value chain is not necessarily the same as social life cycle assessment; each element along the supply chain may have its own individual life cycle. The impact pathways of corporate inputs and outputs, and the midpoints and endpoints of social dimensions are "unclear" (Hutchins & Sutherland, 2008: 1690). For example, "the impact pathway from corporate taxes to improvements in national literacy rates is complex at best and indiscernible at worst" (Hutchins & Sutherland, 2008: 1693). Furthermore, although some relationships had been identified there are others which have not been incorporated within life cycle analysis.

The WBCSD (2017a p. 10) explained that the Social Capital Protocol can be utilised to assess business impacts connected with avoiding illegal activities e.g. child labour and forced labour. These areas may already be reported on but to what extent should companies operating in developed countries communicate their adherence to well established legislation e.g. should companies detail in their annual reports that there are a legally sufficient number of toilets for staff? (Health and Safety Executive, 2017).

Stage 3: Measure and Value

The main focus of Stage 3 concerns the identification of fit-for-purpose indicators and their measurement and valuation.

Step 7: Selection of Valuation Technique

For this step companies identify which valuation technique (quantitative, qualitative, monetary) is most relevant to each impact or dependency. This should be determined by a fit-for-purpose consideration of the objectives to be assessed, the audience, and the availability of time and resources. In a detailed examination of social sustainability indicators and their application to the supply chain Hutchins & Sutherland (2008: 1692) argued that: "a majority of the social indicators are subjective and qualitative;" which is contrary to the stipulations by Darton (2015) to use only quantitative data.

Interestingly, a case study which involved E&Y and Acciona Energy calculated the monetary value of job creation for two different types of energy technology. Generally, policy makers focus only on the cost of energy and not the social and economic impacts but in this study, the two companies were able to identify the "net cost," to society (WBCSD 2017a: 48).

There is obvious value in this wider consideration but is employment the only consideration and are there other factors which might be valued? e.g. lower energy costs for marginalised people might translate into having to work fewer hours. Furthermore, if the issue was about increasing employment then Milton Friedman's experience in Asia makes a salient point. During a visit to the building of a canal, Friedman was surprised to see labourers using spades rather than modern excavation equipment and when he asked why they were not being used was told that this increased employment. Friedman replied, "Oh, I thought you were trying to build a canal. If it's jobs you want, then you should give these workers spoons, not shovels" (Pethokoukis, 2015).

Finally, for this section, it is important to mention that some multi-national firms may adopt different strategies regarding the choice and replacement of suppliers. The reasons for this may be due to social capital factors but may also be associated with the financial opportunities of transfer pricing and low tax regimes (Huh and Park. 2013; Shunko, Do and Tsay. 2017; Xu, Hsu and Niu 2018).

Step 8: List of Indicators and Metrics

Indicators should have SMART characteristics i.e. be: specific, measurable, attainable, relevant, and time bound (Sandhu-Rojon, 2017) and descriptions such as "minor or serious health and safety incident" (WBCSD 2017a: 62) provide insufficient clarity. Proxy indicators may also be used where data is unavailable or where the time scale for impacts to materialise is great. Also, it is suggested, that baselines and counterfactual scenarios might also be applied. Counterfactual scenarios can be used to describe alternative situations which might have resulted had the intervention not happened. Counterfactual considerations have a number of associated problems and can be used inappropriately (Booth, 2003). To avoid these problems, it was recommended that balanced and transparent metrics are used together with any assumptions which are made. Accenture is cited in a case study which describes how the partnership aims to build employment skills in three million people to help them get a job by 2020. The forward looking nature of this calculation naturally involves projections and assumptions.

Comprehensive, accurate and transparent sustainability reporting also presents difficulties for companies. One of the most commonly used and respected frameworks, the Global Reporting Initiative (GRI), has limitations which may not contribute to sustainability (Dumay et al, 2010) and there is the potential for nonfinancial information to be misrepresented (Ballou et al, 2005).

A main challenges for companies is to identify where to begin and what areas to focus upon given: "the plethora of different ways to classify social impacts or dependencies" (WBCSD, 2017a: 14). There are 17 SDGs which possess 169 targets and 230 indicators (United Nations Economic and Social Council, 2016); 834 business indicators (GRI, UNGC and WBCSD, 2017b) (the business indicators were identified from 58 business tools produced by 75 organisations and is not complete); and 150 tools and instruments (Foundation Centre, 2017). These all add up to an immense and potentially insurmountable bureaucratic challenge for organisations. These might then be multiplied by the range of suppliers and products found across the supply chain and which may differ depending on local, national and international markets etc. While this may be just manageable for large organisations with substantial resources it starts to become an impossible mountain to climb for micro, small and medium-sized enterprises.

In addition, compared to the eight Millennium Development Goals, the 169 SDG targets were described as "sprawling," "misconceived," and "a mess" (The Economist, 2015) which makes them difficult to assess and measure. They need to be robustly measured, monitored and followed-up (Lunn et al, 2015); however, Bell and Morse (2008: 1) asked whether sustainability indicators might be "measuring the immeasurable?"

Step 9: Results of Measurement and Valuation

Step 9 involves gathering and analysing primary data (internal business data, surveys, interviews and focus groups) and secondary data (peer reviewed literature, interviews with third parties e.g. experts, external data – government statistics, existing analyses). Once the sources of data are collected they need to be valued taking into account the acceptability of the valuation approach to stakeholders. Also, ethical issues about making trade-offs need to be considered (see below in the discussion about outsourcing); furthermore, double-counting should be avoided, and assumptions made explicit.

Nestle believed that the assumption that people should live to their full potential might mean that all employees would earn a top salary. However, Nestle considered that not only would this result in negative scoring impacts but society's expectations do not uphold this view of living to full potential (WBCSD, 2017a).

An important factor to consider is the availability and complexity of data with which to make assessments of social impact (Hutchins & Sutherland, 2008) and directly gathering this data is not always possible in an extensive value chain. Taking these factors into account, the GRI, UNGC, WBCSD (2015, p. 14) advised that cost and complexity should be proportional to the benefits accrued from measurement.

Yet another consideration is the impact of replacing a supplier in one country with another from a different country which is common practice in global outsourcing. The use of sustainable indicators may not always indicate the true impact on the affected communities (Hutchins & Sutherland, 2008). Which community should take preference or should the company just consider costs?

The criteria for social sustainability within a number of key frameworks e.g. United Nations Commission on Sustainable Development Framework, Global Reporting Initiative, Sustainability Metrics of the Institution of Chemical Engineers, and Wuppertal Sustainability Indicators were found to be not "efficient" (Labuschagne et al, 2005). Moreover, the GRI indicators have limitations (Gray, 2010; Spangenberg, 2016) e.g. for 'Labour/Management Relations' there is only 'Minimum notice periods regarding operational changes' mentioned; and 'Training and Education' does not say who pays for it. Also, GRI4 has several hundred indicators which are unhelpful as a communication tool (Spangenberg, 2016).

To add to the challenges, United Nations (2015b: para. 57) acknowledged that baseline data for some targets were not available. The GRI, UNGC, WBCSD (2015: p. 17) acknowledged that social factors of sustainable development e.g. anti-corruption and poverty eradication, were less frequent due to the difficulties in monitoring and measurement. Moreover, the United Nations Economic and Social Council IAEG (2016: 9) admitted that indicators were affected by levels of methodological development and data availability and to provide some clarity they identified three categories or tiers:

- Tier 1: There is an established methodology and there are widely available data.
- Tier 2: There is an established methodology but no easily available data.
- Tier 3: There is no internationally agreed methodology.

Stage 4: Apply and Integrate

This final stage of the Social Capital Protocol involves analysing the social capital metrics and valuations determined in Stage 3 and applying them to business processes, systems and decision-making. It is suggested that metrics and valuations are collated and presented to suit the company and audience possibly using cost-benefit analysis, total profit and loss account, or total contribution methods. In addition, companies should take action on their results. External audit and verification of the Protocol is not expected but it may provide confidence if undertaken (WBCSD, 2017a).

Step 10: Analysis of Results, Key Assumptions, and Recommended Action

At one stage there were more than 100 ratings agencies (Scalet and Kelly, 2010) which presented problems of compatibility and comparison and although this has declined to a smaller number of internationally recognised agencies the problems still remain (Sakuma and Louche, 2008).

In an analysis of more than 2,500 surveys produced by 1,700 suppliers 'The Sustainability Consortium' (TSC) (2016: 28) noted that the response to 54% of questions addressing environmental or social areas in the supply chain was: "Unable to determine." 27% of responses showed partial supply chain visibility and only 19% demonstrated full supply chain transparency. The TSC concluded that: "perhaps the most important [finding was] that the majority of manufacturers lack visibility into the sustainability performance of their own supply chains." This "lack of visibility" impacts on the ability to manage and improve operations. Greater visibility enables the identification of sustainability issues and allows efforts to be focused on those which will have the greatest effect.

It was acknowledged that some estimation and approximation might be used since precise information may be resource intensive. It was also acknowledged that external factors such as exchange fluctuations might alter an impact even though a company had not changed anything. A case study of Veracel described how the company demonstrated its support for local people it did not employ to avoid unrest and conflict (WBCSD 2017a: 79)

Step 11: Plan for Integrating Social Capital Measurement and Valuation Into Business Systems and Processes.

This penultimate step involves the integration of social capital considerations into business processes. The Protocol's vision is to mainstream social impact measurement to enable companies to integrate people, planet, profit factors to support sustainable growth. The means through which this can be delivered include: strategic planning and goal setting; cost-benefit analysis; impact assessments; management systems; and, external reporting.

It was recognised that this mainstreaming and integration will require time for the company to develop, strengthen and expand its approach. Using this approach AkzoNobel identified that the increase in financial and human capital (€21.74) was 10 times larger than the loss of natural capital (-€1.87) (WBCSD 2017a: 79). This finding may be positive if the natural capital can be replaced; however, if it is a finite resource then this ratio may be of limited value.

Research into the social footprint of three projects by Labuschagne and Brent (2008) was unable to measure all of the social category indicators. Drawing upon these investigations, Hutchins & Sutherland (2008: 1692) concluded that: "Many of proposed frameworks for social sustainability or corporate social responsibility could be difficult to incorporate into decision-making."

Even for developed nations social progress is not a one-way-street with progress sometimes stalling or even going into reverse. Austerity measures in the UK have resulted in the nation flat-lining according to Porter's (2017) 'social progress imperative' which assesses national social development.

Another challenge involves the implicit assumptions made by the SDGs. It was noted above that business of all sizes were expected to sign up to environmental, social and human rights standards (UN 2015b) which implies that business models will be reconfigured to accommodate these. In a critical executive summary, the Institute for Human Rights and Business (2015: 5) argued that: "business is not an adjunct of aid," and that, "Economic activity cannot easily be directed to where the need is greatest." Instead it flourishes when it has the right conditions and opportunities.

Step 12: Plan for Wider Application and Advocacy or Social Capital Measurement and Valuation, Internally and Externally

The final step involves companies returning to Stage 1 in order to identify the next priority areas to address. There was also a "call to action" for businesses to go beyond their own boundaries and contribute towards improving the social capital measurement and valuation practices by producing case studies; providing examples for the company annual report; joining relevant groups and initiatives; and bringing together companies in the value chain. It was acknowledged that there was a long way to go and there were challenges to be faced but that companies such as ArcelorMittal were reporting social and environmental impacts and, when possible, connecting them with industry benchmarks and government priorities (WBCSD, 2017a).

Sustainability reporting has been defined as: "the provision of environmental, social and governance information within documents such as annual reports and sustainability reports" (van Wensen et. al., 2011: 14) and sustainability indicators assist managers in their decision making. Also, many investors also consider this integration of information into the investment process as a means to maximise long-term success (Rahdari and Rostamy, 2015).

With the 12 steps, companies can design a customised approach to reporting by choosing which measurement and assessment approaches within a broader framework. However, it is "not a formal reporting framework" (WBCSD 2017a: 5) and nor do the results have to be reported externally although it is recognised that companies may wish to report their assessments to stakeholders. Environmental impact assessments for new projects or activities are frequently required, but businesses do not have a legal obligation to undertake social impact assessments (WBCSD, 2017b).

This customisation of sustainability reporting has benefits for the organisation and some stakeholders but it does not necessarily enable comparability between organisations. A consensus is required among companies and stakeholders in order that indicators are widely used (Lodhia and Martin, 2014). Initiatives such as The International Integrated Reporting Framework (2013: 7) seek to address this concern and state that: "An integrated report is a concise communication about how an organization's strategy, governance, performance and prospects, in the context of its external environment, lead to the creation of value over the short, medium and long term."

In addition, the large number of tools currently available suggests that there is unlikely to be a universally agreed framework to assess social sustainability in the near future. Moreover, the range of products and services across different supply chains, geographies and time frames makes it difficult to identify: "an appropriate balance between flexibility and prescription… while enabling a sufficient degree of comparability across organizations to meet relevant information needs" (International Integrated Reporting Council, 2013: 7).

There was also an acknowledgment that although social capital impacts and dependencies are frequently specific to context, location and sector the longer term intention is to standardise social capital measurement and valuation. This aspiration still requires further development and the WBCSD (2017b: p. 29) admitted that: "the road ahead is still long."

SOLUTIONS AND RECOMMENDATIONS

Based on the discussions above it is evident that identifying, prioritising, measuring, valuing, integrating and communicating social capital across the supply chain presents numerous challenges for organisations. Among the obstacles are the lack of standardisation; the need for clear geographical, social and temporal boundaries; multiple frameworks and indicators; and incomplete or non-existent methodologies. Some of these limitations arise from the need for flexibility to accommodate different types of organisations and their operations, but this diversity works against a standardised and transparent means of assessment and valuation.

In light of the discussion above, the Social Capital Protocol needs to be assessed against Darton's (2015) seven criteria for sustainability indicators.

To ensure that the application of the Social Capital Protocol is consistent with Darton's criteria, organisations will need to be more precise with their specifications for each of the 12 steps. This should be possible; however, given that there is no legal requirement to conform to the Protocol and that organisations can define their own parameters and ""company ambition level" (WBCSD 2017a: 38)", this presents difficulties in benchmarking and comparing different organisational practices. In the future as social capital accounting becomes more sophisticated, agreed conventions and parameters may emerge and provide a consistent and workable framework which eventually becomes incorporated within a legislative structure. For the moment, we are still enveloped in a fog which the Social Capital Protocol is attempting to dispel.

It appears that the 12 steps in the Social Capital Protocol do not satisfactorily match the criteria for sustainability indicators described by Darton (2015). This does not mean that companies shouldn't attempt to measure and value social capital but they should recognise the challenges they face. Indeed, the WBCSD (2017a) acknowledge that they are at the start of the journey and there are numerous questions to be answered. On this journey we have charted some of the challenges identified by

Table 1. An assessment of degree of fit between the Social Capital Protocol steps and Darton's (2015) criteria for sustainability indicators

	Darton's (2015) criteria for sustainability indicators	Achieved	Not achieved
1	Clear definition of what is to be assessed (the system boundary) and why.		X
2	The nature of the sustainable outcome (economic, environmental, societal) must be defined.		X
3	Coverage of key aspects is necessary.	?	
4	Quantitative data are required, not qualitative judgements.		X
5	Duplication and needless complexity should be avoided.	?	
6	Excluded - Only operational targets and indicators to be used		X
7	Composite weighted indicators used.	?	

Gray (2010: 58) who noted that: "the proposal of any new (albeit organisationally-based) social accounting narrative steers an impossible path between the speculative but ungrounded and the empirical but captured and emasculated."

The SDGs have ambitious targets which also present a range of significant challenges: firstly, the SDGs are not legally binding which means that their successful delivery is dependent upon political commitment (Lunn et. al., 2015). Secondly, the cost of achieving SDG 1 'alleviating poverty' is estimated to be $2-3trillion for the next 15 years (The Economist, 2015). Thirdly, compared to the Millennium Development Goals, the 169 targets were described as "sprawling," "misconceived," and "a mess" (The Economist, 2015) which makes them difficult to assess and measure. Furthermore, they need to be robustly measured, monitored and followed-up (Lunn et al, 2015).

Also, there is the danger that some less scrupulous companies might reap competitive advantage over more sustainably oriented companies through a form of sustainability arbitrage. Voluntary commitment to social capital sustainability is unlikely to be fully successful without legislative enforcement (Gray and Milne, 2004) but getting national and supranational agreement appears distant.

FUTURE RESEARCH DIRECTIONS

There is a growing demand for sustainability reporting by society and these pressures have resulted in the development of the Social Capital Protocol. The analysis of the Protocol in this chapter has been conducted theoretically using examples from a range of secondary sources to identify its strengths and limitations. It is therefore recommended that future research be conducted into the application of all the Protocol's 12 steps in a real world context to identify its full potential.

CONCLUSION

This chapter began with the United Nations' appeal for companies to support the achievement of the Sustainable Development Goals across the supply chain. The three integrated areas of sustainability: social, environmental and economic or 'people, planet, profit' were discussed and it was noted that social capital reporting was less well developed than the other two areas. To address this, the Social Capital Protocol was developed by the World Business Council for Sustainable Development (2017a) and a range of advantages and limitations were identified and assessed using Darton's (2015) criteria for assessing sustainability frameworks.

Bell and Morse (2008: 1) observed that sustainability indicators are "measuring the immeasurable" and although this particularly would appear to be the case with social capital measurement and assessment it is not a justifiable reason for dismissing and ignoring it. We only have one earth and, as Markman and Krause (2016: 9) wrote: Extinction is forever.

REFERENCES

Andersen, M., & Skjoett-Larsen, T. (2009). Corporate social responsibility in global supply chains. *Supply Chain Management*, *14*(2), 75–86. doi:10.1108/13598540910941948

Autry, Ch. W., & Griffis, S. (2008). Supply chain capital: The impact of structural and relational linkages on firm execution and innovation. *Journal of Business Logistics*, *29*(1), 157–173. doi:10.1002/j.2158-1592.2008.tb00073.x

Ballou, B., Heitger, D. L., Landes, C. E., & Adams, M. (2006). The future of corporate sustainability reporting. *Journal of Accountancy*, *202*(6), 65–74.

Banerjee, S. B. (2008). Corporate Social Responsibility: The Good, the Bad and the Ugly. *Critical Sociology*, *34*(1), 51–79. doi:10.1177/0896920507084623

Barnett, M. L. (2007). Stakeholder influence capacity and the variability of financial returns to corporate social responsibility. *Academy of Management Review*, *32*(3), 794–816. doi:10.5465/amr.2007.25275520

Bebbington, J., Unerman, J., & O'Dwyer, B. (2014). *Sustainability Accounting and Accountability*. Abingdon, UK: Routledge.

Bell, S., & Morse, S. (2008). *Sustainability Indicators: Measuring the immeasurable?* London: Earthscan.

Berle, A. A. (1931). Corporate Powers as Powers in Trust. *Harvard Law Review*, *44*(7), 1049–1074. doi:10.2307/1331341

Boele, R., Fabig, H., & Wheeler, D. (2001). Shell, Nigeria and the Ogoni. A study in unsustainable development: II. Corporate social responsibility and 'stakeholder management' versus a rights-based approach to sustainable development. *Sustainable Development*, *9*(3), 121–135. doi:10.1002d.168

Booth, C. (2003). Does history matter in strategy? The possibilities and problems of counterfactual analysis. *Management Decision*, *41*(1), 96–104. doi:10.1108/00251740310445545

Bourdieu, P. (1985). The forms of capital. In J. G. Richardson (Ed.), *Handbook of theory and research for the sociology of education* (pp. 241–258). New York: Greenwood.

Bowen, H. R. (1953). *Social Responsibilities of the Businessman*. New York: Harper.

Calabrese, A., Costa, R., Levialdi, N., & Menichini, T. (2016). A fuzzy Analytic Hierarchy Process method to support materiality assessment in sustainability reporting. *Journal of Cleaner Production, 121*, 248–264. doi:10.1016/j.jclepro.2015.12.005

Carroll, A. B. (1979). A three-dimensional conceptual model of corporate performance. *Academy of Management Review, 4*(4), 497–505. doi:10.5465/amr.1979.4498296

Carroll, A. B. (1991). The pyramid of corporate social responsibility: Toward to moral management of organizational stakeholders. *Business Horizons, 34*(4), 39–48. doi:10.1016/0007-6813(91)90005-G

Carroll, A. B., & Buchholtz, A. K. (2000). *Business & Society. Ethics and Stakeholder Management* (4th ed.). Cincinnati, OH: South Western College Publishing.

Clarkson, M. E. (1995). A stakeholder framework for analyzing and evaluating corporate social performance. *Academy of Management Review, 20*(1), 92–117. doi:10.5465/amr.1995.9503271994

Cochran, P. L. (2007). The evolution of corporate social responsibility. *Business Horizons, 50*(6), 449–454. doi:10.1016/j.bushor.2007.06.004

Colbert, B. A., & Kurucz, E. C. (2007). Three conceptions of triple bottom line business sustainability and the role for HRM. *People and Strategy, 30*(1), 21.

Cousins, P. D., Handfield, R. B., Lawson, B., & Petersen, K. J. (2006). Creating supply chain relational capital: The impact of formal and informal socialization processes. *Journal of Operations Management, 24*(6), 851–863. doi:10.1016/j.jom.2005.08.007

Daily Telegraph. (2017). *Unilever's Paul Polman on why he didn't get angry when Kraft Heinz came to call, and why he'll still keep talking about sustainability*. Retrieved June 19, 2017, from http://www.telegraph.co.uk/business/2017/04/08/unilevers-paul-polman-didnt-get-angry-kraft-heinz-came-call/

Darton, R. C. (2015). Setting a policy for sustainability: the importance of measurement. In J. Klemes (Ed.), *Assessing and Measuring Environmental Impact and Sustainability* (pp. 479–496). Oxford, UK: Butterworth-Heinemann. doi:10.1016/B978-0-12-799968-5.00014-2

Dodd, E. M. Jr. (1932). For whom are corporate managers trustees? *Harvard Law Review, 45*(7), 1145–1163. doi:10.2307/1331697

Dumay, J., Guthrie, J., & Farneti, F. (2010). GRI sustainability reporting guidelines for public and third sector organizations: A critical review. *Public Management Review, 12*(4), 531–548. doi:10.1080/14719037.2010.496266

The Economist. (2015). *The 169 commandments*. Retrieved June 19, 2017, from http://www.economist.com/news/leaders/21647286-proposed-sustainable-development-goals-would-be-worse-useless-169-commandments

Ehrenfeld, J. R. (2008). *Sustainability by Design*. New Haven, CT: Yale University Press.

Elkington, J. (1997). *Cannibals With Forks: The Triple Bottom Line of 21st Century Business*. Oxford, UK: Capstone.

Elkins, P. (2000). *Economic Growth and Environmental Sustainability: The prospects for green growth*. London: Routledge.

Epstein, M. J., & Buhovac, A. R. (2014). *Making sustainability work: Best practices in managing and measuring corporate social, environmental, and economic impacts*. Oakland, CA: Berrett-Koehler Publishers.

European Commission. (2012). *Policies to Encourage Sustainable Consumption, Technical Report 2012-061*. Brussels: European Communities.

Fernando, J. L. (2003). *Rethinking sustainable development. In The Annals of the American Academy of Political and Social Science*. London: Sage Publications.

Florman, M., Klingler-Vidra, R., & Jacinto Facada, M. (2016). *A critical evaluation of social impact assessment methodologies and a call to measure economic and social impact holistically through the External Rate of Return platform*. LSE Enterprise Working Paper # 1602. London: LSE.

Forsman-Hugg, S., Katajajuuri, J. M., Riipi, I., Mäkelä, J., Järvelä, K., & Timonen, P. (2013). Key CSR dimension for the food chain. *British Food Journal, 115*(1), 30–47. doi:10.1108/00070701311289867

Foundation Centre. (2017). *Tools and Resources for Assessing Social Impact*. Retrieved April 13, 2017, from http://trasi.foundationcenter.org/browse.php

Friedman, M. (1970). The social responsibility of business is to increase its profits. New York: Academic Press.

Gao, J., & Bansal, P. (2013). Instrumental and Integrative Logics in Business Sustainability. *Journal of Business Ethics*, *112*(2), 241–255. doi:10.100710551-012-1245-2

Garriga, E., & Melé, D. (2004). Corporate Social Responsibility Theories: Mapping the Territory. *Journal of Business Ethics*, *53*(1-2), 51–71. doi:10.1023/B:BUSI.0000039399.90587.34

Global Reporting Initiative. (2017a). *GRI's History*. Retrieved April 13, 2017, from https://www.globalreporting.org/information/about-gri/gri-history/Pages/GRI%27s%20history.aspx

Global Reporting Initiative (2017b). *The benefits of sustainability reporting*. Author.

Global Reporting Initiative/United Nations Global Compact/wbcsd. (2015). *SDG Compass: The guide for business action on the SDGs*. Author.

Global Reporting Initiative/United Nations Global Compact/wbcsd. (2017a). Retrieved April 12, 2017, from http://sdgcompass.org/business-tools/

Global Reporting Initiative/United Nations Global Compact/wbcsd. (2017b). Retrieved April 12, 2017, from http://sdgcompass.org/business-indicators/

Global Sustainability Standards Board. (2017). *Global Sustainability Standard Board*. Retrieved April 13, 2017, from https://www.globalreporting.org/information/about-gri/governance-bodies/Global-Sustainability-Standard-Board/Pages/default.aspx

Goldin, I., & Winters, L. A. (1995). *The Economics of Sustainable Development*. Cambridge, UK: Cambridge University Press. doi:10.1017/CBO9780511751905

Gouzee, N., Mazijn, B., & Billharz, S. (1995). *Indicators of Sustainable Development for Decision-making*. Report on the UNCSD Workshop of Ghent. Brussels: Federal Planning Office of Belgium.

Governance and Accountability Institute. (2016). *81% of S&P 500 companies published sustainability reports in 2015*. Retrieved July 10, 2018 1 from http://www.ga-institute.com/press-releases/article/flash-report-eighty-one-percent-81-of-the-sp-500-index-companies-published-corporate-sustainabi.html

Gray, R. (2010). Is accounting for sustainability actually accounting for sustainability… and how would we know? An exploration of narratives of organisations and the planet. *Accounting, Organizations and Society*, *35*(1), 47–62. doi:10.1016/j.aos.2009.04.006

Gray, R., & Milne, M. (2004). Towards reporting on the triple bottom line: mirages, methods and myths. In The triple bottom line: Does it all add up? London: Earthscan.

The Guardian. (2010). *Kraft rebuked for broken pledge on Cadbury factory*. Retrieved June 19, 2017, from https://www.theguardian.com/business/2010/may/26/kraft-censured-over-cadbury-takeover-pledge

Guthrie, J., & Farneti, F. (2008). GRI sustainability reporting by Australian public sector organizations. *Public Money & Management*, *28*(6), 361–366. doi:10.1111/j.1467-9302.2008.00670.x

Halpern, D. (2009). *The Hidden Wealth of Nations*. Cambridge, UK: Polity.

Hanifan, L. J. (1916). The rural school community centre. *The Annals of the American Academy of Political and Social Science*, *67*, 130-138.

Health and Safety Executive. (2017). *How many toilets should a workplace have?* Retrieved July 10, 2018, from http://www.hse.gov.uk/contact/faqs/toilets.htm

Hill, R. P., Stephens, D., & Smith, I. (2003). Corporate social responsibility: An examination of individual firm behaviour. *Business and Society Review*, *108*(3), 339–364. doi:10.1111/1467-8594.00168

Huh, W. T., & Park, K. S. (2013). Impact of transfer pricing methods for tax purposes on supply chain performance under demand uncertainty. *Naval Research Logistics*, *60*(4), 269–293. doi:10.1002/nav.21533

Hutchins, M. J., & Sutherland, J. W. (2008). An exploration of measures of social sustainability and their application to supply chain decisions. *Journal of Cleaner Production*, *16*(15), 1688–1698. doi:10.1016/j.jclepro.2008.06.001

Ikelegbe, A. (2005). The economy of conflict in the oil rich Niger Delta region of Nigeria. *Nordic Journal of African Studies*, *14*(2), 208–234.

Institute for Human Rights and Business (2015). *State of play – Business and the Sustainable Development Goals: Mind the gap – Challenges for implementation*. Retrieved April 13, 2017, from http://www.ihrb.org/media/images/reports/state_of_play_reportbusiness_and_the_sdgs.pdf

International Accounting Standards Board (2018). Retrieved July 10, 2018, from https://www.ifrs.org/

International Integrated Reporting Framework. (2013). *The International IR Framework*. Retrieved June 19, 2017, from http://integratedreporting.org/wp-content/uploads/2015/03/13-12-08-THE-INTERNATIONAL-IR-FRAMEWORK-2-1.pdf

International Labour Office. (2017). *Tripartite Declaration of Principles Concerning Multinational Enterprises and Social Policy*. Geneva: International Labour Office.

International Labour Organisation. (1998). *Declaration on Fundamental Principles and Rights at Work*. Retrieved August 10, 2017, from http://blue.lim.ilo.org/cariblex/pdfs/ILO_Declaration_Work.pdf

ISO. (2017). *ISO 14000: Environmental Management*. Retrieved May 3, 2017, from https://www.iso.org/iso-14001-environmental-management.html

Jones, P., Hillier, D., & Comfort, D. (2016). The sustainable development goals and business. International Journal of Sales. *Retailing and Marketing*, *5*(2), 38–48.

Joyner, B. E., & Payne, D. (2002). Evolution and implementation: A study of values, business ethics and corporate social responsibility. *Journal of Business Ethics*, *41*(4), 297–311. doi:10.1023/A:1021237420663

Klassen, R. D., & Vereecke, A. (2012). Social issues in supply chains: Capabilities link responsibility, risk (opportunity), and performance. *International Journal of Production Economics*, *140*(1), 103–115. doi:10.1016/j.ijpe.2012.01.021

Kolk, A. (2003). Trends in sustainability reporting by the Fortune Global 250. *Business Strategy and the Environment*, *12*(5), 279–291. doi:10.1002/bse.370

Krause, D. R., Handfield, R. B., & Tyler, B. B. (2007). The relationships between supplier development, commitment, social capital accumulation and performance improvement. *Journal of Operations Management*, *25*(2), 528–545. doi:10.1016/j.jom.2006.05.007

Labuschagne, C., & Brent, A. C. (2008). An industry perspective of the completeness and relevance of a social assessment framework for project and technology management in the manufacturing sector. *Journal of Cleaner Production*, *16*(3), 253–262. doi:10.1016/j.jclepro.2006.07.028

Labuschagne, C., Brent, A. C., & Van Erck, R. P. (2005). Assessing the sustainability performances of industries. *Journal of Cleaner Production*, *13*(4), 373–385. doi:10.1016/j.jclepro.2003.10.007

Lawson, B., Tyler, B. B., & Cousins, P. D. (2008). Antecedents and consequences of social capital on buyer performance improvement. *Journal of Operations Management*, *26*(3), 446–460. doi:10.1016/j.jom.2007.10.001

Lodhia, S., & Martin, N. (2014). Corporate sustainability indicators: An Australian mining case study. *Journal of Cleaner Production*, *84*, 107–115. doi:10.1016/j.jclepro.2014.05.050

Lunn, J., Downing, E. & Booth, L. (2015). *The Sustainable Development Goals and the post-2015 Development Agenda*. House of Commons Library Briefing Paper 7291. London: House of Commons.

Malthus, T. (1798). *An essay on the principle of population as it affects the future improvement of society*. London: J. Johnson.

Margolis, J. D., & Walsh, J. P. (2003). Misery loves companies: Rethinking social initiatives by business. *Administrative Science Quarterly*, *48*(2), 268–305. doi:10.2307/3556659

Markman, G. D., & Krause, D. (2016). Theory Building Surrounding Sustainable Supply Chain Management: Assessing What We Know, Exploring Where to Go. *The Journal of Supply Chain Management*, *52*(2), 3–10. doi:10.1111/jscm.12105

Matthews, L., Power, D., Touboulic, A., & Marques, L. (2016). Building bridges: Toward alternative theory of sustainable supply chain management. *The Journal of Supply Chain Management*, *52*(1), 82–94. doi:10.1111/jscm.12097

Meadows, D. H., Meadows, D. L., Randers, J., & Behrens, W. (1972). *The Limits to Growth*. New York: Universe Books.

Min, K., Stephen, K., & Chen, H. (2008). Developing social identity and social capital for supply chain management. *Journal of Business Logistics*, *29*(1), 283–304. doi:10.1002/j.2158-1592.2008.tb00079.x

Mohrman, S. A., & Worley, C. G. (2010). The organizational sustainability journey: Introduction to the special issue. *Organizational Dynamics*, *39*(4), 289–294. doi:10.1016/j.orgdyn.2010.07.008

Montabon, F., Pagell, M., & Wu, Z. (2016). Making sustainability sustainable. *The Journal of Supply Chain Management*, *52*(2), 11–27. doi:10.1111/jscm.12103

Nahapiet, J., & Ghoshal, S. (1998). Social capital, intellectual capital, and the organizational advantage. *Academy of Management Review*, *23*(2), 242–266. doi:10.5465/amr.1998.533225

Natural Capital Coalition. (2016). *Natural Capital Protocol – Food and Beverage Sector Guide*. Retrieved April 14, 2017, from www.naturalcapitalcoalition.org/protocol

OECD. (2001). *The Well-Being of Nations: The Role of Human and Social Capital*. Paris: OECD.

Olsen, S., & Galimidi, B. (2008). *Catalog of Approaches to Impact Measurement.* Social Venture Technology Group with Support of the Rockefeller Foundation.

Pedercini, M., Blanco, S. M., & Kopainsky, B. (2011). Application of the malaria management model to the analysis of costs and benefits of DDT versus non-DDT malaria control. *PLoS One*, *6*(11), e27771. doi:10.1371/journal.pone.0027771 PMID:22140467

Pethokoukis, J. (2015). The time when Elizabeth Warren unexpectedly channelled Milton Friedman. *Business Insider.* Retrieved July 1, 2017, from, http://www.businessinsider.com/when-elizabeth-warren-channeled-milton-friedman-2015-6?IR=T

Porter, M. (2017). *FAQ.* Retrieved July 1, 2018, from http://www.socialprogressimperative.org/faqs/

Porter, M., & Kramer, M. R. (2011). Creating Shared Value: How to Reinvent Capitalism – and Unleash a Wave of Innovation and Growth. *Harvard Business Review*, *89*(1/2), 62–77.

PricewaterhouseCoopers (2015). *Make it Your Business: Engaging with the sustainable development goals.* Retrieved May 10, 2017, from https://www.pwc.com/gx/en/sustainability/SDG/SDG%20Research_FINAL.pdf

Pullman, M. E., Maloni, M. J., & Cater, C. R. (2009). Food for Thought: Social Versus Environmental Sustainability Practices and Performance Outcomes. *The Journal of Supply Chain Management*, *45*(4), 38–54. doi:10.1111/j.1745-493X.2009.03175.x

Rahdari, A. H., & Rostamy, A. A. A. (2015). Designing a general set of sustainability indicators at the corporate Level. *Journal of Cleaner Production*, *108*, 757–771. doi:10.1016/j.jclepro.2015.05.108

Raworth, K. (2012). *A safe and just space for humanity: can we live within the doughnut.* Oxford, UK: Oxfam.

Rockstrom, Steffen, Noone, Persson, Chapin, III, Lambin, … Foley. (2009). Planetary boundaries: exploring the safe operating space for humanity. *Ecology and Society*, *14*(2), 32.

Sajjad, A., Eweje, G., & Tappin, D. (2015). Sustainable Supply Chain Management: Motivators and Barriers. *Business Strategy and the Environment*, *24*(7), 643–655. doi:10.1002/bse.1898

Sakuma, K., & Louche, C. (2008). Socially responsible investment in Japan: Its mechanism and drivers. *Journal of Business Ethics, 82*(2), 425–448. doi:10.100710551-008-9895-9

Sandhu-Rojon, R. (2017). *Selecting indicators for impact evaluation*. New York: UNDP.

Scalet, S., & Kelly, T. F. (2010). CSR rating agencies: What is their global impact? *Journal of Business Ethics, 94*(1), 69–88. doi:10.100710551-009-0250-6

Serageldin, I. (1996). Sustainability as Opportunity and the Problem of Social Capital. *The Brown Journal of World Affairs, 3*(2), 187–203.

Setthasakko, W. (2007). Determinants of corporate sustainability: Thai frozen seafood processors. *British Food Journal, 109*(2), 155–168. doi:10.1108/00070700710725518

Seuring, S., & Müller, M. (2008). From a literature review to a conceptual framework for sustainable supply chain management. *Journal of Cleaner Production, 16*(15), 1699–1710. doi:10.1016/j.jclepro.2008.04.020

Shunko, M., Do, H. T., & Tsay, A. A. (2017). Supply chain strategies and international tax arbitrage. *Production and Operations Management, 26*(2), 231–251. doi:10.1111/poms.12629

Spangenberg, J. H. (2016). The Corporate Human Development Index CHDI: A tool for corporate social sustainability management and reporting. *Journal of Cleaner Production, 134*, 414–424. doi:10.1016/j.jclepro.2015.12.043

Spitzeck, H., & Hansen, E. G. (2010). Stakeholder governance: How stakeholders influence corporate decision making. *Corporate Governance: The International Journal of Business in Society, 10*(4), 378-391.

Stiglitz, J., Sen, A., & Fitoussi, J. P. (2009). *The measurement of economic performance and social progress revisited. Reflections and overview*. Paris: Commission on the Measurement of Economic Performance and Social Progress.

Tahir, A. C., & Darton, R. C. (2010). The process analysis method of selecting indicators to quantify the sustainability performance of a business operation. *Journal of Cleaner Production, 18*(16-17), 1598–1607. doi:10.1016/j.jclepro.2010.07.012

Taylor, N., Goodrich, C., Fitzgerald, G., & McClintock, W. (2003). Undertaking longitudinal research. In The international handbook of social impact assessment: Conceptual and methodological advances. Cheltenham: Edward Elgar Publishing.

The Sustainability Consortium. (2016). *Greening Global Supply Chains: From blind spots to hot spots to action*. Author.

UNDP. (2013). *Human Development Report 2013*. New York: UN. Retrieved from http://www.unep.org/documents.multilingual/default.asp?documentid=97&articleid=1503

United Nations. (1948). *UN Universal Declaration of Human Rights*. New York: UN General Assembly.

United Nations. (2011). *Guiding Principles on Business and Human Rights: Implementing the United Nations 'Protest, Respect, Remedy' Framework*. New York: United Nations.

United Nations. (2015a). *Sustainable development goals: 17 goals to transform our world*. Retrieved July 9, 2016 from http://www.un.org/sustainabledevelopment/sustainable-development-goals/

United Nations. (2015b). *Transforming Our World: The 2030 Agenda for Sustainable Development*. Retrieved June 9. 2018, from https://sustainabledevelopment.un.org/content/documents/21252030%20Agenda%20for%20Sustainable%20Development%20web.pdf

United Nations. (2015c). *Guiding Principles Reporting Framework with Implementation Guidance*. Retrieved August 10, 2017, from https://www.ungpreporting.org/wp-content/uploads/UNGPReportingFramework_withguidance2017.pdf

United Nations. (2018). *Sustainable Development Goals: 17 goals to transform our world*. Retrieved July 9, 2018, from https://www.un.org/sustainabledevelopment/sustainable-development-goals/

United Nations Economic and Social Council. (2016). *Report of the Inter-Agency and Expert Group on Sustainable Development Goal Indicators*. Retrieved June 24, 2017, from https://unstats.un.org/unsd/statcom/47th-session/documents/2016-2-IAEG-SDGs-Rev1-E.pdf

United Nations Environment Programme. (1972). *Declaration of the United Nations Conference on the Human Environment*. New York: United Nations.

United Nations Global Compact / KPMG. (2016). *SDG Industry Matrix: Food, Beverage, Consumer Goods: New Sustainable Development Goals to make our world more prosperous; Inclusive, sustainable, resilient*. Author.

van Wensen, K. V., Broer, W., Klein, J., & Knopf, J. (2011). *The state of play in sustainability reporting in the EU*. Study for the European Commission, by CREM BV and Adelphi Consultant.

Vanclay, F. (2003). International principles for social impact assessment. *Impact Assessment and Project Appraisal*, *21*(1), 5–11. doi:10.3152/147154603781766491

Votaw, D. (1973). Genius becomes rare. In D. Votaw & S. P. Sethi (Eds.), *The Corporate Dilemma: Traditional values versus contemporary problems* (pp. 11–45). Englewood Cliffs, NJ: Prentice Hall.

Walker, P. H., Seuring, P. S., Sarkis, P. J., & Klassen, P. R. (2014). Sustainable operations management: Recent trends and future directions. *International Journal of Operations & Production Management*, *34*(5), IJOPM-12-2013-0557. doi:10.1108/IJOPM-12-2013-0557

Wartick, S. L., & Cochran, P. L. (1985). The evolution of the corporate social performance model. *Academy of Management Review*, *10*(4), 758–769. doi:10.5465/amr.1985.4279099

Wilhelm, M. M., Blome, C., Bhakoo, V., & Paulraj, A. (2016). Sustainability in multi-tier supply chains: Understanding the double agency role of the first-tier supplier. *Journal of Operations Management*, *41*, 42–60. doi:10.1016/j.jom.2015.11.001

World Bank (1999).

World Business Council for Sustainable Development. (2015). *Towards a Social Capital Protocol: A Call for Collaboration: Measuring social impacts and dependencies for better business*. Geneva: WBCSD.

World Business Council for Sustainable Development. (2016). *Delivering on the Sustainable Development Goals: The inclusive business approach*. Geneva: WBCSD.

World Business Council for Sustainable Development. (2017a). *Social Capital Protocol: Making companies that truly value people more successful*. Geneva: WBCSD.

World Business Council for Sustainable Development. (2017b). *Forest Products Sector Guide to the Social Capital Protocol: Measuring Social Impact Along the Forest Products Value Chain. Geneva*: WBCSD.

World Business Council for Sustainable Development. (2017c). *Social and Human Capital Protocol*. Retrieved April 14, 2017, from http://www.wbcsd.org/Clusters/Social-Impact/Social-Capital-Protocol

World Business Council for Sustainable Development. (2017d). *Social Capital Protocol*. Retrieved April 14, 2017, from http://www.wbcsd.org/Clusters/Social-Impact/Social-Capital-Protocol/Resources/Social-Capital-Protocol

Xu, J., Hsu, V. N., & Niu, B. (2018). The impacts of markets and tax on a multinational firm's procurement strategy in China. *Production and Operations Management*, *27*(2), 251–264. doi:10.1111/poms.12798

Zhang, M., Ma, L. J., Su, J., & Zhang, W. (2014). Do Suppliers Applaud Corporate Social Performance? *Journal of Business Ethics*, *121*(4), 543–557. doi:10.100710551-013-1735-x

KEY TERMS AND DEFINITIONS

Bruntland Report: The official title of this report is "Our Common Future," which was published by the World Commission on Environment and Development.

Corporate Social Responsibility: A policy through which organizations further social good.

Millennium Development Goals: Eight international development goals identified by the United Nations' Millennium Summit to, for example, eradicate poverty and achieve universal primary education.

Natural Capital Protocol: A framework to support businesses to identify, measure, and value their impacts and dependencies on the environment.

Social Capital: The relationships, institutions, and norms of a society.

Social Capital Accounting: The process of valuing societal relations, institutions, and norms in monetary or other terms.

Social Capital Protocol: A process/framework to enable companies to identify, assess, and value the relationships, institutions, and norms of a society.

Social Impact Assessment: The process of analyzing, monitoring, and managing the positive and negative social consequences of actions.

Supply Chain: The system and resources used to provide goods and services from origin to consumption.

Sustainable Development Goals: The 17 objectives established by the United Nations to end poverty, protect the planet, and support sustainable development.

United Nations: An intergovernmental organization to encourage cooperation and international order.

Chapter 6
Analysis of Internet Financial Planning Based on the Development in China and America

Chi Chien Zhu
Foshan University, China

Wen Yang
Shenzhen University, China

ABSTRACT

Based on an analysis of China residents' financial needs and the main risks of internet financial planning, taking internet financial planning as a breakthrough point, the chapter compares the current situation and development experience of internet finance between developed countries and China from Chinese investors' perspective to analyze the tendency of internet finance development in China. This chapter finds the scale of China residents' financial planning remains to be enlarged. It finds that the gradual improvement of the supervision, the survival of the fittest of financial platform, the development of robot-adviser, and other financial innovations show the optimistic outlook of internet financial planning in China. This study shows theoretical value and practical significance to analyze the future of internet financial planning model and financial product selection in China.

DOI: 10.4018/978-1-5225-7808-6.ch006

INTRODUCTION

Financial product has a pivotal role on the entire financial market. With the continuous improvement of the income level of China residents, the accumulation of funds lying idle in society and the booming of internet finance, the financial planning model based on intelligent terminals has become a new trend. Nowadays, more and more people tend to pay attention to improving the quality of financial planning. Chinese investors do not solely focus on the bank savings as before; instead, they pay more attention to financial freedom, and thus they pursue a personalized financial planning. However, the investment results are rather unsatisfactory in the concrete actual operation due to the limitations of financial knowledge, information asymmetry, etc. Based on the main development tendency of Chinese financial planning, diversified asset allocation is favored by investors, and internet financial planning is their first choice. Compared with the bank, the internet financial planning can seize the long tail market and meet the desire of financial planning of low-income residents. Moreover, the higher rate of return, decreasing risk, not requiring very professional financial knowledge, excellent liquidity, save of time and easier operation make internet financial planning easier to be accepted by Chinese investors. In the past two years, internet finance in China has undergone many changes; moreover, the network loan has gone through the situation from industry booming to industry reshuffle because of more and more strict policy, so the innovative development and transformation and upgrading become the tackling direction of most of the internet financial platform. At present, internet financial industry in China has come into a period of adjustment. Furthermore, the coming of artificial intelligence technology and the big data era also give imagining space and development opportunities to intelligence financial planning model. Therefore, Chinese investors have expectations for the future development of internet financial planning in China.

Therefore, the internet financial planning has its further influence and larger scale as a new way of financial planning, but it is undoubtedly confronted with differences and lag in terms of nature, classification, regulation and risk definition. Moreover, research related to current internet financial planning in China is relatively rare, so it is necessary to conduct the comprehensive study of the internet financial planning issues. This paper attempts to draw lessons from literatures of China and other developed countries involved in researching internet finance. This paper combs the internet financial risks, does a research on trend of Chinese internet financial development and provides reasonable suggestions to investors. Under the great environment of financial inclusion and green finance in China, this paper has certain theoretical guidance value and practical significance for investors' financial planning and investment.

AN OVERVIEW OF INTERNET FINANCIAL PLANNING: THE UNITED STATES AND CHINA

Research on Internet Finance Development in the United States

So far, there is no mention of internet finance in other parts of the world, because the noun was coined in China initially. While the essence of internet finance is finance, and the internet is a technological revolution in terms of academia and the financial industry, but it only provides new financial channels instead of new forms of finance as a tool. However, the form of internet banking has been developed for a long time in developed countries. In fact, similar to Yu E Bao, this internet financing way was originated in the United States. Wang Da (2014) thought that the development of American internet finance can be divided into three stages: the first stage is that rapid development of high-tech and information technology industry, which was fueled by the internet, made e-commerce and finance based on the internet appear initially in 1990s. The second stage is that traditional financial institutions have accelerated the pace of financial informatization and internet after internet experiencing from the climax to the bubble burst in 2000, and the academic circles had in-depth discussions on issues of financial industry and the traditional internet technology integration. After that, pure network financial model and the traditional financial model will form the coexistence of competition and integration became the mainstream view of scholars. The third stage is that the online direct financing model, like Prosper and Lendind Club company, began to rise after subprime mortgage crisis and the global financial crisis, and the development of online crowd-funding and P2P net loan became the latest turnaround of the internet finance in the United States.

Internet finance in the United States has developed rapidly in just forty years. It not only benefited from the innovation and flexibility of the operation model, but also from the perfect legal supervision system and the sound credit reporting system. The US FDIC and the Treasury Department are primarily responsible for the regulation of the third-party payment platform. SEC and the state securities regulators are responsible for protecting investors, and the FDIC and the Consumer Financial Protection Bureau (CFPB) are responsible for maintaining the borrower's equity. While for the supervision of crowd-funding platform, the United States introduced the "Jumpstart Our Business Startups Act" whose regulatory details were developed by SEC to raise the strong supervision on crowd funding platforms. The United States introduced the "money market fund supplement act" in 2010 to make the regulatory requirements that the broker or dealer, which offers money market funds (MMF), must obtain the SEC securities trader license. At the aspect of constructing credit reporting system, the United States has established a sound credit system. Traditional banks, like JP Morgan Chase bank, use the internet, big data

Table 1. The development of Internet Finance in the U.S

Time	Event
1971	The NASDAQ (National Association of Securities Dealers Automated Quotation) system was established to mark the actual operation of new internet financial model
1992	E-TRADE, a franchised online broker, was established to attract customers mainly through Internet channels. It does not rely on the low-price strategy in the offline sales department but provides general sales of product and consulting services.
1995	INSWEB, the first Internet bank in the world, also called "security first online bank" and the pure network insurance company, was established, indicating that the Internet finance has entered a rapid development stage.
	SFNB (the security first network bank) was established in the U.S. It not only was the world's first network bank, but also marked the deepening and expansion of the Internet finance.
1996	Charles Schwab, the network financial traders, were founded, creating new trends of the network bank, insurance and securities.
1999	E-Finance strategy was started.
	JP Morgan Bank created the Lab60 in the field of Internet venture capital to research and invested on the services of the Internet financial innovation.
	PayPal, the world's first Internet money fund, was established. The cash balances in the PayPal user account were automatically invested in the monetary fund managed by PayPal, which can provide the liquidity and increase the returns of investors at the same time.
2005	Prosper, the first P2P loan platform in United States, was established and became a new starting point for the development of Internet credit business in the United States.
2007	Lending Club, the largest Internet loan platform in the United States, was established, which almost realized the real "disintermediation".
2009	Kickstarter, the public financing platform, was formally launched to raise small amounts of money from the public via the network platform, providing creative people with necessary funds for entrepreneurship.
2011	PayPal shut down its Internet money fund, an event represented that the traditional Internet finance model was entering a trough stage while the Internet finance was developing by the transformation in the economic crisis.

technology to obtain customer records to build customer credit system, which will be the combination of internet and finance to build a credit system. In addition, the credit giants like Equifax in the United States integrate non-traditional information using big data technology, in order to carry out the relevant credit scoring service; the financial platforms, like Kabbage, depend on different internet platforms, such as eBay, Yahoo, Amazon, to obtain the dependent third data, for the purpose of constructing their own credit reporting system. The internet financial companies represented by Zest Finance make use of the technology such as big data to provide credit evaluation service to customers, to realize the innovation and improvement of the traditional credit reporting system. From this point of view, the supervision of internet finance in the United States is relatively perfect, not only because of the corresponding specific regulatory units, but also the formation of a multi-level regulatory system. Moreover, the sound credit reporting system can provide protection for the internet finance.

The characteristics of internet finance in United States are long development history, well-developed operation, clear legal status, effective supervision and the relevant supervisory regulations formulated by the existing laws and regulations of financial industry. As a new technology, the U.S. internet finance is only the informational upgradation of traditional finance, not as an independent development of the industry, but as a complementation of traditional financial system. It plays an important role in promoting the allocation of money supply and demand, promoting the informational upgradation of traditional finance and supplement the traditional financial services.

The Development of the Internet Finance in the United States

From the 19th century, the internet finance in the United States began to develop gradually. In 1971, the establishment of NASDAQ system marked the new model of internet finance entering the actual operation. In 1992, E-TRADE, a franchised online broker, was established to develop customers mainly through internet channels. It does not rely on the low-price strategy in the offline sales department, and provides general sales of product and consulting services. In 1995, the world's first internet bank, "security first online bank", and the pure network insurance company, INSWEB, were established, indicating that the internet finance has entered a rapid development stage. In 1995, security first network bank (SFNB) in the United States was established, which not only became the world's first network bank, but also marked the deepening and expansion of the internet finance. The network financial traders, Charles Schwab, was founded in 1996, which makes the network bank, network insurance, network securities become a new trend. E-Finance strategy was started at the end of 1999. JP Morgan Bank created (Lab60) in the field of internet venture capital to a research on the services of the internet financial innovation. Then, the world's first internet money fund, the PayPal money market fund, was established. The cash balances in the PayPal user account were automatically invested in the monetary fund managed PayPal, which can provide the liquidity and improve investors' returns at the same time. In 2005, the first P2P loan platform in United States, Prosper, was established, which became a new starting point for the development of internet credit business in the United states. In 2007, Lending Club, the largest internet loan platform in the United States, was established, which almost realized the real "disintermediation". In April 2009, the public financing platform, Kickstarter, formally launched and it raise small amounts of money from the public mainly via the network platform so that creative people are likely to obtain the necessary funds for entrepreneurship. In 2011, PayPal shut down its internet money fund, representing the traditional internet finance model going into the trough, and the innovation in the emerging areas of internet finance experiencing the transformation in the economic crisis of has been developed.

An Analysis of the Development of the Internet Finance in China

On April 7, 2012, Xie Ping firstly put forward the "internet finance "concept in the "China Finance 40 Forum" (CF40) publicly, which quickly became the focus of academia and industry. Xie Ping (2012) [] proposed that internet finance is different from the indirect financing system of banks and the third financing model of direct financing on capital market. Wu Xiaoqiu (2015) has carried a deep research on the definition and form of internet finance. He defines Internet finance as a new type of financial business that supports big data with the combination of Internet spirit, Internet and cloud computing. It has related financial effects, also known as the third financial form. Therefore, we believe that internet finance is a market using internet technology and mobile communications technology to provide financial services market. Furthermore, the internet financial products are innovative models of internet finance, which are a series of activities based on the internet to gain financial services and financial information to maximize asset returns. Luo Mingxiong (2013) divided the internet finance into six categories including P2P net loan, the third-party payment, crowd funding, big data of finance, informatization of financial institution and internet financial portal to discuss in detail. Nowadays, the main internet financial products on the market are Yu E Bao, CAITONG, Baidu Baizhuan, JD Lingqianbao, Weibo Weicaifu.

On June 2013, Yu E Bao, the first internet financial planning service created in China, began to receive public attention. Driven by the trend of Yu E Bao, all kinds of internet financial products have crashed into the financial market. Especially, the number of P2P net loan platform has increased rapidly. Moreover, those traditional financial institutions rushed by financial crisis also have introduced online financial planning services and all kinds of financial planning tools. Baidu, Alibaba and Tencent quickly occupied in small and micro enterprises, white-collar class and countryside people, which has initially formed a situation of tripartite confrontation pattern of competition, Ping An as the representative of traditional finance, Alibaba and JD as the representative of e-commerce business and Tencent as the representative of social media platform. At the beginning of the second half of 2014, all kinds of internet financial products' problems appeared gradually: the decreasing rate of return of financial products, homogenization of the financial products and the single function, which made the investors upset gradually. Moreover, the phenomenon that the owner of the companies often stopped doing business, lost contact and escaped with money always made the investors nervous. The positive policies and supervision lagging has formed quantities of grey areas, which needed related regulatory policies. In 2015, influenced by five times of decreasing required reserve ratio and decreasing interest rate of the central bank in China, interest rate liberalization and the improvement of the internet financial supervision, the development of internet financial planning products faced more serious challenge; moreover, the whole scale of related financial products was decreasing continuingly, and all the money fund, even the fixed income products, was trapped in recession. Nowadays, 7-days annualized yield of Yu E Bao fluctuates around 2.3%, which is far lower than the high yield of 6.7630% on January 2nd, 2014. While it is different to find relative safe financial planning products with yield higher than 10% on P2P net loan platform which attracts its investors with high rate of return. The positive policies boost internet barbaric growth of finance industry. However, after 2016, the tightening policies cool the financial market, which means that standardization and security become the development tendency of financial industry, and the internet finance services gradually return the nature of raising money.

The internet finance in China grew barbarically at first; then, the innovation of technology and the improvement of regulatory supervision has played an important role in the process of integrating rationally. Nowadays, the internet has become the regular means of financial planning of Chinese residents, but the attention of the public on the internet finance concept is becoming weaker. Instead, the internet finance led by financial technology has entered the new stage of development.

Comparative Analysis of Internet Financial Planning Between the United States and China

Different Legislation System

In 1971, NASDAQ system, pioneered in the United States, promoted the internet finance from the initial idea into the actual operation stage. In 1995, three banks in the United States jointly set up a " Security First Network Bank" on the internet. Then, Internet finance entered a new stage of rapid development and the related financial business model including the internet financial products, PayPal investment fund, ushered in a burst of growth. Nowadays, interest rate liberalization has been fully realized in the United States. There is no more market space for financial products like money market fund. Thus, the business in the United States tends to focus on P2P loans and third-party payment platforms. Lending Club, as top company on P2P net loan industry, one of its characteristics is flexibly suitable for supervision.

Lending Club plays a positive leading role in the response to the internet financial regulation on the P2P industry in the United States. Then, the P2P industry in the United States developed towards more compliant and more flexible under the supervision of SEC; in the meanwhile, SEC also amended the relevant regulatory regulations based on the internet finance industry in the United States to further regulate the internet industry in the United States, which can not only fully protect the legitimate rights of investors, but also give the space of flexible development to internet finance industry.

Different Economic and Financial Condition

Different from the financial market in China, the internet finance industry in the United States has developed from a more comprehensive market, and then the US market has constantly improved its efficiency in the market segments of supplying and demanding. Internet finance in China has shown a situation of diversified business model, highly fragmented service platforms and audience demands and less over-competition. Wang Da (2014) found in the study of the development of the internet finance, that the financial environment of the internet finance in China was more complex than in the United States; moreover, the financial environment in China was facing interest rate reform, unreleased interest rate control, disintermediation of the liabilities of commercial banks and the positive development of the internet finance. On the one hand, the internet finance in China developed actively; on the other hand, the internet finance in China was passive to some degree because the preparation seemed inadequate in the competition with other emerging countries. Compared to the internet finance which was simply driven by technology in the United States, the internet finance industry in China was influenced by the two elements of "deregulation" and "decentration", so it developed more quickly than that in the United States. Moreover, internet finance in China showed its outstanding advantage in the situation of rigidities of current financial market, lacking investment channels, difficulties of financing those small and medium-sized enterprises nowadays. It acted as the connection of investors and financiers and assisted in reaching the equilibrium of supply and demand, which also became the main reason why the internet finance industry, especially the P2P net loan industry, was becoming more and more popular in China.

The demand of Internet Financial planning is largely based on residents' disposal income condition, Internet user's population and social consumption structure. From 2012 to 2016, both China and United. States. have witnessed continuous increase in disposable income per capital, and the figure of later is almost 6 times larger than that in China. However, taking total population and Internet penetration rate into consideration, we could conclude that the development space of Internet Financial

Table 2. Related laws and regulations of Internet Finance in China and the U.S.

Country	Law & Regulation	Objective
United. States.	The Federal Trade Commission Act (FTC Act)	Offline and online privacy and data security
	The Financial Services Modernization Act (Gramm-Leach-Bliley Act (GLB))	The collection, use and disclosure of financial information of financial institutions such as banks, securities firms and insurance companies
	The Fair Credit Reporting Act and the Fair and Accurate Credit Transactions Act	The consumer reporting agency, who use consumer reports (such as a lender) and provide consumer-reporting information (such as a credit card company).
	The Health Insurance Portability and Accountability Act (HIPAA)	Health care providers, data processors, pharmacies and other entities that come into contact with medical information.
	The Controlling the Assault of Non-Solicited Pornography and Marketing Act and the Telephone Consumer Protection Act	The collection and use of e-mail addresses and telephone numbers
	The Electronic Communications Privacy Act and the Computer Fraud and Abuse Act	The interception of electronic communications and computer tampering
	Jumpstart Our Business Startups Act	Emerging growth companies, capital for job creators, crowdfunding, and small entity compliance.
	Judicial Redress Act	Privacy violations when personal information is shared with law enforcement agencies.
	The FCC Privacy Rule	Personal information of browsing history and apps usage
China	The management of payment services for non-financial institutions	Online transaction, issuance and acceptance of prepaid card, Bank receipt, and other related payment methods.
	Electronic banking business management methods	Communication channels or public networks established by banking financial institutions such as commercial banks
	Regulation of Internet insurance business	Internet insurance business of Insurance broker companies

Source: U.S. Securities and Exchange Commission

Planning in China is much greater than in U.S. According to latest Internet data, the population of Internet users in China has reached 721 million, indicating Internet penetration rate is about 52.3% with an average annual increase rate of 2.9%, while the Internet penetration rate in U.S. has been stayed at about 75% for 5 years. Thus, the Internet market in U.S. is nearly saturated, yet that in China is rather prospective.

As for the condition of social consumption and credit loan, the biggest portion of Internet credit loan is spent on real estate in both countries. Under the complete

Figure 1. The legislation system for Internet Finance in the U.S.

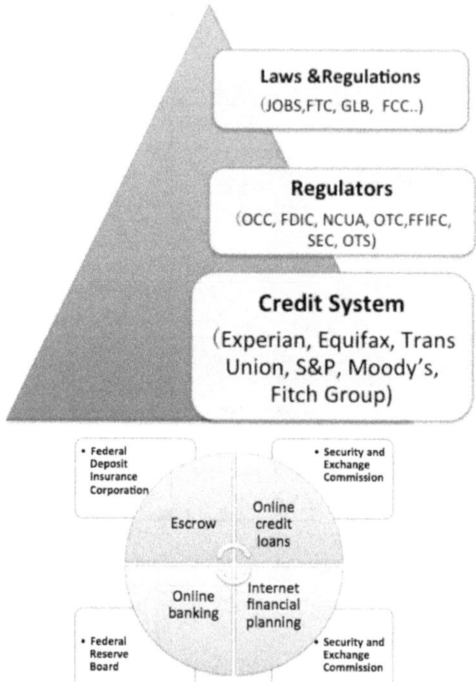

Figure 2. Disposal income per capital in China and United States from 2012 to 2016
Source: International Monetary Fund

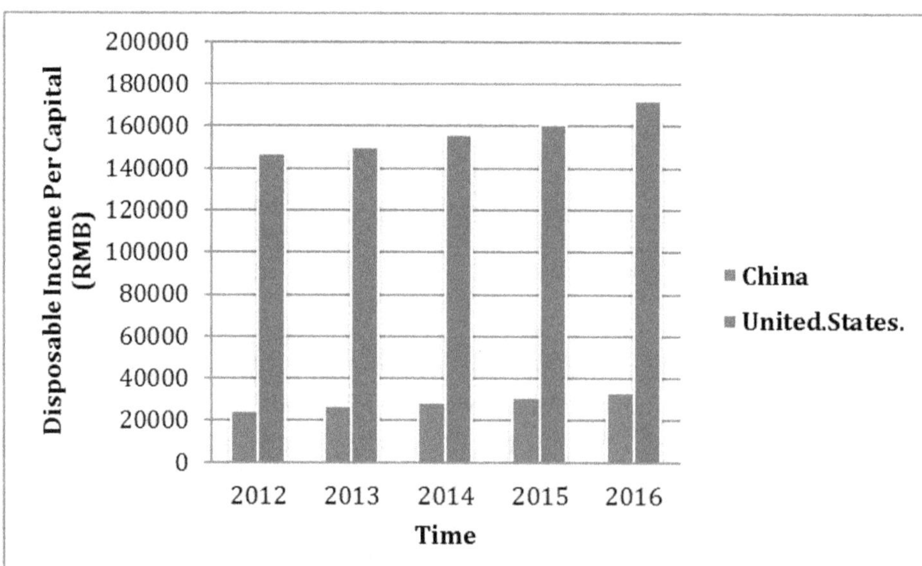

Figure 3. Usage for internet credit loan in China and United States
Source: Winds Database

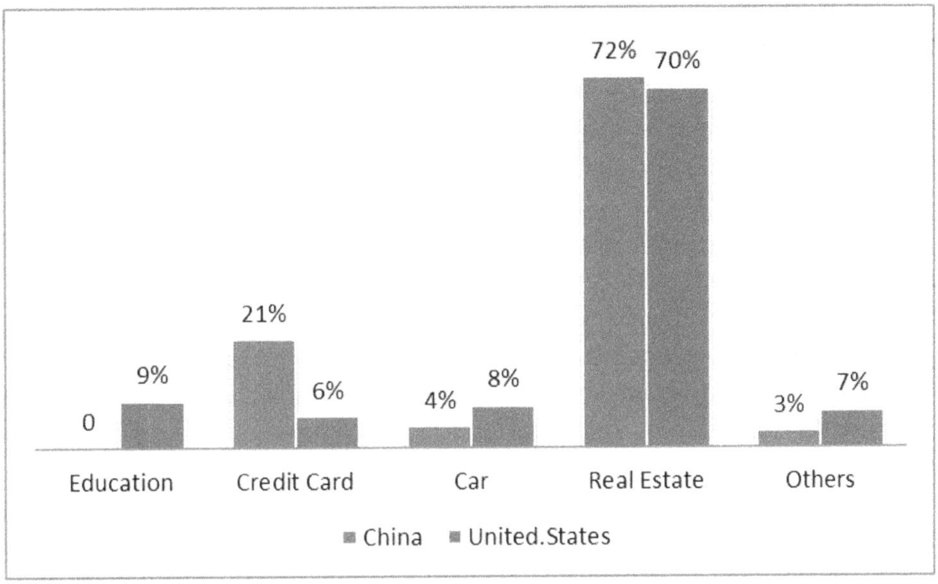

Figure 4. Proportion of consumption credit loan in GDP and consumption expense in China and U.S. from 2012 to 2016
Bar: the proportion of consumption credit loan in GDP
line: the proportion of consumption credit loan in consumption expense
Source: Winds, China Trading Economics

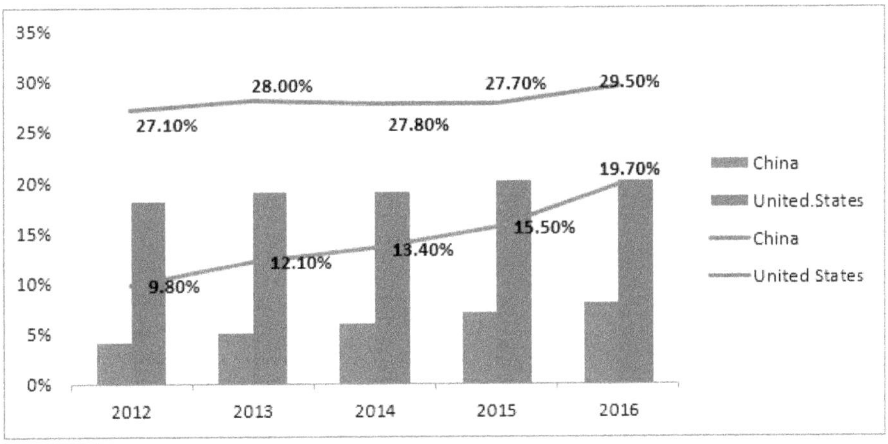

Bar: the proportion of consumption credit loan in GDP
line: the proportion of consumption credit loan in consumption expense

regulatory system and market demand in the U.S., real estate prices remain relatively stable compared to those in China, which is experiencing value increase in land property and investment. Moreover, the consumption credit loan in China is also increasing at a greater speed than in the U.S.

To briefly conclude, the macro and micro economic differences between China and United. States. implying that the development path of Internet Financial Planning in China will be rather distinctive from that in the U.S.

Different Nature of Platforms

The existing Internet finance platform in U.S. majorly comes from two sources: establishment of new companies and transformation of traditional banks. In comparison, Internet financial planning service in China is provided by large companies in three areas: traditional banking, e-commerce business and social media platform.

Net loan platform in the United States is clearly defined as the role of information intermediary, which does not involve any fund lending transaction or duty regarding to the principal and interest. While the role of Chinese online loan platform is ambiguous, which plays dual role of both an information intermediary and credit intermediary. Thus, the internet finance in China not only participates in the entire lending transactions, but also obeys the duty of the entire process of investment transactions. Even if the policy has a clear positioning of information intermediary role that platforms play, part of the platforms are still raising money illegally.

Figure 5. Sources for Internet finance companies in U.S.

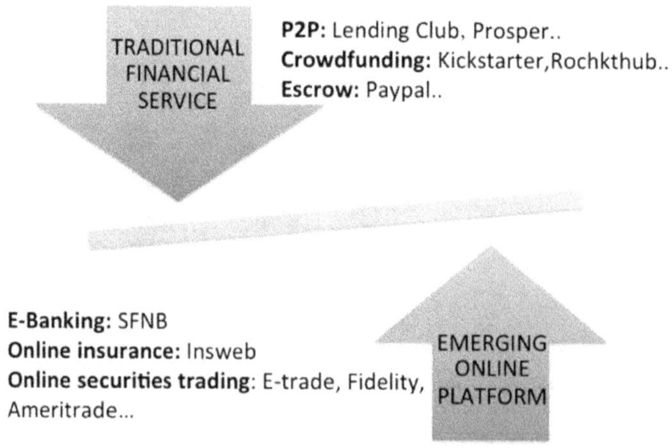

Table 3. Internet finance related companies in the U.S.

Company	Main Business
Lending Club	Credit loan for individual and small business
Prosper	Credit loan, credit transaction and health-care finance
SoFi	Student loan and real estate mortgage
Estimize	Finance prediction and analysis
Mint	Personal financial management
Motif	Personal portfolio management
SigFig	Personal investment management
Realty Mogul	Real estate crowd-funding
Realty Shares	
Fundrise	

Different Credit Information System and Supervisory Laws

The credit system in the United States from institutions credit to personal credit has entered a mature stage, and the mature cognition of the data basis for quantifying credit has been well equipped, such as credit data sources diversified with standard data output system and the integrated consideration of enterprise credit and personal credit. Therefore, the platforms can review online based on relatively official credit data provided by government and the third-party credit agencies. Net loan market in the United States has strict regulatory requirements and high regulatory costs. Under the supervision of SEC, the net loan market in the United States has the requirement of a stringent mechanism of public disclosure assessment and $4 million maintenance margin. Moreover, P2P is also subject to securities law and State laws. While the infrastructure carrying internet finance business model also exists plenty of problems, such as the imperfection of credit system and regulatory policies and the investors' weak awareness of credit and risk, the internet finance industry in China can learn from the credit system and the experience of establishing laws and regulations to break the current development bottleneck, in order to shorten the process of trial and error and the evolution of the whole industry.

Another big difference between the net loan market in China and the United States is that there are lots of institutional investors in the U.S. net loan market. While there are more individual investors in the net loan market in China. The asset securitization market for institutional investors is more developed, so the net loan market is also carrying out a large amount of asset securitization business. And asset securitization is beneficial to improve the liquidity of the net loan market in

U.S, improve the efficiency of capital allocation and reduce the investment risk of the net loan market.

In conclusion, although the internet finance in China was blocked by the credit system, imperfect relevant legislation and not satisfied demand for investment and financing market, the internet finance industry is developing well and there exist opportunities of the mobile internet, cloud computing and big data technology. Thus, the development space of internet finance market in China is still huge, and the power to innovate and upgrade should not be underestimated

An Analysis of Residents' Financial Demand in China

So far, the residents' financial planning strategy in China has gone through three stages: before 1999, residents saved most of their capitals in banks; from 2000 to 2014, house property investment accounted for about 65% of residents' capital allocation; After 2014 was the era of financial products investment, because "double limit" started to limit real estate purchasing, the total value of investment in stocks, trust products, banking products and P2P financial planning experienced a substantial increase.

The Yearly Increase of Disposable Income

From 2008 to 2016, the per capita disposable income of residents in China increased steadily. With more disposable income, the residents profoundly realized the potential growth of asset income. Meanwhile, how to expand the investment solutions for effective wealth management became a new topic of family education.

The Potential Financial Capacity Still Need to Be Stimulated

According to the research data of the marketing data partners on the pan-financial users, Chinese residents only use 27% of income on average for investment. Compared to the "4321 Asset Allocation Rule" (40% investment, 30% living expenses, 20% reserve, 10% insurance), the investment ratio of Chinese residents is clearly too low. According to the Individual Financial Market Research Report of China, China's per capita wealth of is approximately 300,000 RMB, including $11,000 personal financial assets. The per capital wealth in United Kingdom and United States is 7 times that of China while the per capita financial assets in these two countries are nearly 20 times those of China. Considering the saving habit of Chinese, if those cash and deposits are removed from financial assets, the per capita basic financial scale of United Kingdom and United States will be 20 times higher than that of

Figure 6. The per capital disposable income of urban residents
Source: State Statistical Bureau

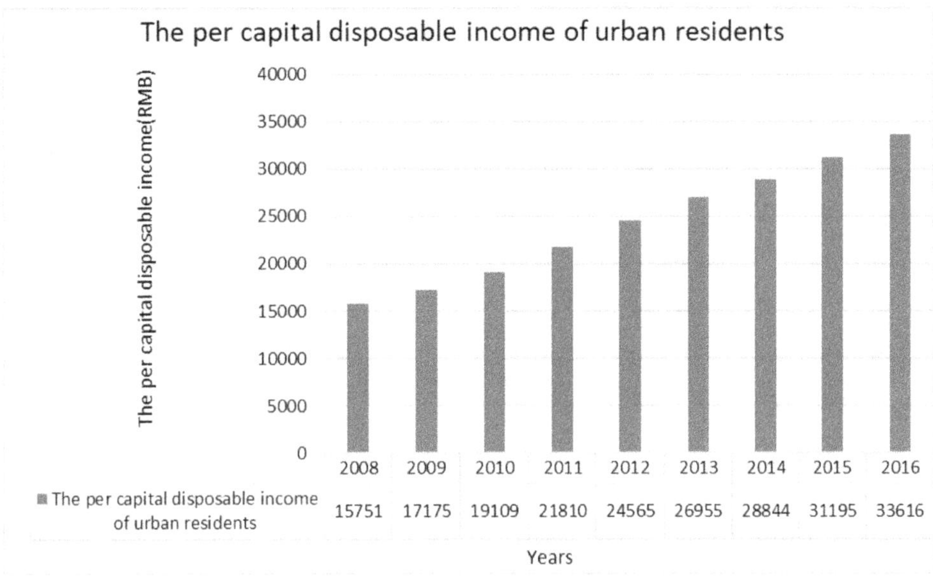

China (shown in figure 7). This means that the potential financial capacity of Chinese residents is still waiting to be developed.

The Major Group of Financial Planning Becomes Younger

The internet financial planning holds several advantages such as low investment threshold, convenient use, simple operation and so on, thus making the young people who have courage to invest in new financial planning model become the main force of P2P financial planning. Considering the saving habit of Chinese, 83% of generation after 80s and 77% of generation after 90s make investment in internet financial planning. Because of the focus on financial freedom, the generation after 80s and 90s tend to choose internet financial planning products with short-term investment cycle, stable income, and good liquidity.

The Diversification of Financial Demands

With the better understanding of internet finance than before, the user's demands begin to expand and they flexibly construct their own "financial pyramid" with diverse products such as regular or current financial planning, preferential funds, gold finance, stock products and overseas funding. Nowadays, the financial service is entering a

Figure 7. A Comparison of the per capita personal wealth and the Per capita financial assets among china, the US and the UK in 2015
Source: Credit Suisse "Global Wealth Report in 2015"
Chinese Family Financial Survey (CHFS) Database

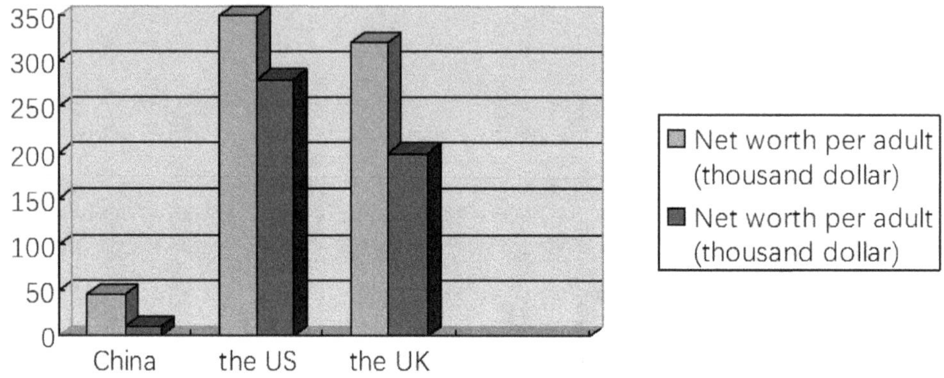

new century with diversity, but the current domestic financial products and financial instruments innovation are lagging behind of this trend -- it is difficult for them to meet the diversified wealth management demands of residents, especially those of the substantial customer group. Due to the consideration of risk diversification and flexibility, diversified asset allocation will dominate the investment market and the new direction of financial institutions innovation will be the product diversification and comprehensive improvement of financial services standard.

Main Risks of Internet Financial Planning in China

The internet financial planning eases the traditional problem of financial information, but it has not only similar risks as those of the traditional way of financial planning, but also its particularity. Wang Hanjun (2013) made the opinion that the internet financial planning must guard against not only the market risk, credit risk and liquidity risk, but also the unique high-tech potential operational risk, legal imperfect legal risk, high linkage caused by the risk of infection and more severe reputation risks than those faced by traditional financial institutions. Xie Pingdeng (2014) pointed out that the internet financial has two prominent risk characteristics. The first one is the risk of information technology, such as computer viruses, computer hacking and financial fishing sites. The second one is the internet financial "long tail" risk caused by the lack of financial knowledge, the weak ability to identify and bear the risk and easiness to be misled. Once the risk happened, although not with a large amount of capita, it will influence great amount of people thus generate greater negative externalities than expected. Therefore, it is necessary to build a macro-prudential regulatory framework, guide the financial platform to accurately locate and strengthen the financial education of investors. The internet Finance National Social Science Fund Major Project Task Force (2015) comprehensively concluded the exchanging results of the 2015 High-level Forum of internet Finance Development. He Fei and Zhang Bing from Nanjing University found that when the platform provides principal and interest guarantee, the investors will tend to lack learning motivation and thus have problems of adverse selection and blind investment behavior. internet financial platform should perform the duty of information disclosure, the borrowers should be responsible for their own credit and consciously regulate the repayment behavior, while the investors should be careful about investment. All the participants should perform their duties and jointly maintain the market order.

THE DEVELOPMENT TREND OF INTERNET FINANCIAL PLANNING IN CHINA

Internet Financial Market Has an Optimistic Outlook

Investors Have Higher Requirements on the Internet Financial Security and Much Rational Risk Preference Than Before

The continued economic downturn and the decline in real economic returns led to the relative reduction in high-yield high-quality assets and the decline in earnings of financial products. Besides, since many investors have gone through losses caused by one-sided emphasis on high-yield and ignorance of the objective risk factors, nowadays they hold a more profound understanding than before. In conclusion, the attitudes of investors are becoming more "conservative", more mature and more rational than before.

Compliance Products and Reliable Platforms Are the Development Trends of Internet Finance

Today, the government and regulators are attaching great importance to platform compliance, product information disclosure, transaction transparency and risk prevention system and meanwhile introducing relevant policies and regulations. Therefore, the internet financial planning platform will focus on their own product designs and financial services to meet the characteristics and financial needs of users, providing them with appropriate financial products and thoughtful financial services. With the development of the internet financial planning market, differentiated and personalized financial platform is the shape of things to come (Sun Ran, 2015). Thus, in order to enhance the stickiness of users, the financial platform should focus on technology and product innovation breakthroughs. Financial platform should select differentiated road to improve the user experience as soon as possible, for example, the financial application scenarios, instant redemption, newly selected financial asset model and intelligent asset management services.

Comprehensive Financial Planning Has Broad Development Space

Comprehensive financial planning satisfies the demand of invertors by highlighting the low threshold, intelligence, mobility, one-stop service and the financial planning function of social financial services. As the integrated financial services become more mature than before, comprehensive financial platform is becoming the best choice for investors. Nowadays, the internet financial giants are positively entering into the comprehensive financial planning of the public financial market, competing to build automatic configuration services and social referral services that help users select products and configuration of assets. The Micro-bank APP strongly promoted "demand +" and "regular +" financial products while Ants Jubao launched a professional financial planning APP for the public to provide comprehensive financial services; Lu Jin built an open platform 3.0 to meet specific wealth management demands in different stages of the users' life cycle; JD Finance also launched the "JD Finance APP3.0", which is positioned as a "one-stop financial life mobile platform." Recently, Lu Jin has gradually shifted its business concentration from P2P business to China's rapidly developing personal financial market, becoming a comprehensive online investment platform, which provides products such as stock, fixed income products and raised funds. Therefore, the internet Comprehensive financial market is the new battlefield of internet finance.

The Integration of Traditional Finance With Internet Financial Platform Development Has Become an Increasingly Obvious Trend

internet finance and traditional financial institutions have their own bright spots. Compared with the internet financial enterprises, the customer resources of banks are mostly high net worth customers. The commercial banks' deep foundation of accumulation of customer, account and capital resources during a long period of time is the prerequisite for business implementation at this stage. Today, the internet financial planning industry has swept to the long tail group which traditional financial institutions feel difficult to serve. Under the strongest supervision, the integration of internet financial planning industry and traditional financial institutions after colliding with each other becomes the trend, whose essence is 'Finance'. Based on the theory of financial function and the research analysis of 36 commercial banks, Mo

Yi Xian (2014) concluded that the internet finance does not increase basic functions of finance but changes the channel, impacts the traditional banking industry and accelerates the business and product innovation of commercial banking. Based on the technology spillover effect and the empirical analysis of 36 commercial banks, Shen Yue (2015) concluded that the internet capital promotes the total factor productivity of commercial banks through the demonstration effect, the competitive effect, the personnel flow effect and the linkage effect, and that shareholding commercial banks as well as urban commercial banks have absorbed the internet financial technology overflow effect most obviously. Viewing financial institutions as a starting point and having concluded the international literature relevant to the impact internet financial has on the traditional finance, Liu Lan Biao (2013) pointed out that there is a greater integration between these two spaces than before. Therefore, the coordinated development of internet financial planning platform and the traditional financial institutions enables them to mine the user value, thereby improving the effectiveness of financial markets to meet the diversified investment needs of investors, bringing investors more financial convenience, income security and stability.

The next wave of the development of cooperation between internet finance and traditional financial institutions will be the mobile payment and smart investment. Meanwhile, the financial institutions with larger traditional scale have begun to acquire some intelligent investment enterprises in this field, regarding this strategy as the next direction of development and holding optimistic opinion that the integration of intelligent investment and traditional financial services hides great wealth.

Intelligent Investment Is a Huge Potential Market and Intelligence Is an Inevitable Trend

Intelligent investment is a kind of artificial wealth management model, combined with artificial intelligence and big data technology to complete the investor risk preference analysis, generate optimal asset allocation program and recommend the best investment strategy. Smart investment is based on Markowitz's portfolio theory, having low service threshold and process standardization, and is not only able to make investment decision-making process objective and rapidly generate investment programs, but also to adjust the asset allocation program according to market dynamics with times and provides services to investors without experience. (As shown in Figure 8). The smart investment appeared in United States in 2005 and began its high growth in 2014. According to Credio statistics, in 2015, the intelligent investment management assets in United States ranged from 256 million to 88.2 billion US dollars, reaching 121.8 billion US dollars in total size. In China, the Smart investment appeared relatively late but quickly became a hot topic of concern. Today, Micro-public banks, ants Jubao and JD Finance have started layout, while other P2P platform are also equipping themselves with intelligent financial planning tools.

As a financial technology performance, the Intelligent investment is the next direction of internet financial planning innovation. First of all, the loss of people's investment before was mainly resulted from avarice. Compared to manual investment, intelligent investment products can overcome the weakness of human nature and greediness. Besides, intelligent investment maintenance costs are low because the cost mainly comes from the initial R & D investment and a large portion of labor costs can be saved after the official use. Secondly, intelligent investment can effectively reduce the degree of dependence on traditional investment advisers by investors and thereby alleviate China's current shortage of investment advisers, which lead to the problem of "unmanned service" state. In addition, as a substation of artificial investment model, this machine uses background data for investment analysis and it can avoid the moral hazard that the traditional manual investment may mislead customers for improving performance. Lastly, compared with the online lending platform where lots of homogeneous financial products exist, the intelligent investment builds its core competitiveness by providing customers with personalized portfolio, personalized precision of intelligent financial services to meet the diversified demands of investors. Meanwhile, the standardized investment services provided by intelligent investment can also meet the regulatory requirements. At present, China's intelligent investment is regarded as securities investment consulting business, which is supervised by the "Securities Investment Advisors Interim Provisions" as well as other relevant laws and regulations, and there has no precise focus on intelligent investment laws and regulations yet.

In the environment of "Inclusive Finance and Green finance", Financial technology has attracted strong market attention. Therefore, the internet financial planning platform must uphold the spirit of financial technology, build up their own intelligent financial planning system with skilled application of artificial intelligence, large data and other high-tech platform, while prevent system security issues. Only if it provides fast, convenient and accurate products as well as services can it compete in the current fierce environment and develop continuously.

Security of Internet Financial Management

Despite the conspicuous trend of making better internet financial services regulation in China, the internet financial model is experiencing such an unprecedented rapid development of innovation that Chinese internet financial regulations are relatively lagging. Considering this situation, investors are required to strengthen risk control consciousness timely and invest prudently. They should rationally choose financial

Figure 8. Schematic of intelligent investment consulting service mode
Source: Stock Planet, CITIC Securities Research Department

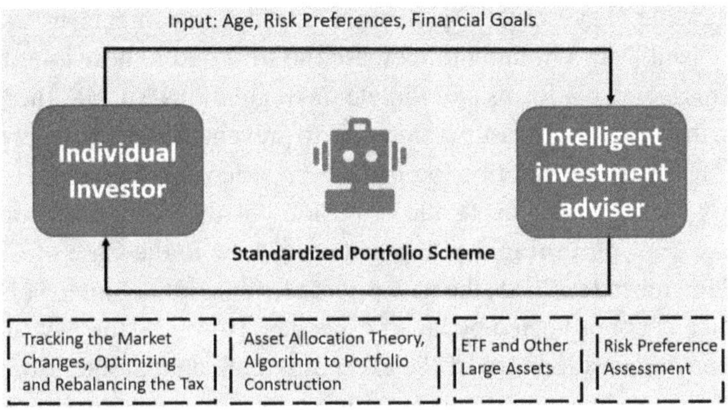

platforms and specific products step by step; thereby effectively guard themselves against financial risks. The followings are specifically introduced some suggestions to controlling the risk of internet financial investment.

Selecting Formal Financial Platforms

Firstly, tips to select the platform. Investors should choose the financial platforms under big companies, such as JD Finance, Ant Financial, Tencent Money management, Baidu Hundred earn and so on, which are relatively reliable. In details, the risk control system of the platforms above is relatively sounder, those platforms are able to fully coordinate the crisis if the borrowers have problems. However, if platforms do not have BAT (Baidu, Alibaba and Tencent) background, investors can consider the platforms' major shareholders. Take Lu Jin as an example, it is a financial platform with Ping An Group as a major shareholders, which provides great supports. However, some platforms claimed that they were invested by big organizations, such as Softbank and Sequoia Capital, cannot prove the platforms' reliability. Because those organizations invest a lot of companies each year.

Secondly, investors should consider the final investors who closely relate to the information disclosure. The investment risks would increase if the issuers conceal the fund allocation, even if they assure to pay investors a few percent of income. By contrast, as the final investors, big companies such as Country Garden, Vanke and Hengda are more reliable, because of their normal cash flow and publicized profitability. Moreover, serious risks will hide in some small businesses, for instance, an unknown timber factory or furniture factory.

Also, the bank will not financially support P2P platforms. In order to enhance investor confidence, some platforms may announce that they have strategic agreements with banks while they actually just have custody agreements in those banks. "Depository bank" does nothing to increase the trust and to bear joint liability for P2P platforms. some platforms still violate the regulations, such as the "false" and "self" traps, though some measures are taken to prevent them escaping with money.

Finally, the interest cannot be too high. It is noticeable that 15% risk and 20% risk are very high. According to the provisions of the Supreme People's Court on Several Issues Concerning the Application of Law in the Case of Civil Loans, issued on September 1st, 2015, the new private lending rate of interest is limited to 24%, of which is not protected by law if exceeded. However, the law supports that the debtor may request a return of the exceeding 36% annual interest rate, though it is paid. Thus, the financial products with interest rate of more than 24% are not protected by law and investors should be cautious when the platforms advertise their high interest rate. At present, the mainstream P2P platform in China generally yield interest rates below 15%. Because high interest rate will give enterprises or individuals excessive borrowing costs, which would delay the repayment, and thus exacerbate investors' risk exposure.

Mastering the Know-How of Buying Internet Financial Products

Firstly, it is important to diversify investments. Investors should make reasonable operational plans and programs based on their actual funds. For example, investors can split a large amount of funds into several small amounts of money, and then invest 4 to 5 platforms to spread the risk of platforms "escaping" with money. At the same time, investors can also diversify their investment period. For example, when the investment periods are all half a year, investors can invest on platform A on the first phase, on platform B on the second phase, and so on, which can avoid the risk caused by operational errors and make it possible to offset investment losses.

Secondly, it is also vital to reasonably plan financial period. Generally, platforms will issue short, medium, and long-term financial products, the longer financial products period, the higher returns. Investors can improve the liquidity of the portfolio on the premise of principal protection. Therefore, investors can flexibly select the medium and short-term products to control the risk of liquidity. In detail, the short-term product is generally 3 to 6 months, which can help investors get principal and interest back on maturity date, ensuring that a part of principal can flow freely. Moreover, the medium-term products are less affected by market fluctuations. In other words, it has relatively stable returns. In this regard, combining the medium-term products with higher and stable returns, and the short-term products with sufficient liquidity, can guarantee the principal and returns, thereby achieving expectations of investors.

Checking a Statement of Your Money at Any Time

After choosing the specific financial products, investors should not pay attention to the expected return, but also investigate the background, process and following progress of the projects and check statement of funds in time. Besides, investors should timely pay more attention to macro-data trends and new trends in capital appreciation to flexibly adjust financial planning according to market changes.

CONCLUSION

Compared with the United States where is the birthplace of internet finance, the internet financial planning in China is developing rapidly, but its scale need to be enlarged. With the sound system of supervision, rapid development of financial planning platforms and the maturity of smart investment, prospects of internet financial planning in China are definitely positive.

The supervision of Chinese internet finance is continually enhanced, which initially forms a unique supervision structure: the parallel authority of the central government, local authorities and self-regulation. In the aspect of law and regulation, China can learn from the US experience on regulatory reforming to improve relevant laws and regulations and to clarify industry threshold and define its behavioral boundary, such as the boundary of supervision, products, and service. In the supervisory aspect, governments should strengthen the supervision of internet finance industry, build up the layout of national financial supervisory network, strengthen the supervision of the internet financial enterprises and their information disclosure. Besides, improving business and personal credit system, accelerating the establishment of large data base, effectively integrating users' credit record on all kinds of internet financial platforms, improving internet financial disciplinary mechanism and seriously punishing internet financial criminal activities are equally significant. In the aspect of self-regulation, it is vital to make industry associations playing functions of business guidance, coordination, services and supervision, to strengthen the protection of rights and interests of consumers of internet finance and to promote internet financial industry to develop positively and healthily.

The internet financial platforms should actively respond to China's financial services in the real economy, promote the national needs of inclusive finance construction, give full play to the advantages of the long tail, broaden the investment channels for investors, and especially help small and micro enterprises, agriculture projects and other financing investment projects. Besides, they should invest more on the research of internet financial technology to alleviate their high technical risks. Moreover, users' stickiness can be improved by stable income, personalized services and diversified advantages. internet finance platforms should positively adapt to the supervision, and clarify their roles as an information intermediary, to improve risk control ability thus better conduct its functions, and to create a good investment environment for investors.

Besides, investors need to enhance their financial knowledge, so as to judge the investment risk more rationally and maturely, to make reasonable funds configuration and planning, and easier to choose a regular platform. According to the quantity of capital and the degree of liquidity, investors can select proper financial products with expected maturity and revenue. Also, they should continuously improve the ability of risk control to effectively ensure the safety of capital.

REFERENCES

Bank. (2003). *Internet Dynamics and Expansion of European Financial Markets: Issues from a Behavioral Finance Perspective*. Springer Berlin Heidelberg.

Basnet, H. C., & Donou-Adonsou, F. (2016). Internet, consumer spending, and credit card balance: Evidence from US consumers. *Review of Financial Economics*, *30*, 11–22. doi:10.1016/j.rfe.2016.01.002

Chen, Z. (2017). *The transition from traditional banking to mobile internet finance: an organization innovation perspective*. Financial Innovation.

Clemons. (2000). The Internet and the Future of Financial Services. The Wharton Financial Institutions Center.

Com Score, Inc. (2009). Nine Out of Ten 25-34-Year-Old U.K. Internet Users Visited a Social Networking Site in May 2009; Internet Users Age 55 and Older More Likely to Visit Social Networking Sites than Business & Finance, Technology and Travel. *M2 Presswire*.

Da Da, W. (2014). On the main mode, evolution and Enlightenment of internet banking in America. *Asia Pacific Economic*, *4*, 70–71.

Da Wang, W. (2014). The development of internet banking in the United States and the comparison of internet finance between China and America -- Research and Reflection Based on the perspective of internet economics. *International Finance Review*, *12*, 47–57.

Dai. (2014). Internet Financial authenticity. *Harvard Business Review*, 4.

Federal Reserve System. (2017). *Consumer and Mobile Finance Services 2016*. Author.

Han. (2016). Conflict and integration of internet Finance and traditional financial model. *Commercial Economy Research*, *15*, 177-179.

Hasen. (2011). Political Equality, the Internet, and Campaign Finance Regulation. *The Forum*, 6.

Hua & Hui. (2015). Internet banking is a new financial instrument or a new financial format. Based on the comparative perspective with the United States. *Asia Pacific Economy, 4*, 31-36.

Jiang & Wu. (2016). Intelligent investment adviser situation and supervision suggestions on the development. *Securities Market Herald*, *12*, 4-10.

Kennickell. (1996). *Saving and Financial Planning: Some findings from a Focus Group*. Author.

Li. (2015). Research on the improvement of credit reporting system under internet financial background. *China North Finance*, *2015*(6), 48-53.

Li, Z. (2016). *American Internet Finance Research*. Jilin University.

Liu. (2014). Xia Ling. Enlightenment of American internet financial development path to China. *Southwest Finance*, *6*, 19-21.

Liu, Xin, & Guo. (2013). Internet financial development and its impact on traditional financial model. *Economics Trends*, *8*, 73-83.

Lu. (2014). Internet financial supervision in the United States and Its Enlightenment to China. *Finance Research in Jilin*, *10*, 27-29.

Lu. (2017). Intelligent adviser: "look at the future". *Expo Financial Chaos (Wealth)*, *2*, 43-46.

Luo, Ying, & Yong. (2013). *Internet finance.* China Finance and Economics Press.

Mo. (2014). The financial industry in the internet era. *Development Pattern of Financial Science, 4*, 1-10.

Nian, W., Guan, D., & Wang, H. (2016). The challenge of internet finance to modern financial intermediary theory -- Concurrently on the impact on financial democratization. *International Economic Review*, *1*, 71–77.

Ping & Zou. (2012). Research of internet financial model. *Financial Research*, 12.

Ping, Zou, & Liu. (2014). The necessity and core principles of internet financial supervision. *International Finance Research*, *8*, 3-9.

Qin, J., Wang, T., & Huang, B. (2016). The Study of Chinese Listed Bank's Efficiency Growth Mode in Internet Finance Era—Based on Full-Combination DEA-PCA Model. *American Journal of Industrial and Business Management*, *06*(11), 11. doi:10.4236/ajibm.2016.611098

SEI. (2016). *The Next Wave of Financial Planning*. SEI.

Sun. (2015). The opportunities and challenges for commercial banks to develop internet financial management. *New Finance, 8*, 36-42.

The Zero One Research Institute. (2016). *Research Report China personal financial market*. Author.

Wang. (2013). Risk challenge of internet banking. *China Finance, 24*, 54-55.

Wang, B. W. (2016). *Crowdfunding and Marketplace Lending - Online Capital Marketplaces as New Asset Classes to Access Funding*. The FinTech Book.

Wu, X. (2015). The Internet Financial Growth Logic. *Finance & Economics, 02*, 5–15.

Yue & Hao. (2015). Internet finance, technology spillover and total factor productivity of commercial banks. *Financial Research, 3*, 160-175.

Zhang & Wu. (2015). Development, risk and Development Forum - internet financial review. *Economic Research, 11*, 183-186.

Chapter 7
Internet Financial Regulation and Law Analysis of China

Chi Chien Zhu
Foshan University, China

Jiye Hu
China University of Political Science and Law, China

ABSTRACT

In recent years, internet finance has developed rapidly in China; however, the inherent characteristics of the internet have magnified the high-risk nature of the financial industry. Consequently, this leads to the complication of risk types, the acceleration of risk propagation, and the increase of interconnection of risk system, and these issues pose a serious challenge to regulation. Including the improvement of internet finance laws and regulations, the establishment of a multi-level internet financial supervision system, and the increase of the internet financial security system, the most effective risk prevention measures can be supplemented by administrative means carried out to resolve the stock risk through the nationwide internet financial rectification. At present, the traditional financial business mode is mainly under the control of the current financial law. This kind of law is rarely related to internet finance. Even if it is involved slightly, it is due to the early formulation time and needs to be revised.

DOI: 10.4018/978-1-5225-7808-6.ch007

INTRODUCTION

Internet finance has played an important part in promoting the economic development in China. However, in recent years, serious accidents and increasing fraud behaviors on e-loan platforms happened frequently. Therefore, the effective role of Internet financial legal supervision and administrative supervision has become a top priority for the development of Internet finance.

Generally thinking, Internet finance is likely to cause adverse effects. Qian Lei (2017) agreed that the Internet finance, as a financial form that relies on the Internet for financial data processing and credit rating, could easily lead to illegal behaviors in addition to the banking financial mode, which is independently participated by financial demanders and suppliers. Magnuson (2017) argued that regulators currently focus on large financial institutions which may cause systemic risks, and ignored the fact that those relatively small but fast-growing financial technology companies also contain risky business activities, and these risks in certain circumstances will turn into higher risks than those came from large financial institutions, or even trigger a new financial crisis; According to Zhao Wenjing (2017), nowadays, Internet finance is developing rapidly, but Internet financial law and regulation still can't catch up with its real-world development timely. Lan Jian and Chen Yixing (2017) believed that the growth rate of investment in e-loan industry is unusual. Once e-loan platforms collapse in large scale, it will cause great economic losses and social impact including family breakdown, higher unemployment rate and unstable society. The rise in crime rates and other bad results will seriously hinder social development.

In terms of legal and administrative supervision, Brownsword and Somsen (2009) showed that the updating speed of laws and regulations are inevitably lagging behind the rea-world development. With the acceleration of innovation, the law of Internet finance is bound to keep pace with the real world; Moses (2011) believed that the ability to prepare financial regulatory laws ahead of time is limited. New types of financial technology will trigger new things, activities or relationships, and it is difficult to clearly define the use of existing regulatory requirements, or their regulated behavior becomes less important due to the development of technology; Brummer (2015) believed that the past regulatory principle is based on the relatively fixed supervision technology and formed the optimal supervision principle. In the past decades, the development of financial technology and internet finance has accelerated the reconstruction of financial market. The supervision model has been unable to adapt to the market environment of financial innovation driven by technology; "Internet financial risk prevention, supervision theory and experience expansion and comparison" research group (2017) found that in the process of Internet financial remediation, The main regulation targets and standards are unclear, the personnel allocation, professional competence and funding of local functional departments are obviously insufficient, the internal risk control mechanism of Internet finance enterprises is not perfect, the progress of e-loan funds is slow and it has docking difficulty; Li Wenhong and Jiang Zeshen (2017) believed that technology companies that have increasingly important impact on financial stability cannot be included in the existing financial regulatory system because they are not engaged in financial business, and there exists a huge regulatory loophole and risks quickly expand; Minsky (1977) argued that there is a fundamental flaw in the economy and it includes capitalist financial institutions, no matter how ingenious and observant the central bankers are, the speculative and innovative features of capitalism will ultimately lead to unstable financial practices and financial relations. Therefore, the most important thing for Internet finance rectification is to establish a central and local joint mechanism, to maintain the bottom line of systemic risk-free financial risks, and to ensure safety and keep control, which is the original way of clearing the source.

The concept of Internet finance has achieved substantial development since it first proposed in China in 2012. It mainly includes two aspects: the first is that traditional financial institutions use Internet communication technology to improve the efficiency of financial business processing, which belongs to the traditional financial science and technology. At the second level, internet companies and financial institutions use big data and Internet technology to carry out financial innovation, transforming from traditional service mode to emerging service mode, relying on big data to realize resource integration, and realizing new financial mode of intermediary services such as fund financing, mobile payment, investment and financial management.

There are four main development modes of Internet finance:

1. Technology companies rely on big data finance for financing: Big data finance is the integration of unstructured data collected by technology enterprises through cloud computing and the analysis of integrated data. Financial institutions can form effective data credit investigation system to understand customer consumption behaviors, and it can also combine with traditional financial models to carry out related fund financing business. Internet technology enterprises can obtain comprehensive customer information through big data. Through reasonable and effective analysis and scientific integration, they can effectively analyze and predict customer consumption behaviors and demands.
2. The third-party payment platform: Now the development of third-party payment is made up of Alipay, WeChat payment, Tenpay, Easy payment, etc. It integrates the gateway payment mode and account payment mode. Most e-commerce companies rely on their own third-party payment platform to provide convenient and free services and attract more small and medium-sized customers. In the

long run, internet technology finance will be promoted to be more and more popular in the future by internet third-party payment, it will not just limited to small payments, large payments between enterprises can be achieved, Internet technology financial enterprises pay attention to the combination of third-party payment platform, which can be online and offline and it will accelerate the popularization of Internet finance and promote the economic development of our country.

3. Internet crowdfunding: A crowdfunding project often receives investment from thousands of people, and the scale benefits are also very impressive. As a new type of financing channel, it can provide some individuals or enterprises which lack of financing channels with a new and efficient way to obtain development funds and achieve innovative development. Besides, the general public can also obtain investment opportunities and obtain certain benefits. The formation of this mechanism is conducive to helping small and micro enterprises to solve the problem of financing difficulties, mobilize the innovation atmosphere of the whole society and promote China's financial reform. Therefore, actively promoting the development of Internet crowdfunding is conducive to an active market economy.
4. Peer to Peer lending(P2P): According to the "2017 China P2P Network Loan Annual Bulletin" released by Zero Think Tank, as of December 31, 2017, the cumulative transaction amount of the national P2P lending industry is conservatively estimated to be about 6.07 trillion yuan, of which the transaction volume in 2017 is about 27,100. 100 million yuan, an increase of 38.8%. In December 2017, the transaction volume was approximately 228 billion yuan, a decrease of 1.3% from the previous month and an increase of 10.1% year-on-year. The annual transaction volume of P2P lending industry turnover is still growing year by year, but the growth rate is gradually slowing down. Considering the regulatory environment and market environment faced by the e-loan industry, it is expected that the total transaction volume in 2018 should be about 3.5-4.0 trillion yuan. As of the end of 2017, the balance of P2P lending (referring to the repayment of principal, the same below) was 1,250 billion yuan, and the interest to be repaid was about 110.9 billion yuan, about 9.2% of the principal. The loan balance increased by 45.1% compared with the same period of last year and decreased by 0.9% from the end of November. It has been declining for three consecutive months. It was due to the risk outbreak in the P2P market, and the arbitrage behavior in bad business had serious impact. In China, there are many negative news about P2P market in its early stage of development, including credit defaults and credit platform "running the road". Nowadays, based on the increasingly perfect national supervision policy, P2P credit will usher in the new development opportunities.

The "barbaric growth" of the P2P lending industry in 2014 and the frequent chaos in 2015 have emerged as the most distinctive events in the development of Internet finance in recent years, which has caused widespread concern in decision-making, regulatory, and academic circles. Under the background of good Internet finance and the industrial ecology development trend, regulate and supervise Internet finance is becoming one of the most important work of regulators. However, there are not many documents that scholars can refer to when they research for Internet financial legal supervision issues, which restricts healthy development of internet finance to some extent. In view of these problems, this paper focuses on systematically summarizing the status quo of China's Internet financial legal supervision. Taking the rapid development of third-party payment as an example, this paper analyzes its development and supervision status, and proposes the regulatory legal theory and supervision direction to adapt to the development of China's Internet finance. The author believes that it will also inspire the development of Internet finance in other countries.

THE CURRENT PROBLEMS IN THE DEVELOPMENT OF INTERNET FINANCE

Internet Financial Regulation Is Not Perfect

From the current point of view, the existing legal system does not effectively regulate Internet finance. First of all, there is no law on Internet financial market access in China. The regulations on relevant regulations and industry regulations on Internet financial market access need to be further improved. Despite the release of the Internet Lending Industry Access Standard in 2013, the e-loan risk has not decreased significantly. In the process of constructing an effective supervision system, we should focus on the supervision of laws and regulations and cannot rely solely on industry self-discipline. Secondly, from the "Company Law" and the existing financial laws and regulations, there is no rules to stipulate what kind of entities can set up an Internet financial enterprise, what kind of specific business can be engaged after setting up an Internet financial enterprise, and what should be done to Internet financial enterprises. The existing legislation and supervision are lagging behind, and it is difficult to meet the actual needs of the rapid development of Internet finance.

The Supervision System of Internet Finance Is Not Perfect

The imperfections of the regulatory system are reflected in the following three points. First of all, in order to cope with the "separate management", the three-party "separate supervision" system formed by the company is essentially institutional supervision. Internet finance has more cross-cutting characteristics and the characteristics of "mixed operation" which made some internet companies confuse about its regulatory agencies, and they have not been effectively supervised. Secondly, the provisions on Internet finance regulatory legislations are not sufficient. The "Guiding Opinions on Promoting the Healthy Development of Internet Finance" mainly targets the macro-level regulation of Internet fund sales. It only stipulates that the CSRC is a regulatory body, but there is no regulation on how to supervise and what measures can be taken. Finally, there are certain flaws in the enforcement of Internet financial supervision. The main reason is that "divisional supervision" is difficult to adapt to the "mixed operation" situation. At the same time, the new Internet finance special legislation does not clearly define the supervision duties, and it is easy to see buck-passing among different regulators.

Risk Prevention Regulations Are Not Comprehensive Enough

Internet finance and traditional finance are intrinsically consistent, which determines that Internet finance has certain risks that traditional finance has. At the same time, because of relying on big data and cloud computing, it has certain risks that traditional finance does not have. First, taking "Yu E Bao" (Alibaba Group designed deposit money fund wealth management products) as an example, the existence of such money market funds is mainly liquidity risk and information disclosure risk. The "Measures for the Supervision and Administration of Money Market Funds" did not set liquidity risk reserves in a targeted manner based on the different reasons for liquidity. At the same time, there was no regulation on the role of big data and cloud computing in monitoring liquidity risks. Secondly, the construction of risk prevention regulations related to Internet finance is not comprehensive enough. Internet finance is closely related to big data and cloud computing, which is prone to bring about long tail risk, technical security risk and interest rate risk. The current legislation does not adequately regulate such risks. Recently, relevant legislation on Internet finance has been mentioned. However, the supporting measures related to the refinement are still lacking.

The Industry Self-Discipline Mechanism Has Not Yet Been Formed

Due to greater coerciveness and effectiveness of government regulation, people tend to pay more attention to and rely more on government regulation and ignore industry supervision. The lack of self-discipline mechanism in internet finance industry can be manifested in the failure to establish a systematic Internet financial industry organization. In the current transitional stage, the corresponding self-regulatory mechanism has not yet formed. On the other hand, it is difficult to form a good mutual complementary relationship between industry self-discipline and government supervision. The Internet Finance Association, established in December 2015, can made up for such defects at a certain level, for example, Tianhong Asset Management Co., Ltd. has joined the Internet Finance Association. But at the same time there are certain deficiencies, China has not yet formed an Internet money market fund association and related industry self-regulation norms.

CONFLICT BETWEEN TRADITIONAL FINANCIAL LAW AND INTERNET FINANCE BUSINESS

Conflict Between the Commercial Banking Act and Third-Party Payments

In 1995, the "Commercial Banking Law" promulgated by China clearly stated that only commercial banks can operate financial services projects, including the securities industry, insurance industry, and trust industry. Moreover, the law clearly stipulates that branch management and branch management should be implemented by three types of financial industries above. China's current structure "one bank and two commissions" (People's Bank of China, China Securities Regulatory Commission, China Banking and Insurance Regulatory Commission) also implements the principle of classified management. With the development of Internet finance business, the payment behavior of third-party non-financial institutions apparently conflicts with the legal provisions of the Commercial Banking Law. In addition, the traditional "one bank and two commissions" model has also led to confusion in the management of "third-party payment," resulting in no entry barrier, no industry standards, and no departmental supervision.

Conflict Between the Securities Law and Crowd-Funding Funds

The scope of the Securities Law includes corporate bonds, company stocks, government bonds, securities investment funds, and other securities issuance and trading behaviors recognized by the State Council. With the development of Internet finance, there are more and more online crowdfunding funds, but this type of crowdfunding does not fall within the scope of the Securities Law. Moreover, the act of crowdfunding is often be suspected of illegal fund-raising and fund-raising fraud. According to Article 10 of the Securities Law, the issuance of stocks to the public through the online platform is suspected of "illegal securities operations". Therefore, the new Internet financial model for public funds for the public needs to be regulated by supporting laws.

Conflict Between the Guarantee Law and Financing

The form of guarantee provided by China's "Guarantee Law" only stipulates traditional economic activities, such as trading, cargo transportation, processing contract, etc. The new Internet financial model does not violate the guarantee law, but the target of trading is a kind of network service. However, the two types of network financing and financial management do not stipulate the corresponding guarantee liability in the Guarantee Law. That is to say, when Internet finance business enters the guarantee business, how to identify and prevent the guarantee risk becomes new legal problem. The law needs to be further improved by imitating other types of clauses or codifying new clauses.

For example, the P2P business in the financing field, the platform always claims to provide the "principal guarantee" to the financier, but if there is a problem with the "risk reserve fund" of the platform company, who should bear the "principal loss" of the financier? If P2P company takes the responsibility, how can we guarantee that the company can afford it? Or in the financing field, Alipay's "Yu E Bao", whose guarantee company is a guarantee company in Shenzhen, has previously promised an annualized rate of return of 8% to the public. If they fail to achieve the goal, how does the third-party guarantee company fulfill its previous commitment? As we all known, what public see is only the influence of "Alipay". There is no way to know the strength of the guarantee company. Once a big loss occurs, investors will bear a huge risk. These issues are not clearly and specifically defined in the current Guarantee Law.

DEVELOPMENT AND SUPERVISION STATUS

P2P

The focus of P2P lending rectification is the regulation of small loan companies. With the announcement of the "Guiding Opinions on Promoting the Healthy Development of Internet Finance" issued by 10 ministries and commissions of the People's Bank of China in August 2015, the network small loan was urgently braked. Since then, the number of microfinance companies plummeted and its number of employees decreased. As of the end of 2017, there were 8551 small loan companies nationwide with 103,988 employees, which were 4.03% and 11.38% lower than 2015 respectively. At present, the limited financing channels, the decline in customer repayment ability, the stigma of civil financial chaos and the weak risk control are the severe challenges facing the development of small loan companies. In December 2017, the P2P Network Lending Risk Special Remediation Leading Group Office issued the "Notice on Doing a Good Job of P2P Network Lending Risk Special Rectification and Reconstruction and Acceptance Work", clearly requiring that all localities should complete the registration and registration of major P2P institutions within their respective jurisdictions by the end of April 2018 and complete them by the end of June. And it further explained the key issues such as creditor's rights transfer, risk reserve fund and fund deposit.

In terms of P2P lending, corresponding countermeasures have been taken across the country. The P2P development of 16 platforms in Shanghai should meet the five requirements: e-loan institutions must play the role of information intermediaries, their businesses must conform to direct lending mode, they must not touch the bottom line, they should standardize the storage and management requirements and complete information disclosure. The 16 Internet financial platforms in Dongguan have received the "Notice Of Rectification and Rectification of Internet Financial Risks in Dongguan", which focuses on problems such as fund storage and management, information security, third-party auditing and loan quota, etc. Internet finance needs to be gradually integrated with financial science and technology, split up P2P business, and turn into comprehensive financial service platform. Shenzhen has issued on-site inspection questionnaire and confirmation and rectification requirements for the special Internet finance renovation by some enterprises. The questionnaire covered four major aspects: basic information of e-loan information intermediaries, products and operations, social contribution and innovative development, and major problems of e-loan intermediaries.

From the current point of view, the development of P2P lending has the following trends: Firstly, the platform compliance cost increases, the market scale growth slows down, and the industry concentration increases. Secondly, relying on the development of new technologies, e-loan will deepen the application of science and technology, and do a good job in risk control management before and after loan. Thirdly, transform and cooperate with traditional financial institutions and other institutions to standardize business, improve infrastructure and achieve all-round upgrading.

Equity Crowdfunding

Equity crowdfunding financing model is a new type of Internet financing model developed after P2P lending. It is a kind of investment behavior with high risk and long term. Its relatively low entry threshold can reduce the cost of small and micro enterprises, which is a natural extension of China's current multi-layer capital market. However, the biggest obstacle to the equity crowdfunding in China comes from the lack of gaps in legal supervision, and the policy definition of the crowdfunding industry is not clear enough. Although the "Implementation Plan for Special Remediation of Internet Financial Risks" and the "Implementation Plan for Equity Crowdfunding Risks" issued in 2016 have strengthened the risk monitoring of equity financing, but the definition of regulatory policy is still vague and it does not meet the operational needs of the current equity crowdfunding industry.

One of the major obstacles to develop equity crowdfunding in China is the unclear industrial policies. The grey area and the red lines of the equity crowdfunding industry regulations are densely intersected, so the development of many equity crowdfunding businesses is hampered, and the advantages of Internet finance in making money and serving the real economy cannot be fully realized. Moreover, the single operating profit model of equity-based crowdfunding platform is another major obstacle to the development of equity-based crowdfunding in China. At present, most equity-based crowdfunding platforms mainly charge transaction fees, in addition to this, there are only a small amount of value-added service fees, and traffic import and marketing fees. In addition, the development of equity-based crowdfunding in China is still at the initial stage, the service system is not perfect enough, and there is no mature system for the follow-up fund demand and investment feedback mechanism.

The equity crowdfunding platform can not operate in a healthy and orderly manner without regulation and legal provisions. In 2017, relevant regulatory policies have been promulgated one after another, and the grey area of the industry is gradually shrinking. It can be seen that the current policy direcitons for the crowdfunding industry is towards strict regulation and standardized development. In order to fundamentally reverse the phenomenon of "bad money drives out good money" of

Figure 1. Pie chart of operation type of crowdfunding platform
Source: Author finishing

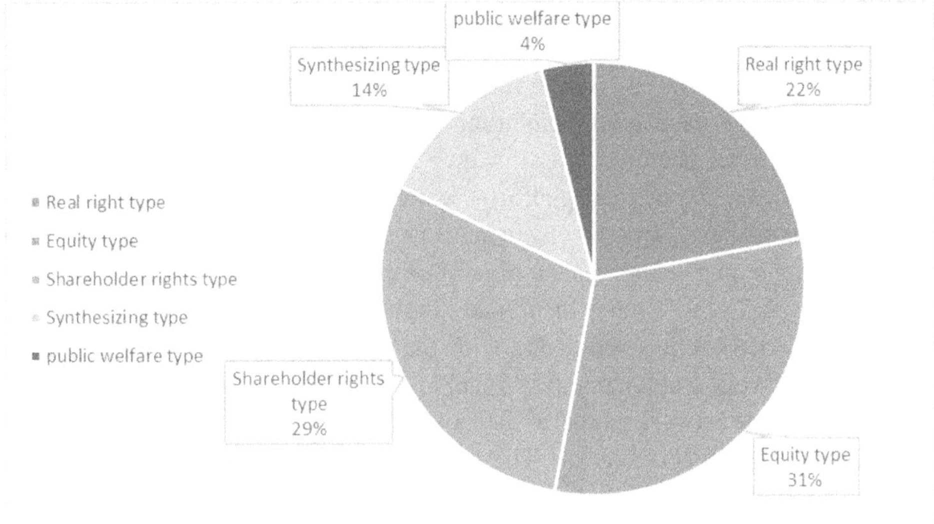

equity-based crowdfunding, the equity-based crowdfunding industry is also actively building a cross-regulatory mechanism of "government + market" industry self-discipline in addition to the regulation of equity-based crowdfunding in policies and regulations. For example, the Zhongguancun Crowdfunding Alliance drafted and published the *"Zhongguancun Crowdfunding Industry Self-discipline Convention (Public Consultation Draft)"*, and China Internet Finance Association issued the *"Questionnaire on the Development of Internet Equity Financing"* to explore the development of the domestic crowdfunding platform and provide reference for the formulation of regulatory policies.

INTERNET INSURANCE

Internet technology has brought a disruptive revolution to China's insurance industry. Traditional large and medium-sized insurance companies have deepened their Internet channels through self-built official websites and e-commerce companies. Some small and medium-sized insurance companies have borrowed Internet technology to enter the Internet insurance market and achieve "overtaking". Large Internet companies and insurance intermediaries have laid out the Internet insurance market. Thanks to the use of Internet technology, the service model of the insurance industry has been updated in depth to meet more fragmented insurance requirements, highlighting the concept of "customer-centric" and greatly expanding the innovation space of insurance products and the scope of the insurance market. Internet insurance premiums have exploded.

Due to the rapid expansion of insurance business and the substantial increase in insurance premiums, the risks in the insurance industry began to accumulate, and some problems have arisen, including the lack of Internet insurance product provisions and insurance consumer disputes arise easily. Internet insurance sales behavior and third-party network platforms which participate in insurance operations need to be standardized. Among which, network mutual aid platforms which violate the publicity and management is the biggest problem in Internet insurance.

In this regard, the China Insurance Regulatory Commission has carried out rectification work in accordance with the "Internet Insurance Risk Special Rehabilitation Work Implementation Plan", requiring local insurance regulatory bureaus to estimate network mutual assistance platforms one by one, including online verification and field certification. The China Insurance Regulatory Commission will classify targets into three categories: The first category refers to platforms which show difference between the public explicit mutual assistance program and the insurance products to public and they do not induce the public to generate rigid claims. The second category refers to platforms which use insurance terminology illegally, occasionally use false advertising or conduct other irregular behaviors, but they do not induce the public to generate rigid claims. The third category refers to

Figure 2. China's Internet insurance scale grew during the 12th five-year plan period
Source: Author finishing

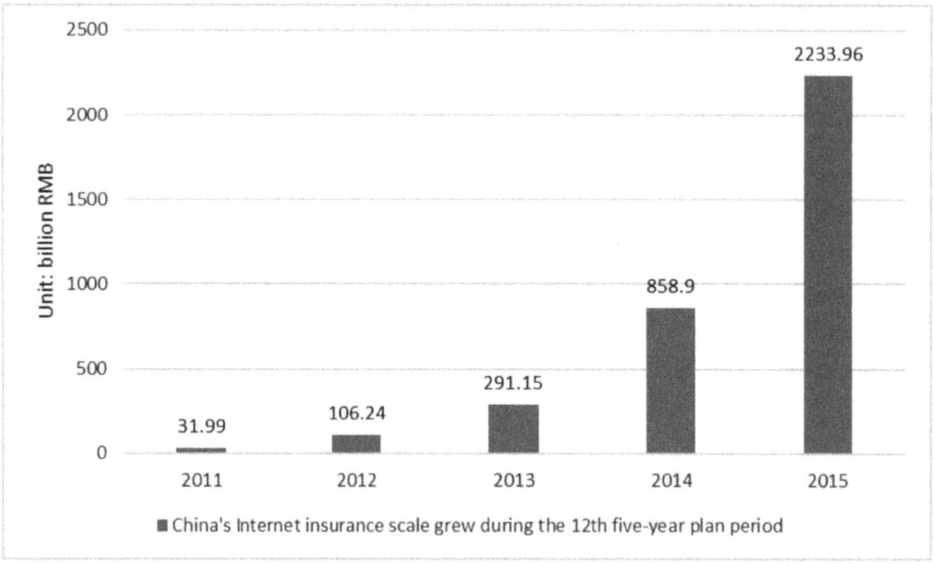

platforms which induce the public to generate rigid claims, or the platforms which collect funds from the public in the name of insurance premiums and illegally establish a pool of funds. Among them, the second and third types of network mutual aid platforms are the targets of special rectification, and the third type of network mutual assistance platform is the focus of rectification.

THIRD PARTY INTERNET PAYMENT

Internet payment as a third-party payment industry is a relatively mature field of Internet finance development in China. After several years of rapid expansion and development, the market growth rate has gradually slowed down. However, there are still some risks that hinder further development of the industry. Relevant entities corresponding remediation measures for reducing risks such as risks related to safety technology, liquidity, money laundering and law.

According to the "China Third-Party Payment Mobile Payment Market Quarterly Monitoring Report for the First Quarter of 2018" which released by Analysys Analyst at the first quarter of 2018, the transaction volume of China's third-party payment in mobile payment market reached RMB 40,364.51 billion, seeing a growth of 6.99%. The scale of transactions by third-party payments in China increased by 260 times from the first quarter of 2010 to the first quarter of 2018, and the development was very rapid. Among them, Alipay occupied the top posit have taken ion of mobile payment with 53.76% market share, and Tencent's financial market share increased to 38.95%, ranking the second in the market. Overall, the market share of both Alipay and Tencent Finance reached 92.71%, occupying an absolute dominant position.

The development of China's third-party payment industry is in stark contrast to the situations in foreign countries:

1. Third-party payments made by China through mobile phones account for 75% of the total transaction volume, and the US data is 20%;
2. 40% of China's retail services are paid through third-party payment companies. Goldman Sachs predict that the figure will reach 68% in 2020; while US third-party payments currently account for 7% of retail sales;
3. Alipay and Tencent are the two largest third-party payment providers, with 870 million and 989 million active users respectively (as of the end of 2017), while the US PayPal has only 227 million active users (as of the end of 2017).

In summary, China's third-party payment industry has shown rapid growth in scale and continuous expansion in application fields in recent years under the huge market capacity of China. The third-party payment industry in China has more development

Figure 3. 2017Q1-2018Q1 China's third-party payment market transaction scale
Source: www.analysys.cn

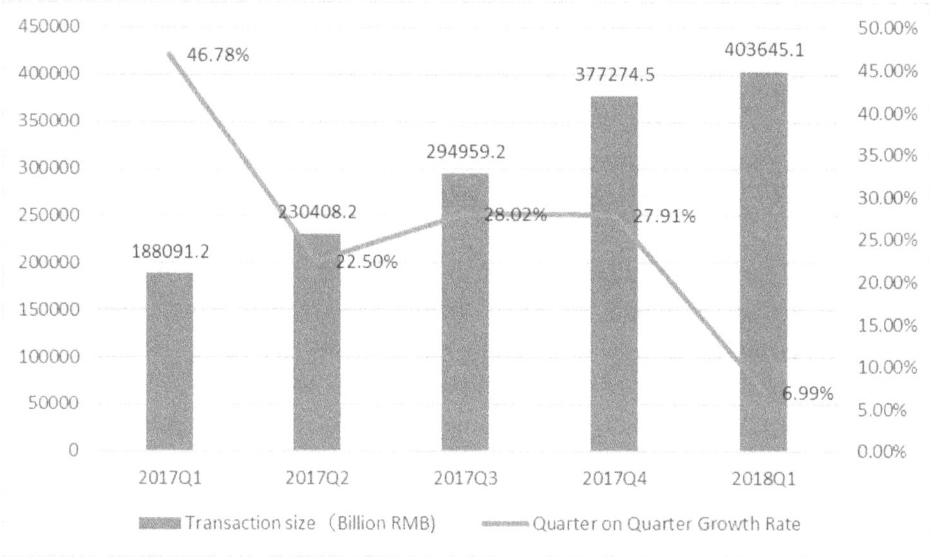

Figure 4. 2018Q1 China's third-party payment market transaction share
Source: www.analysys.cn

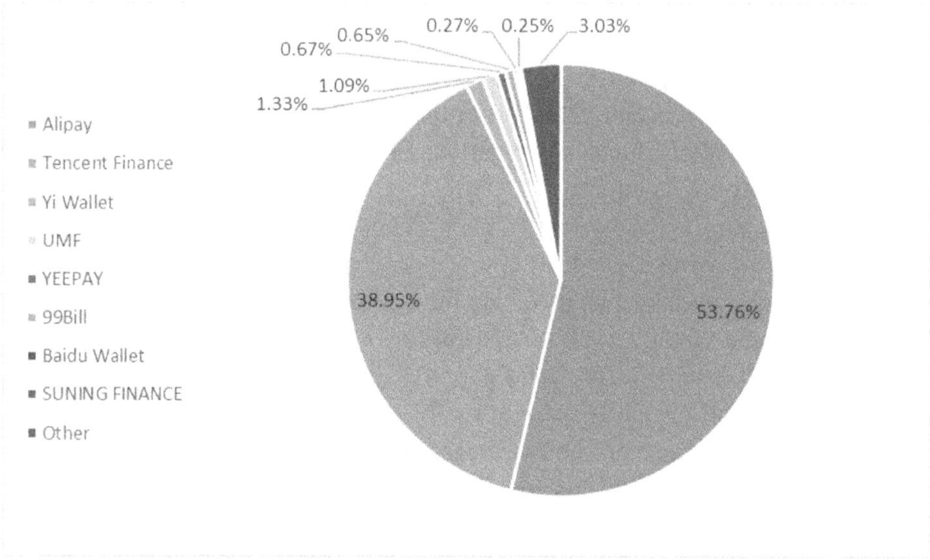

potential than the third-party payment industry in Europe and America. However, as far as the current third-party payment is concerned, the regulatory system still has following problems: Firstly, there is a lack of management regulations for third-party payment. The existing management regulations only involve a certain part of the third-party payment, such as the provisions for payment of license applications, third-party mobile payment platforms, payment links and payment risk regulations. But detailed management measures are still lacking. Secondly, the responsibility of the supervisory party for third-party payment is unclear, and the object of supervision is still not clear enough. At present, the supervision of third-party payment in China is mainly supervised by the People's Bank of China, the China Securities Regulatory Commission, and the Ministry of Industry and Information Technology(MIIT). However, there is no detailed regulation on the regulatory agencies at all stages and the corresponding duties. For the different risks of account-based payment and channel-based payment, there should be differences in the regulatory focus. Thirdly, there is a lack of information exchange mechanism for third-party mobile payment supervision. The third-party payment industry chain involves merchants, consumers, commercial banks, and third-party payment platform companies. The interest relationship is complicated, and the third-party payment users lack awareness of risk, but there is no information exchange mechanism between the development platform and the user.

INTERNET CREDIT REPORTING

At present, in addition to the relatively mature credit information center under the leadership of the People's Bank of China, with the rapid development of Internet information technology, the credit information industry has developed newly – relying on the Internet to launch credit information business. Based on non-traditional credit data, Internet credit institutions analyze the credit status of information subjects through data analysis and data mining, and it provides a wide range of credit information products to credit information demanders including information subjects. The emergence of Internet credit reporting can make up for the deficiencies of traditional credit reporting methods in the types of credit information products, credit reporting costs, and credit coverage.

From January 2015, the People's Bank of China Credit Information Administration issued the "Notice on the Preparations for Personal Credit Information Business", the rudiment of China's Internet credit industry has been formed by mainly personal credit agencies and other multi-disciplinary data source platforms. However, in January 2018, the People's Bank of China has accepted the application for the personal credit information business of Hundreds of Industries Credit Information

Co., Ltd. Hundreds of Industries Credit Information Co., Ltd was jointly established by the China Mutual Gold Association and eight credit bureaus, of which the China Internet Finance Association holds 36% of the shares while the eight credit reporting platforms each hold 8%. So far, China's Internet credit has basically established a regulatory model which indicated that government regulation will play a guiding role, self-regulation of industry will play a major role, and market factors will be introduced.

As far as the current supervision of Internet credit is concerned, efforts can be made mainly from two aspects: Firstly, we can stuff blanks of laws and regulations. The United States has promulgated 17 laws in the process of regulating the credit industry to protect the development of the credit industry. China's current law on credit reporting, the Regulations on the Management of Credit Information Industry, has initially established a multi-level credit reporting system based on national regulations, departmental rules, normative documents and standards. But in the situation of the rapid development of Internet credit reporting nowadays, these laws and regulations are far from enough. The legislation about personal privacy information protection is still premature, large number of legal vacancy and chaos still remain. At present, Internet credit relies on big data to do data mining and analysis. These all involve invasion of privacy and its ambiguous boundaries in law. The second is to improve the data sharing mechanism. The foundation of the credit industry is data, and the sharing of data information is an inevitable requirement for reducing the cost of credit and improving the authority of credit reporting. The construction of the data sharing mechanism can be carried out from two aspects: On the one hand, opening government data to public is important, and the data information generated by the administrative process should be open to the credit reporting agencies in the case of legal compliance. Breaking down data barriers between credit reporting agencies and sharing data in a reasonable and reasonable manner, including data sharing between traditional credit reporting agencies and Internet credit reporting agencies, as well as data sharing between Internet credit reporting agencies.

CASE ANALYSIS OF REGULATORY LAW

On April 27, 2018, in order to standardize the asset management business of financial institutions, unify the regulatory standards for similar asset management products, effectively prevent and control financial risks, and better serve the real economy. The People's Bank of China, the Bank of China Insurance Regulatory Commission, the China Securities Regulatory Commission, and the State Administration of Foreign Exchange jointly issued the "Guiding Opinions on Regulating Asset Management

Business of Financial Institutions" (Yinfa [2018] No. 106, hereinafter referred to as "Opinions") with the approval of the State Council.

The author notes that the main purpose of the "Guidance Opinion" is to "unify the regulatory standards for similar asset management products and effectively prevent and control financial risks...". In other words, one of the main purposes of the Guiding Opinions is to unify the product supervision of various financial institutions such as banks, trusts, securities, funds, futures, and insurance asset management institutions to avoid regulatory arbitrage. The author does not think the relevant requirements to Internet financial platforms in the "Guidance Opinion" are the earliest. In fact, there were similar regulations before.

The contents directly related to the Internet financial platforms in the Guiding Opinions mainly include:

1. Asset management business, as a financial business, belongs to the franchise industry and must be included in financial supervision.
2. Non-financial institutions which conduct irregular behaviors such as using the Internet platform to promote, split up and sell underlying assets that have entry threshold, excessively emphasizing on credit promotion procedures to cover product risks and setting up secondary trading market to attract investors will be punished in accordance with the "Notice of the General Office of the State Council on Printing and Distributing the Implementation Plan for Special Remediation of Internet Financial Risks" (Guo Ban Fa [2016] No. 21) Non-financial institutions may also be held liable for illegal fund-raising, illegally absorbing public deposits and illegally issuing securities.
3. If a non-financial institution violates laws such as conducting asset management business and promising or performing rigid redemption, its penalty will be aggravated.

In fact, the above provisions are mentioned in the normative opinions on relevant laws and regulations concerning Internet finance. For example, the Interim Measures for the Management of Business Activities of Internet Lending Information Intermediaries stipulates that e-loan platforms are prohibited from selling funds for financial products such as wealth management, and selling financial products such as bank wealth management, securities management, funds, insurance or trust products. There are special chapters in the "Implementation Plan for Special Remediation of Internet Financial Risks" that restrict and constrain the Internet financial platforms "to conduct asset management and cross-border financial business through the Internet". In practice, products that need to be purchased by qualified investors, such as nested or split private equity financing products, are subjected to the prohibitions above.

At the same time, the "Guidance Opinions" emphasized that the position of non-financial institutions is information broker rather than credit intermediary. The nature of credit intermediation on the Internet financial platforms has been emphasized in "Guiding Opinions on Promoting the Healthy Development of Internet Finance" and the follow-up laws and regulations on Internet finance.

In addition, "smart investment" business has been carried out by a considerable number of Internet finance platforms, some researchers believed that the introduction of the "Guidance Opinions" has a significant adverse impact on the development of the smart investment business of the Internet financial platforms because the "Guidance Opinions" indicated that, "The financial institutions use artificial intelligence technology and employ robot investment consultants to carry out asset management business with the permission of the financial supervision and management department to obtain the corresponding investment consultant qualification...". It will bring about difficulties and barriers for financial institutions to conduct smart investment business.

In fact, the requirements for investment consultant qualification are stipulated in the Securities Law. The securities business includes securities investment consulting and financial advisors related to securities trading and securities investment activities. No units or individuals may operate securities business without the approval of the securities regulatory authority under the State Council.

In summary, although the "Guidance Opinion" has great significance for the asset management industry with its unified standards and its prevention of regulatory arbitrage, the scope of Internet financial industry regulation has not been enlarged. Nevertheless, relevant regulations and regulations of the Internet financial industry had multiplied, regulations are updated quickly, and the cost of illegal operations is increasing. The Internet financial platforms should pay more attention to compliance management.

SUGGESTIONS AND CONCLUSIONS

To establish and maintain an order for the development of the Internet financial market, it is necessary to attach great importance to the construction of the legal system for Internet financial market access from the source. This chapter discusses methods to improve China's Internet financial supervision legal system from four aspects:

1. It is better to develop and improve laws related to internet finance access, develop a business license system for Internet financial enterprises, establish a clear entry threshold, and clarify the scope of supervision and supervision.

Firstly, regulators must improve the current "Company Law of the People's Republic of China". Considering the specificity of Internet financial enterprises, we need to tighten the access to set up Internet financial enterprises. We need to recognize that market entities can establish Internet financial enterprises according to law from the view of jurisprudence, and we should define the business scope of Internet financial enterprises. The second is to improve the "Criminal Law of the People's Republic of China". Based on actual problems, it is urgent to complement legal loophole of "Internet Finance Crime" which belongs to the Criminal Law of the People's Republic of China and enhance supervision of illegal and criminal activities in Internet financial business like making use of legal loophole.

2. Establish a credit reporting system for Internet finance companies, force greater account information transparency and transact data orderly are essential to prevent the emergence of illegal criminal activities such as money laundering. In the process of Internet finance industry operation, regulators should put more emphasis on the credit of payment institutions, focusing on establishing a sound credit information system, and conduct comprehensive and in-depth analysis and evaluation of relevant transaction information and data such as financing platforms and payment platforms in Internet finance.
3. It is necessary to construct industry self-discipline rules and regulations, formulate regulatory rules and self-discipline standards for virtual financial services industry and promote healthy and rapid development of Internet financial industry. The degree of self-discipline in domestic Internet finance industry and the development of the industry is order or not will largely affect the attitude from regulators and the degrees of financial supervisions. As a useful complement to government supervision, industry self-regulatory organizations will play an important role in self-discipline management.
4. It is suggested to establish an internet financial dispute prevention system, reduce the losses to investors caused by high-risk Internet finance, and increase the protection of investor rights and interests.
5. At the same time, administrative measures can be used to supplement economic methods above. It is necessary to improve remedial methods, implement reform measures, guide financial institutions, carry out administrative punishments and criminal strikes, and accelerate the pace to phase out illegal institutions and business activities from the market.

REFERENCES

An. (2018). Legal Problems and Countermeasures Faced by Internet Finance Supervision in China. *Time Finance, 8*, 55-58.

Brownsword, R., & Han, S. (2009). Law, innovation and technology: Before we fast forward—a forum for debate. *Law Innovation & Technology*, *1*(1), 1–73. doi:10.1080/17579961.2009.11428364

Brummer, C. (2015). Disruptive technology and securities regulation. *Social Science Electronic Publishing*, *84*(3), 977–1052.

Chen. (2018). Research on the Development Model of Science and Technology Financial Service Industry under Internet Thinking. *Journal of Fujian Institute of Financial Management, 1,* 3-9.

Fu & Gao. (2018). Research on Legal Risk Prevention of Internet Finance. *Journal of Beijing Institute of Political Science and Law, 2*, 6-10.

Lan & Chen. (2017). Analysis on the Legal Supervision of Internet Finance under the New Normal——Based on the Perspective of Network Lending. *Chinese Prices, 2*, 49-51.

Lei, Q. (2017). The Difficulties and Countermeasures of Internet Financial Law Supervision. *Business and Economic Review*, *01*, 107–109.

Lu. (2017). On the Improvement of China's Internet Financial Market Access Legal System. *Discussion on Modern Economy, 2*, 88-92.

Magnuson, W. J. (2017). *Regulating fintech*. Social Science Electronic Publishing.

Minsky, H. P. (2009). Banking and a fragile financial environment. *Journal of Portfolio Management*, *3*(4), 16–22. doi:10.3905/jpm.1977.408609

Moses, L. B. (2013). How to think about law, regulation and technology: Problems with 'technology' as a regulatory target. *Law Innovation & Technology*, *5*(1), 1–20. doi:10.5235/17579961.5.1.1

Wu, Han, & Han. (n.d.). Internet finance rectification. *Caixin Weekly,* 30-39.

Zhao. (2017). Discussion on the Legal Supervision of Internet Finance. *Chinese Business Theory, 1*, 44-45.

Zheng, X. (2014). Legal Analysis of Internet Finance. *Journal of Xihua University*, *6*, 68–75.

Chapter 8
Chinese Internet Finance Credit Investigation Issue and Legal Countermeasures

Cheng-Yong Liu
Beijing Institute of Technology – Zhuhai, China

Cheng Chen
National Taiwan University, Taiwan

ABSTRACT

In recent years there has been a phenomenon of "Thirst for Credit Investigation Information" within China's internet finance industry. To compensate for the new credit investigation demands that traditional measures of credit investigation lack, big data credit investigation has been widely recognized as a viable solution. Big data credit investigation however poses greater risks to the rights and interests of the information subject. In order to solve the existing problems associated with the data credit investigation industry, the author advocates that special laws and regulations be revised or formulated on the basis of balancing the rights and interests of the information subject with those of public interests. In the future, the combination of big data credit investigation system with blockchain technology may effectively solve the problems that are harmful to the rights and interests of the information subject, such as information-isolated island and information security.

DOI: 10.4018/978-1-5225-7808-6.ch008

INTRODUCTION

The operation of the modern financial system cannot be separated from the support of credit information. In order to cope with the dilemma this poses, there has been a resulting upsurge of big data credit investigation since 2015. The development of the big data credit investigation industry in China is still however still facing issues surrounding the infringement upon the rights and interests of the information subject; which needs to be actively solved.

The main problems are as follows: (1) The isolated island of credit information caused by the lack of effective information sharing within big data credit investigation agencies; (2) While personal information is being excavated and utilized by multiple subjects, not only the connotation of personal information has changed qualitatively, but also the issue of insufficient protection of the rights and interests of information subjects has become increasingly prominent. In short there is a significant mismatch between big data credit investigation and China's existing credit investigation laws and regulations. In order to solve the above-mentioned problems faced by China's Internet finance industry in big data credit investigation activities, this chapter intends to discuss from the perspective of "Perfecting the laws and regulations of the big data credit investigation", and also points to future research directions of "Combining the big data credit investigation with blockchain technology".

BACKGROUND

Big data credit investigation is often referred to as internet credit investigation or network credit investigation. Compared to traditional credit investigation agencies, the Credit Investigation Center of PBOC for example, has been widely used in the credit risk management of financial agencies.[1] By the end of May 2017, a total of 3,000 agencies had been connected to the database, which included relevant information of 926 million individuals, 23.71 million enterprises and other organizations, effectively solving the problem of information asymmetry and improving the convenience of public financing (Xinhua News Agency, 2017). However, it is difficult for the centre to fully collect information on the liabilities of people with debts outside financial agencies. To prevent the risk of credit default from moving across markets, industries or regions, it is necessary to cultivate some social credit investigation agencies outside the Credit Investigation Center of PBOC,[2] so as to build a diversified and comprehensive credit investigation system compatible with market demands (People's Bank of China, 2017). The big data credit investigation industry has been rapidly developing in China in recent years (Wang Qiang, Qing Sude & Ba Jieru, 2017). It is important to note that credit system based on the big data is only part of the Chinese credit information system, and it is still unable to replace the traditional credit information. For the complete evaluation of the credit status of a specific person, it is still necessary to combine the traditional credit report with big data, the credit report can then be completed. The importance of a credit system based on big data cannot be overemphasized nor can the importance of traditional credit reporting methods.

Big data credit investigation refers to the redesign of the, credit investigation model and algorithm by means of big data, cloud computing depth algorithm, mobile terminal, artificial intelligence and other new technologies. These then collect, sort, store and process the structured and unstructured data produced by individuals or agencies in the use of internet various services that then describe the "Portrait" of the credit subject and present the default rate and credit status of said subject, thereby forming the specific credit products and providing it to information users or directly applying it to a certain preset scenario (Liu Xinhai & Ding Wei, 2014). The establishment of credit investigation agencies in China and the acquisition of the corresponding licenses are bound by the *Regulations on Administration of Credit Investigation Industry*. Big data credit investigation activities in essence still fall within the scope of credit investigation business as defined by this regulation.[3] However, compared to the traditional credit investigation system, it has its own characteristics and can be a useful supplement to the traditional credit investigation system (Shi Mingsheng, 2017).

Big data credit investigation's characteristics are as follows: (1) Comprehensive sources of the credit investigation data: The information source of big data credit investigation includes not only personal Internet financial data but also non-financial internet behavior data of the information subject, such as online shopping, browsing, searching, socializing, travel, online games, online education and other behavioral data can become the contents of information collection (Zhang Yun, Xiao Yu & Zhu Nan, 2016). (2) Complicated types of the credit investigation data: The information handled by big data credit investigation system, in addition to the structured data that can be handled by traditional credit investigation data systems, also include unstructured data such as hypertext, images, sounds, pictures, geographical location information, behavioral data, social relations, etc. (3) Concealled data acquisition and processing: Compared with the standard process of collecting, sorting, processing and forming credit products of traditional credit investigation, big data credit investigation has completely different information collection channels and model design among different agencies. The manner in which these process are conducted results in a relatively low degree of transparency. (4) Multiple application of the credit investigation data: The application of big data credit investigation products, such as credit rating, can be applied not only to the financial credit field targeted by traditional credit investigation business, but also to marriage, dating, accommodation, recruitment, visa, job hunting, renting cars and houses, hotels and tourism and other scenes of life, which gets closer to our daily life.

The concept of what constitutes as "personal information" has undergone many qualitative changes in the context of big data credit investigation. Personal information in this sense refers to information that can directly or indirectly identify the personal information of the subject, and is the identifiable symbols associated with a particular individual, reflecting the characteristics of that individual. Personal information has many different types, and the credit information collected by traditional credit investigation agencies is only one type of the personal information; personal loans, credit cards, guarantees and other credit information collected by the traditional credit investigation system of the Credit Investigation Center of People's Bank of China (PBOC), as well as more than 80 items of data involved in eight types of public information. These include, but are not limited to: payment information of personal housing public accumulation funds, payment and issuance information of the social insurance, vehicle transaction and mortgage information, court judgment and execution information, tax information, communication information, personal subsistence allowance information, professional qualification information, rewards and punishment information (Tu Yongqian & Wang Xiaotian, 2017). Big data credit investigation agencies often portray the credit subject in multiple dimensions to show the default rate and the credit status of the credit subject, and even emphasize that "all data are credit data" (Liu Xinhai & Ding Wei, 2014). As a result, personal information has a new connotation under the background of big data. Personal Internet big data, sensing data, behavioral data, geographic location data and other data can be converted into credit evaluation of individuals through algorithm model. For example, the definition of "Profiling" in Article 4, Paragraph 4, of the General Data Protection Regulation (GDPR) refers to any activity that automates the processing of personal data to evaluate specific aspects of an individual or to analyze and predict specific aspects of an individual, including job performance, financial status, location, health status, personal preferences, trustworthiness, or behavioral performance (European Union, 2016). In the definition mentioned above, only trustworthiness and financial status are involved in the traditional category of personal credit information, and the rest belong to the new connotation of personal credit information under the big data background of "Profiling".

Under the above circumstances, big data credit investigation activities pose more challenges to the protection of the rights and interests of the personal information subject on the grounds that: (1) In the process of collecting and processing personal information, some big data credit investigation agencies don't treat the personal information, traditional credit information and private information differently, resulting in the risk of disclosure and illegal use of personal information (Wang Yong & Wang Pusheng, 2016); (2) Big data mining technology invalidate the traditional regulation measures to the credit investigation activities, in the absence of the new form of regulation, the protection of information rights and interests of the information subject is extremely unfavorable (Li Zhencai, 2016); (3) Big data credit investigation agencies can exempt themselves from the legal system of personal information protection (Wang Rong, 2016) if they use Data Anonymization Technology (Zhang Chenyuan, 2017). However, due to the fact that anonymization is only a temporary state and is characterized by uncertainty and instability, the identity of the information subject may be rediscovered at any time (Sun Guangzhong & Wei Shen, Xie Xing, 2013), so the personal rights and interests of the information subject are still at risk of being infringed upon; Even, personal information transaction industry chain on the "Dark Net" (Liu Yu & Zheng Chenghuan, 2017), also known as "Deep Web" (Liu Tong, 2016), is the main place of infringement of the rights and interests of the information subject. (4) With the rise of Internet society, network security and network transaction involve more non-private personal information which often involve social public interest, national security and other interests, so besides the protection of privacy, the non-private personal information gradually shows the necessity of being independently protected, which can meet the demands of personal information interest protection under the Internet environment (Sun Guomao & Li Meng, 2017).

INFRINGMENT UPON THE INFORMATION SUBJECT'S RIGHTS

Take China's first personal credit score, Sesame Credit is an example of an internationally accepted credit scoring standard, such as the US FICO credit scoring system, which is based on the user's various consumption and behavioral data, combined with traditional financial credit information. By using cloud computing and machine learning techniques, through the various model algorithms, it can obtain a comprehensive score of personal credit status, ranging from 300 to 950 which are divided into five levels of poor, medium, good, excellent, perfect. The higher the score is, the better the credit of the user gets, so as to evaluate the personal credit (Wu Fengjun & Chen Yuyao, 2017). Based on the operating mode and characteristics of the Sesame Credit Score, the data collection dimension is incomplete and the score is difficult to reflect the personal real credit status, there are hidden problems about online personal information and privacy protection, the objection handling and relief face great difficulties (Ye Wenhui, 2015). The lack of protection for the rights and interests of the information subject, under the current practice, big data credit investigation industry mainly focusses on the level of information collection, credit evaluation and industry supervision, as explained below (Kimberly A. Houser & Debra Sanders, 2017).

Infringement on the Level of Information Collection

1. **Non-compliance Procedure:** From practical experience, China's big data credit investigation agencies fail to collect information according to relevant regulations. In accordance with the relevant provisions of Regulations on Administration of Credit Investigation Industry, the collection and utilization of personal information should be limited to credit information, and the right of informed consent of the information subject should be fully guaranteed, as well as the right of objection, correction, privacy and other rights to the credit information derived from it. However, the information collecting process of the big data credit investigation agencies may not be compliant within the following situations:
   a. The measures of information collection may not be legal. The scope of information collected by big data credit investigation agencies is usually beyond the scope of personal credit information. In addition to structured data, such as user registration data, property data, transaction data, payment data, etc., it generally extends to unstructured data such as living habits, behaviors, interests and preferences, sensing data, geographic location data, social data, web behaviors, and psychological testing data (Erica Jaeger, 2014). Big data credit investigation agencies don't consider the correlation between information and credit but rely on their absolute advantages in technology to collect information as much as possible, which can often result in excessive collection. And it isn't clear whether these data contain the prohibited or restricted information, which makes it questionable whether the information collection is used by legal means.
   b. The right of informed consent of the information subject has not been implemented. Firstly, because the information collection technology has the characteristics of concealment and black box processing, it is hard for the big data credit investigation agencies to provide the complete collection list in practice. In the case of ubiquitous information collection, the information subject is unable confirm whether the collected information is true and accurate, let alone exercise the right of informed consent given by law. Secondly, even if the user knows, because of the current situation of using the model of the "Blanket Authorization", it may not be possible to know the scope of the collection, thc purposc of the use, when and where it is copied and disseminated, etc., which results in the fact that the consent right exists in name only and the original intention of consent right cannot be displayed (Harper, Jim, 2011). Furthermore, the data collector is unable to clearly inform the data subject of all possible

data purpose, and it is rather normal for the personal information to be reused beyond the original limitation purpose.

2. **Information Isolated Island:** With the rapid development of Internet and information technology, the scale of personal loans in internet finance is increasing in China. However, big data credit investigation agencies lack in effective information sharing mechanism and face the problem of data integration and sharing, which is harmful to the healthy development of internet financial market.
    a. At present, the credit investigation system of the Credit Investigation Center of PBOC is not open to the big data credit investigation agencies, so it is impossible for them to obtain the precious credit and loan data, and the PBOC can hardly master the credit behavior of enterprises in small loans and leasing finance; The rest of the public data are widely dispersed in the administration of industry and commerce, quality inspection, customs, taxation and other government and business management departments (Tu Yongqian & Wang Xiaotian, 2017). Although the construction of a unified credit information platform has been put on the agenda, the problem of information isolated island is still difficult to solve.
    b. At present, most big data credit investigation agencies have relatively narrow channels of information sources, and the information sources are concentrated in the relevant industries within the group. All agencies regard information as their core assets, and they're unwilling to share or take out the false data, forming a real information isolated island (Wang Qiang, Qing Sude & Ba Jieru, 2017). As a result, individual long loans, excessive loans, fraud loans and other behaviors continue to appear.

Infringement on the Level of Credit Evaluation

In practice, credit evaluation results of some big data credit investigation agencies can difficult to reflect the accurate credit status of the information subject. When the credit products experience issues and the credit evaluation results are the basis for deciding whether to provide other social services, it is obvious that the credit rights and interests of the information subject will not be guaranteed.

1. **Errors in Credit Evaluation Result:** When the information source channel is not comprehensive, and the credit evaluation model is not perfect, the credit evaluation result will inevitably be wrong, thus reflecting a false credit status for the information subject, affecting the reliability and authority of the credit products. The main reasons are: (1) Although the information sources of the big data credit investigation agencies are diversified, with a large

amount of data and rapid updating speed, most are based upon behavioral data, network transaction data, social data from the internet. These data sets are riddled with issues, specifically with highly noise, disorderliness and complex cleaning process, and there is also a lack of a sharing mechanism to regulate data collection from the demand side, so the quality is generally low, and the authenticity and accuracy are difficult to verify effectively. (2) The relationship between different types of data and individual credit remains to be studied and verified in the long term. Taking social data as an example, even if Facebook has applied for a patent for credit evaluation, based on social data in the United States, the role of social data in personal credit evaluation is still under significant controversy and resistance at present (Zhang Yun, Xiao Yu & Zhu Nan, 2016). With respect to the enterprise practice, both success and failure cases have appeared in the practice of reducing the default rate by means of the credit investigation of the social data, but there is no consistent result.

2. **Derivative Application of the Error Result:** If the big data credit investigation agencies expand the credit evaluation result to different application scenarios, without the consent of the information subject, especially when the credit evaluation result is not accurate, it will affect the credit rights and interests of the information subject. As the credit evaluation result is an external evaluation based on personal information, it is also a kind of personal information in essence, and its output and use should obtain the consent of the information subject.[4] In practice, the process of credit evaluation and output of the related results of some big data credit investigation agencies are not regulated, leading to the evaluation results being falsely extended to all aspects of social life, without the prior consent of the information subject. For example, credit scores inquiring based on tourism, social contact, car rental, visa and other application scenarios, in essence, has already been a kind of non-compliance behavior. At the same time, if the credit product doesn't correspond to the true credit status and the credit evaluation result is linked to other social services, that is to say, the decision whether to provide these services is based on such credit evaluation result, the information subject may not be able to fairly obtain related social services, which is obviously more harmful to the rights and interests of the information subject.

Lack of Industry Regulation

The application of big data mining technology to the credit investigation industry has steadily risen in recent years. Due to its characteristics of efficiency and concealment, traditional regulation measures may invalidate the credit investigation activities. Given the current absence of the new regulations, the protection of information rights and interests of the information subject is extremely disadvantaged (Li Zhencai, 2016). According to the provisions of *Regulations on Administration of Credit Investigation Industry*,[5] traditional regulation measures may be taken to the credit investigation industry, including on-site inspection, inquiry and explanation; consulting, copying and the sealing of documents and materials and inspecting related information systems. In addition, according to the provisions of the A*dministrative Measures for Credit Investigation Agencies*,[6] the traditional regulation measures may be taken to the credit investigation agencies, including periodic reporting and the security evaluation of the credit information system. Traditional regulation measures cannot effectively regulate big data credit investigation activities, resulting in serious deficiencies in the regulation of personal information, thus making it difficult to regulate the practices of credit investigation agencies in data mining. As a result, the following challenges arise:

1. **The Regulation of Information Processing is not Timely:** The application of big data credit investigation based on new technology shows the characteristic of high efficiency, so it can complete the mining, analysis and processing of personal information in a very short time. The above-mentioned regulation measures, such as on-site inspection and periodic reporting, are the supervisory measure on providing and inquiring information to the basic database of financial credit information, belonging to the examination of the compliance of structured data in traditional credit investigation. Neither can deal with the flexible and changeable information processing procedure in the big data credit investigation in time.
2. **Absence of Regulation in Information Mining:** Big data credit investigation possesses the characteristic of concealment. Essentially by integrating and processing fragmented, scattered and ambiguous data, it is impossible for the information subject to know exactly what data are used or how they are processed. Regulation measures of the inquiring and consulting mentioned above are only formal examination of the personal credit information that has been formed, and the source and formation process of the personal information is not subject to overall regulation. The data mining process of big data credit investigation agencies lacks in proper regulation, which leads to abuse of data mining technology by credit investigation agencies and infringement on the rights and interests of personal information subject.

SOLUTIONS AND RECOMMENDATIONS

The problems associated with the protection of the rights and interests of information subjects arise on behalf of big data credit investigation may be summarized as a mismatch between the big data credit investigation activities and current laws and regulations of China's existing credit investigation business. To improve the construction of big data credit investigation systems, the author discusses the following contents.

Seeking the Balance of the Conflict Between Multiple Values

The protection of the rights and interests of the information subject in big data credit investigation system should be based on the pursuit of dynamic balance between the rights and interests of the information subject and the public interests. If the big data technology is prohibited from being used in credit investigation activities, it will hinder the development of financial science and technology. As a result, legal resources should be allocated fairly and effectively between personal information protection and financial innovation, which will have appropriate social constraints and a moderate space for the application of technology, so as to provide the conceptual foundation for the big data credit investigation legislative activities. The public interests involved in big data credit investigation, such as: government management, public safety, security of the financial market, economic development, and scientific research prediction, should maintain a dynamic balance between the protection of the rights and interests of the information subject (Wang Yong & Wang Pusheng, 2016).

In pursuit of dynamic balance between the rights and interests of the information subject and the public interests, there are two contents worth exploring:

1. **Personal Information Rights and Interests Should be Appropriately Restricted Under Public Interest Demands:** Based upon the personal information collection for the public interests, citizens have the obligation to appropriately alienate the related personal information. To give full play to the social value of the big data, excessively strict norms should be set up to protect the rights and interests of the information subject (Tu Yongqian & Wang Xiaotian, 2017). For example, the information collected for the purposes of national security, security of the financial market, public health, social intervention, criminal offences, scientific research statistics shall be retained, which should be the exception to the protection of the rights and interests of the information subject in nature.

2. **Personal Information Rights and Interests Should be Highly Protected Under Commercial Demands:** To collect and use for commercial purposes, the rights and interests of the information subject and commercial value should be carefully measured. In practice, the collection and use of personal information based on the purpose of corporate profits, such as data collection for market prediction, accurate sales and other purposes, are more likely to infringe upon the rights and interests of the information subject. In particular, in order to pursue profits, some internet platforms already have such behaviors as indiscriminately collecting and selling personal information and snooping on users' privacy to conduct forced marketing, push information, and cheat on users. Therefore, it is necessary to carefully balance the relationship between commercial value and the rights and interests of the information subject (Shi Mingsheng, 2017).

The author proposes that the closed information limits the possibility of producing values. Thus, the faster the information flows, the greater the value will be produced on society. Only by objectively looking at the positive and negative effects brought by the development of the big data credit investigation and reducing the damage of the rights and interests of the personal information subject on the basis of ensuring data security to the greatest extent, we can actively enjoy the achievements brought by the healthy and orderly development of the industry. Therefore, the technology of big data credit investigation itself is not at fault from an objective perspective, so we shouldn't reject it as if we throw away the apple because of its core. The legislative thinking aimed at the orderly big data credit investigation activities should be aimed to clarify the reasonable boundary of the application of the big data credit investigation technology and to seek a dynamic balance between the expansion of the technical utility and the maintenance of the individual basic rights and interests. That is to say; the protection of the rights and interests of the information subject should be reasonably controlled by public interests.

Implementation of the Maintenance of the Rights and Interests of the Information Subject

At present, China does not have a specific law concerning the protection of personal information. To prevent big data credit investigation agencies from illegally obtaining personal information and infringing on their legal rights and interests, the PBOC has in the past enforced it in accordance with the *Regulations on Administration of Credit Investigation Industry*. In the current situation of the big data industry, there are still many challenges associated with the rights and interests of the information subject as mentioned above. The existing laws and regulations concerning the protection of the rights and interests of the information subject are scattered and even contradictory in content, which indicates that the existing legal system can't solve such realistic problems and is even more difficult to adapt to the new situation of the development of the big data (Xie Jun, 2017). At the same time, China has begun to study the *Personal Information Law of the People's Republic of China (draft)* and regards this law as the fundamental law to maintain the rights and interests of the information subject in the future. This chapter suggests that the new law should pursue the dynamic balance between the rights and interests of the information subject and the public interests. On the premise of protecting such rights and interests, it should take full account of the convenience and cost reduction of the operation of the big data credit investigation agencies, and still pay attention to the following matters to make up the current legal loopholes.

1. **Principle of Necessity in Information Collection:** In order to prevent big data credit investigation agencies from over-collecting, the information collection should conform to the "Minimum Adequacy Principle", which requires that personal information should be collected and processed only within the minimum limit within the scope of legal goal (Tu Yongqian & Wang Xiaotian, 2017). Its purpose is to impose restrictive regulations on personal information, so as to restrain the big data credit investigation agencies from infringing personal information by strict procedures and severe ex-post punishment.
    a. Necessity restriction measures have limitations: In order to implement the principle of necessity,[7] it is advisable to legislate to clearly regulate the types, purpose and usage mode of information that can be collected. Secondly, when big data credit investigation agencies collect unnecessary or irrelevant information that is beyond the required scope of credit investigation business, it should legislate to clearly determine the illegality of their behaviors and make them subject to certain sanctions and bear the corresponding liability for damages. The author thinks that the above-mentioned restrictive measures, which focus on protecting the rights and interests of the information subject, may run counter to the trend of collecting, processing and using personal information under the background of the big data, and there is a phenomenon that legal rules can't comply with scientific and technological innovation, so it should be reviewed.
    b. Principle of necessity should be amended: In order to reconcile the conflict between the security of financial market and the principle of necessity of the protection of personal information, under the background of big data, the principle of necessity should be amended. In order to adapt to the trend of the development of big data, once big data credit investigation

agencies use the Data Anonymization Technology, it will separate the information from the real identity of the information subject (Jin Yao, 2017). As the information has already removed the identifiability of the information subject and is no longer recognized as personal information, so it is free from the regulation of personal information law, including the principle of informed consent, principle of limitation of purpose, and principle of necessity (Zhang Chenyuan, 2017). Because of the diversity of the content of the anonymous information, it also contains behavior information and sensitive information. The data that the information subject originally did not wish to have available publicly, such as medical data and transaction data, will be beneficial for the researchers to use for the relevant research after anonymous processing and will bring better benefit and better service for big data credit investigation agencies. This will also be beneficial to the maintenance of the security of the financial market. It can be seen that, in the development process of the big data credit investigation industry, the construction of the legal system of "Data Anonymization" is of great importance (Wang Rong, 2016). The *Network Security Law of the People's Republic of China* has proposed related provisions concerning the data anonymity at present. Any information that is processed by anonymization and cannot be recovered is not applicable to the relevant legal system of personal information protection.[8] However, with the continuous development of technology, the re-identification technology enables anonymous information to be re-identified (Sun Guangzhong, Wei Wei & Xie Xing, 2013). Resulting in temporary anonymity, whereby the characteristics of uncertainty and instability, and the identity of the information subject may be re-discovered at any time. Therefore, at present, Network Security Law requires that anonymous information can't be re-identified, and such strict restriction is no longer of essential significance. As a result, the construction of the law on "Data Anonymization" should focus on the risks caused by anonymous use and re-identification (Han Xuzhi, 2018), such as the usage procedure for anonymous information, review procedure for the purpose of re-identification, and evaluation procedure for the protection of rights and interests of the information subject after re-identification, etc.

2. **Implementation of the Information Subject's Right to Know:** Internet transactions and the Internet of Things make it impossible to hide the subject of information, and the information subject is often asked for information without knowing it. In order to implement the right to control and the right to choose of the information subject on the level of information collection, it is necessary to legislate to specify the protection norms of the information subject's right

to know, so that credit information can be controlled and rationally applied (Tu Yongqian & Wang Xiaotian, 2017).

a. Firstly, according to the different types of personal information (Nelson & Gregory, 2015), different protection norms of the information subject's right to know should be set up (Yao & Jin, 2017).
   i. Personal sensitive information:[9] Collection and use of personal sensitive information should be cautious, giving priority to the protection of the rights and interests of the information subject (Andrew B. Serwin, 2009). Even if the big data credit agencies are faced with the problems of complicated procedures and increased costs, one should obtain the clear authorization of the information subject in writing or other ways, and the specific authorization shall be listed in detail, and the general authorization of the information subject to the credit investigation agencies shall not be obtained by using the format contract clauses at one time. The authorization of the information subject must be fully indicated by the collectors in order to have effective authorization, and big data collecting agencies has the obligation to indicate the content and position of the clause, including the possible consequences. Once it is necessary to collect information beyond the authorized scope of the information subject in a changing situation, the authorization should be obtained again, so that the right to know and the right to choose of the information subject can be protected and personal information can be over-collected due to the unclear scope.
   ii. Personal general information: Collection and use of personal sensitive information should be flexible to reduce the operating cost of big data credit investigation agencies and into account the efficiency of the credit investigation industry. Even if the express consent of the information subject is not obtained in advance, the "Implied Consent" can be obtained in a presumed manner.[10] In the event of a matter that beyond the scope of implied authorization, an additional implied authorization shall be obtained; under the background of the big data credit investigation, such protection mechanism of the right to know may guarantee the basic control ability of the information subject to its own information.
   iii. Bad information: In view of the loosest requirements for bad information,[11] big data credit investigation agencies only need to inform the information subject about "Basic information of the credit investigation agencies, contents of the collected information, users and purposes of the credit information". There is no need to get the

consent of the information subject. Experience from EU legislation shows that the bad information can be collected only with the consent of the information subject. Generally, people choose not to collect bad information to have a better credit evaluation. In the long run, big data credit agencies will eventually find themselves in trouble in the development of the industry.

b. Secondly, in the process of using information, it is also necessary to ensure the information subject's right to know (Zhencai & Li, 2016). In other words, once the information is used by the relevant agencies and it is unfavorable to the information subject, such as making a negative decision on the information subject on the basis of the credit report, the information user shall be responsible for informing the information subject of this situation, the information source and the basic information of the credit report provider.

Perfecting the Regulation of Network Financial Credit Investigation

As mentioned above, traditional regulation measures cannot effectively deal with big data credit investigation activities, thus a new form of regulation for the big data credit investigation model should be constructed, which should not limit the creativity of the market but should prevent risks in advance (People's Bank of China, 2017).

1. **Moderate Regulation Principle:** At present, big data credit investigation is still in its infancy. In order to adapt to the development trend of "Internet + Credit Investigation", it is necessary to create a suitable environment for the development of big data credit investigation industry on the basis of protecting the legal rights and interests of the information subject. In other words, the regulation should be comprehensive and based on the principles of encouraging innovation and focusing on risk, so as to guide the big data credit investigation business to be carried out in an orderly manner and direct big data credit investigation agencies to standardize their own business rules, improve various business operation processes and internal control system.
2. **Quality Regulation of Big Data Credit Investigation Products:** At present, there are many errors and distortion in big data credit investigation products, which may be due to the poor data accuracy caused by operational omissions, modeling technology and mining technology. Therefore, if the design for the quality regulation system of the big data credit investigation can be carried out by means of internal verification, scientific and transparent regulation, dispute

data processing procedures and so on, it may improve the maximum possible accuracy of personal information.

a. In order to protect the rights and interests of the information subject, big data credit investigation agencies should set up an internal verification system to regulate the data collection and analysis scientifically and transparently. That is to say, big data credit investigation agencies should be required to verify the credit investigation data before submitting the data. In order to ensure the correctness of information mining and analysis, big data credit investigation agencies should be required to conduct scientific regulation on the credit investigation data, variables and basic methods used by them, and timely disclose to the information subject.
b. For the disputed credit report, it is necessary to perfect the objection mechanism of the parties. When the information subject questions the accuracy and completeness of his personal information, and the case cannot be confirmed as incorrect after verification, the existing law only requires to record the verification situation and the contents of the objection.[12] It should be explicitly stipulated that big data credit investigation agencies and the objector should conduct joint investigation together, or empower the objector with the right to request the competent authorities to alter the scope of personal information collection prior to determining the accuracy and validity of the information.

3. **Regulation on the Application of Big Data Credit Investigation Products:** In the era of internet big data, with the application of new technologies and new data in the credit investigation industry, the big data credit investigation products have new forms, and the application of these products should be properly regulated (Wang Lin, 2015). Therefore, considerably more big data credit investigation products should be included into the regulatory scope. In other words, risk evaluation of big data credit investigation industry is different from that of traditional credit investigation industry, and the new big data credit investigation products may not fall within the regulation scope of the *Regulations on Administration of Credit Investigation Industry*,[13] so it is not subject to the existing laws. For example, derivative credit investigation products based on credit information including products based on fraud scoring,[14] collection scoring, etc.[15] Although these products don't belong to the credit risk scoring but belong to the operational risk scoring, they still have the substantial impact on the credit of the information subject, ensuring these products are included in the scope of legal regulation (Zhencai & Li, 2016).

FUTURE RESEARCH DIRECTIONS

The combination of big data credit investigation systems and the use of "Blockchain Technology" is the major points of interest for future research. (Mikella Hurley & Julius Adebayo, 2016). Blockchain Technology is a decentralized and shared transaction database, which utilizes the encrypted chain-type block structure and the distributed node consensus algorithm to perform data verification, storage and update (Hua Jie, 2018). Due to the problems of information isolated island and information security in big data credit investigation industry, some scholars began to explore the feasibility of applying blockchain technology to the field of the personal credit investigation; After China proposed the *G20 High-level Principles for Digital Finance Inclusion* at the G20 Hangzhou Summit in 2016, the research began to receive widespread attention and consideration. The current application of blockchain technology in China's big data credit investigation industry is mainly based on the information exchange platform model and the co-construction and sharing information platform mode. The former is cheap to construct but has many disadvantages, while the latter is difficult to implement but has many advantages (Zhang Zhongbin & Liu Yansong, 2017).

At present, the combination of blockchain technology in big data credit investigation system will help to solve the problems of credit information isolated island and information security. Firstly, blockchain distributed storage provides the physical basis for information sharing, and information sharing is an effective solution to the problem of information isolated island, which is more beneficial to alleviate the problem of information asymmetry and reduce the credit risk in the financial system (Wang Qiang, Qing Sude & Ba Jieru, 2017). Secondly, the credit investigation industry, based on its role status, bears the dual responsibility of information sharing and information protection, so its development has to be restricted by this contradiction. The combination of "Blockchain Technology" and "Encryption Algorithm" in the big data credit investigation system will ease the contradiction between information sharing and information protection, and it will be able to maintain personal information security while sharing information (Zhang Xian, Jiang Yuzhao, & Yan Ying, 2017). Even so, there are still many problems in the application of blockchain credit investigation in China, such as blockchain technology conflicts with user's right to be forgotten,[16] traditional credit investigation regulation does not apply to blockchain credit investigation (Zhou Ruijue, 2017), and the loss of private key damages the rights and interests of the information subject (Zhang Cai, 2016). These foregoing problems are topics that should be deeply studied in the future, hoping that it can help to update the technology and the legal system in the future to meet the demands of the future Chinese market.

CONCLUSION

Compared with the traditional credit investigation, the big data credit investigation has greatly improved in efficiency, which is helpful to avoid human interference to prevent moral hazard and solve the problem of information asymmetry in financial market more effectively. Although it contributes to the improvement of financial security, it also poses a greater risk to the rights and interests of the information subject under the current situation of the industry. The main reason is that big data credit investigation does not match with the regulations of China's existing credit investigation business. Therefore, it is necessary for China to revise or formulate special laws and regulations for the existing development and future trend of big data credit investigation industry. The construction of the relevant legal system should protect the rights and interests of the information subject and should take the dynamic balance between the rights and interests of the information subject and the public interests as the basic thinking to harmonically seek personal information protection, financial innovation and financial security, thus enjoying the achievements brought by the healthy and orderly development of the data credit investigation industry. In the future, the combination of the blockchain technology and the big data credit investigation is highly promising, hoping that it can attract more attention and more research can be conducted, and its feasibility also needs to be proved in practice.

REFERENCES

Cai, Z. (2016). Principle, application and suggestion of blockchain technology. *Software, 11*, 51–54.

European Union. (2016). *Regulation (EU) 2016/679 of the European Parliament and of the Council of 27 April 2016 on the protection of natural persons with regard to the processing of personal data and on the free movement of such data, and repealing Directive 95/46/EC (General Data Protection Regulation)*. Retrieved August 13, 2018, from http://eur-lex.europa.eu/legal-content/EN/TXT/?uri=CELEX:32016R0679

Han, X. (2018). Legal Regulation of Anonymous Information in the Age of Big Data. *Journal of Dalian University of Technology, 4*, 64–75. doi:10.100711595-018-1786-z

Harper, J. (2011). *Reputation Under Regulation: The Fair Credit Reporting Act at 40 and Lessons for the Internet Privacy Debate*. Retrieved August 13, 2018, from https://ssrn.com/abstract=2033360

Houser, K. A., & Sanders, D. (2017). The Use of Big Data Analytics by the IRS: Efficient Solutions or the End of Privacy as We Know It? *19 Vand. J. Ent. & Tech., L*, 817.

Hurley, M., & Adebayo, J. (2016). Credit Scoring in the Era of Big Data. *18 Yale J. L. & Tech., 148*, 150–215.

Jaeger, E. (2014). Facebook Messenger: Eroding User Privacy in order to Collect, Analyze, and Sell Your Personal Information. *31 J. Marshall J. Computer & Info., L*, 393.

Jie, H. (2018). The application and legal regulation of blockchain technology and intelligent contracts in the confirmation and transaction of intellectual property rights. *Intellectual Property*, *2*, 14–15.

Jun, X. (2017). The Legal Position of "Privacy" and "Personal Information" in the Network Environment. *Journalism Lover*, *02*, 50–53.

Kim & Just. (2018). Potential Antitrust Risks in the Development and Use of Blockchain. *31 J. Tax'n F. Inst. 5*.

Li, Z. (2016). Regulation thinking of big data credit investigation: Inspiration from the *Fair Credit Reporting Act. Credit Investigation*, *11*, 32–37.

Lin, W. (2015). Research on the application of collection scoring technology in small and micro enterprises of commercial banks in China. *Hainan Finance*, *6*, 33–35.

Liu, X., & Wei, D. (2014). Application and enlightenment of the big data credit investigation: A case study of American internet finance company - ZestFinance. *Tsinghua Financial Review*, *10*, 93–98.

Nelson, G. (2015). *Practical Implications of Sharing Data: A Primer on Data Privacy, Anonymization, and De-Identification.* Retrieved September 25, 2018, from http://support.sas.com/resources/papers/proceedings15/1884-2015.pdf

People's Bank of China. (2017). *Announcement of Information Related to Baihang Credit Co. Ltd. (Under Preparation).* Retrieved August 13, 2018, from http://www.pbc.gov.cn/rmyh/105208/3456248/index.html

People's Bank of China. (2017). *Public Notice on the Relevant Situations of Baixing Credit Information Co., Ltd.* Retrieved September 25, 2018, from http://www.pbc.gov.cn/rmyh/105208/3456248/index.html

Qiang, W., Qing, S., & Ba, J. (2017). Discussion on the application of blockchain in credit investigation industry. *Telecommunications Network Technology*, *5*, 37–41.

Rong, W. (2016). Legal regulation of data anonymization. *Communications Technology*, *4*, 38–44.

Serwin. (2009). Privacy 3.0 - The Principle of Proportionality. *42 U. Mich. J.L. Reform, 869.*

Shi, M. (2017). Research on big data credit investigation and the protection of the rights and interests of the personal information subject. *Credit Investigation*, *5*, 38–43.

Sun, G., & Meng, L. (2017). Research on the application of blockchain technology in the field of personal credit investigation - Based on the perspective of digital inclusive finance. *Corporate Finance Research*, *1*(15), 121.

Sun, G., Shen, W., & Xing, X. (2013). De-anonymization technology and its application in the big data era. *Communications Technology*, *6*, 52–57.

Tong, L. (2016). Design of visual Deep Web collection platform based on Hadoop, *Computer. Engineering and Science*, *2*, 217–223.

Tu, Y., & Wang, X. (2017). Legislative perfection of the protection of the personal credit information in the context of big data. *China Internet*, *5*, 43–53.

Wu, F., & Chen, X. (2017). Legal Protection of Personal Information in Internet Credit: Taking Sesame Credit as an Example. *Internet Finance*, *9*, 11–16.

Xian, Z., Jiang, Y., & Ying, Y. (2017). Overview of blockchain privacy techniques. *Journal of Information Security Research*, *11*, 981–989.

Xinhua News Agency. (2017). *The People's Bank of China: The basic database of financial credit information has collected the information of 926 million natural persons*. Retrieved August 13, 2018, from http://news.xinhuanet.com/fortune/2017-06/20/c_1121179605.htm

Yao, J. (2017). Legal Basis and Norm Reconstruction of De-identification of Personal Information. *Law Review*, *3*, 120–130.

Ye, W. (2015). Operational Models and Regulatory Countermeasures of Big Data Credit Information Agencies—Taking Sesame Credit as an Example. *Internet Finance*, *7*, 60–63.

Yong, W., & Wang, P. (2016). Privacy risks and countermeasures in big data credit investigation. *Studies in Dialectics of Nature*, *7*, 118–122.

Yu, L., & Zheng, C. (2017). Research on Deep Web crawler based on Scrapy. *Design Research and Application*, *7*, 112.

Yun, Z., Yu, X., & Nan, Z. (2016). A preliminary study on the reliability of social data in personal credit investigation. *Shanghai Finance*, *3*, 50–54.

Zhang, C. (2017). Legal regulation on data anonymization processing. *Journal of Chongqing University of Posts and Telecommunications*, *6*, 52–58.

Zhang, Z., & Liu, Y. (2017). Application and Prospect of Blockchain Technology in Credit Investigation Industry. *Credit Investigation*, *7*, 47–49.

Zhou, R. (2017). Research on the legal regulation of blockchain technology. *Journal of Beijing University of Posts and Telecommunications*, *3*, 39–43.

KEY TERMS AND DEFINITIONS

Big Data Credit Investigation Agencies: The credit investigation agencies that collect, sort, store and process structured data and unstructured data on the internet by using big data technology to redesign the model and algorithm of credit investigation and form specific credit products.

Credit Information: Refers to the information produced when the information subject participates in the social economic activities. This information is obtained by the credit investigation agencies from the credit information provider and provided to the information users as the credit level of the information subject after the analysis and processing. If the information refers to personal identification information, account information, association information, public records, and bad records, personal activity information and private information that are unrelated to social and economic activities should be excluded from credit information.

Identification of the Information Subject: Includes direct and indirect identification. Direct identification can point to a specific individual based on the information itself, such as ID number, telephone number, home address, etc. Indirect identifiability refers that it can point to a specific individual after combining the information with other information.

Information Isolated Island: A computer application system whose functions are not related to each other, information is not shared and exchanged, and information is disconnected from business processes and application.

Information Subject's Right to Know: Any civil subject, whose information has been collected by big data credit investigation agencies, has the right to know the collected information as well as the specific contents and forms of credit investigation products produced according to the information.

Minimum Adequacy Principle: Requires that personal information should be collected and processed only within the minimum limit of the legal target.

Personal Information: May contain (1) sensitive personal information relating to personal privacy, which is the personal information consisting of information about racial or moral origins, political views, religious beliefs or other similar beliefs, union affiliation, physical or psychological status, sexual agency or alleged agency relationship of the data objects, or related litigation, etc.; and (2) trivial personal information that does not involve personal privacy, which refers to materials that are clearly not unduly infringed on the right to privacy of the recorded person.

Traditional Credit Investigation Agencies: Combining with the identity verification of the identity authentication center, the credit investigation agencies can provide credit inquiring services to the banking system and personal credit reports to individuals by using the data submitted by commercial banks and other social organizations.

ENDNOTES

1 Credit Investigation Center of People's Bank of China, as a directly-affiliated public institution, is especially responsible for the construction, operation and maintenance of the enterprise and individual credit investigation system (namely the basic database of the financial credit information, also known as the basic database of the credit information of the enterprise and individuals). It regards the bank credit information as the core and also includes public information on social insurance, housing fund, environmental protection, outstanding taxes, the civil adjudication and enforcement, etc.; At the same time, the center has access to various lenders such as commercial banks, rural credit cooperatives, trust companies, finance companies, auto finance companies, small loan companies, etc.; The information inquiry ports of the credit investigation system are spread throughout the country's financial institutions, and its credit information service network covers the whole of China.

2 The China State Council issued the *Outline for the Construction of Social Credit System (2014-2020)* in 2014, hoping to basically build a credit information system covering the whole society based on the sharing of credit information resources by 2020. In 2015, eight institutions were allowed to start their personal credit investigation business.

3 Article 1 of the *Regulations on Administration of Credit Investigation Industry*: The term "Credit Information" as mentioned in this regulation refers to the activities of collecting, sorting, storing, and processing the credit information of enterprises, institutions and other organizations and the credit information of individuals, and providing it to information users.

4 Article 19 of the *Regulations on Administration of Credit Investigation Industry* stipulates that "If the credit investigation agencies or information providers or information users obtain the consent of the information subject by adopting the format contract clauses, it shall make a prompt sufficient to attract the attention of the information subject in the contract and make a clear explanation according to the requirements of the information subject."

Article 20 stipulates that "The information user shall use personal information for the purposes agreed by the personal information subject and shall not use it for any purpose other than those agreed upon and shall not provide it to any third party without the consent of the personal information subject."

5 Article 33 of the *Regulations on Administration of Credit Investigation Industry* stipulates that "The credit investigation industry regulation and administration departments of the state council and its agencies may, in accordance with the laws, administrative regulations and the provisions of the state council, perform the regulation and administration duties on the credit investigation industry and institutions operating the basic databases of the financial credit information, and may adopt the following regulation and administration measures: (1) Go into the credit investigation institutions and institutions operating the basic databases of the financial credit information for on-site inspection, and check the compliance of the institutions providing or inquiring information to the basic databases of financial credit information with the relevant provisions of this regulation; (2) Inquire parties, units and individuals involved in the incident under investigation and ask them to explain the related matter; (3) Consult and copy documents and materials related to the incident under investigation and seal up those documents and materials that may be transferred, destroyed, concealed or altered; (4) Check related information systems."

6 Article 28 of the *Regulations on Administration of Credit Investigation Industry* stipulates that "An individual credit investigation agency shall report to the People's Bank of China on the credit investigation of the previous year at the end of the first quarter of each year, while an enterprise credit investigation agency shall report the credit investigation of the previous year to the record-keeping administrative institutions at the end of the first quarter of each year. The contents of the report shall include credit information collection, development of credit investigation products, credit information service, objection handling, construction of the credit information system and information security guarantee, etc."

Article 29 stipulates that "An individual credit investigation agency shall, in accordance with relevant regulations, submit to the People's Bank of China materials such as statistical statements of credit investigation business, financial and accounting reports, auditing reports and other information. An enterprise credit investigation agency shall, in accordance with relevant regulations, submit to the record-keeping administrative institutions materials such as the statistical statements of credit investigation business, financial and accounting reports, and auditing reports, etc. The credit investigation agency shall be responsible for the authenticity, accuracy and completeness of the reports and materials submitted."

7 In order to implement the principle of necessity, traditionally, the forbidding provisions concerning the collection of credit information to the big data credit investigation agencies will be clearly stipulated at first, such as Article 14 of the *Regulations on Administration of Credit Investigation Industry*:" The credit investigation agencies shall not collect personal religious beliefs, genes, fingerprints, blood types, diseases and medical history, as well as other personal information prohibited by laws and administrative regulations, and the credit investigation agencies shall not collect information on individual income, deposits, securities, commercial insurance, real estate and total amount of paid tax. Unless the credit investigation agencies explicitly inform the information subject of the possible adverse consequences of providing such information, and obtain the written consent of the information subject, such information shall not be collected."

8 Article 42 of the *Network Security Law of the People's Republic of China* which came into force on June 1, 2017, stipulates that "The network operator shall not disclose, alter or damage the personal information it collects; No personal information shall be provided to others without the consent of the person whose information is collected. However, the exception is if the information is unable to identify a specific individual and can't be restored."

9 Information Security Technology Guide for the Protection of Personal Information in Public and Commercial Service Information Systems classifies the personal information into personal sensitive information and personal general information. The personal sensitive information refers to "the personal information which, once exposed or modified, will adversely affect the identified personal information subject. The specific contents of the personal sensitive information in each industry is determined according to the willingness of the personal information subject receiving services and the respective business characteristics. For example, personal sensitive information can include ID number, cell phone number, race, political views, religious belief, gene, and fingerprints, etc."

10 In China's practical experience, many cases of the personal information collection often adopt the implied consent. For example, many mobile App applications can only be used by users by simply clicking the "Next Step". Once a service is used, it is deemed to agree to the information collection clauses.

11 Article 44 of the *Regulations on Administration of Credit Investigation Industry* stipulates that "Bad information refers to information that has a negative impact on the credit status of the information subject. It includes information that the information subject fails to fulfill its obligations under the contract in the activities of borrowing, buying on credit, guaranteeing, leasing, insurance, using credit cards, etc., information on the administrative punishment of the information subject, information on the obligations of the information subject and compulsory execution on the information subject that judged or determined by the people's courts, and other bad information as prescribed by the credit investigation industry regulation and administration departments of the state council."

12 Article 44 of the *Regulations on Administration of Credit Investigation Industry* stipulates that "If the information subject believes that there are errors or omissions in the information collected, stored or provided by the credit investigation agencies, it shall have the right to raise the objection to the credit investigation agencies or the information providers and request them to correct it. If a credit investigation agency or an information provider receives an objection, it shall, in accordance with the provisions of the credit investigation industry regulation and administration departments of the state council, mark the relevant information, verify and deal with the objection, and reply the results to the objector in writing within 20 days after receiving the objection. After verification, if any error or omission is confirmed in the relevant information, the information provider or the credit investigation agency shall correct it; If it is confirmed that there are no errors or omissions, the objection notes shall be cancelled; If it can't be confirmed after verification, the verification situation and contents of the objection shall be recorded."

13 Article 2 of the *Regulations on Administration of Credit Investigation Industry* stipulates that "This regulation shall apply to the credit investigation business and related activities within the territory of China. The term "Credit Investigation Business" as mentioned in this regulation refers to the activities of collecting, sorting, storing, and processing the credit information of enterprises, institutions and other organizations (Hereinafter referred to as "enterprises") and the credit information of individuals, and providing it to information users."

14 The fraud risk scoring model includes:(1) Fraudulent application risk scoring model, which can predict the probability of fraud in credit card application and provide scientific basis for the bank to discover and reject the fraudulent application; (2) Transaction fraud risk scoring model is to use advanced data mining and model technology to predict the probability of fraud in credit card transaction, and provide scientific basis for the bank to discover and reject fraudulent transactions.

15 Due to the small loan amount of the small-sized enterprise and the insufficient pledge for the guarantee, the traditional collection model for the large and medium-sized enterprise brings higher cost and lower efficiency. Therefore, adopting differentiated collection strategy and process for small and micro-sized enterprise with collection scoring technology can realize the refinement and intensification of collection management and effectively improve the effect and efficiency of the collection.

16 Article 16 of the *Regulations on Administration of Credit Investigation Industry* stipulates that "The time limit for the credit investigation agencies to keep bad personal information shall be 5 years from the date of the termination of the bad behavior or the event; If the time limit exceeds 5 years, it shall be deleted."

Chapter 9
The Role of Banks in Renewable Energy Finance:
An Analysis of Turkey

Meryem Filiz Baştürk
Uludag University, Turkey

ABSTRACT

In today's world, global warming and environmental problems resulting from fossil waste have directed economies' attention to renewable energy. Renewable energy has become quite important to developing countries, in particular those that depend on foreign energy sources and confront continuously increasing energy demand since they need renewable energy to be able to achieve their goal of sustainable growth and do this without destructing the environment and by reducing their foreign dependency. Higher costs of renewable energy investment when compared to traditional energy investment affect the investment made in this field, though. The fundamental problem in renewable energy investment is how to finance it as it is not economically rational to invest in sectors with high costs. This chapter explores the role of banks in financing renewable energy by focusing on Turkey.

INTRODUCTION

Global climate change is a common concern today, and the policies on sustainability focus mainly on environmental destruction caused by solid/fossil waste. Although such concerns are global, the problem has another aspect regarding sustainability for developing countries. These countries are generally dependent on foreign energy sources, and this is seen as a big obstacle to realizing the objectives of sustainability.

DOI: 10.4018/978-1-5225-7808-6.ch009

Renewable energy is a way of reducing the foreign dependency of these countries. In addition to helping countries become less dependent, renewable energy stands out as an environmentally-friendly energy type. In this regard, making investment in renewable energy is becoming more and more important especially for the countries that have continuously-increasing energy consumption and that heavily rely on foreign energy sources. This hence leads them to making more investment in renewable energy sources (Buchner, 2018). Besides increasing investment in renewable energy, how to finance this investment is a significant issue since the national renewable energy market of every country has unique features. It is necessary to take these features into consideration while determining the policies. In fact, it is not possible to implement the same finance policy in every country because of the unique features of countries (Brown, et. al., 2012: 21; Hamilton, 2010: 5). In addition to these features, the size and variety of renewable energy sources, the technological infrastructure that they require, and the marketing process also differ. This requires the implementation of an economical finance management that improves economic efficiency both at different stages of a renewable energy policy and for every renewable energy project (Lindlein & Mostert, 2005: 9; IDFC, 2014: 17). This obviously shows that one fundamental problem relating to renewable energy is how to finance it.

Banks are one of the institutions that provide finance for renewable energy. In the financial system, they act as financial intermediaries between the economic units with funding gaps and the ones with fund surplus. This is very common particularly in developing countries in which banking system has a huge share since financial markets in these economies do not have a sufficient depth when compared to developed countries. The loans that the banks provide in developing countries have an important impact on economic growth. Banks inevitably become a main actor in financing renewable energy in an economy where banking system has a decisive role in its financial system. However, it is important not to restrict the banks to commercial banks since national and bilateral/multilateral development banks play an important role in financing renewable energy projects. It is also essential not to ignore the loans provided by the international financial institutions.

The studies on renewable energy draw more attention as there is now more awareness of renewable energy; renewable energy investment is increasing both in Turkey and all around the world, and this investment is likely to increase in the future. The limited number of the studies discussing this issue by focusing on Turkey is the main motivation for writing this paper. In this regard, this study is believed to contribute to the literature. Revealing how renewable energy has been financed in Turkey so far will give a chance to make comparison with the practices in similar countries. Carrying out more studies on the practices in developing countries will help find optimal methods for renewable energy finance in the long term by considering the specific features of every country.

This study firstly discusses the importance of renewable energy and the developments in the renewable energy investment, followed by the presentation of the methods adopted in financing renewable energy. Then it discusses renewable energy market in Turkey in general terms.The study finally examines the renewable energy finance in Turkey and presents a general evaluation.

THE IMPORTANCE OF RENEWABLE ENERGY: TRENDS AND EXPERIENCES

Energy is the main source of economic growth. Without energy, economies cannot achieve their goal of sustainable growth. On the other hand, the environmental destruction casued by solid/fossil fuel leads to global climate change. As a result of the growing concerns about the climate change, Paris Climate Change Agreement (COP21) that introduced legal obligations about climate change was signed in December 2015 by 195 countries[1]. The signatory countries to the agreement confirmed that they would reduce carbon emission, and the global temperature would decrease below 2 degrees Celcius (REN21, 2016: 110-111). This brings about a trade-off. On one hand, economies have to achieve their goal of sustainable growth. On the other hand, they have to do this without leading to a global temperature rise. The solution to this trade-off is renewable energy. The reason why renewable energy emerges as a solution to this trade-off results from its benefits to the economy. The first and possibly the most important benefit is that it ensures the security of energy supply. Renewable energy sources help reduce the dependency on foreign countries by improving the security of energy supply, which is very important for the developing countries that highly depend on energy import. The increase in renewable energy sources in these countries both offer a variety of energy supply and contribute to economic growth by decreasing foreign source dependency. It also enhances the resistance of the economy to the price fulctuations in fossil fuel. Secondly, it reduces climate change since renewable energy sources are clean and environmentally friendly, which is their unique feature when compared to other energy sources. Thirdly, investment in renewable energy projects encourages employment growth as it provides new job opportunities. Fourthly, renewable energy helps provide basic social services to rural areas where there are no national power grids. Finally, there is globally a high level of interest in and awarenes of renewable energy investment. Because of the advantages of renewable energy, most governments have set goals relating to renewable energy and have also started to implement policies to achieve these goals (IDFC, 2014: 3; Kaygusuz, 2007: 79-80; Müller, et al., 2011: 9; Philibert, 2011: 5-9; Kılıç & Aslan, 2017: 2).

It is important to look at the course of renewable energy investment on a global scale to have a general idea about the issue. Figure 1 shows the investment made in renewable energy between 2004 and 2017 under three categories. The reason for having a third category instead of categorizing the countries as developed and devoloping is to show the increase in renewable energy investment in China, India, and Brazil called the "big three". The share of these three countries is higher when compared to other developing countries, but China is the key factor in this. In fact, the investment made by China in renewable energy in 2017 was 126.6 billion $, about 12 times more than that made by India and 21 times more than that made by Brazil. India's investment in renewable energy is 10.9 billion $, while Brazil's is 6.0 billion (UNEP, 2018: 14-15). These countries can sustain the high growth rate they have achieved only if they can meet the increasing energy demand. These countries invest in renewable energy to meet increasing energy demand, ensure the security of energy supply, and do this without giving harm to the environment (Kumar, et al., 2010). As seen in Figure 1, renewable energy investment notably increased both in the countries called the "big three" and in other developing countries between 2004 and 2017. This shows us that the awareness of renewable energy investment has increased in developing countries. After the 2008 financial crisis the investment of developed countries in renewable energy reduced whereas it increased in the developing countries especially thanks to the contribution of the China's in the " "big three" (Hamilton, 2010: 7; Brown, et. al., 2012: 34-36). Another remarkable point that the figure shows is that while the investment made by the developed countries was higher until 2015, this changed in 2015. Since then, developing countries have made more investment in renewable energy than developed countries[2]. 63 percent of the global investment in renewable energy in 2017 belonged to developing countries (UNEP, 2018: 20-21; REN21, 2018: 141).

After this general evaluation, it is also necassary to analyze the investment in renewable energy based on sectors. Figure 2 and Figure 3 show the investment made by the developed and developing countries in renewable energy between 2010 and 2017 based on sectors. The investment made by the developing countries in wind energy in 2010 was 6.5 billion $ more than the amount made by the developed countries. The investment made by the developed countries in solar energy is more, though. It can be seen that although there is not a big difference between developing and developed countries in terms of biomass and waste to energy, biofuels and small hydro, developing countries seem more adventageous (UNEP, 2011: 19). The most notable point in the investment made by the developing and developed countries in renewable energy in 2011 on sectoral basis is the remarkable increase in the investment of developed countries in solar energy. This results from the support made by the developed countries to solar photovoltaic (PV) (Zhang & He, 2013: 394). While the investment in wind energy comes first in developing countries, an

Figure 1. New investment in renewable energy (billion $)
Source: Global Trends in Renewable Energy Investment 2018, (UNEP, 2018).

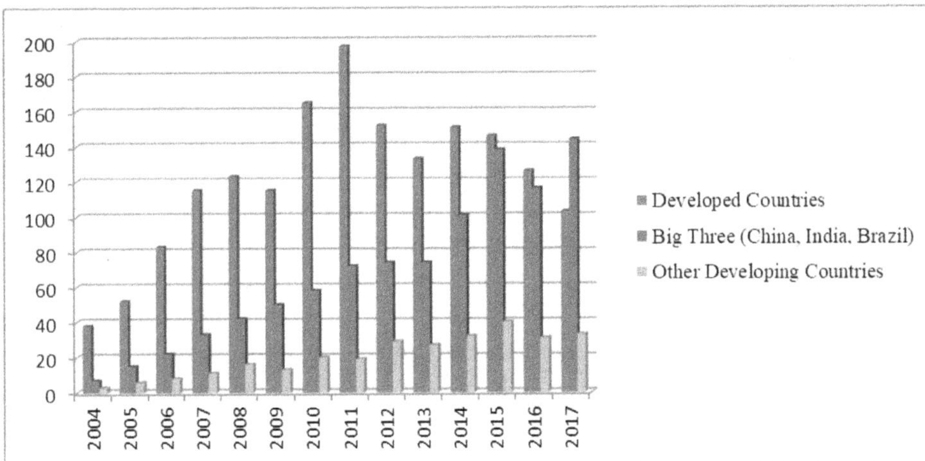

increase in solar investment can also be observed (UNEP, 2012: 21). For 2012, solar investment ranked first both in developed countries and in developing countries, followed by wind energy investment of 35 billion $ for developed countries and 45.3 billion $ for developing countries. Investment in other renewable energy sources is at quite lower levels for both developing and developed countries when compared to the investment in solar energy and wind energy (UNEP, 2013: 21-22). While solar investment ranked first in developed countries for the period of 2013-2015, wind energy investment and solar investment came first in developing countries in 2013 and between 2014 and 2017, respectively. Between 2014 and 2016, geothermal and small hydro investment was higher in developing countries while biomass and waste-to-energy investment ranked first in developed countries (UNEP, 2015: 20-21; UNEP, 2016: 21). In 2017, among renewable energy investment, the solar investment made (115.4 billion $) by the developing countries was far higher than that (45.4 billion $) of developed countries. The biggest contribution to the increase in solar photovoltaic (PV) investment made by developing countries belongs to China, which is a result of the support made by the government since March 2009, particularly between 2011 and 2015. A notable increase in solar photovoltaic investment in developing countries can be observed since 2011 (Zhang, et al., 2017: 867; Zhang & He, 2013: 394). Although the wind investment graphs are very close for both types of countries (for developing countries: 54.8 billion $; for developed countries: 52.4 billion $), developing countries outstripped developed countries (UNEP, 2018: 21). For both developed and developing countries, there is more wind and solar PV investment compared to the investment in other renewable energy sources, which depends on the financial incentives and technology. The decrease in costs as a result of advancing technology also has a decisive role in the increasing renewable energy investment (IRENA, 2014: 88-89; Kalamova, et.al., 2011: 20). While solar energy costs started to decrease after 2008, wind energy costs showed a notable decrease as of mid-1980s (IDFC, 2014: 13). This can be observed in the investment made by the developing countries in wind energy. In the Figures showing the period of 2010-2017, it can be seen that the investment made by developing countries in wind energy is higher that the amount made by developed countried for the whole period.

Renewable energy has become that much important for both developed and developing countries, which is the main motivation for the increasing emprical studies on this issue. Sadorsky (2009) analyzed the relation between renewable energy consumption and income level for eighteen emerging economies, concluding that the increase in income has a positive and statistically significant impact on renewable energy consumption. Apergis and Payne (2010a) explored the causality relationship between economic growth and renewable energy consumption. They carried out this search by using the panel data method for the period of 1992-2007 for thirteen countries within the borders of Eurasia. They found a bilateral relation between renewable energy consumption and economic growth both in the short term and in the long term. Another study by Apergis and Payne (2010b) was on the relation between renewable energy consumption and economic growth for twenty OECD countries for the period of 1985-2005. Similar to the results of their previous study, they found out that there was a bilateral relation between renewable energy consumption and economic growth in the short term and long term. Apergis and Payne (2011) did the same study for six Central American countries for the period

Figure 2. Developed countries renewable investment by sector (billion $)
Source: UNEP, 2011, 2012, 2013, 2014, 2015, 2016, 2017, 2018.

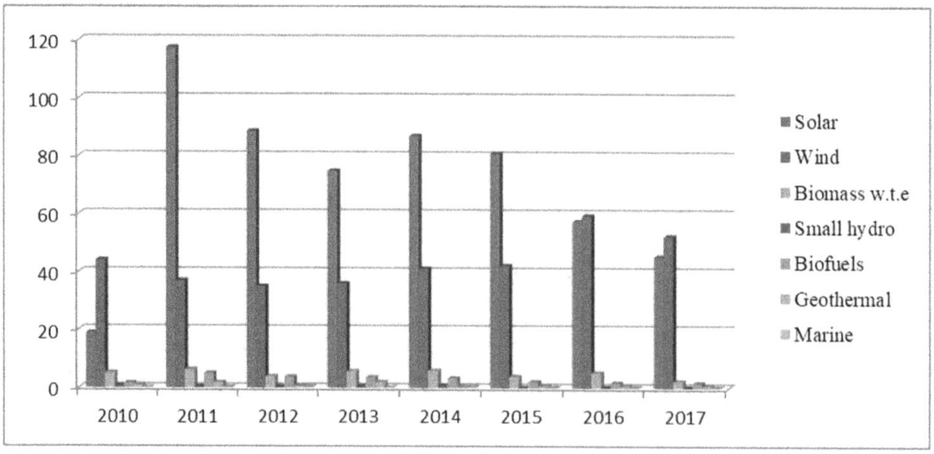

Figure 3. Developing countries renewable investment by sector (billion $)
Source: UNEP, 2011, 2012, 2013, 2014, 2015, 2016, 2017, 2018.

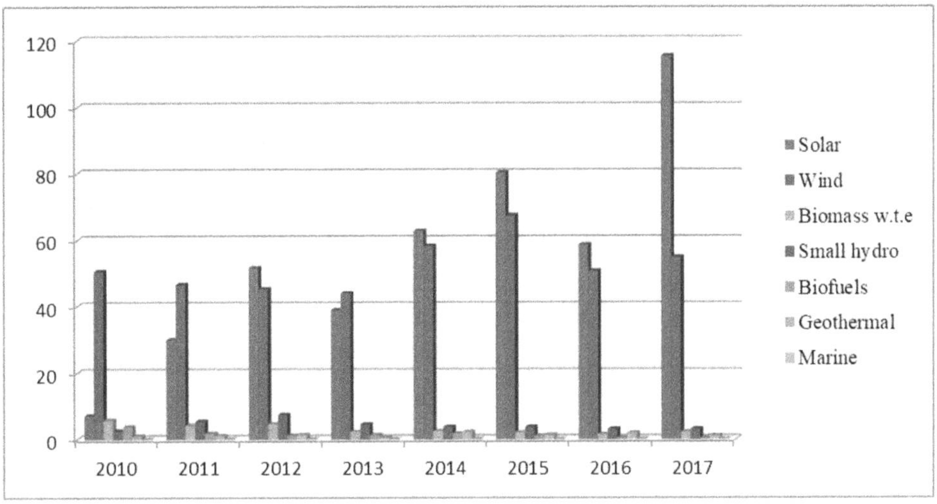

of 1980-2006. They reached the same findings as their two previous studies: there is a two-way relation between renewable energy consumption and economic growth in the short run and the long run. Although Apergis and Payne (2010a, 2010b, 2011) studied different countries for different periods, their studies show that renewable energy has become important to all countries analyzed and has an impact on economic growth. Lin and Moubarak (2014) analyzed the relation between renewable energy consumption and economic growth in China. In their study focusing on the period of 1977-2011, they found a bilateral causal relation between renewable energy consumption and economic growth in the long term. Çınar and Yılmazer (2015) carried out a study for the period of 1990-2013 for the developing countries (Brazil, India, China, Turkey, Mexico, South Africa, Chili, Indonesia) by using the panel data analysis, and they found out that renewable energy sources had a positive effect on growth. Bakırtaş and Çetin (2016) analyzed the relation between renewable energy consumption and economic growth in 18 countries out of G-20 countries for the period of 1992-2010 and found that the increase in real GDP per capita increased renewable energy consumption in the long term. They argued that when the analysis were carried out separately for every single country (Brasil, India, Japan, South Korea, Russia, and the United Kingdom), the increase in real GDP per capita would increase renewable energy consumption per capita in the long term. Kılıç and Aslan (2017) analyzed the impact of renewable and nonrenewable energy on economic growth for 28 OECD countries for the period of 1990-2013. They found out that in all the countries analyzed, renewable energy supported economic growth in the long run.

RENEWABLE ENERGY FINANCE MECHANISM

The common feature of "renewable energy" and "financial sector" is that they both have a rapid technological advancement and play a key role in economy. The fundamental motivation for investors is to increase the returns on their investment. This leads them to being in a search of new investment, and they also want to diversify the fields that they invest in. In this regard, renewable energy that contributes to countries development become more and more attractive for investors (Lindlein & Mosert, 2005: 1). Although there is more and more interest in renewable energy, the financial problems that result from the unique features of renewable energy investment cause some barriers to investors. It is neccassary to briefly mention these costs before moving to finance instruments. Firstly, renewable energy investment includes higher costs in the beginning stages. Secondly, the scale is smaller when compared to traditional investment. Thirdly, renewable energy investment requires long-term finance. Fourthly, renewable energy investment is considered riskier than conventional energy investment by investors (Kandır & Yakar, 2017: 87). Much as technology cost of renewable energy investment has decreased, finance for renewable energy projects is not at satisfactory levels due to market obstacles and high-risk perception (IRENA, 2016: 19).

There are three basic methods for financing the investment made in renewable energy that depends on several factors like the availability of natural resources, technical advancement, financial profitability, and governmental policies. These methods are debt, equity, and grants and subsidies. In addition to them, there is also a type of finance called mezzanine finance that is the combination of bank debt and equity. Different financial sources play a key role in different stages of renewable energy investment (Lam & Law, 2018: 937-938; Kalamova, et al., 2011: 14). This can be seen in the table below.

Table 1. Technology development and sources of finance in the renewable energy sectors

Development Stage	Basic Tecnology Research	Technology Development	Establishing Commercial Viability	Large-scale Deployment
Financial Tools	Public Finance Grants and Subsidies	Venture Capital Public Equity Development Loans Green Bonds Private Equity Corporate Loan Bank Debt		

Source: Kalamova et.al., 2011: 15; Lam & Law, 2018: 940; UNEP, 2018.

Basically, those that develop renewable energy projects find capital from two sources: they can prefer bank loans or they can export equity capital (UNEP, 2009: 3; Lindlein & Mostert, 2005: 17). However, newly-established companies or companies that will invest in a new field have difficulty in accessing to these sources in the early stage. At this phase, the support made by the government or public finance come to the forefront (Hamilton, 2010: 14-15) as the first stage of renewable energy investment -technology research- includes high costs. The stage of technology development is usually financed by venture capital and private equity, though. While venture capital is appropriate for the early phase of technology development, private equity is suitable for the following phase. Venture capital investors demand more yields in return of more risks when compared to private equity investors. During the commercialization stage of the project, low interest rates and loan guarantees play a key role since it is difficult for investors to find capital in the market or find commercial loans at this stage since their projects have not become matture enough (Kalamova, et al., 2011: 29; UNEP, 2009: 6-19; Lam & Law, 2018: 938-39). After the projects become commercially viable, they become a field in which commercial banks can invest since what is important for the banks is to be paid off. Commercial banks abstain from investing in a field that is highly costly in the beginning (Hamilton, 2010: 14-15).

In developing countries, development banks make the projects financially attractive by providing support to projects that are appropriate for commercialization. In this regard, it can be seen in the practices of developing countries that national development banks play an important role in financing renewable energy projects (Lindlein & Mostert, 2005: 52-58). For instance, national development banks in Turkey, Brazil, and Mexico provide funds for several long-term renewable and clean energy projects that cannot find sufficient support from private banks. This is undertaken by state-owned or public sector banks in India. The four biggest state-owned banks in China provide funds for renewable energy projects. Green investment banks were established in some developed countries (USA, United Kingdom) to provide funds for renewable energy projects (Alexander, 2016: 10-14). Also, the loans provided directly by the World Bank, multilateral and bilateral development banks for wide-scale projects and indirectly (via national banks or financial institutions) for small-scale projects are also of great importance (Brown, et al., 2012: 26; Ata, 2012: 105).

In addition to bank loans, borrowing can be in the form of bond issue. In this regard, green bonds draw the most attention. Green bonds are issued by governments, banks, bilateral development banks and multilateral development banks/agencies (Lam & Law, 2018: 938). Green bonds were first issued by the EIB (European Investment Bank) in 2007, and they were then also issued by the World Bank in 2008. These bonds started to be used by international, regional, and national development banks for financing green investment (Griffith-Jones, et al., 2012: 28-30). Figure 4 shows the level of green bonds issue, which started in 2007, for 2007-2017. It can be seen in the Figure that there started a gradual increase in green bonds issue as of 2012. Green bonds issue drawing the attention of more and more investors was 95.1 billion $ in 2016 (REN21, 2017: 117). The green bonds issue increased by 67 percent in 2017, reaching 163.1 billion $ (REN21, 2018: 147). It is thought that green bonds issue that has increased particularly in recent years is likely to continue in the following years.

To sum up, it is essential to draw the attention of private sector to this field so that investment in renewable energy can increase. However, this highly depends on whether or not the private sector finds renewable energy as profitable. In this regard, it is necessary to remove the constraints on private sector investment and introduce incentives appealing to the private sector. Public finance plays an important role in this process (IRENA, 2016: 19-27). Besides, the support provided by the national and bilateral development banks and multilateral international institutions particularly to the renewable energy projects in developing countries is notable. The recent increase observed in the green bond issue- a highly new tool- underlines a good chance that it will be of high importance in the following years. Also, it is thought that the share of institutional investors- making up a big part of the private sector- (pension funds, insurance companies, endowments and sovereign wealth funds) in renewable energy investment will increase (IRENA, 2016: 24-25).

Figure 4. Total green bonds in the world (billion $)
Source: Global Trends in Renewable Energy Investment 2018, (UNEP, 2018).

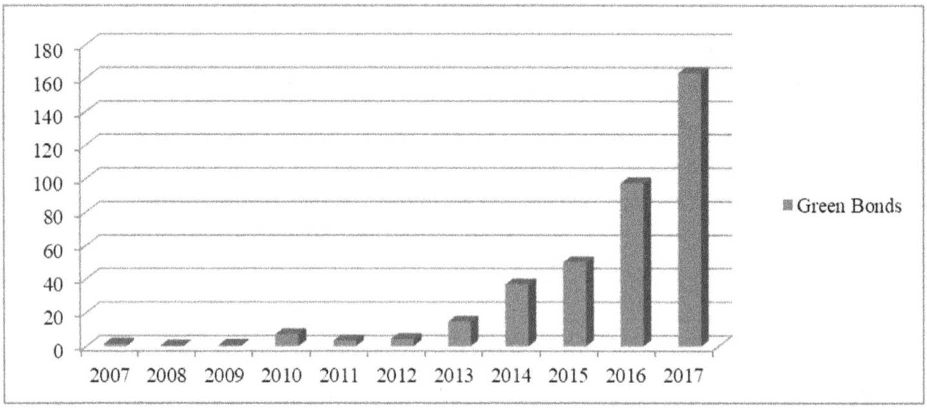

RENEWABLE ENERGY IN TURKEY

To have a sustainable economic growth, Turkey is trying to meet its increasing energy demand on the one hand and to ensure the security of energy supply by reducing its dependency on foreign energy sources on the other hand. Within this context, the reason why renewable energy investment is becoming more and more important in Turkey is its continuously increasing need for energy and its dependency on foreign sources to meet this need. It can also be claimed that global awareness of environmental problems also has an impact on attaching more importance to renewable energy investment. When the fact that the demand for energy in Turkey will increase in the future is taken into consideration, the need for renewable energy seems obvious. The importance of this issue was also emphasized in the National Renewable Energy Action Plan (NREAP) (2014: 10-22) and some specific goals were set. Turkey's renewable energy targets for 2023 are to increase the share of renewable energy in general energy consumption to 20%, meet at least 30% of total electrical energy demand and 10% of transportation sector by renewable energy.

Turkey is among the OECD countries with the fastest-growing energy demand and has the highest increase in energy demand after China (Karagöl et al., 2016: 6). In fact, when the trend of primary energy consumption in Turkey by years is analyzed, it can be observed that domestic and renewable energy sources need to be increased. As can be seen in Figure 5, primary energy consumption has increased by years. While the primary energy consumption was 100.4 million tonnes of oil equivalent (mtoe) in 2007, it increased to 157.7 mtoe in 2017 (BP, 2018). This upward trend is likely to continue in the future. The main problem is that the share of imported energy consumption in primary energy consumption is quite high, and this makes Turkey dependent on foreign energy sources. Cyclical fluctuations in particular both affect Turkish economy adversely and endanger the security of its energy supply (Simsek & Simsek, 2013, 521-22). In this regard, National Energy Efficiency Action Plan (NEEAP 2017-2023) was prepared by the Ministry of Energy and Natural Sources. This action plan includes steps to achieve national targets on energy efficiency. According to the plan, the goal is to increase domestic and renewable energy consumption. The target for 2017-2023 period is to decrease Turkey's primary energy consumption by almost 23.9 million tonnes of oil equivalent (or by about 14%).

The Law on the use of renewable energy sources in Turkey (Renewable Energy Law, REL, Law No.5346) was put into effect in 2005. Renewable energy investment remained at an unsatisfactory level until 2010 because of the relatively low feed-in tariff levels and lack of secondary legislation. Some amendments relating to higher feed-in tariff levels for some sources and monetary or non-monetary incentives were introduced to the Renewable Energy Law in December 2010. The revision to

Figure 5. Primary energy consumption in Turkey (millon tonnes of oil equivalent)
Source: BP Statistical Review of World Energy 2018.

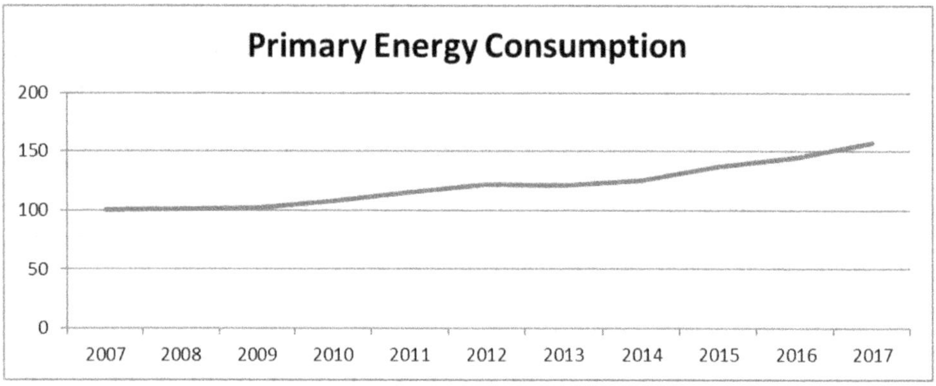

feed-in tariff levels in particular led to an increase in investors interest in renewable energy and helped the sector gain momentum (MENR, 2014: 11). As a result, the total installed power in renewable energy increased from 15.5 (gigawatts) GW in 2009 to 34.2 GW in 2016, an increase of more than two times (Karagöl & Kavas, 2017: 18). The total capacity is aimed at reaching 61 gigawatts (GW) by 2023 (IEA, 2016: 169). To achieve these goals, the investment in renewable energy has increased particularly in recent years. The investment increased from 1.9 billion $ in 2015 to 2.2 billion $ in 2017. When the renewable energy investment made by 10 European countries in 2017 is analyzed, it is seen that Turkey ranks fifth (UNEP, 2018: 25; Karagöl & Kavas, 2017: 19).

Figure 6. Renewable energy investment in Europe
Source: Global Trends in RenewableEnergy Investment 2018, (UNEP, 2018).

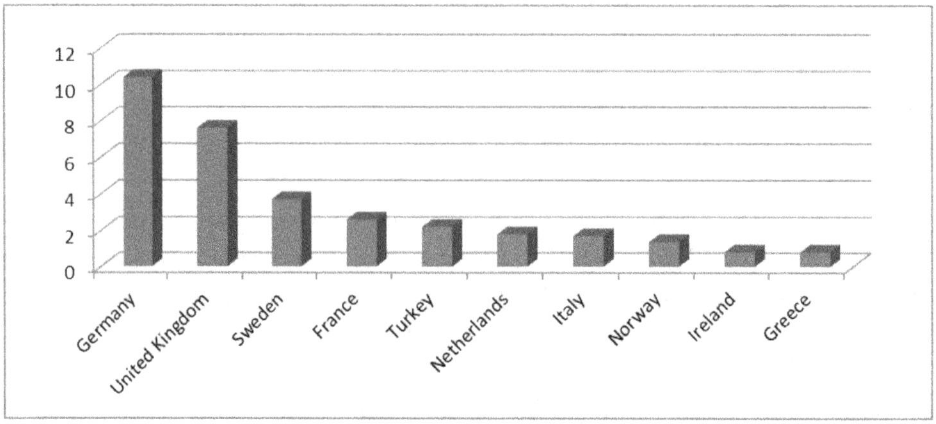

Although the investment in renewable energy has increased, the share of renewable energy consumption is still at low levels despite the increase by years. Figure 7 compares Turkey's renewable energy consumption with that of the "big three" of China, India, and Brazil between 2007 and 2017. Although there is not a big difference among them in 2007, it gets bigger by 2017, with China going well ahead and Turkey having the lowest renewable energy consumption.

Figure 7 does not include hydroelectricity consumption. When compared to other renewable energy sources, hydroelectricity is used the most in electricity generation both in the world and in Turkey (Karagöl & Kavas, 2017: 20). Hydroelectricity consumption in Turkey is also at lower levels than that in the "big three".

Figure 7. Renewable energy consumption in turkey and in the "big three" countries[3]
Source: BP Statistical Review of World Energy 2018.

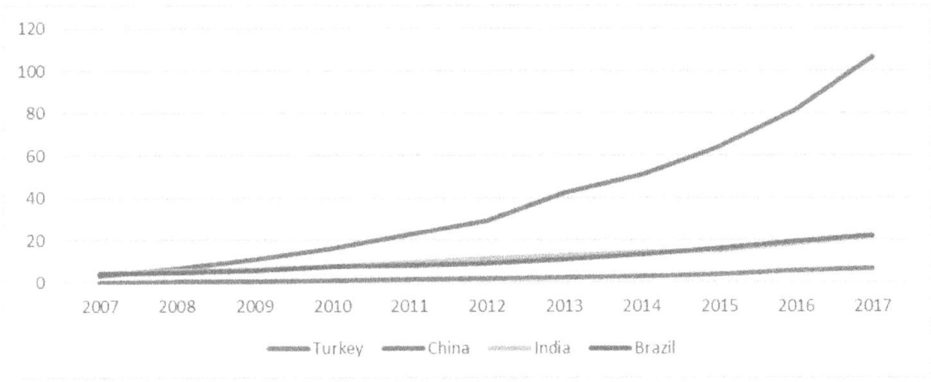

Figure 8. Hydroelectricity consumption in Turkey and in the "big three" countries[4]
Source: BP Statistical Review of World Energy 2018.

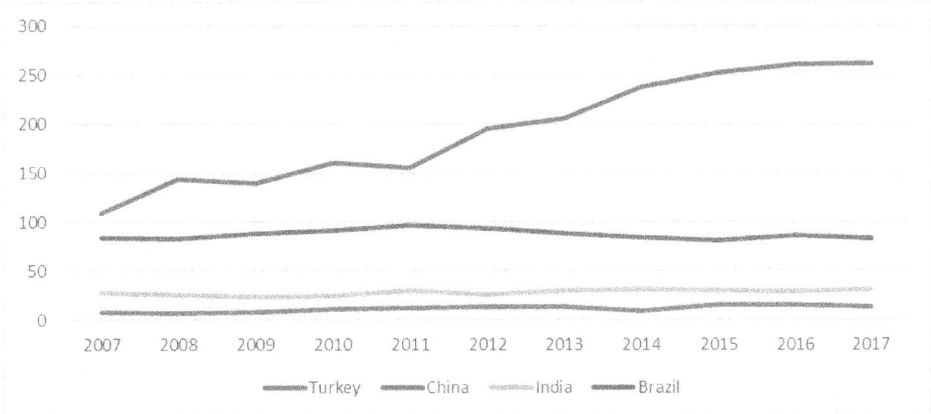

Turkey has a high potential of hydro, wind, solar, and geothermal energy thanks to its convenient geographical location and favourable climatic conditions (IEA, 2016: 21-22). Despite its high potention for renewable energy generation, it can not be argued that Turkey benefits from this potential enough due to some factors primarily like the high costs. Since the initial investment requires advanced technology, it causes high costs. Apart from the costs, another obstacle to renewable energy investment is lack of financial sources (Simsek & Simsek, 2013: 529; Karagül & Kavas, 2017: 27-30). Renewable energy consumption in Turkey is hence lower when compared to emerging market economies with high energy demand. However, the goals set by the government relating to renewable energy for 2023, the support provided, the increase in investment year by year, high social awareness of renewable energy are all promising.

RENEWABLE ENERGY FINANCE IN TURKEY: THE ROLE OF BANKS

Banks play a key role in Turkish financial system. Therefore, they become one of the financial intermediaries to finance renewable energy. Similar to the practices in other developing countries, national development banks play a significant role in financing renewable energy. Also, the loans provided by bilateral and multilateral development banks and international funds is the key to financing renewable energy in Turkey. The private sector is provided loans through intermediary banks or financial institutions (Ata, 2012: 105-106).

Industrial Development Bank of Turkey (TSKB) has a leading role in financing renewable energy projects in Turkey. TSKB has been supporting renewable energy projects since the early 2000s by raising funds from the institutions like the World Bank, European Investment Bank (EIB), Agency of French Development (AFD), German Development Bank (KfW), European Bank for Reconstruction and Development (EBRD) (TSKB, 2017: 32). The number of renewable energy projects financed by TSKB since 2002 increased to 245 by the end of 2017. The total amount of investment in renewable energy projects was 9.6 billion $ between 2003 and 2017, and 4.1 billion $ of this amount was provided by TSKB. It can be seen that almost half of the financial support to renewable energy projects was provided by TSKB (TSKB, 2018: 66), which clearly shows the importance attached by TSKB to sustainability and environmental awereness[5]. It was also the Industrial Development Bank of Turkey that issued the first green/sustainable bonds in 2016. Under the coordination of 7 banks, five-year term green bonds of 300 million $ was issued to the international market (Bitlis, 2016; Kandır& Yakar, 2017: 100). Green bonds are used in financing green investment projects. Green/sustainable bonds issued by

TSKB have an aspect of sustainability besides having the features of green bonds. In this regard, the purpose was to support both the green projects and the projects with social benefits (TSKB, 2017: 99). Finally, "Subordinated Sustainable Bond" was issued by TSKB in March 2017, which was a first within this context. The purpose was to support environmental projects like renewable energy and social projects with a ten-year term bond of 300 million $ (TSKB, 2018: 71).

The loans provided by the commercial banks in Turkey for renewable energy investment are generally the funds raised from the international financial institutions. In this regard, it is necessary to focus on two programs initiated in Turkey by the European Bank for Reconstruction and Development (EBRD). The first one is "Turkey Sustainable Energy Financing Facility" (TurSEFF), and the second one is "Turkey Mid-Size Sustainable Energy Financing Facility" (MidSEFF).

"Turkey Sustainable Energy Financing Facility" was initiated on July 14, 2010 by the European Bank for Reconstruction and Development (EBRD) with the support of the Clean Technology Fund and European Union. The program was developed for the energy efficiency of small and medium sized enterprices (SMEs) and for renewable energy investment. The loans provided by ERBD are granted to the investors via the following common banks (Akbank, Deniz Bank, Garanti Bank, Türkiye İş Bankası, Vakıf Bank, Yapı Kredi). The loans provided by TurSEFF and their upper limits are shown in the table below. Since its establishment, TurSEFF has provided 538 million Euro to 1006 projects (TurSEFF, 2018; EBRD, N.A.).

"Mid-Size Sustainable Energy Financing Facility" (MidSEFF) supported by the European Investment Bank (EIB) and the EuropeanUnion (EU) was also implemented in 2011 by the European Bank for Reconstruction and Development (EBRD). MidSEFF has granted loans of 1 billion Euro for mid-sized investment projects for renewable energy, energy efficiency, and waste-to-energy via the following Turkish

Table 2. The loans provided by TurSEFF

The Category of Loans		Upper limit for Loans
Energy Efficiency Loans	Small-sized energy efficiency Loans	Up to 250.000 Euro
	Medium-sized energy efficiency Loans	> 250.000 – 5 million Euro
Energy Efficiency Loans for Commercial Buildings		Up to 5 million Euro
Renewable Energy Efficiency Loans		Up to 5 million Euro
Supplier's Loans		Up to 1 million Euro
Supplier's Credit		Up to 5 million Euro

Source: EBRD (N.A.)

banks (Akbank, Denizbank, Finansbank, Garanti, Türkiye İş Bankası, Vakıfbank, Yapı Kredi) (MidSEFF, 2018).

In addition to the programs introduced, the commercial banks interest in renewable energy investment is increasing day by day in Turkey, which is consistent with the global trend. For instance, Garanti Bank declared its "Climate Change Action Plan" in late 2015, committing that it would make 60% of its energy investment in renewable energy. Garanti Bank revised its commitment in 2016 to minimum 70% renewable energy investments will be within new energy invetments by 2020. Garanti Bank supports wind power projects in particular and was the leader in 2017 in terms of the investment made in this field with a market share of 30.2% (Garanti Bankası, 2018a: 66-100). Other renewable energy sectors are also supported by the Bank[6]. Solar energy loans can be given as an example to this. Garanti Bank supports solar energy and unlicenced electricity generation projects of 1 MW (megawatt) and below 1MW through its loan called "Solar Energy Loans" (Garanti Bankası, 2018b). Türkiye İş Bankası (İşbank) provides loans called "Unlicenced Electricity Generation Loans" to the companies that would like to generate electricity of 1 MW and below 1 MW from renewable energy sources (Türkiye İş Bankası, 2018). A similar type of loan called "Credit Package for SMEs" provided by Halkbank. The purpose was to support the renewable energy projects (the installation power of which is up to 1MW) of SMEs that generate electricity from solar and wind energy sources. Another renewable energy loan provided by the Bank was "Green Energy Loan", whose purpose was to make electricity and heat energy generation from biomass energy sources common (Halkbank, 2018a). Halkbank granted loans of 171.25 million TL to 49 renewable energy projects in 2017 with the funds raised from the international financial institutions like the Agency of French Development (AFD) and European Investment Bank (Halkbank, 2018b: 42).

The role of banks in Turkey in renewable energy finance can be exemplified with a few case studies. For instance, a long-term (fifteen-year term) financing package of 720 million $ was provided to Efeler Geothermal Project that belongs to Güriş Holding in Germencik, Aydın (a province in the Aegean Region of the country) by EBRD in 2015 (TSKB, 2016). In this regard, a financial support of 200 million $ was provided to the Project by EBRD. For the Project, a loan of 325 million $, 130 million $, and 65 million $ was provided by Türkiye İş Bankası, TSKB, Black Sea Trade and Development (BSTDB) respectively (Rosca, 2015a). Wits its 232.3 MW power, Efeler geothermal plant is the biggest plant in Turkey and the second biggest one in Europe (Tenva, 2015). Another example is Kızıldere III geothermal power plant, which belongs to Zorlu Energy. For financing the second unit of Kızıldere III geothermal power, having 65,5 MW power, a loan contract of 190 million $ was signed with EBDR, Akbank, Türkiye İş Bankası, TSKB. This was a thirteen-year term loan, two-year of which was nonrecourse loan (Zorlu Energy, 2017:17). Enerjisa

Bares wind power plant in Balıkesir 2012 and Rotor wind plant in Osmaniye 2009 can be given as examples of two biggest energy plants in Turkey for which direct finance is provided by EBRD (Rosca, 2015b).

CONCLUSION

Economies need energy to be able to achieve their growth targets. Energy generated from solid/fossil fuel causes global climate change, environmental destruction, and greenhouse gas emissions, though. To overcome these problems, economies have directed their attention to renewable energy. Renewable energy stands out as the greatest choice since it reduces the dependency of countries on foreign sources, particularly solid/fossil fuel as well as being environmentally-friendly. Besides its importance, renewable energy thus becomes a prior target for the countries that face continuously increasing energy demand and that are dependent on foreign energy sources to fullfil this demand. The countries that have recently made investment in renewable energy the most are hence those whose energy demand is continuously increasing (China, India, and Brazil in particular). Besides the growing interest in renewable energy investment, how to finance this investment stands out as a quite important issue since the structure and depth of countries financial systems differ from one another. Also, renewable energy market of every country is unique. Hence, it is neccassary to determine the policies to be implemented by considering all these differences. Higher initial costs of renewable energy investment when compared to traditional energy investment also affect the decisions of potential investors. In this regard, one fundamental problem faced in renewable energy investment is how to finance it.

The underlying reason for attaching more importance to renewable energy in Turkey is its increasing need for energy and its dependency on foreign sources to meet this need. Renewable energy investment seems as a solution to ensure the security of energy supply by reducing its foreign-dependency. It is difficult in countries like Turkey to raise fund for energy and development projects. When there is insufficient capital accumulation or lack of financial depth, banking system gains importance as a powerful actor in the financial system. Banks but particularly national development banks play an important role in financing renewable energy in Turkey. The loans that commercial banks get from multilateral development banks or international financial institutions also have a big share. To illustrate, TurSEFF and MidSEFF programs initiated in Turkey by the European Bank for Reconstruction and Development (EBRD) within this context have provided finance to various renewable energy investment. In addition to these programs, banks in Turkey have preferred to extend their portfolio of renewable energy investment in line with the global awareness of renewable energy. For example, Garanti Bank committed itself to increasing the share of its renewable energy investment in new energy investment to minimum 70% by 2020.

With these sources, the target is to increase the share of renewable energy in total energy consumption to one third by the mid-2020s. This target is important to have a sustainable development in Turkey. The goal of sustainable growth in developing countries should be closely monitored. In addition, the sustainable energy policies of Turkey have a different importance on a global scale since Turkey has one of the highest upward trends in energy demand in the world. The effort to meet the increasing energy demand with renewable energy sources is a policy that needs to be seen valuable in terms of global environmental problems.

REFERENCES

Alexander, K. (2016). *Greening banking policy*. Retrieved April 10, 2018, from http://unepinquiry.org/wp-content/uploads/2016/09/10_Greening_Banking_Policy.pdf

Apergis, N., & Payne, J. E. (2010a). Renewable energy consumption and growth in Eurasia. *Energy Economics*, *32*(6), 1392–1397. doi:10.1016/j.eneco.2010.06.001

Apergis, N., & Payne, J. E. (2010b). Renewable energy consumption and economic growth: Evidence from a panel of OECD countries. *Energy Policy*, *38*(1), 656–660. doi:10.1016/j.enpol.2009.09.002

Apergis, N., & Payne, J. E. (2011). The renewable energy consumption–growth nexus in Central America. *Applied Energy*, *88*(1), 343–347. doi:10.1016/j.apenergy.2010.07.013

Ata, S. U. (2013). Sürdürülebilir enerjinin finansmanı [Financing of Sustainable Energy]. In Türkiye'de İklim Değişikliği ve Sürdürülebilir Enerji [Climate Change and Sustainable Energy in Turkey]. İstanbul: ENİVA- Enerji ve İklim Değişikliği Vakfı.

Bakırtaş, İ., & Çetin, M. A. (2016). Yenilenebilir enerji tüketimi ile ekonoik büyüme arasındaki ilişki: G-20 Ülkeleri. *Sosyoekonomi*, *24*(28), 131–145. doi:10.17233e.43089

Bitlis, M. (2016). Green bonds. *Escarus Blog*. Retrieved April 15, 2018, from http://www.escarus.com/green-bonds

BP. (2018). *BP Statistical Review of World Energy*. Retrieved June 25, 2018, from https://www.bp.com/content/dam/bp/en/corporate/pdf/energy-economics/statistical-review/bp-stats-review-2018-full-report.pdf

Brown, J., Makinson, S., & Magallon, D. (2012). *Financial mechanisms and investment frameworks for renewables in developing countries*. International Renewable Energy Agency (IRENA), Retrieved April 15, 2018, from http://www.irena.org/publications/2013/Jan/Financial-Mechanisms-and-Investment-Frameworks-for-Renewables-in-Developing-Countries

Buchner, B. (2018). *Global landscape of renewable energy finance*. International Renewable Energy Agency (IRENA). Retrieved April 15, 2018, from https://www.irena.org//media/Files/IRENA/Agency/Publication/2018/Jan/IRENA_Global_landscape_RE_finance_2018.pdf

Çınar, S., & Yılmazer, M. (2015). Yenilenebilir enerji kaynaklarının belirleyicileri ve ekonomik büyüme ilişkisi: Gelişmekte olan ülkeler örneği. *Dokuz Eylül Üniversitesi İktisadi ve İdari Bilimler Fakültesi Dergisi*, *30*(1), 55–78.

EBRD. (n.d.). *Türkiye Sürdürülebilir Finansman Programı*. Retrieved February 12, 2018, from https://www.ika.org.tr/upload/duyurular/Turkiye-Surdurulebilir-Enerji-Programi-aciklanmistir-526300.pdf

Garanti Bankası. (2018a). *Garanti Bankası 2017 Entegre Faaliyet Raporu*. Retrieved June 24, 2018, from https://surdurulebilirlik.garanti.com.tr/media/1233/garanti-bankasi-2017-entegre-faaliyet-raporu.pdf

Garanti Bankası. (2018b). Retrieved from https://www.garanti.com.tr/tr

Griffith-Jones, S., Ocampo, J. A., & Spratt, S. (2012). *Financing renewable energy in developing countries: Mechanisms and responsibilities*. European Report on Development. Retrieved March 5, 2018, from http://policydialogue.org/files/publications/Financing_Renewable_Energy_in_Developing_Countries.pdf

Halkbank. (2018a). Retrieved from https://www.halkbank.com.tr/

Halkbank. (2018b). *Sürdürülebilirlik Raporu 2017*. Retrieved June 24, 2018, from https://mediaservice.halkbank.com.tr/media/document/Halkbank/Biz/Surdurulebilirlik/raporlarveetkinlikler/Halkbanksrtr2017.pdf

Hamilton, K. (2010). *Scaling up renewable energy in developing countries: Finance and investment perspectives*. Energy, Environment & Resource Governance Programme Paper 02/10. Retrieved March 15, 2018, from http://www.chathamhouse.org/sites/default/files/public/Research/Energy,%20Environment%20and%20Development/0410pp_hamilton.pdf

IDFC. (2014). *Scaling up renewable energy investments*. Retrieved March 15, 2018, from https://www.idfc.org/Downloads/Publications/02_other_idfc-expert_documents/IDFC_Sustainable_Infrastructure_Paper_01-12-14.pdf

IEA. (2016). *Energy policies of IEA countries Turkey 2016 review*. Retrieved January 25, 2018, from https://www.iea.org/publications/freepublications/publication/EnergyPoliciesofIEACountriesTurkey.pdf

IRENA. (2014). *REmap 2030: A renewable energy roadmap*. Retrieved January 25, 2018, from http://www.irena.org/-/media/Files/IRENA/Agency/Publication/2014/IRENA_REmap_Report_June_2014.pdf

IRENA. (2016). *Unlocking renewable energy investment: The role of risk mitigation and structured finance*. Retrieved January 25, 2018, from https://www.res4med.org/wp-content/uploads/2017/11/IRENA_Risk_Mitigation_and_Structured_Finance_2016.pdf

Kalamova, M., Kaminker, C., & Johnstone, N. (2011). *Sources of finance, investment policies and plant entry in the renewable energy sector*. OECD Environment Working Papers, No.37. OECD Publishing. doi:10.1787/5kg70680l1hb-en

Kandır, S. Y., & Yakar, S. (2017). Yenilenebilir enerji yatırımları için yeni bir finansal araç: Yeşil tahviller. *Maliye Dergisi*, *172*, 85–110.

Karagöl, E. T., & Kavaz, İ. (2017). *Dünyada ve Türkiye'de yenilenebilir enerji* [Renewable Energy in the World and Turkey]. SETA. Retrieved April 4, 2018, from https://setav.org/assets/uploads/2017/04/YenilenebilirEnerji.pdf

Karagöl, E. T., Kaya, S., & Koç, Y. E. (2016). *2016'da Enerji* [Energy in 2016]. SETA. Retrieved April 4, 2018, from https://www.setav.org/2016da-enerji/

Kaygusuz, K. (2007). Energy for sustainable development: Key issues and challenges. *Energy Sources. Part B, Economics, Planning, and Policy*, *2*(1), 73–83. doi:10.1080/15567240500402560

Kılıç, R., & Aslan, V. (2017). Yenilenebilen ve yenilenemeyen enerjinin iktisadi büyüme üzerindeki etkisi: 28 OECD ülkesi üzerine ampirik bir çalışma. *Eskişehir Osmangazi Üniversitesi İİBF Dergisi*, *12*(1), 1–12.

Kumar, A., Kumar, K., Kaushik, N., Sharma, S., & Mishra, S. (2010). Renewable energy in India: Current status and future potentials. *Renewable & Sustainable Energy Reviews*, *14*(8), 2434–2442. doi:10.1016/j.rser.2010.04.003

Lam, P., & Law, A. (2018). Financing for renewable energy projects: A decision guide by developmental stages with case studies. *Renewable & Sustainable Energy Reviews*, *90*, 937–944. doi:10.1016/j.rser.2018.03.083

Lin, B., & Moubarak, M. (2014). Renewable energy consumption – economic growth nexus for China. *Renewable & Sustainable Energy Reviews*, *40*, 111–117. doi:10.1016/j.rser.2014.07.128

Lindlein, P., & Mostert, W. (2005). *Financing renewable energy: Instruments, strategies, practice approaches.* KfW Discussion Paper. Retrieved January 14, 2018, from http://docplayer.net/76204320-Financing-renewable-energy.html

MENR. (2014). *National renewable energy action plan for Turkey*. Retrieved April 24, 2018, from http://www.ebrd.com/documents/comms-and-bis/turkey-national-renewable-energy-action-plan.pdf

MENR. (2018). *National energy efficiency action plan (NEEAP) 2017-2013*. Retrieved May 24, 2018, from http://www.yegm.gov.tr/document/20180102M1_2018_eng.pdf

MIDSEFF. (2018). Retrieved from http://www.midseff.com/

Müller, S., Brown, A., & Ölz, S. (2011). *Renewable energy policy considerations for deploying renewables.* Information Paper. IEA. Retrieved April 4, 2018, from https://www.iea.org/publications/freepublications/publication/Renew_Policies.pdf

Philibert, C. (2011). *Interactions of policies for renewable energy and climate.* Working Paper. IEA. Retrieved March 10, 2018, from https://www.oecd-ilibrary.org/docserver/5kggc12rmkzq-en.pdf?expires=1527756748&id=id&accname=guest&checksum=E7B1DF8C7058B42939CD1A5A11B1ACC9

REN-21. (2016). *Renewables – Global Status Report: 2016.* Retrieved June 4, 2017, from http://www.ren21.net/wp-content/uploads/2016/05/GSR_2016_Full_Report_lowres.pdf

REN-21. (2017). *Renewables – Global Status Report: 2017.* Retrieved April 28, 2018, from http://www.ren21.net/wp-content/uploads/2017/06/17-8399_GSR_2017_Full_Report_0621_Opt.pdf

REN-21. (2018). *Renewables – Global Status Report: 2018.* Retrieved September 28, 2018, from http://www.ren21.net/wp-content/uploads/2018/06/17-8652_GSR2018_FullReport_web_final_.pdf

Rosca, O. (2015a). *EBRD co-finances Turkey's largest geothermal power plant.* Retrieved July 18, 2018, from https://www.ebrd.com/news/2015/ebrd-cofinances-turkeys-largest-geothermal-power-plant-.html

Rosca, O. (2015b). *EBRD supports Turkey's shift to renewable energy.* Retrieved July 18, 2018, from https://www.ebrd.com/news/2015/ebrd-supports-turkeys-shift-to-renewable-energy.html

Sadorsky, P. (2009). Renewable energy consumption and income in emerging economies. *Energy Policy, 37*(10), 4021–4028. doi:10.1016/j.enpol.2009.05.003

Simsek, H. A., & Simsek, N. (2013). Recent incentives for renewable energy in Turkey. *Energy Policy, 63*, 521–530. doi:10.1016/j.enpol.2013.08.036

TENVA. (2015). *Turkey's Biggest Geothermal Power Plant "Efeler GPP" Opened.* Retrieved June 11, from http://www.tenva.org/en/turkiyenin-en-buyuk-jeotermal-santrali-efeler-jes-acildi/

TSKB. (2016). *Project Finance, III.* GGDP Roundtable, Reykjavik. Retrieved July 18, 2018, from https://www.esmap.org/sites/esmap.org/files/DocumentLibrary/TSKB_Hepkaya.pdf

TSKB. (2017). *Entegre Rapor 2016.* Retrieved June 24, 2018, from http://www.tskb.com.tr/i/assets/document/pdf/TSKB_Entegre_Rapor_2016.pdf

TSKB. (2018). *Entegre Rapor 2017.* Retrieved June 24, 2018, from http://www.tskb.com.tr/i/assets/document/pdf/TSKB_2017_Entegre_Raporu.pdf

Türkiye İş Bankası. (2018). Retrieved from https://www.isbank.com.tr/TR/ana-sayfa/Sayfalar/ana-sayfa.aspx

TURSEFF. (2018). Retrieved from http://www.turseff.org/sayfa/facility

UNEP. (2009). *Private financing of renewable energy – A guide for policymakers.* Retrieved July 4, 2017, from https://www.chathamhouse.org/sites/default/files/public/Research/Energy%2C%20Environment%20and%20Development/1209_financeguide.pdf

UNEP. (2011). *Global trends in renewable energy investment 2011: Analysis of trends and issues in the financing of renewable energy.* Retrieved June 4, 2017, from http://fs-unep-centre.org/sites/default/files/media/sefi2011finallowres.pdf

UNEP. (2012). *Global trends in renewable energy investment 2012.* Retrieved June 4, 2017, from http://fs-unep-centre.org/sites/default/files/publications/globaltrendsreport2012.pdf

UNEP. (2013). *Global trends in renewable energy investment 2013*. Retrieved June 4, 2017, from http://fs-unep-centre.org/system/files/globaltrendsreportlowres_0.pdf

UNEP. (2014). *Global trends in renewable energy investment 2014*. Retrieved June 4, 2017, from http://fs-unep-centre.org/system/files/globaltrendsreport2014.pdf

UNEP. (2015). *Global trends in renewable energy investment 2015*. Retrieved June 4, 2017, from http://fs-unep-centre.org/sites/default/files/publications/15028nefvisual9mediumres.pdf

UNEP. (2016). *Global trends in renewable energy investment 2016*. Retrieved March 4, 2018, from http://fs-unep-centre.org/sites/default/files/publications/globaltrendsinrenewableenergyinvestment2016lowres_0.pdf

UNEP. (2017). *Global trends in renewable energy investment 2017*. Retrieved March 4, 2017, from http://fs-unep-centre.org/sites/default/files/publications/globaltrendsinrenewableenergyinvestment2017.pdf

UNEP. (2018). *Global trends in renewable energy investment 2018*. Retrieved May 5, 2018, from http://fs-unep-centre.org/sites/default/files/publications/gtr2018v2.pdf

Zhang, D., Wang, J., Lin, Y., Si, Y., Huang, C., Yang, J., ... Li, W. (2017). Present situation and future prospect of renewable energy in China. *Renewable & Sustainable Energy Reviews*, *76*, 865–871. doi:10.1016/j.rser.2017.03.023

Zhang, S., & He, Y. (2013). Analysis on the development and policy of solar PV power in China. *Renewable & Sustainable Energy Reviews*, *21*, 393–401. doi:10.1016/j.rser.2013.01.002

Zorlu Energy. (2017). *Enerjimiz gelecek için, Zorlu Enerji Elektrik Üretim Anonim Şirketi 01 Ocak-30 Eylül 2017 Dönemi Faaliyet Raporu*. Retrieved May 5, 2018, from http://console22.zorluenerjigrubu.com/Upload/Document/9.11.2017-ZORENFR0917_YK_Faaliyet_Raporu.pdf

KEY TERMS AND DEFINITIONS

Big Three: Renewable energy investments are higher in China, India, and Brazil when compared to other developing countries. For that reason, they are called the "big three."

Geothermal Energy: This energy comes from heating from the earth and it may have fluid forms kind like mineral or hydro water.

Green Bonds: Green bonds are used by international, regional, and national development banks for financing green investment.

MidSEFF (Turkish Mid-Size Sustainable Energy Financing Facility): The program which developed by EBRD has provide loans of 1 billion Euro for renewable energy projects (wind energy, geothermal energy, etc) via the following Turkish banks (Akbank, Denizbank, Finansbank, Garanti, Türkiye İş Bankası, Vakıfbank, Yapı Kredi).

National Energy Efficiency Action Plan (NEEAP 2017-2023): This action plan includes steps to achieve national targets on energy efficiency.

National Renewable Energy Action Plan for Turkey (NREAP): The purpose of this program is to increase the share of renewable energy in general energy consumption to 20%, meet at least 30% of total electrical energy demand and 10% of transportation sector by renewable energy in 2023.

Renewable Energy: Renewable energy is the energy obtained from the natural sources such as solar, wind, biomass, geothermal.

Renewable Energy Financial Instruments: It includes various financial instruments (such as grants, venture capital, green bonds, etc.) used to finance renewable energy investments.

Solar Energy: Solar energy is the energy generated from the sun.

TurSEFF (Turkey Sustainable Energy Financing Facility): The program which developed by EBRD aims to finance small and medium-sized enterprises (SMEs) through participating banks (Akbank, Deniz Bank, Garanti Bankası, Türkiye İş Bankası, Vakıf Bank) in Turkey.

Wind Energy: Wind energy is the energy generated from wind turbines.

ENDNOTES

1 However, the USA withdrew from Paris Agreement on June 2, 2017.

2 In UNEP (2017) report, it is stated that developed countries invested in renewable energy more than developing countries in 2016. However, in UNEP (2018) report, it is seen that developing countries invested more in renewable energy than developed countries. The figures in this paper are based on the figures in UNEP (2018) report.

3 Based on gross generation from renewable sources including wind, solar, geothermal, biomass and waste not accounting for cross border electricity supply.

4 Based on gross primary hydroelectric generation and not accounting for cross-border electricity supply.

5 TSKB was selected the as the sustainable bank of the year in the Eastern Europe for three subsequent years (2008, 2009, 2010) (TSKB, 2017, p. 32).

6 All kinds of loans granted by the Bank within the context of sustainability can be accessed on the website of the Bank.

Chapter 10
Green Finance for Sustainable Global Growth:
Costs and Benefits of Green Buildings Compared With Conventional Buildings

Elizabeth Motunrayo Ojo-Fafore
University of Johannesburg, South Africa

Clinton Aigbavboa
University of Johannesburg, South Africa

Wellington Thwala
University of Johannesburg, South Africa

Pretty Remaru
University of Johannesburg, South Africa

ABSTRACT

Green buildings have become one of the most famous and fastest growing construction concepts. As the world is becoming environmentally viable, all investors and contractual workers will need to know the figures of green financing and if the dangers of contributing are justified regardless of the arrival sum. This chapter aims to compare green building and conventional building using the cost differences and economy impact to ascertain the benefits of green building over the conventional building of green building. Data was collected through questionnaire survey from 50 construction professionals. The result of this chapter shows that green buildings are more expensive than conventional buildings; however, the benefits accrue from green building makes green building cheaper in the long run.

DOI: 10.4018/978-1-5225-7808-6.ch010

INTRODUCTION

With increasing environmental concerns globally, it has become important for the finance sector to become responsive to environmental issues which give rise to the Green finance (Goel, 2016) Green Finance thus involves making investments in environmentally sustainable products and projects which aims at reducing or avoiding greenhouse gas emissions, controlling industrial pollution, water sanitation, waste management and overall biodiversity protection. It also includes green investments. Green building is part of green investments.

As cited in Hwang et al., 2017, the green building revolution is sweeping across most of the world. The goal of a green building is to take responsibility for achieving energy and resource efficiency, realizing long-term economic, environmental and social health (Sahamir & Zakari 2013, Yoon, Zhao, Hwang & Lee 2016). The development of green building is often discouraged by the perceived higher costs compared to traditional buildings; despite the fact tht green building have economic, social and environmental benefits (Dodge Data & Analytical, 2016).

In South Africa, operation of the building sector accounts for 23% of greenhouse gas emissions, while emissions from the manufacture of the major materials for the building sector amounts to around 18mtCO2 per year, or around 4% of total CO2 emissions (CIDB, 2009). Although buildings are a large contributor of greenhouse gases, they have received little attention in international global warming protocols and initiatives, which tend to focus on industry and transport (GSBSA, 2009). Dodge Data and Analytics (2016) reported that the green expansion would continue in developed countries such as the United States, Germany, and the United Kingdom. However, in South Africa this is still a relatively new concept, although awareness has dramatically increased (GSBSA, 2009). The world Green Building Council has a mission to achieve green building for everyone. To achieve this, it is imperative for construcion professionals and all stakeholders to know the cost implications and benefis of Green building. In the light of this perception this study investigates the green finance of green building, the benefits of green building and compare the cost of green building to conventional building in Johannesburg, Gauteng, South Africa.

BACKGROUND

It seems that green building has reached a tipping point. Any dabble into the real estate world will yield articles advertisements and discussion about green products and designs, as well as the stories about the latest green building. Yet the financing of green building is seldom discussed (Environmental Design & Construction 2007).

There is no standard definition of green financing. Green financing is a phenomenom that combines the world of finance and business it environmentally behaviour (Jayasubramanian & Shanti 2014). Green finance is a broad term that can refer to financial investments following sustainable projects and initiatives, environmental products nd policies tht encourage the developement of a more sustainable econonmy (Gilbert et al., 2012). It is defined as a financial support for green growth which reduces greenhouse gases and air pollutants emissions significantly. Also defines as a new financial pattern that integrates environmental protection with econmoics profits, emphasizing green and finance. Green finance covers the improvement of the areas of environmental degradation. It must be eco-friendly and can contriute to poverty alleviation. Green finance is an innovative financial pattern aimed at the environmental protection and the accomplishment of sustainable utilization of resources. Wang & Zhi 2016 defined Green finance as a phenomenon that combines the world of finance and business with enviromentally freindle behaviour.

From all the above definitions, it can be deduced that Green finance is all about environmental compliance, using sustainable resource while maximizing profit.

The term 'green' building refers to the use of environmentally friendly techniques and technologies in the design and construction of the built environment (Love et al., 2012). According to the United Nations Environment Programme (UNEP, 2009), 30% to 80% cut in energy consumption of buildings is attainable if the right green technologies are used. Additionally, the World Green Building Council (WorldGBC, 2014) reported that the design of an office building impacts the health, well-being, and productivity of its occupants. Therefore, green buildings also bring social and financial benefits to key stakeholders. Green buildings have environmental, economic, and social benefits. Green buildings first benefit the environment. Globally, buildings are responsible for 40% of annual energy consumption, including 12% of all fresh-water use and produce up to 40% of our solid waste (UNEP, 2011). Moreover, buildings were responsible for about one-third of greenhouse gas (GHG) emissions in the world (WorldGBC, 2013). Therefore, the building sector could lead to a great and efficient reduction of GHG emission if appropriate green technologies, materials, and construction methods were used (Wu et al., 2014). Green buildings also bring economic benefits to the key stakeholders involved. Green buildings can bring about energy and water savings, which lower operating costs. Fowler & Rauch (2008) reported that some green buildings consumed 26% less energy and saved 13% of maintenance costs when compared to average commercial buildings (Carpenter, 2009). According to a publication of the US Environmental Protection Agency (2014), green building can be defined as the practice of creating structures and the use of environmentally responsible and resource-efficient processes throughout a building's life cycle starting from its siting and extending to its design, construction, operation, maintenance, renovation and deconstruction

2. LITERATURE REVIEW

2.1. Benefits of Green Building

There is growing evidence that green building bring multiple benefits. The benefits of green buildings can be grouped within three categories: Environmental, Economic and Social.

2.1.1. Environmental Benefits

- The building sector has the largest potential for significantly reducing greenhouse gas emissions compared to other major emitting sectors (UNEP, 2009.)
- This emissions savings potential is said to be as much as 84 gigatonnes of CO2 (GtCO2) by 2050, through direct measures in buildings such as energy efficiency, fuel switching and the use of renewable energy (UNEP, 2016).
- The building sector has the potential to make energy savings of 50% or more in 2050, in support of limiting global temperature rises to 2°C (above pre-industrial levels) (UNEP, 2016)
- Green buildings achieving the Green Star certification in Australia have been shown to produce 62% fewer greenhouse gas emissions than average Australian buildings, and 51% less potable water than if they had been built to meet minimum industry requirements.
- Green buildings certified by the Indian Green Building Council (IGBC) results in energy savings of 40 - 50% and water savings of 20 - 30% compared to conventional buildings in India.
- Green buildings achieving the Green Star certification in South Africa have been shown to save on average between 30 - 40% energy and carbon emissions every year, and between 20 - 30% potable water every year, when compared to the industry norm.
- Green buildings achieving the LEED certification in the US and other countries have been shown to consume 25 per cent less energy and 11 per cent less water, than non-green buildings.

2.1.2. Economic Benefits

Green buildings offer a number of economic or financial benefits, which are relevant to a range of different people or groups of people. These include cost savings on utility bills for tenants or households (through energy and water efficiency); lower construction costs and higher property value for building developers; increased occupancy rates or operating costs for building owners; and job creation. Since the publication of WorldGBC's groundbreaking 2013 report

Global energy efficiency measures could save an estimated €280 to €410 billion in savings on energy spending (and the equivalent to almost double the annual electricity consumption of the United States (European Commission, 2015)

2.1.3. Social Benefits

Green building benefits go beyond economics and the environment, and have been shown to bring positive social impacts too. Many of these benefits are around the health and wellbeing of people who work or live in geen buildings.

2.2. Barriers to Adoption of Green Building

Adoption of green building practices faces many challenges. Researchers across the globe have conducted studies to identify various potential barriers that militate against green building adoption. After an extensive review of literature on the barriers to green building, some barriers were identified. These barriers listed below have the potential to hinder the adoption of green building practices.

- Initial construction costs of green buildings are high (Samari et al. 2013, Ametepey et al. 2015, Azad and Akbar2015, AlSanad 2015, Persson and Grönkvist 2015, Ghazilla et al. 2015, Ali et al. 2016, Timilsina et al. 2016).
- Cost of green technologies and materials are high (Hwang et al., 2017).
- Green incentives are not sufficient (Ghazilla et al. 2015, Al Sanad, 2015, Timilsina et al. (2016), Ali et al. 2016).
- There are no sufficient investors (Leung and Chau, 2013).
- Customers unwilling to pay (Tian & Li, 2018).
- Inadequate construction standards and legislation (Samari et al. 2013, Bohari et al. 2016, Persson and Grönkvist 2015, Ghazilla et al. 2015, Azad and Akbar 2015, Ametepey et al. 2015, Akadiri 2015, Wang et al. 2016, Ali et al. 2016).

- Inadequate way to empower green building. (Wang et al. 2016, Ghazilla et al. 2015, Azad and Akbar 2015, Ametepey et al. 2015, Samari et al. 2013, Azad and Akbar 2015, AlSanad, 2015, Persson and Grönkvist 2015, Ghazilla et al. 2015, Ali et al. 2016, Timilsina et al. 2016).
- Lack of advanced technology (Ghazilla et al. 2015, Azad and Akbar 2015, Ametepey et al.2015)
- Lack of proficient Knowledge (Azad and Akbar 2015, Ametepey et al. 2015, Samari et al. 2013,
- Ahn et al. 2013, Wang et al. 2016, Bohari et al. 2016, Williams and Dair 2007, Kasai and Jabbour 2014, Ali et al. 2016).
- No accurate data to easily convince decision maker. (Wang et al. 2016, Ghazilla et al. 2015, Azad and Akbar 2015, Ametepey et al. 2015, Samari et al. 2013).
- Researchers do no empirically support the benefit of green building (Persson and Grönkvist 2015, Ghazilla et al. 2015, AlSanad,2015, Akadiri, 2015, Wang et al. 2016, Timilsina et al. 2016, Ali et al. 2016)

2.3. Drivers of Green Building

Drivers of green building are noted by different researchers. Each of these drivers is examined below.

2.3.1. Request by Stakeholders

Bond and Perrett (2010) found that about portion of the partners questioned in a review appointed by the GBCA demonstrated that inhabitant request is driving their inclusion with green working, regardless of the occupants' refusal to pay additional to rent a Green appraised fabricating. Financial specialists likewise trust that it might be troublesome later on to offer or rent a structure that is not Green star appraised and this incentivizes them to construct green.

Moreover, the Vancouver Economic Development Commission (2009) places that the green building part has extensively changed in the course of the most recent decade. Two conceivable explanations behind this incorporate solid government initiative and new strategies and rating frameworks, for example, LEED. As per US Green Building Council (2003), inside three years of the LEED rating framework's dispatch, three percent of new plug ventures had enrolled for accreditation.

2.3.2. Financial Benefits of Going Green

Specialists in another paper opposed declined working expenses are an essential intention in green building, Tzschentke et al (2004). This is supported by different studies showing that organizations that seek after green activities, for example, diminishing the vitality expended, can decrease vitality related working expenses, Joseph (2013), Buys and Hurbissoon (2011).

2.3.3. Reduced Environmental Impact

According to Intel Corporate Responsibility Report (2008) Objectives, for example, decreasing a structure's ecological effect, reducing the structure's influence to greenhouse gas releases, and giving a more advantageous workplace to tenants regularly figure the choice to construct a Green evaluated assembling. As indicated by Kats (2003) a green building utilizes assets, for example, arrive, vitality, water and materials substantially more effectively than does a traditional structure, and with the persistent utilization of common lighting and enhanced indoor air quality, it adds to the general wellbeing, solace, and profitability of its inhabitants.

Other drivers that are noted by Yudelson (2010) towards executing green building development include: lower lifecycle costs, the accessibility of an industry (Green Star) rating system, Maintenance fee decreases, Employment and retention of important workers.

The key partners and their separate parts in the green building procedure are represented in this segment:

2.3.4. The Professional Team and Their Involvement in Green Building

Allen and Potiowsky (2008) The development industry contains numerous key players and unmistakable exchanges. As per Elforgani and Rahmat (2010), architectural, mechanical and electrical outlines are the most powerful in the "green" building plan prepare in light of the fact that these frameworks influence the building envelope, selections of materials and vitality proficiency. They assist contend that the constrained association of other industry partners in the outline procedure can impact the execution of green plans. As per Buys et al (2011) despite the fact that contractual workers assume an essential part in green working, because of their inclusion in the venture conveyance framework and contract particulars, a temporary worker's association in the plan procedure is regularly constrained.

2.3.5. The Green Building Council

According to Green Building Council of South Africa (GBCSA 2007) their mission is to advance improvement and support green building practices through market-based arrangements.

2.3.6. Building Materials and Construction Industry

There is a massive variety in the organizations occupied with the building store network, from area buying and advancement through to materials, development, building use and decommissioning. The development business is immense, various and complex. At the worldwide level, most development is completed by the private division, running from casual, small scale ventures to multinational organizations. All are impacted by the motivating forces in the business sectors they work, and react to government direction where it influences their exercises. There are different records and registries of green building experts and suppliers, however there are no complete information on the sorts and size of organizations taking part in green building. Improved data would diminish exchange costs, enhancing proficiency and rivalry, which would help the business as a rule (Kalra and Bonner, 2012) furthermore give the establishments to enhancing manageability. Perceiving the assorted qualities of on-screen characters inside development and materials creation, and the contrasting motivations and requirements of SMEs and of substantial firms, is vital to advancing a business market for green structures.

2.3.7. Financial Institutions

Money related foundations important to green development range from mindful property financial specialists or effect speculators who have solid ecological objectives (even prerequisites of natural profits for ventures), to business performing artists looking for business sector rate returns on individual home loans or substantial credits to property designers. Drawing in monetary establishments requires both information. Furthermore, cost motivating forces to put resources into green development; however venture choices have a tendency to be immovably established in transient financial picks up as opposed to in long haul reserve funds in vitality costs (UN Habitat, 2011).

2.3.8. Research and Educational Institutions

Research associations can address information holes and add to checking and assessment (M&E) work. Instructive organizations can build up the aptitudes required to incorporate green practices with business exercises, for instance through professional auxiliary and tertiary training and preparing for those working in the manufactured environment.

In Brazil, a study by Gomes et al. (2007) found that little had changed regarding planning and extending research exercises subsequent to 2004, when difficulties were distinguished (e.g. the requirement for a solid life cycle investigation database, regionalisation of supportability appraisal and reporting and characterized provincial execution benchmarks and markers). This is mostly because of absence of political backing and absence of coordination.

2.4. Financing Green Building

As a result, conventional buildings are not providing sufficient eco-friendly and energy saving equipments. Green buildings have minimum energy efficiency, water conservation, indoor air quality, and waste recycling standards etc. Not all the municipalities of the world developed the green building policies, but the increasing acceptance of green building practices in many cities is reflected in the adoption of policies by cities, counties, and states. The United States Green Building Council (USGBC), a national non-profit membership organization, the Leadership in Energy and Environmental Design (LEED) and the Tokyo Green Building Program (TGBP) of Japan provide a guideline and rating system for green buildings. The goal of the TGBP is to encourage building owners to carry out voluntary environment conscious efforts and create a more environmentally emerging market with high quality buildings and structures. The founder of LEED, describes green building as the "design and construction practices that significantly reduce or eliminate the negative impact of buildings on the environment and occupants in five broad areas such as sustainable site planning, safeguarding water and water efficiency, energy efficiency and renewable energy, conservation of materials and resources, and indoor environmental quality" (USGBC 2001). The fields for the idealization of green buildings are as follows (Yoshida and Sugiura 2011, Opportunities in Green Finance 2009):

- Reduction of thermal loads, such as, proper designing of the envelope of the building to reduce its heat load and use of spectral selective glasses for structural glazing and heat reflective walls, roofs, floors, and windows for the building.
- Use of renewable energy, such as, use of natural light, photovoltaic power generation, wind power generation, solar thermal system, and other renewable energy.

- Indoor environmental quality, for example, maintaining indoor thermal and visual comfort, and air quality.
- Maximum use of onsite sources and sinks like by bio climatic architectural practices.
- Using the natural resources available at site like trees as natural sun sheds to the advantage of the building and use excavated earth for landscaping.
- Energy saving, such as, use of energy efficient equipment for water heating, floor heating, ventilation, and air conditioning.
- The landscape design to supplement the proposed solar passive structures for the building, thus reducing the overall heat load of the building including developing small artificial water bodies which creates local air flow, thus making air natural cooling of the building.
- Use of eco-friendly materials, such as, use of recycled aggregates in concrete, blended cement (e.g., blast-furnace slag coarse cement), recycled steel, and other recycled building materials.
- Using locally available products also saves money and helps the environment, avoiding the effects of a long supply chain thus reducing the emissions due to transport and lesser carbon foot prints.
- Use of rain water harvesting structures to charge the aquifer and use of stored water.
- Use of techniques like vermin compost as a waste recycling strategy.
- Long-life design of the building, such as, flexible structure enabling easy maintenance, renovation, and conversion (e.g., configuration of plumbing, beams, floor height, etc.); physical durability (e.g. quality of cement, the covering depth of reinforced concrete, and exterior material).
- Maximize use of renewable energy sources, specially use of solar power for electricity with solar panels mounted on the roofs, thus effecting dual benefit of generation of electricity as well as low heat transfer to the roof slab.
- Water circulation, such as, circulation of rain and waste water by on-site sewage treatment; using rainfall infiltration.
- Recycling water from washrooms for watering the plants and lawns in the garden. To minimize the wastage of water through controlled water flushing system and recycling through sewage treatment plant.
- Planting, such as, a larger area of planting, planting on the wall and roof of building, optimal mix of shrub and arbour, coordination with surrounding green areas, attention to the local eco-system.
- Mitigation of the urban heat island phenomenon, such as, covering ground by plants, water, or materials with water retention capability; covering building walls and roofs by plants, water, materials with water retention capability,

or high-reflectivity coating; shape and configuration of buildings to improve wind flows.

- Use minimum energy to power the building with energy efficient intelligent lighting, heating, ventilation and air-conditioning.

2.5. Cost Difference Between Green and Conventional Buildings

This chapter serves to evaluate in detail the cost difference of green and conventional buildings. As the world is becoming environmentally viable all investors and contractual workers will need to know the figures of practicing environmental safety and if the danger of contributing is justified regardless of the arrival sum. The most condemned issue about developing these manageable structures is the cost included. The advancements included in it tend to cost more than customary structures. Most green structures cost a premium of more than 2% however return 10 times more advantages over whole life cycle of building Kats et al. (2003).

Kats (2006) examined the setup and improvement cost of 30 green schools unconcerned spots in the United States and almost considered that green schools incline to cost around 2% more than standard ones.

In a later study, the same researcher Kats (2010) drove a review for more than 100 designers, building proprietors, counsellors to procure information about the green cost premium of more than 170 green structures in the United States and some diverse countries and assumed that most green structures cost fairly higher than conventional structures. The researcher found that the reported green cost premium for the whole illustration stretching out from 0% to 18%. Regardless, the battles that the cost premium of more than 75% of the researched green structures falls inside the range from 0%to 4%. The researcher moreover battles that examining the incremental cost of green structures using particular procedures yields the same results. The dominant part of this expense is because of the utilization of premium materials, high-effectiveness apparatus, and extra layers of procedure work process.

In New Zealand, Rehm and Ade (2013) matched the real price of 17 green office structures, ensured as green by the New Zealand Green Building Council's evaluating device (Green Star NZ Version 1.0), against cost models created utilizing expense guides and handbooks for the same structures. The creators utilized non-parametric Wilcoxon coordinated sets marked positions test to figure out if the real cost is considerably greater than the demonstrated expense. They establish that green buildings expenses were higher by and large when contrasted with displayed cost estimates, yet the distinction is not factually huge. In the same study they audited 631 engineers to separate cost partition between customary advancement procedures and green structures. Of the engineers inspected, (a) 86% trusted green structures costs were more than conventional improvement, (b) 13% trusted cost refinement was Negligible and (c) only 1% trusted green advancement costs less (Rehm and Ade, 2013). Results from their data examination did not support the producers' announcement that using green building sharpens grows advancement costs.

Another study by Gregory and Kats (2003) finished a study which laid out that "Green structures are commonly seen to be essentially more excessive than ordinary structures and routinely not worth regard the additional price charge. For instance, a mid 2003 article in the New York Times was authorised permitted "Not Building Green Is Called a Matter of economics."In requesting to pick the expense of inserting green showed up distinctively in connection to customary course of action, a few dozen building specialists and coordinators were come to secure the expense of 33 green structures from over the United States emerged from routine outlines.

The standard premium for these green structures is to some degree under 2%. The more prominent piece of this cost is an outcome of the greater architectural and designing outline period, showing costs and time essential to join sensible building rehearses into projects. All things considered, the earlier green building parts are joined into the setup set up, the lower the cost.

Green buildings are commonly perceived to be a lot more expensive than conventional buildings. For example, an early 2003 article in the New York Times was entiles '' No Building Green is called a matter of economics. In order to determine the cost of building green compared o conventional building, several dozen building representatives and architect were contacted To secure the costt of 33 green buildings from across the United States compared the conventional designs for those same buildings.

The *report* compiled by the Green Building Council South Africa (GBCSA), the Association of SA Quantity Surveyors (ASAQS) and the University of Pretoria (UP) and released in July 2016, found that the average cost premium of building green over and above the cost of conventional construction – or green cost premium – is a mere 5.0% and can be as low as 1.1%.

This study, combined with the annual *MSCI/GBCSA Sustainability Index*, which consistently shows that in South Africa green buildings yield a higher return on investment, make a very strong business case for green buildings to developers, property owners and corporate.

3. RESEARCH METHODOLOGY

The research was conducted in two stages: Quantitative, using a well-structured questionnaire. The questionnaire was administered to 50 construction professionals who are at present working or have been involved in green building in Johannesburg,

40 were returned and they were all usable, which shaped the premise of the study. The convenience sampling was used in the study. A five-point likert scale was utilized to decide the cost difference between conventional and green building and benefits of green building in Johannesburg. The embraced scale was as per the following:

1=Very low
2= Low
3= Neutral
4= High
5= Very high

The other scale used was as follows:

1= Strongly disagree
2= Disagree
3= Neutral
4= Agree
5= Strongly agree

The mean score (MIS) was computed for each item as follows:

$$MIS = \frac{1n_1 + 2n_2 + 3n_3 + 4n_4 + 5n_5}{\Sigma N} \quad (1)$$

Where:

n_1 = Total of respondents for factor 1
n_2 = Total of respondents for factor 2
n_3 = Total of respondents for factor 3
n_4 = Total of respondents for factor 4
n_5 = Total of respondents for factor 5
N = Total number of respondents

After scientific calculations, the criteria are then positioned in descendent order of their mean thing score (from the utmost to the lowermost).

4. FINDINGS

4.1. Benefits of Green Buildings

Table 1 shows the respondents ranking of benefits of green buildings in Gauteng province. The table reveals that: Green building provide better health for building occupants due to the improved indoor quality and lead to the development of more energy-efficient products and services were ranked first with a 4.50 score; Green building improve comfort, satisfaction and well-being of building occupants was ranked second with a score of 4.43, the environmental and emissions costs of green buildings are lower was ranked third with a score of 4.40; green buildings enjoy the support of climate change protocols was ranked forth with a score of 4.35; improve the quality of life for individuals was ranked fifth with a score of 4.28; use less natural resources and so as to protect the ecosystem was ranked sixth with a score of 4.23; Economic life of green building is extended since plant and equipment are more robust to alternative uses was ranked seventh with a score of 4.19; lead to the reduction of annual water cost savings and Increase the occupant safety and security was ranked eighth with a score of 4.03; lead lower operational and support costs was ranked ninth with a score of 3.85; Waste disposal costs in the green buildings are lower was ranked tenth with a score of 3.75; Make risk management manageable (economic, financial, market, etc.) was ranked eleventh with a score of 3.73 and the cost of maintenance in green building is greatly reduced was ranked last with a score of 3.53.

4.2. Barriers to Green Building

Table 2 shows the respondents ranking of barriers of green buildings in Gauteng province. The table reveals that: initial construction costs of green buildings are high when compared to conventional building was ranked first with a 4.15 score; Cost of green technologies and materials are high when compared to conventional building was ranked second with a score of 4.10, There is a shortage of professionals with suitable experience and government incentives are not enough to encourage green building movement were ranked third with a score of 3.53, There is no sufficient number of investors for the construction of green buildings was ranked forth with a score of 3.43; Customers are unwilling to pay for the green building projects due to high costs associated with it and inadequacy of construction standards and Inadequate way to empower green building were ranked fifth with a score of 3.40, Non-presence of government financing was ranked sixth with a score of 3.10; Lack of advanced technology was ranked seventh with a score of 2.90; Lack of proficient knowledge was ranked eighth with a score of 2.85, There is not accurate information to easily

Table 1. Benefits of green buildings (Source: Ojo et al., 2018)

Benefits of Green Buildings	MIS	Rank (R)
Provide better health for building occupants due to the improved indoor quality	4.50	1
Lead to the development of more energy-efficient products and services	4.50	1
Improve comfort, satisfaction and well-being of building occupants	4.43	2
The environmental and emissions costs are lower.	4.40	3
Enjoy the support of climate change protocols	4.35	4
Improve the quality of life for individuals	4.28	5
Use less natural resources and so as to protect the ecosystem.	4.23	6
Economic life of green building is extended since plant and equipment are more robust to alternative uses.	4.19	7
lead to the reduction of annual water cost savings.	4.03	8
Increase the occupant safety and security.	4.03	8
Lead lower operational and support costs.	3.85	9
Waste disposal costs in the green buildings are lower.	3.75	10
Make risk management manageable (economic, financial, market, etc.).	3.73	11
The cost of maintenance in green building is greatly reduced.	3.53	12

convince decision makers was ranked ninth with a score of 2.83, and Researchers do not empirically support the benefits of green buildings was ranked last with a score of 2.55.

4.3. Drivers of Green Buildings

Table 3 shows the respondents ranking of drivers of green buildings in Gauteng province. The table reveals that: Reduced Environmental Impact was ranked first with a 4.48 score; Increased green building education was ranked second with a score of 4.43; The Green Building Council which promotes the improvement and encourage green building practices through market-based solutions was ranked third with a score of 4.30; Financial Benefits of Going Green and Financial institutions involvement in Money related foundations to green development were ranked forth with a score of 4.15; Recruitment and retention of key employees and the availability of an industry (Green Star) rating system and Maintenance cost reductions were ranked fifth with a score of 4.05, Lower lifecycle costs was ranked sixth with a score of 4.03, Government policy was ranked seventh with a score of 3.85 and Building code (marketing) was ranked last with a score of 3.75.

Table 2. Barriers of green buildings (Source: Ojo et al., 2018)

Barriers of Green Building	MIS	Rank (R)
Initial construction costs of green buildings are high when compared to conventional building.	4.15	1
Cost of green technologies and materials are high when compared to conventional building.	4.10	2
Government incentives are not sufficient to encourage green building movement.	3.53	3
There is a shortage of professionals with suitable experience.	3.53	3
There is no sufficient number of investors for the construction of green buildings.	3.43	4
Customers are unwilling to pay for the green building projects due to high costs associated with it	3.40	5
Inadequacy of construction standards and additionally legislations	3.40	5
Inadequate way to empower green building	3.40	5
Non-presence of government financing.	3.10	6
Lack of advanced technology	2.90	7
Lack of proficient knowledge	2.85	8
There is not accurate data to easily convince decision makers	2.83	9
Researchers do not empirically support the benefits of green buildings.	2.55	10

Table 3. Drivers of green building (Source: Ojo et al., 2018)

Drivers of Green Building	MIS	Rank (R)
Reduced Environmental Impact.	4.48	1
Increased green building education.	4.43	2
The Green Building Council which promotes the development and encourages green building practices through market-based solutions.	4.30	3
Financial Benefits of Going Green.	4.15	4
Financial institutions involvement in Money related foundations to green development.	4.15	4
Recruitment and retention of key employees.	4.05	5
The availability of an industry (Green Star) rating system.	4.05	5
Maintenance cost reductions.	4.05	5
Lower lifecycle costs	4.03	6
Government policy.	3.85	7
Building code (marketing).	3.75	8

4.4. Cost Difference Between Conventional and Green Buildings

Respondents were asked to rank cost contributions towards conventional buildings, the results are illustrated Table 4. Extra layers of procedure work process was ranked first with a 3.65 score; design procedure and degree scope and utilization of premium materials was ranked second with a 3.38 score; using high effectiveness equipment and greater architectural and designing outline period were ranked third with a 3.28 score, design fees was ranked fourth with scores of 3.20; LEED documentation was ranked fifth with a 2.73 score; level of LEED certification required was ranked sixth with a score of 2.68, and Advanced technology were ranked last with 2.58 score.

Respondents were asked to rank cost contributions towards green buildings, the results are illustrated in Table 5. Level of LEED certification required, LEED documentation and advanced technology were ranked first with a score of 4.30; design fees was ranked second with score of 4.23; design procedure and degree scope were ranked third with a score of 4.05; greater architectural and designing outline period were ranked forth with a score of 3.90; using of high effectiveness equipment was ranked fifth with a score of 3.80; utilization of premium materials was ranked sixth with a score of 3.68 and extra layers of procedure work process was ranked last with a score of 3.50.

Tables 6, 7, and 8 show the case of cost difference between conventional buildings and green buildings. The results shows that there is the cost of green buildings are higher than of conventional building for example there is a cost difference of R5 132.18 per m^2 between the construction of Alexander Forbes head office with an amount of R22 733.42 per m^2 and construction of Mary Moodley office facility with an amount of R17 601.24 per m^2, there is a cost difference of R3 171.02 per

Table 4. Cost contributions towards conventional buildings (Source: Ojo et al., 2018)

Cost contributions towards conventional buildings	MIS	Rank (R)
Extra layers of procedure work process.	3.65	1
Design procedure and degree scope	3.38	2
Utilization of premium materials	3.38	2
Using of high-effectiveness equipment	3.28	3
Greater architectural and designing outline period	3.28	3
Design fees	3.20	4
LEED documentation	2.73	5
Level of LEED certification required	2.68	6
Advanced technology	2.58	7

Table 5. Cost contributions towards green buildings (Source: Ojo et al., 2018)

Cost contributions towards green buildings	MIS	Rank (R)
Level of LEED certification required	4.30	1
LEED documentation	4.30	1
Advanced technology	4,30	1
Design fees	4.23	2
Design procedure and degree scope	4.05	3
Greater architectural and designing outline period	3.90	4
Using of high-effectiveness equipment	3.80	5
utilization of premium materials	3.68	6
Extra layers of procedure work process.	3.50	7

m^2 between the construction of Nedbank head office with an amount of R27 906 976.74 and construction of Garankuwa office facility with an amount of R20 235,23, there is a cost difference of R6 594.04 per m^2 between the construction of Aurecon's Century City office with an amount of R26 829.27 and construction of Desmond Tutu Office facility with an amount of R23 658.25 and there is a cost difference of R236 943.80 per m^2 between the construction of Hotel Verde with an amount of R252 631.58 and construction of protea hotel with an amount of R15 687.78.

Table 6. Cost of green building (Source: Ojo et al., 2018)

Type of building (Green Buildings)	Size (m^2)	Cost	Cost per m^2
Alexander Forbes Head office	36 950 m^2	R840 000 000.00	R22 733.42
Nedbank Head office	43 000 m^2	R1 200 000 000 000	R27 906 976.74
Aurecon's Century City office	3 280 m^2	R88 000 000.00	R26 829.27
Hotel Verde	950 m^2	240 000 000.00	R252 631.58

Table 7. Cost of conventional building (Source: Ojo et al., 2018)

Type of building (Conventional)	Size (m^2)	Cost	Cost per m^2
Mary Moodley Office Facility	852 m^2	R14 996 258.00	17 601.24
Garankuwa office facility	950 m^2	R19 223 468.89	R20 235, 23
Protea Hotel	800 m^2	R12 550 221.98	R15 687.78
Desmond Tutu Office facility	1000 m^2	R23 658 254.78	R23 658.25

Table 8. Cost difference between green building and conventional building (Source: Ojo et al., 2018)

Type of building	Cost per m²		Cost difference
	Green	Conventional	
Office	R22 733.42	R17 601.24	R5 132.18
	R26 829.27	R23 658.25	R3 171.02
	R26 829.27	R20 235.23	R6 594.04
Residential	R252 631.58	R15 687.78	R236 943.80

5. CONCLUSION AND RECOMMENDATIONS

The literature on the costs variance of green structures contrasted with customary is certain. It encourages the observation that green buildings development expenses are higher than that of traditional ones. More than half of the writing states that green structures cost much higher than customary ones with a portion of the reasons being high material expenses and green accreditation, high-proficiency equipment to say only a couple.

The writing on the benefits of green building calls attention to a few advantages which are said not to be characteristics of customary structures. These are ecologically friendly, interior environment quality, thermal comfort, wellbeing and efficiency and economic benefits. There was no single article read which restricted this declaration.

The writing on the barriers of green building points out numerous factors that hinders the development of green building which conventional buildings don't encounter. These are Higher cost, absence of limit of development, absence of innovative technology, absence of proficient knowledge, absence of government support and motivating forces, absence of public responsiveness to name few.

Nevertheless, there was not abundant writings on the drivers of green buildings, a little ideas were identified which emphasised the drivers of green building development, such drivers are request by Stakeholders, money related Benefits of Going Green, reduced environmental impact, need for corporate/social responsibility, lower lifecycle costs, the availability of an industry (Green Star) rating system, to mention just a few. And further sketched out the key partners and their separate parts in the green building process, which are: The Professional Team, The Green Building Council, Clients, Building materials and construction industry, financial institutions, Research and educational institutions.

This chapter examined the benefits of green buildings in Johannesburg and compares the costs of green building to conventional building. The study used a quantitative and a case study approach to collect empirical data. The data indicated that green buildings provide better health for building occupants due to the improved indoor quality, lead to the development of more energy-efficient products and services increase luxury, satisfaction and welfare of building tenants, improve the value of lifetime for individuals, the ecological and emissions costs are lower, enjoy the support of climate change protocols) and uses less natural resources and so as to protect the ecosystem, Economic life of green building is extended, to the reduction of annual water cost savings were identified as the top ten benefits of green buildings in Johannesburg. Based on these findings, it can be concluded that clients, contractors and consultants need to take consideration of the benefits of green buildings and start investing in green building construction.

Also, the case study revealed that the cost of green buildings is higher than of conventional building. Level of LEED certification required, LEED documentation, advanced technology, design fees, design procedure and degree scope, utilization of premium materials, greater architectural and designing outline period were the major cost contributions towards green buildings in Johannesburg. Therefore, it can be concluded that the cost difference between conventional and green buildings are due to the components that green building incorporates and that results in greater benefits to the occupants and environment.

This chapter gave an insight to the accrue benefit of green buildings to all stakeholders. Also encourage investors on financing green buildings as well as the South African government to encourage green buildings movements. This will in turn help in developing the country's green rating system.

This research is limited by its small sample size and the location of a case study approach. Nonetheless, it provides factual evidence of the benefits of green building and the cost difference between green building and conventional building

ACKNOWLEDGMENT

This research is supported by the university of Johannesburg research funding.

REFERENCES

Ali, A. N. A., Jainudin, N. A., Tawie, R., & Jugah, I. (2016). Green initiatives in Kota Kinabalu Construction industry. *Procedia: Social and Behavioral Sciences*, *224*, 626–631. doi:10.1016/j.sbspro.2016.05.453

Allen, J. H., & Potiowsky, T. (2008). Portland's Green Building Cluster. *Economic Development Quarterly*, *22*(4), 303–315. doi:10.1177/0891242408325701

AlSanad, S. (2015). Awareness, drivers, actions, and barriers of sustainable construction in Kuwait. *Procedia Engineering*, *118*, 969–983. doi:10.1016/j.proeng.2015.08.538

Ametepey, O., Aigbavboa, C., & Ansah, K. (2015). Barriers to successful implementation of sustainable construction in the Ghanaian construction industry. *Procedia Manufacturing*, *3*, 1682–1689. doi:10.1016/j.promfg.2015.07.988

Bohari, A. A. M., Skitmore, M., Xia, B., & Zhang, X. (2016). Insights into the adoption of green construction in Malaysia: The drivers and challenges. *Environment-Behaviour Proceedings Journal*, *1*(4), 45–53.

Bond, S. (2010). *Best of the Best in Green Design: Drivers and Barriers to Sustainable Development in Australia*. Lincoln University Digital Dissertation.

Buys, F., & Hurbissoon, R. (2011). Green buildings: A mauritian built environment stakeholders' perspective. *Acta Struct.*, *18*, 81–101.

Carpenter, S. (2009). Do green buildings really save energy? *Building*, *59*(2), 22.

Chuck, W. F., & Kim, J. T. (2011). Building environmental assessment schemes for rating of IAQ in sustainable buildings. *Indoor and Built Environment*, *20*(1), 5–15. doi:10.1177/1420326X10397780

CIDB. (2009). *Greenhouse gas emission reduction: potentials from buildings*. Construction Industry Development Board (CIDB) discussion document. Retrieved from www.cidb.org.za

Djokoto, S. D., Dadzie, J., & Ohemeng-Ababio, E. (2014). Barriers to Sustainable Construction in the Ghanaian Construction Industry: Consultants Perspectives. *Journal of Sustainable Development*, *14*(1). doi:10.5539/jsd.v7n1p134

Dodge Data & Analytics. (2016). *World green building trends: Developing markets accelerate global green growth. Smart Market report*. Design and Construction Intelligence.

Eisenberg, D., Done, R., & Ishida, L. (2002). *Breaking down the barriers: Challenges and solutions to code approval of green building*. Tucson, AZ: Development Center for Appropriate Technology.

Elforgani, M. S., & Rahmat, I. (2010). An investigation of factors influencing design team attributes in green buildings. *American Journal of Applied Sciences*, *7*(7), 7. doi:10.3844/ajassp.2010.976.986

Ellis, K. (2011). *Green Growth Opportunities and Requirements in Egypt*. Eschborn: Deutsche Gesellschaftfür Internationale Zusammenarbeit.

Erten, D. (2011) Istanbul: The Challenges for Sustainable Buildings in Emerging Economies. Leverkusen: *UNEP-SBCI Symposium on Sustainable Buildings*.

Fowler, K. M., & Rauch, E. M. (2006). *Sustainable Building Rating Systems Summary, Pacific Northwest National Laboratory*. Richland, WA: PNNL. doi:10.2172/926974

Ghazilla, R. A. R., Sakundarini, N., Abdul-Rashid, S. H., Ayub, N. S., Olugu, E. U., & Musa, S. N. (2015). Drivers and barriers analysis for green manufacturing practices in Malaysian SMEs: A preliminary findings. *Procedia CIRP*, *26*, 658–663. doi:10.1016/j.procir.2015.02.085

Goel, P. (2016). *Green Finance: A step towards sustainable financial system*. Abhnav Publications.

Goering, J. (2009). *Sustainable real estate development: The dynamics of market penetration*. Academic Press.

Gomes, V., Gomes da Silva, M., Lamberts, R., Vespoli, M. T., & Sangoi de Oliveira, M. (n.d.). Sustainable Building in Brazil. *International Initiative for a Sustainable Built Environment.*

Green Building Council South Africa. (2007). Available online: http://www.gbcsa.org.za

Habitat, U. N. (2011). *Sustainable Building Practices for Low Cost Housing: Implications for Climate Change Mitigation and Adaptation in Developing Countries. Shelter Initiative for Climate Change Mitigation and Adaption*. SICCMA.

Häkkinen, T., & Belloni, K. (2011). Barriers and drivers for sustainable building. *Building Research and Information*, *39*(3), 239–255. doi:10.1080/09613218.2011.561948

Hwang, B. G., Zehu, L., Wang, Y., & Cheong, X. (2017). Green Building construction projects in Sngapore; Cost premiums & Cost performance. *Project Management Journal*, *48*(4), 67–79. doi:10.1177/875697281704800406

Hydes, K. R., & Creech, L. (2010), Reducing mechanical equipment cost: the economics of green design. *Building Research & Information, 1*(1). Available at: http://www.tandfonline.com/loi/rbri20

IntelC. R. R. (2008). Available online: http://www.intel.com/

Joseph, C. (n.d.). *What Are the Benefits of Going Green for a Business?* Available online: http://www.smallbusiness.chron.com/

Kalra, R., & Bonner, R. (2012). *Addressing Climate Change with Low-Cost Green Housing*. Washington, DC: World Bank.

Kats, G. (2003). *Green Building Costs and Financial Benefits.* Massachusetts Technology Collaborative.

Kats, G. (2010). *Greening Our Built World: Costs, Benefits, and Strategies.* Washington, DC: Island Press.

Kats, G., Alevantis, L., Berman, A., Mills, E., & Perlman, J. (2003). *The costs and financial benefits of green buildings.* A report to California's sustainable building taskforce. Retrieved from http://www.usgbc.org/Docs/News/News477.pdf

Kibert, C. J. (2008). Sustainable Construction: Green Building Design and Delivery (3rd ed.). Wiley.

Lau, K.T., Tan, K.T., Lee, A.R., & Mohamed. (2009). A comparative study on the energy policies in Japan and Malaysia in fulfilling their nations' obligations towards the Kyoto Protocol. *Energy Policy, 37*, 4771–4778.. doi:10.1016/j.enpol.2009.06.034

Liu, J. Y., Low, S. P., & He, X. (2012). Green practices in the Chinese building industry: Drivers and impediments. *Journal of Technology Management in China, 7*(1), 50–63. doi:10.1108/17468771211207349

Love, P. E. D., Niedzweicki, M., Bullen, P. A., & Edwards, D. J. (2012). Achieving the green building council of Australia's world leadership rating in an office building in Perth. *Journal of Construction Engineering and Management, 138*(5), 652–660. doi:10.1061/(ASCE)CO.1943-7862.0000461

McGraw Hill Construction. (2013). *World Green Building Trends.* Bedford, MA: Author.

OECD. (2003). *Environmentally Sustainable Buildings, Challenges and Policies.* Paris: Organisation for Economic Co-operation and Development.

OECD/IEA & AFD. (2008). *Promoting Energy Efficiency Investments: Case studies in the residential sector*. Paris: International Energy Agency.

Ofori, G., & Kien, H. L. (2004). Translating Singapore architects' environmental awareness into decision making. *Building Research and Information*, *32*(1), 27–37. doi:10.1080/09613210210132928

Persson, J., & Grönkvist, S. (2015). Drivers for and barriers to low-energy buildings in Sweden. *Journal of Cleaner Production*, *109*, 296–304. doi:10.1016/j.jclepro.2014.09.094

Rehm, M. & Ade, R. (2013). Construction costs comparison between "green" and conventional office buildings. *Build. Res. Inf.*, *41*, 198–208. http://dx..2013.769145 doi:10.1080/09613218

Richard, L., & John, E. (2009). *Urban Construction Project Management. McGraw-Hill.*

Riesa, R., Bileca, M.M.,Gokhanb, N.M., & Needy, K.L. (2006). The Economic Benefits of Green Buildings: A Comprehensive Case Study. *The Engineering Economist: A Journal Devoted to the Problems of Capital Investment, 51*(3), 259-295.

Sahamir, S. R., & Zakaria, R. (2013). Green assessment criteria for public hospital building development in Malaysia. *Procedia Environmental Sciences*, *20*, 106–115. doi:10.1016/j.proenv.2014.03.015

Samari, M., Ghodrati, N., Esmaeilifar, R., Olfat, P., & Shafiei, M. W. M. (2013). The investigation of the barriers in developing green building in Malaysia. *Modern Applied Science*, *7*(2), 1–10. doi:10.5539/mas.v7n2p1

Shi, Q., Zuo, J., & Zillante, G. (2012). Exploring the management of sustainable construction at the programme level e a Chinese case study'. *Construction Management and Economics*, *30*(6), 425–440. doi:10.1080/01446193.2012.683200

Shi, Z., & Huang, H. (2013). Identifying the critical factors for green construction e an empirical study in China. *Habitat International*, *40*(1), 1–8. doi:10.1016/j.habitatint.2013.01.003

Shrestha, P.P & Pushpala, N. (2012). *Green and non-green school buildings*: an empirical comparison of construction cost and schedule. *Constr. Res. Congr.*, 1820–1829. doi:10.1061/9780784412329.183

Tian, X., & Li, Y. (2018). Key factors of People's willingness to pay for green building in a less develop region in China. A pilot research effort in Shaxi province. *International Review for Spatial Planning and Sustainable Development, 6*(3), 78-93.

Timilsina, G. R., Hochman, G., & Fedets, I. (2016). Understanding energy efficiency barriers in Ukraine: Insights from a survey of commercial and industrial firms. *Energy*, *106*, 203–211. doi:10.1016/j.energy.2016.03.009

Trainer, T. (2013). Can the world run on renewable energy? A revised negative case. Renewable Energy, 29, 88-104.

Tzschentke, N., Kirk, D., & Lynch, P. (2004). Reasons for going green in serviced accommodation establishments. *International Journal of Contemporary Hospitality Management*, *16*(2), 116–124. doi:10.1108/09596110410520007

UNEP. (2009). *Buildings and climate change—Summary for decision-makers*. Retrieved from http://www.unep.org/ sbci/pdfs/sbci-bccsummary.pd

USGBC. (2003). *Building Momentum—National Trends and Prospects for High Performance Green Buildings*. U.S. Green Building Council. Available online: http://www.org/Docs/

Vancouver Economic Development Commission (VEDC). (2009). *Green Buildings in Vancouver*. Available online: http://www.vancouvereconomic.com/userfiles/file/green-building-profile.pdf

Wang, T., Li, X., Liao, P.-C., & Fang, D. (2016). Building energy efficiency for public hospitals and healthcare facilities in China: Barriers and drivers. *Energy*, *103*, 588–597. doi:10.1016/j.energy.2016.03.039

Wang, Y., & Zhi, Q. (2016). The role of green finance in environmental protection: Two aspects of market mechanism polices. *Energy Procedia*, *104*, 311–316. doi:10.1016/j.egypro.2016.12.053

World, G. B. C. (2013). *The business case for green building—A review of the costs and benefits for developers, investors and occupants*. Retrieved from http://www.worldgbc.org/files/1513/6608/0674/Business_Case_For_Green_Building_Report_WEB_2013-04-11.pdf

World, G. B. C. (2014). *Health, wellbeing and productivity in offices—The next chapter for green building*. Retrieved from http://www.worldgbc.org/ files/6314/1152/0821/WorldGBC__ Health_Wellbeing__productivity_Full_Report.pdf

Wu, P., Xia, B., & Zhao, X. (2014). The importance of use and end-of-life phases to the life cycle greenhouse gas (GHG) emissions of concrete—A review. *Renewable & Sustainable Energy Reviews*, *37*, 360–369. doi:10.1016/j.rser.2014.04.070

Yoon, S. W., & Lee, D. K. (2003). The development of the evaluation model of climate changes and air pollution for sustainability of cities in Korea. *Landscape and Urban Planning*, *63*(3), 145–160. doi:10.1016/S0169-2046(02)00186-X

Yu, C. W. F., & Kim, J. T. (2010). Buildingpathology,investigationofsick buildings—VOC emissions. *Indoor and Built Environment*, *19*(1), 30–39. doi:10.1177/1420326X09358799

Yudelson, J. (2008). *The Green Building Revolution*. Washington, DC: Island Press.

Yudelson, J. (2009). *Cost of green buildings, Green Building through Integrated Design. McGraw-Hill Professional.*

Yudelson, J. (2010). *Greening Existing Buildings*. McGraw Hill Companies Inc.

Zhao, X., Hwang, B. G., & Lee, H. N. (2016). Identifying critical leadership styles of project managers for green building projects. *International Journal of Construction Management*, *16*(2), 150–160. doi:10.1080/15623599.2015.1130602

Zuo, J., & Zhao, Z. (2014). Green building research–current status and future agenda: A review. *Renewable and Sustainable Energy Reviews, 30*, 271-281.

KEY TERMS AND DEFINITIONS

Benefit: An advantage or profit gained from something.

Building: A structure with a roof and walls such as house or factory.

Construction: The action of building something.

Conventional Building: Refers to the traditional method of construction.

Cost: An amount that needs to be paid or spent to buy or obtain something.

Environment: It is everything that is around us. It could be living or nonliving things.

Green Building: It refers to both structure and the application of processes that are environmentally responsible and resources efficient throughout a building lifecycle.

Green Finance: It is an innovative financial pattern aimed at the environmental protection and the accomplishment of sustainable utilization of resources.

Occupants: The action or fact of occupying a place.

Chapter 11
An Analysis of Green Taxation in Turkey for Sustainable Growth

Erdal Eroğlu
Çanakkale Onsekiz Mart University, Turkey

ABSTRACT

Ecological problems such as global warming, climate change, and loss of biodiversity are at the top of governments' agendas as negative externalities like fewer water sources, food and energy shortage, drought, desertification, and migration have recently been deeply felt by societies. Environmentally related taxes are one of the most important instruments of fiscal policy used to internalize "negative externalities" to prevent environmental pollution and to ensure sustainable growth. This type of tax represents the ideal principle that "the polluter pays." Most of the European and OECD countries today have revised their tax systems to stop environmental destruction and have begun to implement environmental taxation. The purpose of this chapter is to carry out an analysis of green taxation in Turkey for sustainable growth. In this regard, this study aims to analyze green taxation practices and regulations within the scope of a sustainable economy in Turkey and offer solutions by considering the practices in various countries with effective green taxation policies.

DOI: 10.4018/978-1-5225-7808-6.ch011

INTRODUCTION

In order to carry out an international fight against such environmental problems as global warming, climate change, water, air and other types of pollution, various common plans and programs have recently been introduced by the international organizations (EU, OECD, WB, etc.). The main purpose stated in these documents is to ensure a sustainable growth and leave the next generations a livable life. To this end, authorities have started to put taxes on areas causing environmental pollution, to introduce public incentives for biodiversity conservation, an effective environmental management, wild-life protection, and efficient energy use, and to implement renewable energy policies. These policies are in general terms called green budget reform in the literature (Schlegelmilch, 1999; Gale & Barg, 2014). The implementations are mostly related to taxation, though (Kreiser, 2012).

Within the scope of green taxation, tax should have an impact that deters people from causing environmental distortion, contributing to a less polluted environment (Ballet et al., 2007). To prevent environmental problems, introducing new taxes is not enough on its own. It is also necessary to remove the tax incentives and tax reliefs that pose a danger for the environment and make the current taxes environmentally-friendly (OECD, 2001). Within the general scope of green budgeting, every stage of an economic activity should be restructured by considering the environment. Negative externalities that are seen as the reason for the state's intervention in the market or regarded as a market failure by the neo-classical approach establish the theoretical basis of green taxation. A negative externality is defined a cost that is suffered by a third party as a result of an economic transaction. With green tax, negative externalities are included into price, and the cost of pollution is minimized.

The neoclassical theory argues that the need for public intervention in the market may result from the problem of negative market externalities. Not including the cost of pollution into prices or not having enough gains from market intervention leads to market failure. When considered from the perspective of property rights, one result of lack of exactly stated and implemented property rights or liability rules is that economic activities are carried out with less concern for the environment and the next generation (Ciocirlan and Yandle, 2003: 204).

While public policies are implemented via taxes for including the cost of externalities into prices (Pigouvian Approach), regulations (Plott Approach), subsidies, charges, pollution permits, and direct controls, there are measures like 'Coase theory', 'Hicks-Kaldor' and 'Scitovsky' as market solutions (Kargı and Yüksel, 2010). Green taxation stands out as a public policy solution to include externalities into economy.

The environmental problems that have become a global issue with its wide-range impacts have forced countries, international institutions and organizations to take some specific measures all together. When the current and possible adverse impacts of wasteful and extravagant consumption resulting from global competition for the world sources are taken into consideration, it can be argued that green taxation will continue being discussed for a long period in the future. It is, therefore, of great importance to carry out an analysis of this issue. In this regard, the purpose of this study is to analyze green taxation practices and regulations within the scope of a sustainable economy in Turkey and offer solutions by considering the implementation in various countries with effective green taxation policies.

In this regard, the purpose of this study is to analyze green taxation practices and regulations within the scope of a sustainable economy in Turkey and offer solutions by considering the implementations of various countries with effective green budgeting policies. The importance of this study lies on possible contribution to literature on green taxation that is a newly discussed subject in Turkey and also it hopes to offer policy suggestions. The methodological framework of the study is qualitative. The data to be used in this study are gained from central administration budget revenues and expenditures published by the Turkish Ministry of Finance. To analyze the regulations on green taxation, the Tax Law numbered 213 and the activity reports of Revenue Administration will be used. The study has five sections. The first section presents a literature review about green taxation and sustainable growth, followed by the practices and implementation in some European countries. The third section deal with international efforts for sustainable growth and green taxation. The fourth section offers a general evaluation on Turkish tax legislation and policy goals. The final section analyzes the implementation of green budgeting and the regulations on it in Turkey.

LITERATURE REVIEW: GREEN TAXATION AND SUSTAINABLE GROWTH

It can be said that green taxation was firstly discussed in the 1920s by Arthur C. Pigou, an economist from Britain (Ciocirlan and Yandle, 2003: 203; Daugbjerg and Svendsen, 2001: 7). Pigou argues that external impacts should be regulated through taxes (Wallart, 1999: 9). The concept of externality is generally defined as the impact- either positive or negative- of a decision taken by an economic actor on another economic actor (Zerbe, 1980: 90). According to Pigou, enhancing the welfare is the most important factor enabling to achieve social benefit. The most important factor that prevents reaching optimum welfare level in the economy is the difference between marginal social product and marginal private product. This difference is defined as externality by Pigou (Pigou, 2017: 40). According to Pigou's analysis, the problem of externality is solved when the parties come to an agreement as they are considered independent of each other (Baştürk, 2014: 145). In this case, governments support industries by introducing taxes or intervene by introducing regulations. For instance, there is economic efficiency in a goods market when the demand and the supply for the good balances. And at this point, marginal private cost is equal to marginal benefit. However, when the environmental costs are included into this analysis, it is necessary to consider not only the private cost but also the total cost in order to achieve economic efficiency. In this case, the total of marginal private cost and marginal external cost should be equal to total social cost. In other words, the total of private cost and external cost is equalized to social cost (Wallart, 1999: 46). In their decisions during the market process, producers and consumers consider only the private cost but ignore the external cost, though. In this case -regarded as market failure- Pigouvian tax introduces a pricing system -defined as usage cost - as a solution (Määttä, 1997: 7). In other words, when there is negative externality, the total of marginal private cost and Pigouvian tax is equalized to total demand, thus enabling economic activity. Pigouvian tax helps producers and consumers consider not only the private cost but also the social cost in their economic activities by pricing negative externalities (Wallart, 1999: 47).

Pigou actually introduced an environmental tax to solve the problem of externality that occurs as environmental pollution. Pigouvian-style tax is determined at a level equal to the value of negative externality and is directly related to the amount of pollution. This type of tax represents the ideal principle that "the polluter pays" (Gündüz and Agun, 2013: 60). According to Pigou, *"economic welfare might be increased by taxes upon things which are desired for their uncommonness and by bounties on things that are desired for their commonness"* (Pigou, 2017: 218).

Plott (1966) states that Pigou's theory of levying tax on the production of X that leads to negative externality is inadequate and even wrong under quite restrictive conditions. According to Plott, if external cost (environmental pollution) is to be regulated via tax, the tax should be levied on the output or on the source input. For instance if you want to regulate the environmental pollution (external cost) resulting from a factory via tax, you should put tax on the smoke that comes from the factory's chimney or on the factory's input that causes the smoke (Plott, 1966: 84). In fact, according to Plott "*the first problem, that of determining just exactly what variable should be taxed, becomes just as difficult as the second problem, that of determining what the optimum tax should be*" (Plott, 1966: 87).

Pigouvian-style tax is criticized by another economist Ronald Coase. According to Coase, the problem of the Pigou's conception "*is to declare that there is a divergence between social and private costs, and that the producer creating the externality should be discouraged by government policies such as taxes, subsidies, or regulation*" (Pigou, 2017: 55). With these measures, the efficiency of resource allocations will increase, and the output will be at an optimal level. Coase sees this analysis inadequate in many aspects. Firstly, Pigou's framework compares a laissez-faire state, where externalities are not internalized, to an ideal state, where externalities are corrected by a government policy. *"A better approach would seem to be to start our analysis with a situation approximating that which actually exits, to examine the effects of a proposed policy change and to attempt to decide whether the new situation would be, in total, better or worse than the original one"* (Coase, 2013: 876). Secondly, externalities are not unilateral as argued by Pigou but are based on bilateral relations. Pigou sees one side as the one causing harm and the other side as a victim (affected by the harm), arguing that those causing the harm should compensate that harm (Medema, 1994: 79). According to Coase, *"The real question that has to be decided is: should A be allowed to harm B or should B be allowed to harm A?"* (Coase, 2013: 837). Thirdly, the attempts to internalize the externalities have an operational cost. The governmental action is not cost-free; in some cases, the cost of the policy designed to internalize the externalities may be higher than the benefit gained from decreasing or removing the externalities (Coase, 2018: 845).

As seen, whether to levy tax on the activity itself that causes externality or on the input or output in the production or consumption process during which externality emerges is a subject of discussion. There is also a discussion on whether to put an amount of tax that is equal to the external cost or to determine tax according to a different tax basis. The literature review also shows a recent discussion about how to use the tax revenue gained from environmental pollution: to compensate the externality or to finance tax cuts in other fields (Kargı and Yüksel, 2010: 191). Green taxation is not adequate on its own to show that countries have environmentally-friendly fiscal policies. To argue this, it is necessary to analyze the budget compositions of countries that include revenue and expenditure policies (Downes, 2018). Environmental taxation is considered as a reform to find financial sources necessary to solve environmental problems. Green taxation reform or ecological tax reform does not only mean introducing new environmental taxes. Green taxation reform includes removing financial incentives and tax relief that are hazardous to the environment and restructuring them in an environmentally-friendly way as well as implementing various new financial market tools that take the environment at every stage of economic activity into consideration (Öz and Kutbay, 2016: 248).

Green taxation found a place on governments' agenda particularly in the aftermath of the Second World War as environmental awareness started to rise among the societies. Today, it can be observed that sustainable growth, environmental awareness, and the concepts of green taxation, green procurement, and green budget make sense when they are considered all together (Ahsan and Rahman, 2017; Staropolli, 2017; Bina, 2013, Kates et al., 2016). When sustainable growth is mentioned, it certainly refers to sustainable environment, or green sustainability. The concept of sustainable growth or development has been adopted and included into their programs by big enterprises, governments, social reformers, and environmental activists (Giddings et al., 2002: 189; Bina, 2013). In Brundtland's report, the classical definition of sustainable development is as follows: "*meeting the needs of present without compromising the ability of future generations to meet their needs*" (Walters, 1991: 423). In addition to this definition, the concept has many other definitions, some of which are: (Leal, 2000: 9-10);

- *"The modality of development that enables countries to progress, economically and socially, without destroying their environmental resources (here referring to country policies)";*
- *"The type of development which is socially just, ethically acceptable, morally fair and economically sound (here referring to the social ramifications of development)";*
- *"The type of development where environmental indicators are as important as economic indicators (here referring to the close links it bears with economic Growth".*

As it can be seen, sustainable development has economic, social, cultural, and environmental aspects (Leal, 2000). Environmental policies within the scope of sustainable development are based on four basic principles (Güzel, 2001: 1): the principle of "the polluter pays", the principle of "the user pays", the principle of "caution", and the principle of "locality". In the first principle ("the polluter pays"), the whole cost of protection and control is put on the value of the good and the service produced. In the principle of caution are there the policies to be developed to achieve sustainable development. The principle of locality aims to raise the level of participation in policy-making process and to help local authorities to solve the local problems by determining the policy-making process.

MAJOR ENVIRONMENTAL TAXES AND CURRENT SITUATION

Environmental problems and pollution have recently become an important subject on the agenda of modern societies, and important conferences and workshops have been organized by international organizations and various non-governmental organizations so far to find solutions (Giddings et al., 2002: 187). This has contributed to the relevant literature a lot. While defining environmental taxes or green taxes, OECD emphasized that the purpose of this type of tax is not to generate additional revenue for the budget but only to protect the environment and help change production and consumption preferences in favor of the environment (Barde, 1998: 1).

When tax practices in different countries are analyzed, it is seen that there are various types of environment taxes. There are also different categorizations in the literature, some of which are as follows: indirect taxes introduced specifically for environmental goals, indirect taxes that were not introduced for environmental goals but started to have environmental goals in time, and direct taxes for environmental goals (Kazıcı, 1992: 19). The classification of Ekins (1999) is as follows: (1) Cost-covering charges: *"taxes levied purely with the intention of changing environmentally damaging behavior by increasing the marginal cost of polluting"* (2) Incentive taxes: *"where parties using particular environmental resources contribute to the cost of monitoring or mitigation"* (3) Revenue-raising taxes: *"all environmental taxes yield revenue, which may contribute towards overall public finances or reductions in employment or product taxes"* (Ekins, 1999: 42-43). Another classification that belongs to the OECD and the EU is: (1) energy taxes, (2) transportation taxes, (3) pollution taxes, (4) natural resources taxes (Ferhatoğlu, 2003: 3). Table 1 shows some of the environmentally related taxes in OECD countries. Some of these taxes (Motor Vehicle Tax, FUEL tax, Solid Waste Tax, etc.) are also implemented in Turkey.

In European countries, some environmental taxes are as follows; motor vehicle tax, FUEL tax, waste tax, alcoholic beverage surtax, soft drink surtax, beverage container tax, pesticide fee, energy taxes, air and water pollution tax, battery-accumulator-packing wastes taxes, rubber tire tax, oil waste tax, oil pollution control fee, transportation taxes (Özdemir, 2009: 16).

Table 1. Environmentally related taxes: OECD

Vehicle	*Motor vehicle registration fee:* Tax on import cars, Tires Tax, Railway Tax, Duty of airway security *Motor vehicle tax (payment/year):* Gas guzzler tax *Road tax (€/year):* Tax on congestion, tax on permits to enter historical city district
Energy	*Energy consumption Tax:* Tax on installing nuclear equipment *Air pollution tax:* Tax on CO2 emissions in petroleum activities
Waste	*Packaging charges:* Duty on tires, Hazardous waste. *Waste Deposit Levy:* Tax on the landfilling and incineration of waste, Charge on exceeding of GHG emission limits.
Water	*Water pollution tax:* Tax on pesticides, Charge to discharging of wastewater, Oil release charge *Taxes on water quantity:* Tax on ground water
Other	*Duty on ozone depleting chemicals:* Duty on raw materials
Carbon/Energy/ Fuel Taxes	The principal environmental motivation behind the introduction of carbon/energy/ fuel taxes has been the desire to control CO2 emissions, the main greenhouse gas responsible for global warming and climate Change (Ekins, 1999: 44).

Source: Sebastian Miller and Carlos Ludena, "Green Taxes for a Greener Environment", June, 2012.

Table 2. Environmentally related tax revenue as a share of each country's total tax revenue (%)

Country	2000	2001	2005	2006	2007	2008	2009	2010	2011	2012	2013	2014
Australia	7,9	8,1	6,9	6,7	6,5	6,8	7,2	7,0	6,8	7,6	7,8	
Austria	7,0	7,3	7,7	7,4	7,1	6,9	7,0	6,9	7,1	6,9	6,7	6,7
Belgium	5,7	5,8	6,0	5,4	5,3	5,0	5,3	5,3	5,3	4,9	4,5	4,5
Brazil	2,1	2,1	3,1	3,1	3,1	2,8	2,5	2,8	2,8	2,2	1,9	1,8
Canada	3,8	3,8	3,7	3,6	3,6	3,6	3,8	3,9	3,8	3,7	3,7	3,7
Switzerland	6,8	7,2	7,4	7,1	6,8	6,8	6,7	7,0	6,8	6,7	6,6	6,6
China	3,1	4,6	5,3	5,2	4,9	4,7	7,5	8,0	7,4	7,4	7,3	7,1
Czech Republic	7,5	7,8	8,1	7,9	8,0	8,0	8,4	8,4	8,6	8,4	8,1	7,9
Germany	6,3	7,0	7,1	6,8	6,2	6,0	6,3	6,1	6,1	5,8	5,6	5,4
Denmark	10,6	10,7	10,6	10,4	10,5	9,7	9,1	9,2	9,3	8,9	9,0	8,2
Spain	6,5	6,3	5,6	5,3	5,1	5,2	5,5	5,2	5,1	4,9	5,7	5,6
Estonia	5,2	6,6	7,7	7,3	7,1	7,3	8,3	8,8	8,6	8,6	8,1	8,0
Finland	6,8	6,8	7,1	7,0	6,5	6,4	6,2	6,6	7,2	7,0	6,8	6,6
France	5,2	4,8	4,7	4,6	4,4	4,4	4,5	4,4	4,4	4,3	4,3	4,4
United Kingdom	8,2	7,7	7,0	6,6	6,8	6,8	7,5	7,5	7,2	7,2	7,2	7,2
Greece	6,8	7,6	6,5	6,4	6,4	6,1	6,0	7,6	7,8	7,8	7,9	7,7
Italy	7,1	7,6	6,9	6,8	6,2	6,2	6,6	7,6	8,1	8,6	8,4	8,8
Japan	6,5	6,6	6,4	6,1	5,9	5,8	6,2	5,8	5,6	5,4	5,1	
Korea	12,3	13,2	11,4	10,7	10,8	10,4	9,5	11,0	9,3	9,6	9,2	
Luxembourg	7,1	7,1	7,9	7,4	7,1	7,1	6,6	6,4	6,4	6,2	5,6	5,2
United States	3,4	3,4	3,3	3,2	3,1	3,1	3,4	3,4	3,3	3,2	3,0	2,8
South Africa	8,0	7,3	6,2	5,9	5,9	5,4	7,2	8,6	8,7	8,8	8,6	8,2
Turkey	***11,5***	***11,0***	***17,0***	***15,1***	***15,0***	***14,0***	***14,3***	***15,0***	***13,4***	***13,1***	***13,9***	***13,3***
OECD	***5,8***	***6,0***	***5,8***	***5,4***	***5,3***	***5,1***	***5,6***	***5,7***	***5,5***	***5,3***	***5,3***	***5,1***

Source: OECD Stat, https://stats.oecd.org/Index.aspx?DataSetCode=ENV_ENVPOLICY

Taking the variety of the environmental taxes in both EU and OECD countries into consideration, it is seen that green taxation is attached more and more importance. While preparing their budgets, countries prioritize environmentally-friendly policies and set the goal of sustainable growth. However, the results of the implementation show that the current situation needs to be improved. Table 2 reveals the share of environmental tax revenues in total tax revenues in some OECD and EU countries by years. For instance, the countries with the highest share of environmental taxes in total tax revenues are as follows: Turkey; 13,3, Italy; 8,8, Denmark; 8,2, South Africa; 8,2, and Estonia; 8. The countries with the lowest share are as follows: Brasil; 8, the United States; 2,8, Canada; 3,7, and France; 4,4.

When the share of environmentally related taxes in total tax revenues is analyzed for Turkey (Graph 1), it is seen that Turkey has a higher share than OECD countries for each term between 2000 and 2014. For 2014, while the environmentally related tax revenue as a share of each country's total tax revenue is 5,1 in OECD countries, this figure is 13,3 in Turkey. It is undoubtedly impossible to reveal the level of environmental consciousness of a country only with this share. When the OECD'S indicators of green growth, namely air pollution, carbon productivity, land resources, green innovation, and environmental taxes are analyzed; different results are observed (OECD, 2017).

For instance, the indicators are as follows for OECD and Turkey:

- Share of environmental patents, % of all patents: OECD (11,54), Turkey (6,27)
- Change in built-up area, %: OECD (31,59), Turkey (57,41)
- Change in population, %: OECD (18,35), Turkey (39,52)
- Production-based CO2 productivity: OECD (3,91), Turkey (4,53)
- Population exposed to pollution levels above WHO guidelines, %: OECD (75,16), Turkey (99,92)

These indicators show that the environmentally related taxes in Turkey were not determined to achieve sustainable growth or to help prevent environmental pollution. As seen in detail in the analysis, the environmentally related taxes in Turkey are used as an important source of public revenue more like corporate taxes and revenue taxes.

Figure 1. Trends of Environmentally related tax revenue as a share of each country's total tax revenue 2000-2014
Source: OECD Stat, https://stats.oecd.org/Index.aspx?DataSetCode=ENV_ENVPOLICY

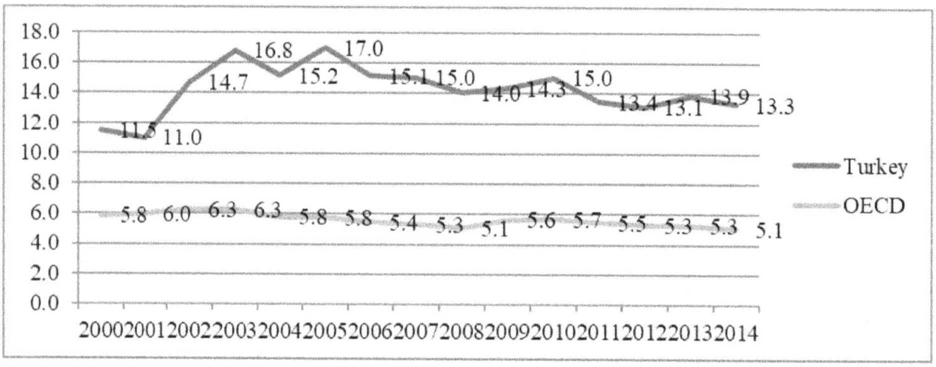

INTERNATIONAL EFFORTS FOR SUSTAINABLE GROWTH AND GREEN TAXATION AND CURRENT SITUATION

As mentioned above, the first scientific study on environmental problems and suggestions for public solution was carried out in the 1920s by Pigou. The most important international step taken for the environment (1972) was the conference on the environment organized by the UN in Stockholm as well as its result-Stockholm Declaration. This declaration is the first document in international environmental law to recognize the right to a healthy environment (Sohn, 1973; Handl, 2012). The subjects discussed in general terms in Stockholm were as follows: environmental planning and management in the settlement areas, natural sources and sea pollution, recognition and audit of environmentally-hazardous substances (Aksu, 2011: 13). The declaration contains a set of "*common principles to inspire and quid the peoples of the world in the preservation and enhancement of the human environment*" (Sohn, 1973: 423). Many of the principles stated in the Declaration are now considered within the scope of the general international law. Some of them have become binding on the states. Article 21 of the Declaration in particular gained the characteristic of hard law in time: *"States may exploit their resources as they wish but must not endanger others"* (Pallemaerts, 1997: 613). Stockholm Declaration was followed by another important document, Brundlant Report in 1987. The importance of the Report is its emphasis on sustainable growth (Daly, 1990: 1; Redclift: 2005). The concept of sustainable development *"was launched: social and economic advance to assure human beings a healthy and productive life, but one that did not compromise the ability of future generations to meet their own needs" (Walters, 1991: 424).* Another focus of the report is as follows*: "Ecology and economy are becoming ever more interwoven - locally, regionally, nationally, and globally-into a seamless net of causes and effects"* (Walters, 1991: 424). Brundlant report contributed to the non-governmental organization' being considered as an important party about environmental and developmental subjects. This contribution reached a peak with the Earth Summit held in 1992 in Rio de Janeiro (Redclift, 2005: 218). With 172 states' participation, the Earth Summit is an unprecedented UN conference in terms of its size, and it yielded five fundamental international documents: the Rio Declaration on Environment and Development, Agenda 21, the UN Framework Convention on Climate Change, the UN Framework Convention on Biodiversity Change, and the Statement of Forest Principles. In the conference, the action plan called *Agenda 21* and the *Rio Declaration* are seen as important steps taken for sustainable economy and green taxation.

The UN Framework Convention on Climate Change was put into effect on March 21, 1994, and it became the institutional framework for sustainable development for the countries. In addition to 196 countries, the EC (European Communities) is a party to the Convention. The main objective of the Convention is to reduce carbon dioxide (CO2) and greenhouse gas emissions and keep the current greenhouse gas concentrations in the atmosphere at a level not threatening human health (UN, 1992). The Convention was based on the idea that some countries should take on more responsibility in the combat against climate change as they emitted more greenhouse gases into the atmosphere following the industrial revolution. The principle of *"common but differentiated responsibilities and respective capabilities"* envisages that countries will participate in this global combat against climate change under their own socio-economic circumstances. In this regard, the Convention categorizes the countries under three groups according to their differentiated obligations: The countries in the first group (Annex 1) are obliged to *"reduce greenhouse gas (GHG) emissions, to protect and develop sinks, and to report the measures they take to prevent climate change and data about GHG emissions". This category comprises 42 countries and EC. The countries in this category (Annex II) are "obliged to transfer environment friendly technologies to specially developing countries and to take all necessary steps to encourage, facilitate and finance access to these technologies on top of other responsibilities they have as being Annex I countries"*. There are 23 countries and EC in Annex II (MFA) The countries under the last category are encouraged to reduce GHG emissions, to cooperate on research and technology and to protect sinks but are not bound by other obligations like the Annex I and II countries. Annex III compromises 153 countries (Ministry of Foreign Affairs). The Kyoto Protocol was signed in 1997-three years after the enactment of the Convention- in the meeting held in Kyoto, Japan by the UN by the signatories of the UN Framework of Climate Change.

Another important step taken for sustainable growth relating to environmental problems is the Vienna Convention for the Protection of Ozone Layer and Montreal Protocol on Substances that Deplete the Ozone Layer. Vienna Convention was adopted in 1985. With 196 parties, Montreal Protocol is regarded as the most successful multilateral agreement on the environment. For the implementation of the Montreal Protocol, Multilateral Fund (MLF) was established with the contributions of the developed countries in London in 1990 (Ministry of Foreign Affairs).

In 2000, the world leaders gathered in the UN's office in New York and announced the Millennium Declaration. The Millennium Declaration set out 8 development goals (to eradicate extreme poverty and hunger, to achieve universal primary education, to promote gender equality and empower women, to reduce child mortality, to improve maternal health, to combat HIV/AIDS, malaria and other diseases, to ensure environmental sustainability, and to develop a global partnership for development) and 18 sub-goals. These goals were to be achieved by 2015. The parties to the Protocol agreed on the majority of the goals (Adams, 2006; Aksu, 2011).

The World Summit on Sustainable Development was held in Johannesburg in 2002 with the broad participation of 104 heads of State and Government as well as non-governmental organizations and committees. The Summit yielded two documents: Johannesburg Declaration and Action Plan. The Declaration states the common responsibilities of the countries for regional and global sustainable development and emphasized their obligations for the protection and sustainability of the environment. The Declaration also underlines the importance of simultaneous movement of economic development and environmental sustainability and focuses on the global cooperation in this regard. Deforestation, loss of biodiversity, global warming, the increase in natural disasters, continuing air, water, and sea pollution are the fundamental environmental problems mentioned in the Declaration (UN, 2002: 16-23).

Finally, Paris Agreement, which forms the framework of the climate change regime, was adopted in UNFCCC 21st Conference, Paris in 2015. The Agreement entered into force on November 4, 2016 after the condition that minimum 55 parties that cause 55% of the global greenhouse gas emissions approve the agreement was met. Paris Agreement aims to enhance the global socio-economic strength against climate change after 2020. The long-term goal of the Agreement is to keep the increase in global average temperature far below 2°C (over pre-industrial levels). This goal requires parties to gradually reduce their use of fossil fuel (petroleum, coal) and raise their share of renewable energy in their consumption (Ministry of Energy and Natural Resources).

LEGISLATION, PLAN AND POLICY GOALS FOR SUSTAINABLE GROWTH AND GREEN TAXATION IN TURKEY

A "Survey on the Perception of Climate Change and Energy Preferences in Turkey"[1] recently conducted with citizens has revealed that citizens in Turkey have high awareness about climate change. 86.8% of the participants answered 'yes' to the question 'Do you believe that there is global warming?' while only 10% said 'no' and 3.2% preferred not to answer the question. Another remarkable question is 'Are you worried about the climate change? If yes, how much worried are you?' which was the question in the European Social Survey conducted in 18 countries in 2017. To this question, 25% of the participants answered "very worried" while 50% answered "worried". Most of the participants (75%) seem worried about the climate change. When the election manifestos declared by five parties [Justice and Development Party (the ruling party), Republican Peoples' Party, Peoples' Democratic Party, İYİ Party and Saadet Party (the opposition parties)] during the latest election (June 2018) process are analyzed it is obvious that environmental problems are attached more importance compared to their previous ones. Besides, the opposition parties criticize the ruling party (Justice and Development Party) for not introducing adequate policies on sustainable development and renewable energy, for causing and economy of unearned income based on construction, and for destroying green areas.

Although citizens, non-governmental organizations, and political parties have recently become more aware of climate change and ecological problems, it can be observed that there is not enough improvement in terms of practices.

In Turkey, the first policies on the environment were included in Five Year Development Plan (1979-1983). During this plan period, Prime Ministry Secretariat of Environment was established, and "The Environment Law" was introduced in line with the principle of sustainable development of the environment in 1983. Emphasizing that it is the responsibility of everyone to protect, improve the environment and prevent the pollution, the Law includes the principle of sustainable development, the principle of participation, the principle of prevention, the principle of "the polluter pays", the principle of absolute liability, the right to information and application, market based mechanisms and education on the environment (Aksu, 2011: 20). In 1995, the preparation process for "National Environmental Strategy and Action Plan" started with the technical support of the Ministry of Environment and the financial aid of the World Bank, and several goals were accordingly set. These goals are as follows (Kırıcı, 2010):

- To improve the life quality
- To raise environmental awareness and consciousness
- To improve environmental management
- To have a sustainable economic, social, and cultural development
- To harmonize national environmental policies with the approaches adopted in 1992 Rio Declaration and Agenda 21

In line with these goals, the State Planning Organization prepared National Environmental Action Plans regarding 'Land Use and Coastal Zone Management', 'Preservation of Natural History and Cultural Values', 'Training and Participation', 'Air Pollution Resulting from the Energy Sector', 'Population and the Environment', 'Management of Water Sources', 'Management of Hazardous Waste' (DPT, 1997). The State Planning Organization also prepared a timetable so that the goals could be achieved in the short-term (1), medium-term (5-10), and long-term within a period of two decades.

Turkey supports international cooperation in the environmental area. The agreements and protocols to which Turkey is a party are as binding as Turkish Environment Law and also form a part of its national legislation. 'Mediterranean

Action Plan" has been carried out by the Mediterranean Countries and European Community since 1975 to implement the Convention for the Protection of the Mediterranean Sea against Pollution (Barcelona Convention) and its additional protocols. This plan moved forward taking measures against the sea pollution following the Rio Conference held in 1992 and turned into a plan aiming to ensure sustainable development in the Mediterranean Region. After becoming a party to Barcelona Convention and its subsequent protocols, the Presidency of Special Environmental Protection Institution was established. 14 Special Environmental Protection Areas have been declared so far. In line with the principles determined following Stockholm Environment Conference in 1972, the Convention on the Conservation of the Wildlife and Natural Habitats (Bern Convention) was signed in 1979. Turkey became a party to the Convention in 1984. Another treaty that Turkey is a party to is the "Convention on the Wetlands" (Aksu, 2011: 21; Yüksek, 2010: 120-121).

The first and the most significant step taken in the international arena was the UN Framework Convention on the Climate Change signed in Rio de Janeiro in 1992. The Convention entered into force in March 1994 and the EU is a party to this convention in addition to 196 countries including Turkey. Turkey became a party to this Convention on May 24, 2004. In 1997, Kyoto Protocol was signed by the parties to the UNFCCC in 1997, but Turkey does not have an obligation of digitized emission restriction/reduction. Turkey became a party to Montreal Protocol on December 19, 1991 and accepted all the amendments introduced by the Protocol. Lastly, Turkey signed Paris Convention on April 22, 2016 in New York (Ministry of Energy and Natural Resources).

AN ANALYSIS OF GREEN TAXATION IN TURKEY

This section analyzes the green taxation implementation in Turkey. Although taxes that can be considered as green taxes in Turkey have an important share in total tax revenue, it should be noted that they are not for environmental purposes. The 'green' taxes included in this study cover Motor Vehicle Tax, Special Consumption Tax (List I Tariff A and B – List II), tax on fuel consumption and vehicle purchase that are within the scope of Special Consumption Tax, Environment and Sanitation Tax, and Electricity Consumption Tax. Finally, natural gas, petroleum, and their products as well as all other energy products, motor vehicle purchase-sales are subject to Value Added Tax.

Motor Vehicle Tax

Introduced with the Motor Vehicle Tax Law dated 18.02.1963 and numbered 197, Motor Vehicle Tax is a type of special property and wealth tax levied on land, air, and sea transportation motor vehicles. While the amount of motor vehicle tax was determined according to a vehicle's weight, cylinder capacity, and age, it changed as of 1.1.2004 with the law dated 25.12.2003 and numbered 5035. The amount of tax is now determined according to a vehicle's cylinder capacity and age. As the vehicle gets older, the amount of tax decreases, which shows that the main purpose of this type of tax is not to protect the environment.

Special Consumption Tax (FUEL Consumption and Vehicle Purchase Tax)

The Special Consumption Tax (SCT) Law numbered 4760 was put into effect in 2002. The goods that can be included into this type of tax are categorized under four lists. List (1) includes petroleum products like petroleum, diesel oil, fuel oil, natural gas. List (II) contains motor vehicles; List (III) comprises there alcoholic and nonalcoholic beverages as well as tobacco and tobacco products; and List (IV) involves electronic products, white goods, some luxurious consumer goods (Canpolat, 2009: 140). SCT's environmentally related taxes can be found under List I. List I/ Category A includes various types of petroleum products and oil types such as aviation gasoline, unleaded normal gasoline, unleaded super gasoline, leaded super gasoline, leaded normal gasoline, natural gas, fuel oil, lubricating oils, differential oil, base oil, jet fuel and motor while List I/ Category B is related to benzene, solvents, varnishes, pentane, ethers, thinners and etc., (Özdemir, 2009:

Table 3. Motor vehicle tax

Tariff	Tax Object	Criterion
List I	Cars, motorbikes, off-road vehicles and etc., and motorcycles	Engine capacity (cm3) and age
List II	Except for the list I; minibus, panel van, motor caravans (engine capacity), bus and etc., (seating place), truck, tractor and etc., (maximum total weight)	The type of the vehicle, seating place, maximum total weight and age
List III	Removed from law according to Article 2 of the Law No. 5897 dated 6/5/2009	-
List IV	Airbus and helicopter	The type of the vehicle, maximum take-off weight and age

Source: Law No. 197 on Motor Vehicles Tax, Retrieved from www.mevzuat.gov.tr.

29). Fuel consumption and vehicle purchase taxes were included in the scope of SCT in 2002. Fuel consumption tax levied on the purchase of petroleum products was included in List I while vehicle purchase tax determined with Motor Vehicle Tax Law was included in List II. Both types of taxes have environmental features as they are products that cause environmental pollution. OECD/EEA considers fuel consumption tax and vehicle purchase tax that were implemented in Turkey and SCT's List (I) and List (II) that are today implemented as environmentally related taxes (Canpolat, 2009: 140-141).

Environmental Sanitation Tax and Electricity Consumption Tax

Environmental sanitation tax and electricity and gas consumption tax were regulated in the articles 44 and 34-39 in the Law on Municipal Revenues numbered 2464. The central management determines the rate, basis, and reduction of the environmental sanitation tax, but municipalities collect and benefit from this type of tax. Also, the central management is authorized to determine the rate and basis of electricity and gas consumption tax. This tax is also collected by the municipalities even if it is indirectly. All of this tax revenue remains to the municipalities. Environmental sanitation tax covers "the buildings -used as houses, workplaces, or in other ways within the borders of the municipalities and urban areas- that benefit from the municipalities' environmental sanitation services", and the taxpayers are those that use these buildings in general. The tax basis is the amount of water consumption. Electricity consumption tax is levied only on electricity consumption. This type of tax is about electricity consumption within the border of municipalities and urban areas, and its taxpayers are electricity users (Gündüz ve Agun, 2013: 74).

Methodology

A qualitative method has been adopted in this study. It aims to reveal the level of green taxation for sustainable growth in Turkey. In this regard, it firstly presents a literature review on the green taxation legislation and the international agreements to which Turkey is a signatory. It also discusses the green programs and objectives accordingly introduced. Secondly, the level of green taxation in Turkey is revealed based on an analysis of tax revenues. The data are obtained from central management budget tax revenues and municipal budget tax revenues. Both data sets are found on the websites of the General Directorate of Public Accounts, the Ministry of Finance. The data were analyzed to find out whether these taxes are an effective deterrent against economic activities that destroy the environment and to what extend the tax revenues are used for the benefit of the environment. As green economy covers a broad literature, this study is restricted to the analysis of the environmentally related

Table 4. The amount of taxes on some products that are under List I and List II

	Type	Tax Amount (Turkish Lira)	Amount of tax /tax rate	Unit
List I- Tariff A	Aviation gasoline	2.5000	0	Liter
List I- Tariff A	Unleaded gas (95 octane)	2,3765	2,3765	Liter
List I- Tariff A	Unleaded gas (98 octane)	2,4985	2,4985	Liter
List I- Tariff A	Jet fuel	2,5000	0	Liter
List I- Tariff A	Diesel fuel	1,7945	1,7945[)]	Liter
List I- Tariff A	Distillate fuel (marine fuel)	1,7945	1,7945	Liter
List I- Tariff A	Oil fuel	0,2370	0,2370	Kilogram
List I- Tariff A	High-sulfur fuel oil	0,2240	0,2240	Kilogram
List I- Tariff A	Natural gas which in use motor vehicles	0,8599	0,8599[)]	Cubic meter
List I- Tariff A	Natural gas and etc.,	0,0230	0,0230	Cubic meter
List I- Tariff B	Benzoyl (Benzene)	2,4985	2,4985	Kilogram
List I- Tariff B	Toulon (Toluene)	2,4985	2,4985[(1)]	Kilogram
List I- Tariff B	Xylol (Xylene)	2,4985	2,4985[(1)]	Kilogram
List I- Tariff B	Solvent naphtha	2,4985	2,4985[(1)]	Kilogram
List I- Tariff B	Hexane	2,4985	2,4985[(1)]	Kilogram
List I- Tariff B	Heptane	2,4985	2,4985[(1)]	Kilogram
List I- Tariff B	Pentane	2,4985	2,4985[(1)]	Kilogram
List II	Attractants for semi-trailers		% 4	-
List II	Self-moving freight vehicles not equipped with lifting equipment for carrying goods at short distances in factories, warehouses, ports or airports Attractors of the kind used on railway station platforms; and parts of these vehicles		% 4	-
List II	Especially designed for moving on snow, with compression ignition internal combustion piston engine (diesel or semi-diesel) or internal combustion piston engine with spark ignition		6,7	-

Source: SCT Law No 4760, Retrieved from www.mevzuat.gov.tr.

taxes. Green public procurement and environmentally-friendly expenditure policies are not included into the scope of this study.

Findings

An analysis of the structure of tax revenues in Turkey shows that the most important source of Inland Revenue is taxes on goods and services (%41). Among them have the value-added tax (VAT) and special consumption tax (SCT) the biggest shares. The share of VAT in total tax revenue is 11% while SCT's share is 26%. The shares of some other tax revenues are as follows: Income tax is 21%, corporate tax is 9% and motor vehicle tax has a share of 2%.

When the shares of taxes called environmentally-related taxes within the scope of Turkish Tax System are analyzed, the findings are as follows: The share of Motor Vehicle Tax is 2,31%, the share of tax on petroleum and natural gas included in the list of Special Consumer Tax I is 12,26%, and the share of tax on motor vehicles included in the list of Special Consumer Tax II is 4,11%. In total, the share of taxes considered within the scope of environmentally related tax in central administration budget tax revenue is 18,55%. Graph 2 shows that this percentage increased from 15,58% in 2000 to 18,55% in 2016, showing an upward trend till the end of 2005 but a downward trend since then. The underlying reason for this is the increase in the income tax and the corporate tax which increased the total tax revenue.

It can be seen that taxes considered as environmentally related taxes have an important share in Turkish budget's tax revenues. The contribution of special consumption tax to this high share should be noted down. SCT in Turkey is different from that in EU and OECD countries (Ferhatoğlu, 2003: 5; Batırel, 2002:5; Özdemir, 2009: 30). The taxes levied on goods and services in these countries increase the cost of the goods and services. With the price increase, it is aimed that the consumers will substitute them with the ones that are not harmful to the environment. In other words it can be observed that special consumption tax is used by these countries to influence the producers' and consumers' choices in various areas from energy save to transportation and environment besides its financial objectives. In Turkey, though, it is seen that more importance is attached to the financial gains of SCT rather than its effects that may prevent the harm to the environment. The scope of SCT in Turkey is a lot wider than the implementation of SCT in the EU. While taxes are levied on the substances and goods that are harmful to health and environment in the EU countries, the substances and goods that do not have such harmful impacts are within the scope of this tax in Turkey. It is possible for the special consumption tax to have a deterrent impact on environmental pollution only with an increase in the price of fuel oil that will thus lead to a restrictive consumption. In practice, the harm that the fuel gives to the environment is determined based on the amount of consumption (kg, liter, etc.) not on its emission, and the tax ratio differs depending on the type of the fuel (gasoline, diesel, auto gas, etc.). This shows that not the environmental aspect but the financial aspect of the tax is attached particular importance (Çelikkaya, 2011: 111).

When Motor Vehicle Tax in Turkey is analyzed, the price of motor vehicles increase, and this leads to a decrease in the use of vehicles and less carbon emission, thus having a positive impact on the environment. With the amendments to the Law (dated 25.12.2003 and numbered 5035), the amount of taxes to be levied on vehicles is now determined according to the cylinder capacity and age rather than their weight. The reason for basing the amount of tax on cylinder capacity is that

Table 5. Environmentally related tax revenue and share of total tax revenues (Thousand TL and %)

	2011	2012	2013	2014	2015	2016
Total Tax Revenues (TTR)	253.809.179	278.780.848	326.169.164	352.514.457	407.818.455	459.001.741
Motor Vehicles Tax Revenues (MVT)	6.003.994	6.716.446	7.353.299	7.786.841	8.948.684	9.986.415
MVT/TTR (%)	***2,36***	***2,40***	***2,25***	***2,33***	***2,30***	***2,31***
Special Consumption Tax (SCT)	64.188.786	71.705.544	85.461.561	91.095.043	105.922.766	120.401.507
SCT-List I (Petroleum and Natural Gas Products)	33.572.623	35.934.622	45.158.151	45.628.139	50.829.553	56.296.381
SCT-List II (Motor Vehicles)	8.567.837	8.408.972	10.564.665	12.850.802	17.026.579	18.872.615
SCT/TTR (%)	**25,28**	**25,72**	**26,20**	**25,84**	**25,97**	**26,23**
SCT- List I/TTR (%)	**13,22**	**12,88**	**13,84**	**12,94**	**12,46**	**12,26**
SCT- List II/TTR (%)	3,37	3,01	3,23	3,64	4,17	4,11
Transportation: Road Bridge-Tunnel Fee Revenues (TL)	20.677	28.043	23.736	33.839	28.739	20.207
Environmentally related tax revenue /Total Tax Revenues (%)	***21,34***	***18,32***	***19,34***	***18,80***	***18,83***	***18,55***
Environmentally related tax revenue/GNDP*	***3,06***	***3,25***	***3,48***	***3,24***	***3,28***	***3,26***

Source: Ministry of Finance, General Directorate of Accounting, Retrieved from www.muhasebat.gov.tr

the more a vehicle's capacity is the more fuel it consumes and the more harmful gas it emits into the environment. As the cylinder capacity of a vehicle increases, the amount of the tax levied on it increases; therefore, this criterion leads the consumers to preferring motor vehicles with lower cylinder capacity, thereby having a more positive environmental impact. The tax to be paid decreases as the vehicle gets older, though. This is completely in contrast with the environmental benefits of the tax. Motor Vehicle Tax in this case encourages using old vehicles that cause more pollution compared to new vehicles as lower tax is levied on them. It should be, however, noted that the government introduced a new bag bill in 2018 to encourage buying new cars, which will be applicable by December 31, 2019. The owners of the vehicles (automobiles, panel vans, minibuses, buses, vans, trucks) older than 16 year-old are allowed to have a Special Consumption Tax reduction of maximum 10 thousand lira on the condition that their vehicles are registered as end-of-life vehicles to be disposed. Although it is argued that the main purpose is not to reduce environmental pollution, it can be said that this change may have a positive impact on the environment. Looking at the share of Motor Vehicle Tax in total revenues, it is seen that it does not have an important share with an average around 2,30%.

An analysis of the environmental sanitation tax whose main purpose is to levy tax on services with a hazardous effect on the environment and which is collected by the municipalities shows that their share in municipal tax revenues is quite low, with a share of 3,87%. The fiscal autonomy of local authorities can be claimed to be rather low (Eroğlu ve Serbes, 2018). Municipalities are financially dependent on the central management. Their own revenues are also at low levels. This can cause the municipalities to be inadequate for fighting against environmental problems. The most important tool that municipalities can use in this fight is green taxation. And the only tax that they have in practice is their environmental sanitation tax that has a very low share in total their revenues.

CONCLUSION

Environmental problems are one important result of the accelerated capitalism that has found itself a new area of valuation- a new form of capitalism known for more consumption, more production, more energy, more fuel, more electricity, more tree cut-downs, and the commodification of the nature more and more. In capitalist economies, the problems related to the environment are discussed within the scope of externalities, and the solutions suggested are generally about pricing the damage. These solutions do not suggest any possibilities for the removal of the damage made to the environment.

Table 6. Environmental Sanitation Tax in Municipalities (%)

	2011	2012	2013	2014	2015	2016
Environmental Sanitation Tax Revenue	386.997	383.329	384.679	361.814	395.296	474.733
Total Tax Revenue	6.878.140	7.232.437	8.196.251	9.283.644	10.839.017	12.225.548
Environmental Sanitation Tax Revenue/Total Municipalities Tax Revenues	5,61	5,29	4,68	3,88	3,64	3,87

Source: Ministry of Finance, General Directorate of Accounting, Retrieved from www.muhasebat.gov.tr

Figure 2. Environmentally related tax revenue /total tax revenues (%)
Source: Ministry of Finance, General Directorate of Accounting, Retrieved from www.muhasebat.gov.tr

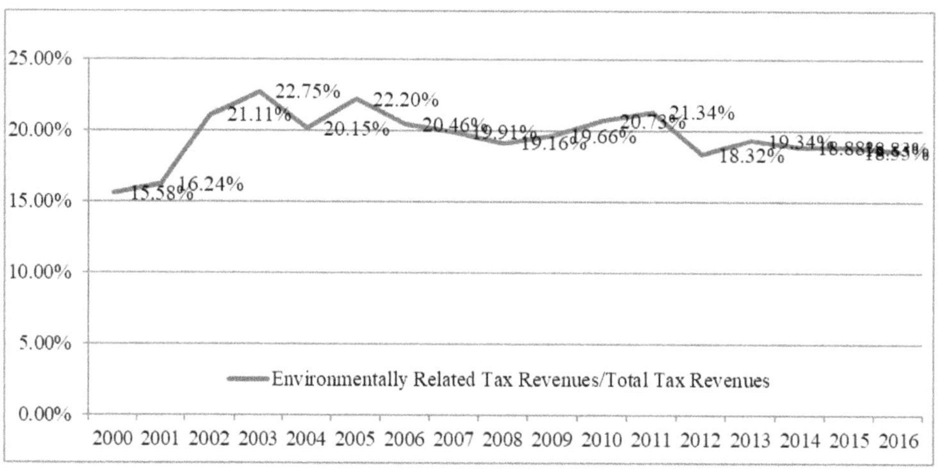

There has been more academic research focusing on environmental problems, contributing to social awareness, though. Governments, international organizations (UN, WHO, EU, OECD), and non-governmental organizations also deal with these problems by organizing conferences, symposiums, and introducing binding agreements that restrict the activities with hazardous effects on the environment. Green taxation has also been suggested as an important policy solution. Although all these efforts are valuable, they are not enough when the indicators of health, environment, and poverty are analyzed. The environmental tax to tax revenue or GDP ratio seems quite low. It is, hence, necessary to increase both green taxes and use the tax revenues to make investment for an environmentally-friendly and sustainable development.

When environmentally-related taxes are analyzed in terms of their ratio to total tax revenues in Turkey, they have a relatively big share compared to OECD countries, but it can be argued that the aim of raising these taxes is not to achieve sustainable growth or to protect the environment. The main purpose of these taxes can be claimed to be rather financial-or to generate revenue for the budget. The indicators alone, hence, do not reveal that Turkey has a green economy. To exemplify with a simple example, Turkey levies the highest tax on fuel in the world, and this tax makes up an important source of revenue for the budget. As a result, it cannot be claimed that the environmentally related taxes in Turkey actually lead individuals or corporations to act in an environmentally-friendly way or to protect the environment. These taxes do not have an impact that reduces the environmental pollution. In this regard, it can be asserted that among the OECD countries, Turkey is one of the countries that benefit from environmentally related taxes the least. With its growing economy, population, industrialization, increasing tourism and urbanization, Turkey needs more inputs like energy and fuel, and this increases industrial waste, environmental pollution, and air pollution. Therefore, it is necessary to introduce new regulations that help producers and consumers to change their preferences with hazardous impacts on the environment rather than the current practices focusing on fiscal goals.

It can be said that the main purpose of the SCT, MVT and Environmental Sanitation Tax analyzed in the scope of the study is not mainly for environmental protection but they indirectly have positive effects on environment. By rearranging these taxes with environmental priority, both sustainable development and environmentally- friendly budgeting can be realized. For example, SCT can be used for environmental purposes by expanding the product range (fuel oil, etc.) to achieve the goal of environmental protection. Similarly, the aspect of MVT that encourages the use of old vehicles can be restructured. Finally, the share of the environmental sanitation tax, which has a relatively small share in municipal revenues but is directly related to the environment, should be increased. This tax benefit principle can be made functional and structured to protect the environment and finance environmental services.

REFERENCES

Adams, W. M. (2006). The Future of Sustainability: Re-thinking Environment and Development in the Twenty-first Century. Report of the IUCN renowned thinkers meeting.

Ahsan, K., & Rahman, S. (2017). Green Public Procurement Implementation Challenges in Australian Public Healthcare Sector. *Journal of Cleaner Production*, *152*, 181–197. doi:10.1016/j.jclepro.2017.03.055

Aksu, C. (2011). Sürdürülebilir Kalkınma ve Çevre. *Güney Ege Kalkınma Ajansı*, 1.

Ballet, J., Banzin, D., Lioui, A., & Touahri, D. (2007). Green Taxation and Individual Responsibility. *Ecological Economics*, *63*(4), 732–739. doi:10.1016/j.ecolecon.2007.05.005

Barde, J. P. (1998). Environmental Taxes in OECD Countries an Overvıew. *Workshop on Environmental Taxes in China and OECD Member Countries*, CCNM/CHINA/EPOC(98)4.

Batırel, F., Ö. (2002). Büyüme Dostu Vergileme ve Türkiye Uygulaması. *Journal of Life Economics, 2*(4), 1-8.

Baştürk, M. F. (2014). Mülkiyet Problemi, Dışsallıklar ve Coasean Çözüm. *Yönetim ve Ekonomi: Celal Bayar Üniversitesi İktisadi ve İdari Bilimler Fakültesi Dergisi*, *21*(1), 143–154.

Bina, O. (2013). The Green Economy and Sustainable Development: An Uneasy Balance? *Environment and Planning. C, Government & Policy*, *31*(6), 1023–1047. doi:10.1068/c1310j

Brunnée, J. (2009). *The Stockholm Declaration and the Structure and Processes of International Environmental Law. In The Future of Ocean Regime-Building* (pp. 39–62). Brill.

Canpolat, S. (2009). *Çevre Vergileri ve Türkiye Uygulaması. Ankara Üniversitesi Sosyal Bilimler Enstitüsü.* Yayımlanmamış Yüksek Lisans Tezi.

Coase, R. H. (2013). The Problem of Social Cost. *The Journal of Law & Economics*, *56*(4), 837–877. doi:10.1086/674872

Ciocirlan, C., & Bruce, Y. (2003). The Political Economy of Green Taxation in OECD Countries. *European Journal of Law and Economics*, *15*(3), 203–218. doi:10.1023/A:1023390126187

Çelikkaya, A. (2011). Avrupa Birliği Üyesi Ülkelerde Çevre Vergisi Reformları ve Türkiye'deki Durumun Değerlendirilmesi. *Anadolu University Journal of Social Science*, *11*(2), 97–120.

Daly, H. E. (1990). Toward Some Operational Principles of Sustainable Development. *Ecological Economics*, *2*(1), 1–6. doi:10.1016/0921-8009(90)90010-R

Daugbjerg, C., & Svendsen, G. (2001). *Green Taxation in Question: Politics and Economic Efficiency in Environmental Regulation.* Springer. doi:10.1057/9780230595538

Downes, R. (2018). *Green Budgeting can Spur Governments to Improve Our Planet's Bottom Line*. Retrieved from http://oecdinsights.org/2018/01/19/green-budgeting-can-spur-governments to-improve-our-planets-bottom-line/

DPT. (1997). *Ulusal Çevre Eylem Planı*. Retrieved from http://okulonceciyiz.biz/upload/ulusal-cevre-eylem-plani-egitim-ve-katilim.pdf

Ekins, P. (1999). European Environmental Taxes and Charges: Recent Experience, Issues and Trends. *Ecological Economics*, *31*(1), 39–62. doi:10.1016/S0921-8009(99)00051-8

Eroğlu, E., & Serbes, H. (2018). Fiscal Autonomy of Sub-Central Governments in Turkey. In *Financial Sustainability and Intergenerational Equity in Local Governments* (pp. 83–100). IGI Global. doi:10.4018/978-1-5225-3713-7.ch004

Ferhatoğlu, E. (2003). Article. *Avrupa Birliği'nde Ortak Çevre Politikası Çerçevesinde Çevre Vergileri*, *3*, 1–7.

Giddings, B., Hopwood, B., & O'Brien, G. (2002). Environment, Economy and Society: Fitting Them Together into Sustainable Development. *Sustainable Development*, *10*(4), 187–196. doi:10.1002d.199

Gale, R., & Barg, S. (Eds.). (2014). *Green Budget Reform: An International Casebook of Leading Practices*. Routledge. doi:10.4324/9781315070636

Gündüz, O., & Agun, B. H. (2013). Çevre Vergilerinin Yerel Yönetim Düzeyinde Uygulanması: Avrupa Birliği ve Türkiye Uygulaması. *Maliye Finans Yazıları*, *27*(99), 55–79.

Güzel, A. (2001). Sürdürülebilir Kalkınma'da Yerel Yönetimlerin Mali Sorumlulukları. *Çevre ve Sürdürülebilir Kalkınma Paneli*, 2023.

Handl, G. (2012). Declaration of The United Nations Conference on the Human Environment (Stockholm Declaration), 1972 and the Rio Declaration on Environment and Development, 1992. *United Nations Audiovisual Library of International Law, 11*.

Kargı V., & Cihan Y. (2010). Çevresel Dışsallıklarda Kamu Ekonomisi Çözümleri. *Maliye Dergisi*, *159*, 183-202.

Kates, R. W., Parris, T. M., & Leiserowitz, A. A. (2005). What is Sustainable Development? Goals, Indicators, Values, and Practice. *Environment (Washington DC)*, *47*(3), 8–21.

Kayapınar, E. Y. (2006). *Ulusal Çevre Stratejisi Eylem Planı*. Çevre ve Orman Bakanlığı ÇED ve Planlama Genel Müdürlüğü, Sunum.

Kazıcı, S. (1992). *Vergilendirme ve Çevre. Vergi Dünyası.* Aralık.

Kırıcı, M. (2010). *Avrupa Biriliği'nde ve Türkiye'de Çevre ve Ulaştırma Sektör Politikalarının Bütünleştirilmesi ve Uygulamaların Karşılaştırılmalı Olarak İncelenmesi, 5.* Ulusal Çevre Mühendisliği Kongresi.

Kreiser, L. A., Sterling, A. Y., Herrera, P., Milne, J. E., & Ashiabor, H. (Eds.). (2012). *Green Taxation and Environmental Sustainability* (Vol. 12). Edward Elgar Publishing. doi:10.4337/9781781952184

Leal Filho, W. (2000). Dealing with Misconceptions on the Concept of Sustainability. *International Journal of Sustainability in Higher Education, 1*(1), 9–19. doi:10.1108/1467630010307066

Määttä, K. (2006). *Environmental taxes: an introductory analysis.* Edward Elgar Publishing.

Medema, S. G. (1994). *Ronald H. Coase.* London: The Macmillan Press.

Ministry of Foreign Affairs (MFA). (n.d.). Retrieved from http://www.mfa.gov.tr/united-nations-framework-convention-on-climate-change-_unfccc_-and-the-kyoto-protocol.en.mfa

Ministry of Energy and Natural Resources. (n.d.). Retrieved from http://www.enerji.gov.tr/en-US/Pages/International-Negotiations

Ministry of Finance. (n.d.). *General Directorate of Accounting.* Retrieved from www.muhasebat.gov.tr

OECD. (2011). *Environmentally Related Taxes in OECD Countries: Issues and Strategies.* OECD Publication Service.

OECD. (2017). *Green Growth Indicators.* Retrieved from http://www.oecd.org/greengrowth/green-growth indicators/

Öz, E., & Kutbay, H. (2016). Ekolojik Vergileme: Seçilmiş Bazı Dünya Ülkeleri ile Türkiye Verilerinin Karşılaştırılması. *Eskişehir Osmangazi Üniversitesi İİBF Dergisi, 11*(1), 247–272.

Özdemir, B. (2009). Article. *Küresel Kirlenme Sürdürülebilir Ekonomik Büyüme ve Çevre Vergileri Maliye Dergisi, 157,* 1–36.

Pallemaets, M. (1997). Stocholm'den Rio'ya Uluslararası Çevre Hukuku: Geleceğe Doğru Geri Adım mı? (trans.) Bülent Duru. *Ankara Üniversitesi SBF Dergisi, 52*(1), 613–632.

Pigou, A. (2017). *The Economics of Welfare*. Routledge. doi:10.4324/9781351304368

Plott, C. R. (1966). Externalities and Corrective Taxes. *Economica, 33*(129), 84–87. doi:10.2307/2552274

Redclift, M. (2005). Sustainable Development (1987–2005): An oxymoron comes of age. *Sustainable Development, 13*(4), 212–227. doi:10.1002d.281

Schlegelmilch, K. (1999). *Green Budget Reform in Europe: Countries at the Forefront: With 20 Figures and 142 Tables*. Springer Science & Business Media. doi:10.1007/978-3-642-58637-8

Sebastian, M., & Carlos, L. (2012). *Green Taxes for a Greener Environment*. IDB. Retrieved from http://www.imf.org/external/np/seminars/eng/2012/rio/pdf/smcl.pdf

Sohn, L. B. (1973). Stockholm Declaration on the Human Environment. *The Harv. Int'l. LJ, 14*, 423.

StaropoliC.SteinerM. (2016). *Green Public Procurement*. Retrieved from https://www.webssa.net/files/slides_coursegpp-2017.pdf

UN. (1992). *United Nations Framework Convention on Climate Change*. Retrieved from https://unfccc.int/sites/default/files/conveng.pdf

UN. (2002). National Implementation of Agenda 21: A Summary. *Johannesburg Summit 2012*. Retrieved from http://www.un.org/esa/agenda21/natlinfo/

UN. (2012). Rio Declaration on Environment and Development. *United Nations Conference on Environment and Development,* A/CONF.151/26. Retrieved from http://www.undocuments.net/rio-dec.htm

Yüksek, M. (2010). *Sürdürülebilir Kalkınma ve Türkiye'de Çevre Politikaları. Gaziantep Üniversitesi Sosyal Bilimler Enstitüsü*. Yayımlanmamış Yüksek Lisans Tezi.

Zerbe, R. O. (1980). The Problem of Social Cost in Retrospect. *Research in Law and Economics, 2*, 83–102.

Wallart, N. (1999). *The Political Economy of Environmental Taxes. In New Horizons in Environmental Economics*. Cheltenham, UK: Edward Elgar.

Walters, M. (1991). Ecological Unity and Political Fragmentation: The Implications of the Brundlant Report for the Canadian Constitutional Order. *Alberta Law Review, 29*(2), 420–449.

KEY TERMS AND DEFINITIONS

Environmental Problems: Ecological problem is degradation in ecological system as a result of global warming, climate change, loss of biodiversity.

Environmental Sanitation Tax: It is a kind of environmental tax collected from housing and workplaces that uses the cleaning services of municipalities.

Externalities: An externality is a positive or negative consequence of an economic activity experienced by unrelated third parties.

Green Taxation: Green taxation is a state intervention for negative externality. With green tax, negative externalities are included into price, and the cost of pollution is minimized.

Motor Vehicle Tax: A tax on motor vehicles. Land motor vehicles registered to traffic bureaus or offices; also, helicopters and airplanes registered to the Directorate General of Civil Aviation are subject to the tax.

Negative Externalities: Negative externality is defined a cost that is suffered by a third party as a result of an economic transaction.

Special Consumption Tax: Special consumption tax (SCT) is levied only for once at one stage of consumption process of the goods within the scope of four lists annexed to the SCT Law No. 4760.

Sustainable Development: Meeting the needs of present without compromising the ability of future generations to meet their needs.

Sustainable Growth: Sustainable economic growth means a rate of growth that can be maintained without creating other significant economic problems, especially for future generations.

ENDNOTE

1. İklim News and Konda Research and Consultancy Company cooperated for the "Survey on the Perception of Climate Change and Energy Preferences in Turkey" carried out with 2595 citizens based on face-to-face interviews.

Chapter 12
Nonlinear Effect of Financial Efficiency and Financial Competition on Heterogeneous Firm R&D:
A Study on the Perspective of Sustainable Finance

Min Xiao Du
Yingkou Institute of Technology, China

Yang Gao
Dalian University of Technology, China

Yu Wang
Dalian University of Technology, China

Bei Bei Chen
Dalian University of Technology, China

Sang-Bing Tsai
https://orcid.org/0000-0001-6988-5829
University of Electronic Science and Technology of China Zhongshan Institute, China & Civil Aviation University of China, China & WUYI University, China

ABSTRACT

Green finance focuses on the coherence and sustainability of finance. This chapter studies the influence of financial scale, financial efficiency, and financial competition on enterprise R&D investment, which includes the different side effects of financial quantity and quality, and to some extent reflects the coherence and sustainability of financial development. The authors use manufacturing company data, regional financial quantity, and quality indicators from 2005 to 2007. The results reveal that

DOI: 10.4018/978-1-5225-7808-6.ch012

(1) less developed area enterprises, or low- and medium-technology enterprises, a large amount of financial quantity expansion cannot support the R&D activities of high innovation efficiency, and (2) financial efficiency and financial competition have a nonlinear effect on firm R&D. Low financial efficiency leads to a lack of efficient firm R&D financial development. The results of the chapter reveal a crucial approach to improve the effect of financial inefficiency on firm R&D by changing from merely expanding financial quantity to improving quality instead.

INTRODUCTION

Enhancing the key role of the market mechanism in the allocation of resources, encouraging enterprise innovation and technological progress, and improving the investments of financial capital in the real economy are crucial to achieving sustained economic growth, industrial upgrading, and avoiding China's "middle income trap". Nevertheless, the financial sector has double characteristics. On one hand, as the core role of modern economic resource allocation, the efficient operation of the financial industry is conducive to the promotion of the development of the real economy. On the other hand, both the sharp expansion of financial scale and excessive speculation will lead to the departure of the initial objective of financial services in the real economy. Financial development theory does not clearly define how to invest limited capital into a firm's innovation and technological progress at the micro level. Since 2015, China's economic growth has entered the "New Normal," and from 2016 to 2020, potential gross domestic product (GDP) growth will increase from 5.7 to 6.7%. Besides, an apparent L-type downward trend indicates that profit driven industrial capital is pursuing short-term profits through the penetration of the financial sector, which leads to a shortage of core technologies in the entity sector, a decline in investment rate, and unsustainable economic growth. While China's financial development is undergoing a quantitative expansion, it is relatively inefficient. Thus, from this point of view, it is of great theoretical value to study the influence of financial development on enterprise innovation. Howbeit, current studies on the relationship between financial development and innovation investment, most of which concentrated on either financing constraints or the interests and challenges of financial structures, lacked integration of the quality level of the financial sector resulting from financial efficiency and financial competition. So it is hard to explicate the demand for the logical shift of financial development from scale expansion to efficiency improvement. Thus, in view of the vital factor of enterprise heterogeneity characteristics—i.e., total factor productivity—this chapter chooses the relationship among financial efficiency, financial competition, and micro-level firm R&D investments as its basic research object. This chapter draws the conclusion through empirical tests: The threshold effect exists when the financial efficiency and financial competition affect the innovation investment of enterprises. Only improvements in financial efficiency and moderate competition can promote firm R&D significantly. In order to effectively reduce the impact of financial inefficiency on R&D in China's companies, it is vital to change from merely expanding financial quantity to improving quality.

FINANCIAL DEVELOPMENT AND HETEROGENEOUS FIRM R&D

Financial Development

Due to the rise of the research on the influence of financial development on the real economy, micro-enterprises financial development or economic innovation investment research has received extensive attention. From the perspective of financial structure, this chapter analyzes the comparative advantage of promoting R&D investment in the banking and market-oriented financial structures, as well as the inflow of foreign capital under the opening of the financial markets. On the basis of studies on bank-dominated financial structure, such as Baum (2011), financial intermediation is good at collecting and processing information, which is conducive to resources collection and economic development. Nevertheless, On the basis of studies on market-dominated financial structures such as Gustav (2010), financial markets can provide more flexible financial risk products and risk management tolls; nevertheless, banks are generally cautious, which is detrimental to innovation and growth. With the opening and deepening of financial markets, the inflow of foreign capital has continuously enhanced the role of domestic financial structure in promoting innovative investments in the real economy. In addition, countries with high efficient financial systems export financial intermediation functions to countries with low efficiency; therefore, this will help achieve innovative capital allocation and risk diversification functions, increasing firm R&D, as Bertrand (2009) pointed out.

The Impact of Productivity Level on Firm R&D Input Level

Many studies have also considered the impact of corporate characteristics on R&D while studying the impact of financial development on firm R&D investments. Schumpeter's research on the influence of internal factors (ranging from scale to capital intensity, age, profit, and human resource differences) on firm R&D was the first study in the field. But these factors rarely include the core of firm heterogeneity:

productivity levels. A large number of studies have focused on the impact of R&D on corporate productivity but have not noticed that corporate productivity usually reflects the contribution of non-productive factors, such as institutional environment or technological progress (Shen, Yan, & Tzeng, 2017). Different productivity levels can often reflect significant differences in technological level or innovation efficiency of enterprises, and innovation behavior is different in R&D. In addition, the sensitivity to external factors is also various (Jefferson, Huamao, Xiaojing, & Xiaoyun, 2006; Salomon & Shaver, 2005). Yang integrated firm R&D (Yang, Chiao, & Kuo, 2010), productivity, and exports into the overall analysis framework by using the three-stage ordinary least square (OLS) method. The method indicates that the improvement of firm R&D productivity leads to a change in and choice of the firm's own R&D activities after the export of self-selection behavior. That is to say, the higher the productivity level of the enterprise, the stronger the motivation of R&D, and the higher the corresponding R&D investment (Booth, Ntantamis, & Zhou, 2015; Yang & Chen, 2012).

China's Financial Development

When we combine the analysis of the impact mechanism of macro-financial development on firm R&D investment with the self-characteristics of heterogeneous firm R&D, we find that with the financial development of the economy, the financial sector should effectively use funds to firms with higher R&D capability and efficiency so as to better improve the optimal innovation scale and promote the sustainable development of the real economy (Chu et al., 2017). Thus, it is of great importance to judge whether China's financial development is conducive to the flow of financial resources to more efficient companies. First, the complexity and uncertainty of the high-tech R&D projects are very outstanding. A large number of SMEs (Czarnitzki & Hottenrott, 2011a), especially in the early stages of high-tech enterprises, lack guaranteed assets. Next, there is a fundamental conflict between capital requirements bank credit security principles, which makes it difficult to obtain bank credit financing. Second, in the context of information opaqueness and a lack of asset liquidity, financiers have to depend on their own backgrounds and special advantages to intervene and guide the flow of resources in the financial sector. This phenomenon mainly relies on the enterprise's own reputation or security. Especially in state-owned enterprises, the implicit guarantee of the government or the country has led to the reverse selection of R&D financing of state-owned financial institutions for non-state enterprises (Artz, Norman, Hatfield, & Cardinal, 2010; Bougheas, Gorg, & Strobl, 2003). Therefore, this chapter develops hypothesis 1.

Hypothesis One: Expansion of the financial scale can lead to the deviation of financial funds from supporting high-efficiency firms for R&D input, resulting in financial inefficiencies to appear.

FINANCIAL EFFICIENCY, FENANCIAL COMPETITION, AND FIRM R&D

Financial Efficiency and Firm R&D

According to the financial scale, quantitative growth cannot automatically lead to improved financial efficiency. Nevertheless, financial efficiency plays a key role in the financing process that promotes economic development. The level of financial efficiency determines financial strength and financial costs. Thus, financial efficiency largely determines the overall level of economic efficiency (Beck & Levine, 2002). For countries in transition, only through the promotion of real economy growth can we really establish the strong supporting mechanisms of a financial system in the real economy (Silva & Carreira, 2012), especially the entity firm R&D needs to speed up financial reform (Sher & Yang, 2005) and financial innovation, and improve financial efficiency. Compared to firm R&D, the core function of financial development is to choose the most innovative entrepreneurs and effectively allocate funds to support entrepreneurs' innovation and entrepreneurship activities to achieve sustained economic growth (Anwar & Sun, 2011; Dehesa, Druck, & Plekhanov, 2007).

The financial structure dominated by China's big banks and the difficulties in financing for SMEs have led to the frictionless financial inefficiency scale, which has constrained financing scale of these enterprises, thus thereby suppressing the level of innovation and investment (Cull, Davis, Lamoreaux, & Rosenthal, 2006). Financial capital flows to inefficient state sectors, making it difficult to increase the scale and efficiency of financial development (Beck & Levine, 2002; Rajan & Zingales, 2003). In the Chinese banking sector, the higher the proportion of government ownership, the smaller the credit inefficiency affects SME innovation, and even more negative (Xiao & Zhao, 2012). Therefore, under the condition of the low efficiency in financial markets, the pure financial expansion cannot effectively promote more efficient businesses and may even inhibit firm R&D at innovative and efficient enterprises without political or government guarantees. As a result, this chapter develops hypothesis 2.

Hypothesis Two: Financial efficiency has a threshold effect on firm R&D. Only by improving financial efficiency and strengthening the quality of financial development can we promote firm R&D efficiency.

Financial Competition and Firm R&D

Improving and enhancing financial efficiency is crucial—especially in transition economies and in China, where the banking industry is highly monopolistic. Only through a fully competitive financial market can the Pareto optimal allocation of financial resources—namely financial efficiency—be realized. When perfect competitive is difficult to achieve, the Pareto improvement of financial resource allocation should be achieved by encouraging competition and developing competitive financial markets. In the credit market, financial enterprises, as the main bodies of organizing deposits and issuing loans, often compete for achieving management goals and strengthening businesses. As capital providers, these companies also transport capital to the highest-income economic field, seeking efficient capital allocation. The degree of financial market competition is a qualitative financial development index which is parallel with the scale and efficiency of the financial intermediation development (Beck & Levine, 2002; Rajan & Zingales, 2003). In the case of a distorted financial structure, cooperation between foreign direct investment and private enterprises can encourage banks to provide loans to the private sector, which can offset distortions and help to improve financial efficiency. However, whereas financial competition has promoted the expansion of the financial system, increased financial efficiency and improved the innovation of entities, excessive competition may lead to impulsive, blind and disorderly financial markets, and may even result in confusion in the country's macro-financial order and economic and social disorder. In particular, China is transitioning from an old system to a new one, with local government intervention hidden behind financial competition; this kind of intervention has distorted the local financial structure as an exogenous force in the process of capital deepening, causing it to deviate from the optimal financial structure determined by the local factor endowment structure and leading to a deadline of financial efficiency in this capital deepening process (Borck, Caliendo, & Steiner, 2007; Edmark & Ågren, 2008). Thus, this chapter develops hypothesis 3.

Hypothesis Three: Financial competition has a threshold impact on firm R&D input. Moderate financial competition can effectively improve inefficiencies in innovation capital allocation in the financial sector, thereby increasing firm R&D.

RESEARCH DESIGN

Research Samples and Data Sources

This chapter adopts enterprise statistical data of the "China Industrial Enterprise Database" (2005–2007), which is solicited and compiled by the National Bureau of Statistics from all state-owned and non-state-owned enterprises. Limited by the time range of industrial enterprises' innovation investment data, this chapter selects the time span from 2005 to 2007, because the number of enterprises is large, the coverage is extensive, and the panel data is wide and short. Financial development indicators (regional financial efficiency indicators, regional financial institution loan balances and regional financial competition indicators, and others) are from the "China Financial Yearbook" (2011) and "China's Marketization Index - The Relative Process of Marketization in Various Regions 2009 Report." In this chapter, we will adopt the Access 2010 and Stata11.0 statistical software packages to complete the data processing by screening 35,859 samples, all with positive R&D investment.

Selection and Definition of Variables

Definition and Measurement of Quantitative and Qualitative Indicators of Financial Development

1. In order to select the size of the financial development (fd) indicators, Goldsmith (1969) put forward the concept of a financial correlation ratio: total financial assets and all tangible assets—the value of national wealth—to measure the level of financial development. However, Beck (2002) pointed out that it should not just compare the quantitative differences among different qualitative projects. Therefore, this chapter draws on the research results of Lu (2009) and uses the ratio of total loans to GDP of financial institutions in various regions rather than the quantitative scale of financial development to study its influence on firm R&D.
2. According to the Beck's definition of financial efficiency (Beck & Levine, 2002) and Ranjian's choice of financial efficiency indicators (Rajan & Zingales, 2003), financial efficiency indicators are selected. (1) LDR (decre) bank loans have the greatest impact on investment growth in different regions; thus, we use the year-end loan balance / year-end deposit balance of provincial financial institutions to reflect the conversion efficiency of savings investment in the banking system, which represents the micro-efficiency of the banking system. (2) The loan proportion of non-state-owned enterprises (credit) is equal to the loan amount of non-state enterprises / total loan amount. Market activities

should enable capital to flow to more efficient industries under the condition socialist market economy (Org, 2004). Non-state-owned enterprises become active market participants because of their high operating efficiency and should deserve financial support commensurate with their contribution. This situation shows that the financial allocation efficiency of social resources is an important aspect of macroeconomic financial efficiency inspection (Chen, Sun, Tang, & Wu, 2011).

The data are represented by the proportion of non-state-owned loans to financial institutions in China's market-oriented index report, which contains short-term loans, long-term loans, and loans provided by financial institutions to all non-state-owned enterprises. (3) With regard to the savings investment conversion rate (dein), the savings raised by financial institutions can only increase value when converted into capital and flow through the production sector. On the premise of a high savings rate, the efficiency of investment savings reflects the ability of regional finance to create wealth, which is a key aspect of financial development efficiency. Therefore, this chapter uses the ratio of total capital formation (the total amount of fixed capital and the value of inventory changes over a period of time) to the deposit balance of financial institutions in various regions to express the conversion rate of savings investment, which stands for the impact of micro-banks on macroeconomic efficiency.

3. As for the selection of financial competition indicators, this chapter learns from and complements Beck and Rajan's (Beck & Levine, 2002; Rajan & Zingales, 2003) selection method and divides them into the following concepts. (1) We use non-state financial institutions to absorb deposits as a percentage of deposits in all financial institutions to reflect the level of competition in the domestic credit market, and the data come from the China market-oriented index report. (2) China's financial system is represented by a banking monopoly that is openness to the outside world and the inflow of foreign capital. The competitive landscape of local financial institutions will inevitably be affected by these changes. Therefore, this chapter uses the proportion of provincial foreign direct investment to GDP (FDI) to measure the level of competition associated with financial liberalization.

Selection of Other Major Variables

1. Enterprise innovation input level (R&D) (Brown, Fazzari, & Petersen, 2009; Lai, Lin, & Lin, 2015) refers to the proportion of firm innovation investment in total assets.

2. As for the productivity of heterogeneous enterprise (tfp), this chapter adopts the HTFP method to measure the total factor productivity index of enterprises, the C-D production function as the research object, LnQ to represent the natural logarithm of the firms' output Q, LnK to represent the natural logarithm of enterprise capital K, LnL to represent the natural logarithm of the labor force, and the logarithmic approximation of total factor productivity, LnTFP, to represent the residuals obtained by using OLS as a linear regression without interception, that is, the enterprise's "Solow residual value." In this chapter, the lagged variable of enterprise productivity is introduced into the model as an explanatory variable.
3. With respect to enterprise internal cash flow (cf), this chapter uses the ratio of an enterprise's net cash flow from operating activities and assets to measure internal cash flow (Brown & Petersen, 2009), i.e., net cash flow / assets.
4. Export (ex) represents the ratio of exports to total sales revenue. Since the export variables have many zero observations, in order to avoid the estimation deviation caused by too many missing values, we introduce the form ln(1+ex/sales). We introduce the lagged export variables into the model as explanatory variables to avoid the endogenous problems caused by enterprise export and R&D intensity (Wang, Lu, Huang, & Lee, 2013; Shen, 2017).
5. Enterprise capital intensity (k/l) refers to the total fixed assets / total number of employees of the company.
6. Industry concentration (HHI) uses the Herfindahl-Hirschman Index (Matsumoto, Merlone, & Szidarovszky, 2012; Matsumoto, Merlone, & Szidarovszky, 2008) to control the competitive structure within the industry.
7. Regarding enterprise size (Size) (Shin & Kim, 2011), we use the logarithm of sales revenue as the proxy variable of enterprise size.
8. Enterprise age (Age) refers to the time span from the start-up to the statistical year of the enterprise.
9. Industry (Industry) and annual dummy variables (Year) are introduced as control variables (Shen, 2017; Czarnitzki & Hottenrott, 2011b).

EMPIRCIAL RESULTS

Descriptive Statistical Analysis of Variables

Table 1 reports the descriptive statistical analysis of the variables. In Table 1 and the analysis below, we use the winsorization method for all variables to handle extreme values at the 1% and 99% levels (Anton & Bostan, 2017) in order to mitigate the impacts of outliers.

Table 1. Descriptive statistical analysis of the characteristics of each variable

Variables		Average variables	Median variables	Standard deviation	Minimum	Maximum
Financial scale	Fd	1.092	0.962	0.365	0.612	2.234
Financial efficiency	Dein	0.329	0.337	0.124	0.098	0.877
	Decre	0.710	0.713	0.095	0.348	0.929
	Credit	10.140	10.59	2.088	2.690	13.150
Financial Competition	Nonde	8.106	8.160	1.873	-3.980	11.010
	FDI	4.066	4.140	2.044	-0.010	9.390
R&D	RDI	0.021	0.006	0.052	4.04E-07	2.557
Heterogeneity	TFP	3.919	3.771	0.769	0.449	7.787
Control variables	CF	0.053	0.581	0.305	-13.870	23.955
	EX	4.811	0.011	5.340	0.000	19.014
	K/L	4.223	4.059	1.261	-3.215	14.058
	HHI	0.145	0.039	0.301	0.018	0.911
	SIZE	11.589	10.535	1.678	4.868	19.047
	AGE	14.698	7.000	16.097	0.000	407

Data source: "China Industrial Enterprise Database"(2005-2007), "China Financial Yearbook" (2011) and provincial statistical yearbook, each metric contains 35859 samples.

Impact of Financial Development on Heterogeneous Firm R&D Research

Construction of Measurement Model

This section examines the influence of the quantitative expansion of financial development on R&D of heterogeneous corporates, and further explores the R&D configuration efficiency of heterogeneous enterprise finance development. Therefore, we take firm R&D as an explained variable, and other variables such as financial development scale, firm heterogeneity characteristics (total factor productivity) as explanatory variables. We develop the following panel model according to the academic standard modeling methods (Hanh, 2014):

$$R\&D_{\mathrm{it}} = \beta_0 + \beta_1 \mathrm{FD}_{it} + \beta_2 TFP_{it-1} + \beta_3 CF_{it} + \beta_4 EX_{it-1} + \beta_5 (K/L)_{it} + \beta_6 HHI_{it} + \beta_7 SIZE_{it} + \beta_8 AGE_{it} + \sum Year_t + \sum Industry_j + \varepsilon_{it} \quad (1)$$

In equation (1), i denotes the enterprise, t denotes the period, and j denotes the industry category. See the definitions of the variable names above.

Empirical Results Analysis

Table 2 shows the results of the effect of the development of financial scale on heterogeneous firm R&D divided by enterprise ownership type, industry differentiation, and regional economic development level. (1) For state-owned enterprises and private enterprises, financial quantitative development has a significant positive effect on the R&D of the former (rather than the latter). This result reveals that under the monopoly of China's state-owned banks, the quantitative development of finance has constrained banks' credit resources and allocated them to either the government or elite state-owned enterprises with close ties to the government. (2) For high-, middle-, and low-tech companies, the quantitative development of finance positively affects high-tech companies, but it does not affect low- and medium-technology companies. This result shows that as China's high-tech industry is protected by national policies and local governments, the development of the banking system will help the innovation activities of enterprises that rely more on external capital. (3) For enterprises in developed areas and underdeveloped areas, financial quantitative development also has a positive impact on the former and a negative impact on the latter as in economically underdeveloped areas, enterprises are usually small and the returns are relatively low. Moreover, it is hard to get innovative financing from large banks and financial markets. When the financial function does not exist, funds cannot be effectively configured.

Table 2 also represents the influence of enterprises' heterogeneity (productivity) on their own innovation investment. Generally speaking, the total factor productivity of enterprises has a positive impact on R&D among enterprises with different ownership systems, in different industries, and in different regions, indicating that high productivity enterprises have strong innovation capabilities. On the contrary, we find that the productivity of enterprises has a more significant impact on the private sector, economically underdeveloped regions, and low-tech industries. Therefore, such firms or firms in this region have stronger incentive to innovate and try to increase their competitiveness through innovation. Nevertheless, these companies do not obtain enough innovation financing from their own country's financial scale development, encountering internal cash flow restrictions.

Table 2. Impact of financial development on heterogeneous firm R&D research

	Divided by ownership		Divided by industry		Divided by region	
Variables	**State-owned enterprises**	**Private enterprise**	**High-tech industry**	**Middle and low-tech industry**	**Developed regions**	**Underdeveloped regions**
Fd	0.0040127**	0.0011563	0.00494***	-0.0018923***	0.0034215***	-0.0012009
	(2.90)	(0.23)	(5.48)	(-3.03)	(4.89)	(-0.48)
Tfp	0.0088791***	0.0331841***	0.0141752***	0.0177676***	0.0185776***	0.0117284***
	(10.77)	(21.38)	(28.31)	(25.36)	(28.77)	(21.72)
Ex	0.0003967***	0.0003579*	0.0002584***	0.0001246	0.0002265**	0.0005444***
	(3.56)	(1.69)	(3.97)	(1.29)	(2.33)	(6.90)
Cf	0.0003128	0.0028265*	0.0016551	0.0024428*	7.36e-07	0.0021157*
	(0.35)	(1.91)	(1.51)	(1.72)	(0.45)	(1.77)
k/l	1.80e-07**	0.0000195***	3.40e-06***	6.15e-07***	7.70e-07***	6.01e-07**
	(2.63)	(9.07)	(8.20)	(4.28)	(5.65)	(2.17)
HHI	-0.00421*	-0.00417*	-0.00438*	-0.00455*	-0.00468*	-0.00472*
	(-1.73)	(-1.68)	(-1.81)	(-1.92)	(-1.98)	(-2.04)
Size	0.0046862***	0.0069438***	0.0055577***	0.006587***	0.006202***	0.0064398***
	(11.84)	(7.05)	(20.91)	(19.08)	(18.70)	(23.77)
Age	-0.0000763***	0.0000603	-0.0000567***	0.0000677*	-0.0000445**	0.0000267
	(-3.42)	(0.54)	(-3.06)	(1.99)	(-2.29)	(1.15)
cons.	0.0480681***	-0.0208204*	0.0418401***	0.0317505***	0.0445082***	0.049962***
	(10.43)	(-1.92)	(14.32)	(7.09)	(7.29)	(12.67)
R2	16.95	17.36	15.56	14.58	14.54	15.87
statistic F	27.27***	76.6***	159.42***	115.78***	141.45***	133.57***
N	2565	6762	6322	5631	14862	4522

NOTE: () is for the variable t statistics; *, **, *** indicate that they passed the test at significant levels of 10%, 5%, 1% respectively; each model contains dummy variables "industry (Industry) and year (Year)" which are not listed in the table to save space. The definition of high-tech industry is based on the "Catalog of High-tech Industry Statistics" issued by the National Bureau of Statistics in 2006. It can be viewed on the website: http://www.stats.gov.cn/tjbz/t20061123_402369836.htm; This chapter defines eastern China as economically developed regions, which contains Beijing, Tianjin, Hebei, Shanghai, Jiangsu, Zhejiang, Fujian, Shandong, Guangdong, Joan, Liaoning and other 11 regions, and the rest of central and western China are defined as economically underdeveloped regions.

Impact of Financial Efficiency and Financial Competition on Private Firm R&D Research

Measurement Model Construction and Inspection

In this section, we examine the effect of financial development qualitative improvements on heterogeneous firm R&D and further explore the effect of financial development on the distribution efficiency of heterogeneous firm R&D. Therefore, we take firm R&D as the explained variable, the qualitative indicators of financial development (financial efficiency, financial competition) as the threshold variables of financial scale development, and enterprise heterogeneity (total factor productivity) and other variables as explanatory variables. We create the following threshold panel model using the Hansen (1999) modeling method:

$$R\&D_{it} = \alpha_0 + \alpha_1 TFP_{it-1} + \beta' control_{it} + \theta_1 \mathrm{FD}_{it} \cdot I(q_{it} \leq \gamma_1) + \theta_2 \mathrm{FD}_{it} \cdot I(\gamma_1 < q_{it} \leq \gamma_2) + \theta_3 \mathrm{FD}_{it} \cdot I(q_{it} > \gamma_2) + \varepsilon_{it} \quad (2)$$

In equation (2), i represents the enterprise and t represents the period. See the definitions of the variable names above. β' represents the coefficient vector of the control variable, controlit represents the control variable vector, including enterprise internal cash flow CFit, export EXit-1, capital intensity K/Lit, industry intensity HHI, age AGEit, size SIZEit, and industry and year control variables, θ represents the coefficient of the threshold variable, I(·) is the indicator function, γ represents the specific threshold value, qit represents a threshold variable (including various types of financial efficiency and financial competition indicators), and εit represents random disturbance items, when qit≤γ, I(qit≤γ)=1; in contrast, when qit>γ, I(qit>γ)=1.

In this chapter, based on the principle of panel threshold model estimation, the measurement model is estimated without considering threshold effect, a threshold value, and two threshold values. We also test the threshold effect of the explained variable at significance levels of 1%, 5%, and 10%, and Table 3 shows the test results of the threshold effect. In the 95% confidence interval, financial efficiency has a single-threshold effect on firm R&D and financial competition has a double-threshold effect on firm R&D.

Table 3. Threshold effect test of each variable

Indicator	loans by non-state-owned enterprises		LDR		Conversion of savings to investment		Deposits of non-state banks			Foreign capital inflow		
	Single/double threshold		Single/double threshold		Single/double threshold		Single/double/three threshold			Single/double/three threshold		
F value	9.43	2.97	13.83	3.41	11.51	3.33	19.02	8.76	1.84	6.33	6.29	3.15
P value	0.004	0.102	0.001	0.112	0.002	0.095	0.000	0.012	0.143	0.010	0.015	0.091
99%	8.16	8.46	8.25	8.87	8.33	8.75	7.19	7.94	8.85	6.22	6.44	6.51
95%	3.88	3.25	3.62	3.78	3.72	3.81	3.66	3.81	3.62	3.32	3.34	3.24
90%	2.64	2.55	2.33	2.62	2.45	2.71	2.82	2.91	2.39	2.27	2.31	2.25
Threshold value	11.05		0.78		0.51		(7.03,10.51)			(3.34,6.13)		

Empirical Results Analysis

The results of the effect of financial qualitative indexes development on private firm R&D are shown in Table 3. First, generally speaking, the influence of financial efficiency on heterogeneous firm R&D indicates that each financial efficiency indicator negatively affects firm R&D on the side lower than the threshold value but positively affects firm R&D on the side higher than the threshold value. This result shows that improvements in financial quality has a positive impact on private firms with high R&D, which is clearly different from the impact of simple financial quantitative development on firm R&D as shown in Table 2. Nevertheless, different financial efficiency indicators have different impacts on firm R&D. (1) The LDR indicator on the side of higher than the threshold value does not significantly improve the level of firm R&D, showing that China's bank industries invest more capital into the innovative financing of state-owned enterprises, while private enterprises have limited capital. (2) The efficiency of the conversion of savings to investment on the side of higher than the threshold value in the banking industry can promote private firm R&D, showing that when the whole society forms fixed assets, bank deposits positively affect private firm R&D for private enterprises are the main factor in participating social activity and the factor influencing efficiency improvements. (3) The ratio of non-state enterprises loans in the whole society on the side of higher than the threshold value has a positive impact on R&D of private enterprises. In other words, as the non-state economy gains more loans, private enterprises with higher innovation efficiency can obtain more financing, and the efficiency of macroeconomic also improves.

Second, with respect to the impact of competition on heterogeneous firm R&D, (1) the deposits absorbed by non-state banks represent the level of competition in the domestic credit market. However, when domestic credit market competition is lower than (6.03) or higher than (9.01), the threshold values is conducive to the private firm R&D. Only within the limits of two thresholds can this competition significantly boost firm R&D. This result shows that when the domestic financial market competition is weak, the banking system monopoly income makes it difficult to improve financial efficiency and the supply's credit market invests more money on safer business or projects. In spite of this, when the domestic financial market is more competitive, financial capital is detrimental to the innovation activities of enterprises and the quantitative expansion of financial development caused by fierce competition forces banks must turn to more lucrative investment projects. Howbeit, at the present stage, the reason for this unobvious negative trend is that China's financial marketization process is still not deep enough and financial competition has not reached a high level. Only when the level of financial competition in China is within a reasonable limit can the company vigorously promote R&D. (2)

Foreign capital inflow is actually similar to China's credit competition, but there is no statistical significance on either side of the threshold. This result shows that the participation of foreign capital in domestic financial markets and moderate competition can improve the innovative financing constraints of private enterprises, but the relationship between foreign investment and domestic enterprises is not close.

Table 4. Impact of financial efficiency, financial competition on private firm R&D research

Indicator	Efficiency indicator			Competition indicator	
Variable	Loans ratio by non-state-owned enterprises	LDR	Conversion of savings to investment	Deposits of non-state banks	Foreign capital inflow
Tfp	0.0317***	0.0315***	0.0315***	0.0308***	0.0318***
	(20.42)	(20.32)	(20.32)	(19.82)	(20.28)
Ex	0.00034*	0.00037*	0.00035*	0.00031*	0.00032*
	(1.74)	(1.77)	(1.75)	(1.63)	(1.65)
Cf	0.00240*	0.00246*	0.00249*	0.00233*	0.00242*
	(1.76)	(1.78)	(1.80)	(1.65)	(1.77)
k/l	0.0000173***	0.0000177***	0.0000182***	0.0000181***	0.0000185***
	(7.94)	(8.03)	(8.14)	(8.11)	(8.21)
HHI	-0.00428*	-0.00436*	-0.00441*	-0.00425*	-0.00429*
	(-1.84)	(-1.96)	(-2.03)	(-1.79)	(-1.86)
Size	0.00868***	0.00862***	0.00865***	0.00852***	0.00892***
	(8.91)	(8.86)	(8.87)	(8.80)	(9.15)
Age	0.00013	0.00016	0.00018	0.00011	0.00010
	(1.13)	(1.15)	(1.16)	(1.09)	(1.08)
$fd(q \leq \gamma 1)$	-0.0013	-0.0010	-0.0008	-0.0024**	-0.0001
	(-1.58)	(-1.26)	(-1.20)	(-2.10)	(-0.16)
$fd(\gamma 1 < q \leq \gamma 2)$	0.0032**	0.0021	0.0039***	0.0034**	0.0011
	(2.67)	(1.53)	(3.13)	(2.71)	(1.30)
$fd(q > \gamma 2)$	-	-	-	-0.0015	-0.0011
	-	-	-	(-1.58)	(-1.28)
Sample size	6762	6762	6762	6762	6762

NOTE: () is for the variable t statistics; *, **, *** indicate that they passed the test at significant levels of 10%, 5%, 1% respectively; each model contains dummy variables "industry (Industry) and year (Year)" which are not listed in the table to save space.

Robustness Examination

Impact of Financial Efficiency and Financial Competition on Low- and Medium-Technology Firm R&D Research

Table 5 shows the results of the impact of financial qualitative indicators development on the R&D of low- and medium-technology company. The influence of financial competition and financial efficiency on firm R&D on both sides of different threshold values is similar to that shown in Table 4, however, the specific path of impact is slightly different. In the case of lower the threshold value, the financial efficiency indicator, LDR, the proportion of loans by non-state-owned enterprises and the conversion of savings to investment have no significant negative impacts on firm R&D, suggesting that low financial efficiency is not conducive to low- and medium-technology firm R&D. In the case of higher than the threshold value, LDR and the conversion of savings to investment positively affect firm R&D, but the proportion of loans by non-state-owned enterprises has no significant effect on firm R&D. This result shows that when more bank deposits are converted to loans and then effectively converted into all social assets, low- and medium-technology firm R&D can benefit from this kind of transformation because these firms buy advanced equipment or technology to improve their competitiveness and therefore behave as a manifestation of technological advance characteristics. There is no significant positive influence on the proportion of loans exceeding the threshold of non-state-owned enterprises, indicating that the macroeconomic efficiency of the China's financial system's impact on low- and medium-technology firm R&D has not yet reached an overall high level.

Regarding the financial competition indicator, credit competition in China that is either too low or too high has an obvious inhibitory effect on low- and medium-technology firm R&D. But moderate competition can actively promote innovation investment and innovation financing. Within a certain range, foreign capital inflow can also effectively promote firm R&D, while lower or higher foreign participation has a negative impact on business innovation but is not statistically significant.

Impact of Financial Efficiency and Financial Competition on Underdeveloped Area Firm R&D Research

Table 6 shows the effect of financial qualitative indicators development on firm R&D in underdeveloped regions. The negative impact of financial efficiency and financial competition indicators on firm R&D is lower than the threshold value. The result shows that lower financial efficiency and lower degree of financial competition are not conducive to strengthening firm R&D in these regions. In the case of higher than the

Table 5. Impact of financial efficiency, financial competition on middle and low-tech firm R&D research

Indicator	Efficiency indicator			Competition indicator	
Variable	Loans ratio by non-state-owned enterprises	LDR	Conversion of savings to investment	Deposits of non-state banks	Foreign capital inflow
Tfp	0.0188***	0.0188***	0.0188***	0.0180***	0.0175***
	(19.62)	(19.68)	(19.67)	(18.67)	(17.94)
Ex	0.00011	0.00012	0.00012	0.00012	0.00012
	(1.01)	(1.26)	(1.26)	(1.42)	(1.36)
Cf	0.0023*	0.0022*	0.0022*	0.0026*	0.0025*
	(1.69)	(1.68)	(1.68)	(1.77)	(1. 76)
k/l	0.0000167***	0.0000171***	0.0000175***	0.0000179***	0.0000181***
	(7.58)	(7.83)	(7.96)	(8.03)	(8.10)
HHI	-0.00412*	-0.00424*	-0.00436*	-0.00415*	-0.00422*
	(-1.75)	(-1.87)	(-1.93)	(-1.78)	(-1.83)
Size	-0.0068***	-0.0064***	-0.0064***	-0.0063***	-0.0061***
	(-14.63)	(-13.60)	(-13.59)	(-13.38)	(-13.07)
Age	0.000061*	0.000068*	0.000071*	0.000063*	0.000061*
	(1.67)	(1.75)	(1.79)	(1.69)	(1.67)
$fd(q \leq \gamma 1)$	-0.0001	-0.0002	-0.0001	-0.0021***	-0.0001
	(-1.05)	(-1.19)	(-1.08)	(-3.73)	(-0.23)
$fd(\gamma 1 < q \leq \gamma 2)$	0.0010	0.0012*	0.0033***	0.0014*	0.0017*
	(1.60)	(1.68)	(4.57)	(1.74)	(1.88)
$fd(q > \gamma 2)$	-	-	-	-0.0011*	-0.0008
	-	-	-	(-1.65)	(-1.52)
Sample size	5631	5631	5631	5631	5631
Threshold value	11.65	0.73	0.50	(7.4, 10.06)	(3.71, 7.21)

NOTE: () is for the variable t statistics; *, **, *** indicate that they passed the test at significant levels of 10%, 5%, 1% respectively; each model contains dummy variables "industry (Industry) and year (Year)" which are not listed in the table to save space.

threshold value, the ratio of conversion of savings to investment and foreign capital inflow has a significant positive effect on firm R&D. This result indicates that the increase in social fixed assets and foreign investment can effectively promote firm R&D in less developed regions and acts as a powerful embodiment of technological progress and technological progress in foreign inflow spillovers. Other indicators have no significant effect on the above threshold value.

Table 6. Impact of financial efficiency, financial competition on undeveloped firm R&D research

Indicator	Efficiency indicator			Competition indicator	
Variable	**Loans ratio by non-state-owned enterprises**	**LDR**	**Conversion of savings to investment**	**Deposits of non-state banks**	**Foreign capital inflow**
Tfp	0.0110***	0.0109***	0.0104***	0.0108***	0.0106***
	(15.22)	(15.01)	(14.43)	(14.94)	(14.68)
Ex	0.0003**	0.0002*	0.0003**	0.0002**	0.0003**
	2.78	1.65	2.54	2.32	2.72
Cf	0.0025*	0.0023*	0.0020*	0.0023*	0.0024*
	(1.84)	(1.76)	(1.70)	(1.75)	(1.79)
k/l	-0.0000***	-0.0000***	-0.0000***	-0.0000***	-0.0000***
	(-3.62)	(-3.71)	(-3.59)	(-3.33)	(-3.52)
HHI	-0.00471*	-0.00470*	-0.00472*	-0.00473*	-0.00474*
	(-1.98)	(-1.94)	(-2.05)	(-2.11)	(-2.13)
Size	-0.0045***	-0.0042***	-0.0043***	-0.0044***	-0.0044***
	(-12.41)	(-11.56)	(-11.85)	(-12.16)	(-12.25)
Age	0.0001*	0.0001**	0.0001*	0.0001**	0.0001*
	(1.79)	(2.17)	(1.69)	(2.28)	(1.96)
fd(q≤γ1)	-0.0016***	-0.0008**	-0.0024***	-0.0009**	-0.0009**
	(-4.88)	(-2.37)	(-6.49)	(-2.64)	(-2.62)
fd(q>γ1)	0.0006	0.0000	0.0011***	0.0004	0.0031***
	(1.39)	(0.11)	(3.55)	(1.09)	(8.01)
Sample size	4522	4522	4522	4522	4522
Threshold value	10.96	0.82	0.47	8.36	3.74

NOTE: () is for the variable t statistics; *, **, *** indicate that they passed the test at significant levels of 10%, 5%, 1% respectively; each model contains dummy variables "industry (Industry) and year (Year)" which are not listed in the table to save space.

CONCLUSION

This chapter analyzes the R&D impact of firm through a lot of Chinese industrial enterprises data samples and quantitative and qualitative indexes of regional financial development, in combination with the characteristics of enterprise heterogeneity, panel data, and the threshold panel method. The chapter draws the following conclusions. (1) In this period, China's extensive fiscal growth could not effectively support innovation motivation, as well as the R&D activities of efficient private enterprises, middle-, and low-tech enterprises, and enterprises in less developed areas have the problem of financial inefficiency. (2) The threshold effect exists when the financial efficiency affects the firm R&D. When the financial efficiency is low, the quantitative expansion of financial development cannot actively promote the innovation investment of enterprises with higher innovation efficiency, and there are inefficiencies; when the financial efficiency is improved, along with the improvement of financial development quality, the financial expansion will help to promote innovation investment of enterprises with higher innovation efficiency. (3) The threshold effect exists when the financial competition affects the firm R&D. The financial efficiency loss caused by high degree of monopoly in the financial sector, low level of competition or excessive financial competition will inhibit the financial development and reduce the innovation input of enterprises; while moderate financial competition can effectively improve the inefficient allocation of innovative capital in the financial sector and increase the innovation investment of enterprises. China's main problems are the low levels of financial efficiency and financial competition, which can effectively improve the financial development inefficiencies of firm R&D by changing the mere expansion of the quantitative financial scale and improving financial qualitative development.

POLICY RECOMMENDATIONS

According to the research in this chapter, this chapter has the following policy recommendations. First, in China, financial system reform has lagged behind the reform of the economic system, and due to the extensive financial expansion, the efficiency of China's financial system still has much room for growth. Financial capital has not been appropriately optimized and allocated, leading to the waste of financial resources, which is detrimental to the transformations of China's economic growth pattern and optimizing and upgrading the industrial structure. In particular, the financial development process in underdeveloped regions must improve the efficiency of the financial system by improving the internal governance level of financial institutions and cooperation among regional financial institutions to ensure the balanced development of interregional finance. As a result, China's future financial system reform and development should pay more attention to "qualitative" development, optimizing the financial structure, and improving financial functions to gradually improve the situation in which financial development is adequate quality development is lacking.

Second, the nonlinear relationship between financial scale and financial system efficiency in firm R&D reveals that the contribution of financial development to firm R&D in the future is relatively dependent on the efficiency level. Policy-making departments and local governments therefore should pay full attention to efficiency. Taking into account the "threshold effect" among financial development, financial efficiency, and firm R&D processes, policy-making departments and local governments should develop relevant financial development strategy at the regional level. When financial expansion reaches a certain effective limit, it should be transformed to improve efficiency and adjust the structure, great efforts should be made to break through the impact of financial scale on firm R&D bottleneck, and a sound interaction mechanism should be established to expand the financial scale, improve financial efficiency and R&D growth, prevent excessive liquidity of asset bubbles, and reduce the harm caused by the excessive development of financial scale which result in deviations from R&D in the real economy.

Third, the construction of financial functions should be strengthened and the technical level of financial employees should be raised. We cannot reduce the risk of innovation fund allocation through financial ownership discrimination due to the need to strengthen the risk screening procedures for innovation projects. Social capital should be properly introduced, emphasizing the coordinated development of direct financing and indirect financing. For different companies, especially SMEs, we should take different measures to provide multi-level and multi-channel financing systems. The marketization of interest rates should be accelerated and original banks should pay less attention to becoming the new gods of the private sector, which requires them to increase their risk management levels accordingly.

Fourth, the financial markets construction should be improved and the financial structure should be optimized. Traditional manufacturing and new services or technology innovation companies all need equity, but banks cannot provide equity and other financial institutions are in short supply. On one hand, China's trillions in large bank deposits cannot be lent out. On the other hand, the real economy badly needs equity capital, but it is very difficult to get financing from the domestic capital market. The "limited supply of financial assets" price will rise rapidly if we cannot open up more channels for the use of funds. Large and deep financial markets can alleviate the problem of credit rationing caused by imperfect bank reform, prevent asset bubbles and rapidly absorb excess liquidity in the economy. Besides, problems such as complex listing approval processes, high thresholds, single nominal interest rates, hidden fees for non-state-owned enterprises that increase costs exist in China's corporate bond market. Reforms can include reviewing content, canceling traditional methods of first and second batches for the entire year and converting them into approval methods after maturity. However, the risk control mechanism should be standardized, appropriately lowering the debt issuance threshold to increase the supply of corporate bonds. In terms of distribution, interest rates should be used as benchmarks and reflect different allocations of company differential pricing. In addition, the Chinese corporate bond market should enter the track of healthy development under market-oriented operations, thus becoming a vital part of the financial market.

ACKNOWLEDGMENT

This research was supported by the Junior Fellowships of CAST Advanced S&T Think-tank Program (DXB-ZKQN-2017-021); Science Foundation of Ministry of Education of China (16YJC790105); Liaoning S&T Project (2017050262); Basic Research Projects of Dalian University of Technology (DUT18RC(4)020, DUT17RC(4)30).

REFERENCES

Anton, S., & Bostan, I. (2017). The Role of Access to Finance in Explaining Cross-National Variation in Entrepreneurial Activity: A Panel Data Approach. *Sustainability*, *9*(11), 1947. doi:10.3390u9111947

Anwar, S., & Sun, S. (2011). Financial development, foreign investment and economic growth in Malaysia. *Journal of Asian Economics*, *22*(4), 335–342. doi:10.1016/j.asieco.2011.04.001

Artz, K. W., Norman, P. M., Hatfield, D. E., & Cardinal, L. B. (2010). A Longitudinal Study of the Impact of R&D, Patents, and Product Innovation on Firm Performance. *Journal of Product Innovation Management*, *27*(5), 725–740. doi:10.1111/j.1540-5885.2010.00747.x

Baum, C. F., Schäfer, D., & Talavera, O. (2011). The impact of the financial system's structure on firms' financial constraints. *Journal of International Money and Finance*, *30*(4), 678–691. doi:10.1016/j.jimonfin.2011.02.004

Beck, T., & Levine, R. (2002). Industry growth and capital allocation: Does having a market- or bank-based system matter? *Journal of Financial Economics*, *64*(2), 147–180. doi:10.1016/S0304-405X(02)00074-0

Bertrand, O. (2009). Effects of foreign acquisitions on R&D activity: Evidence from firm-level data for France. *Research Policy*, *38*(6), 1021–1031. doi:10.1016/j.respol.2009.03.001

Booth, L., Ntantamis, C., & Zhou, J. (2015). Financial Constraints, R&D Investment, and the Value of Cash Holdings. *The Quarterly Journal of Finance*, *05*(04), 1550011. doi:10.1142/S2010139215500111

Borck, R., Caliendo, M., & Steiner, V. (2007). Fiscal Competition and the Composition of Public Spending: Theory and Evidence. *Finanz-Archiv*, *63*(2), 264–277. doi:10.1628/001522107X220107

Bougheas, S., Görg, H., & Strobl, E. (2003). Is R & D Financially Constrained? Theory and Evidence from Irish Manufacturing. *Review of Industrial Organization*, *22*(2), 159–174. doi:10.1023/A:1022905102446

Brown, J. R., Fazzari, S. M., & Petersen, B. C. (2009). Financing Innovation and Growth: Cash Flow, External Equity, and the 1990s R&D Boom. *The Journal of Finance*, *64*(1), 151–185. doi:10.1111/j.1540-6261.2008.01431.x

Brown, J. R., & Petersen, B. C. (2009). Why has the investment-cash flow sensitivity declined so sharply? Rising R&D and equity market developments. *Journal of Banking & Finance*, *33*(5), 971–984. doi:10.1016/j.jbankfin.2008.10.009

Chen, S., Sun, Z., Tang, S., & Wu, D. (2011). Government intervention and investment efficiency: Evidence from China. *Journal of Corporate Finance*, *17*(2), 259–271. doi:10.1016/j.jcorpfin.2010.08.004

Chu, C. C., Tsai, S. B., Chen, Y., Li, X., Zhai, Y., Chen, Q., ... Li, B. (2017). An Empirical Study on the Relationship between Investor Protection, Government Behavior, and Financial Development. *Sustainability*, *9*(12), 2199. doi:10.3390u9122199

Cull, R., Davis, L. E., Lamoreaux, N. R., & Rosenthal, J. (2006). Historical financing of small- and medium-size enterprises. *Journal of Banking & Finance*, *30*(11), 3017–3042. doi:10.1016/j.jbankfin.2006.05.005

Czarnitzki, D., & Hottenrott, H. (2011). Financial Constraints: Routine Versus Cutting Edge R&D Investment. *Journal of Economics & Management Strategy*, *20*(1), 121–158. doi:10.1111/j.1530-9134.2010.00285.x

Czarnitzki, D., & Hottenrott, H. (2011). R&D Investment and Financing Constraints of Small and Medium-Sized Firm. *Small Business Economics*, *36*(1), 65–83. doi:10.100711187-009-9189-3

Dehesa, M., Druck, P., & Plekhanov, A. (2007). Relative Price Stability, Creditor Rights, and Financial Deepening. *IMF Working Papers, 7*(139).

Edmark, K., & Ågren, H. (2008). Identifying strategic interactions in Swedish local income tax policies. *Journal of Urban Economics, 63*(3), 849–857. doi:10.1016/j.jue.2007.06.001

Hanh, P. T. H. (2014). *Financial Development, Financial Openness and Trade Openness: New evidence.* FIW Working Paper.

Hansen, B. E. (1999). Threshold effects in non-dynamic panels: Estimation, testing, and inference. *Journal of Econometrics, 93*(2), 345–368. doi:10.1016/S0304-4076(99)00025-1

Jefferson, G. H., Huamao, B., Xiaojing, G., & Xiaoyun, Y. (2006). R&D Performance in Chinese industry. *Economics of Innovation and New Technology, 15*(4-5), 345–366. doi:10.1080/10438590500512851

Lai, Y., Lin, F., & Lin, Y. (2015). Factors affecting firm's R&D investment decisions. *Journal of Business Research, 68*(4), 840–844. doi:10.1016/j.jbusres.2014.11.038

Lu, S. F., & Yao, Y. (2009). The Effectiveness of Law, Financial Development, and Economic Growth in an Economy of Financial Repression: Evidence from China. *World Development, 37*(4), 763–777. doi:10.1016/j.worlddev.2008.07.018

Martinsson, G. (2010). Equity financing and innovation: Is Europe different from the United States? *Journal of Banking & Finance, 34*(6), 1215–1224. doi:10.1016/j.jbankfin.2009.11.015

Matsumoto, A., Merlone, U., & Szidarovszky, F. (2008). Cartelizing groups in dynamic linear oligopoly with antitrust threshold. *International Game Theory Review, 10*(04), 399–419. doi:10.1142/S0219198908002011

Matsumoto, A., Merlone, U., & Szidarovszky, F. (2012). Some notes on applying the Herfindahl–Hirschman Index. *Applied Economics Letters, 19*(2), 181–184. doi:10.1080/13504851.2011.570705

Org, Z. (2004). Finance and Growth: Theory and Evidence. *Social Science Electronic Publishing, 1*(5), 37–40.

Rajan, R. G., & Zingales, L. (2003). The great reversals: The politics of financial development in the twentieth century. *Journal of Financial Economics, 69*(1), 5–50. doi:10.1016/S0304-405X(03)00125-9

Salomon, R. M., & Shaver, J. M. (2005). Learning by Exporting: New Insights from Examining Firm Innovation. *Journal of Economics & Management Strategy*, *14*(2), 431–460. doi:10.1111/j.1530-9134.2005.00047.x

Shen, K. Y. (2017). Compromise between Short-and Long-Term Financial Sustainability: A Hybrid Model for Supporting R&D Decisions. *Sustainability*, *9*(3), 375. doi:10.3390u9030375

Shen, K. Y., Yan, M. R., & Tzeng, G. H. (2017). Exploring R&D Influences on Financial Performance for Business Sustainability Considering Dual Profitability Objectives. *Sustainability*, *9*(11), 1964. doi:10.3390u9111964

Sher, P. J., & Yang, P. Y. (2005). The effects of innovative capabilities and R&D clustering on firm performance: The evidence of Taiwan's semiconductor industry. *Technovation*, *25*(1), 33–43. doi:10.1016/S0166-4972(03)00068-3

Shin, M., & Kim, S. (2011). The effects of cash holdings on R&D smoothing of innovative small and medium sized enterprises. *Asian Journal of Technology Innovation*, *19*(2), 169–183. doi:10.1080/19761597.2011.630501

Silva, F., & Carreira, C. (2012). Do financial constraints threat the innovation process? Evidence from Portuguese firms. *Economics of Innovation and New Technology*, *21*(8), 701–736. doi:10.1080/10438599.2011.639979

Wang, C., Lu, Y., Huang, C., & Lee, J. (2013). R&D, productivity, and market value: An empirical study from high-technology firms. *Omega*, *41*(1), 143–155. doi:10.1016/j.omega.2011.12.011

Xiao, S., & Zhao, S. (2012). Financial development, government ownership of banks and firm innovation. *Journal of International Money and Finance*, *31*(4), 880–906. doi:10.1016/j.jimonfin.2012.01.006

Yang, C. H., & Chen, Y. H. (2012). R&D, productivity, and exports: Plant-level evidence from Indonesia. *Economic Modelling*, *29*(2), 208–216. doi:10.1016/j.econmod.2011.09.006

Yang, K. P., Chiao, Y. C., & Kuo, C. C. (2010). The Relationship Between R&D Investment and Firm Profitability Under a Three-Stage Sigmoid Curve Model: Evidence From an Emerging Economy. *IEEE Transactions on Engineering Management*, *57*(1), 103–117. doi:10.1109/TEM.2009.2023452

Chapter 13
The Use of Carbon Finance for Struggling With Climate Change

Filiz Konuk
Sakarya University, Turkey

ABSTRACT

The developments in science and technology have brought a lot of problems with them. The most important of these is climate change, which appears at the global level. The effect of climate change, which comes first as an environmental problem, cannot be ignored. Management, which has had serious income and economic losses because of weather conditions, has taken several precautions in order to reduce climate change risks. One of these is weather derivations. Weather derivations are a safety type that makes the determined payments if there are defined weather events. However, the most commonly used are weather option agreements, weather swap agreements, and weather future agreements. In the chapter, climate change and the weather derivations that are a means that managements use to avoid climate change risks will be explained.

INTRODUCTION

When the acquisitions which industrialization and development process in 18th century provided and the cost of this process on the physician environment of earth is compared, whether the result is profit or loss has become one of the most debated subjects of our day (Saraç, 2010). Along with the fact that it is difficult to reveal the result of this numeral cost benefit analysis, there is a known fact that this huge

DOI: 10.4018/978-1-5225-7808-6.ch013

development and change process is a feedback for human as climate change and global warming today (Yalçın, 2010).

The desire for economic growth and development has brought about the increased need for fossil energy. Increasing fossil fuel consumption and unconscious human behavior have caused an increase in atmospheric concentrations of the gases. These gases prevent the ray energy to go up to upper atmosphere after hitting Earth and the cooling of atmosphere layers close to Earth and land (Samur,2007) caused an increase in atmospheric concentrations (Başoğlu &Telatar, 2013). The earth atmosphere functions as the mirror of greenhouse effects. Therefore, this resulting effect mechanism is called 'greenhouse effect'. This mechanism enables the short wave radiation of the sun to come but it holds the long wave radiation reflected by the world (Saraç, 2010). That is to say, the short wave radiation from the sun are again reflected to the earth by the greenhouse gases in the atmosphere in the form of long wave radiation after hitting the earth (Alper & Anbar 2008:226).

Gasses such as carbondioxide (CO_2), methane (CH_4), diazotmonoxit (N_2O), halogenated compounds containing hydrophlorone carbones (HFC_s) sulphurhexafluoride (SF_6) have greenhouse effect (Demireli & Hepkorucu, 2010). CO_2 which has an atmospheric life ranging between five to two hundred years and whose increase can be attributed to heavy fossil fuel consumption, is one of the major factors which is increasing infrared radiation (Başoğlu & Telatar, 2013, p. 10). In addition, CO_2 is a greenhouse gas type which forms approximately 80% of the greenhouse gas effect of developed countries and approximately 60% of total greenhouse effect globally. The density of this gas in the atmosphere has increased 40% compared to the period before industrial revolution due to fuel consumption and incorrect land usage. Before industrial revolution, the density which was 280 ppmv (one molecule in million volume or a piece of one million) has become 391 ppmv during 2011 (Liu et al., 2009).

The greenhouse gas emissions in previous years also has an effect on today' s density level of greenhouse gases in atmosphere. Global greenhouse gas emissions between years 1970-2004 has increased 70%. IPCC emission scenarios, private report asserts that global greenhouse gas emissions will increase 25% to 90% between years 2000-2030 (IPCC,2007). The report prepared by OECD asserts that greenhouse gas emissions will increase 50% by 2050 unless the needed precautions are taken (Şaylan, 2010).

The increase in greenhouse gas densities in the atmosphere destroys the energy balance on earth. This is the reason why the radiation from Erath is prevented from reaching space by being kept in atmosphere by greenhouse gases and left again and earth is heated more. The increased burning of carbon containing fossil fuels like petrol, natural gas and coal since 19th century and incorrect land usage policies which have led to mass deforestation have greenhouse gas densities in the atmosphere.

Figure 1.
Source: http://scrippsco2.ucsd.edu/graphicsgallery/mauna_loa_record/mauna_loa_record.html

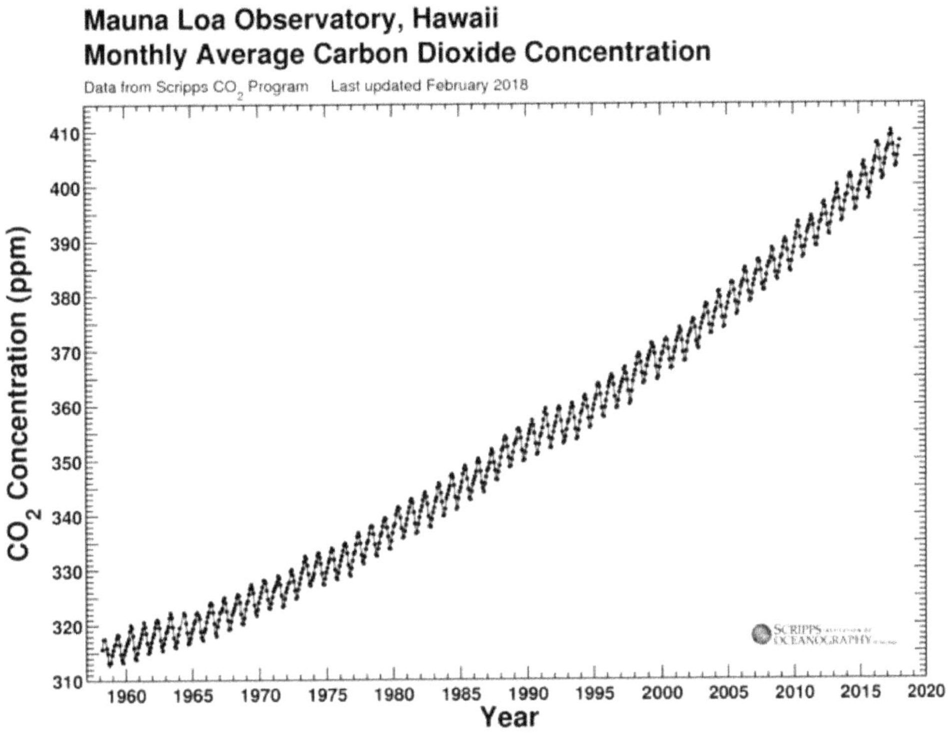

This has caused temperatures to rise in lower layers of the earth and the atmosphere (Türkeş, 2012). The greenhouse effect is the cause of global warming and climate change (Bayrak, 2012).

Most of the observed increase in global average temperatures since the mid-20th century is very likely due to the observed increase in anthropogenic GHG concentrations. İt is likely that there has been significant anthropogenic warming over the past 50 years averaged over each continent. (IPCC, 2007)

According to the first Studying Group, fifth Assessment Report, all 10 year periods for the global temperature data recorded since 1850 have become hotter consecutively for the last 30 years. Climate data show that 1983-2012 period was probably the hottest 30 year period of the last 1400 years in northern hemisphere. While the global average (land and ocean) surface temperature between the periods 1800-1900 and 2003-2012 total warming was 0.78 degrees Celsius, it showed a

Figure 2. Distribution curve of climatic events
Source: Alper and Anbar (2008, p. 228)

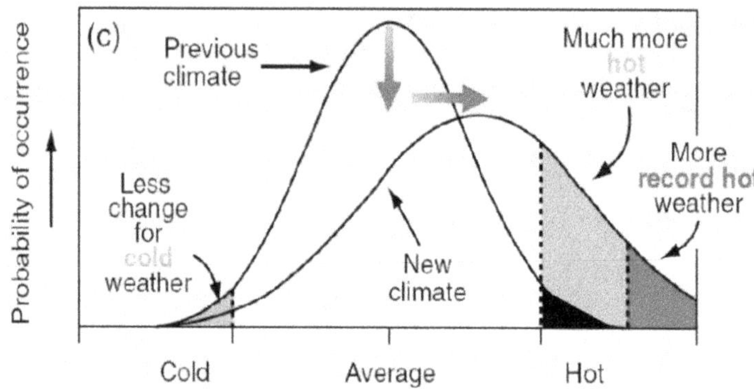

linear warming tendency of 0.85 degrees Celsius between 1880-2012 period; 0.89 degrees Celsius between 1901-2012 period (IPCC, 2007).

The climatic changes as a result of the increase in densities of greenhouse gases also causes changes in climatic events. There is also a change and shift in the distribution curve of climatic events related to climate changes as it is seen in Figure 1. The curve is moving right and flattening. This points out that less cold will be experienced and extreme climate events will increase in coming years (Alper & Anbar, 2008, p. 228).

Global warming affects glaciers and sea level in a negative way as well. While a 3.5%-4.1% decrease in 10 year periods between years 1979-2012 was experienced in the density of sea glaciers of North Pole, there were risings at sea level. This rising was 0.83 mm/year between years 2005 and 2009, while it was 0.62 mm/years between 1971 and 2009 (IPCC, 2013, pp. 8-9).

The effect of temperature increase on global scale has a negative effect on natural systems. For example, it is estimated that the yearly average river flow and attainability of water until this century will increase by 10% at high latitudes and in some rainy tropical regions and it will decrease around 10%-30% in some dry regions at middle latitudes. And this will lead to drought in some regions, flood and spate in some regions (because of heavy rain conditions). It is estimated that there will be important changes in eco-system form and function, the ecologic interactions and geographic distribution of species if the increase in global temperature is above 2.0 degrees Celsius and if this is accompanied by carbon dioxide condensation in atmosphere (Özdemir, 2008). The increased global warming has negative effects on both all living things and the environment.

THE ECONOMIC EFFECTS OF CLIMATE CHANGE

The source of the global warming is the greenhouse gases stemming from economic activities. Economic grow and development improves the welfare of people. So, there is a reversal relation between the improvement of welfare of people related to economic developments and the negative effect of green houses stemming from economic activities on global warming and human life. In this case, people will either compromise from their welfares by reducing their economic activities or they will experience the negative effects of climate change directly or indirectly. While developed countries are more sensible to climate change, developing countries are less sensible towards taking precautions for reducing climate change by saying that this will affect economic growth and development in a negative way. Therefore, this makes them the biggest part of the community who are affected the most by climate change. Along with this, a 2 degrees Celsius increase is accepted as a safety threshold (UNEP, 2006, p. 4) and an increase above this will affect both developed and developing countries in a negative way.

The most important effect that climate change has on economy is the cost of natural disasters formed by climate change. Thus, the economic costs as a result of increased natural disasters between the period 1985-1999 and became 2.5% of Gross National Product, 13.4% of developing countries (OECD, 2005, p. 223). On the other hand, 85% of 8820 natural disasters which happened worldwide between the years 1960-1999 are related to air and the economic loss of about 75% (Coleman, 2003). In the EU region, the cost of storms in 1999 was 13 billion Euros and the cost of floods was 13 billion Euros. In Europe, the cost of hot airwave in 2003 that caused the death of 27,000 people was 10 billion Euros. Hot air wave is said to be the highest temperature of 1000 years and it is predicted that the possibility of similar hot airwaves to happen is more than 100 times in the coming 10 years. In

Table 1. The economic effects of climate change on developed and developing countries

	Temperature Increase	The Effect of Temperature Increase
Developing Countries	The increase of temperatures in a negative way	Generally economic loss when temperatures increase
Developed Coutries	an increase up to 2 degrees celcius	Net economic income
	an increase between 2 and 3 degrees celcius	Neutral or income loss
	an increase above 3 degrees celcius	Net loss

Source: Dlugolecki and Lafeld (2005, p. 11)

EU region, the cost of disasters related to climate change has reached 8 billion Euros by doubling in the last 20 years. The yearly costs of floods are likely to increase 20 times by the year 2070 (Dlugolecki & Lafeld, 2005, p. 14). The total cost of natural disasters in the world was 230 billion dollars in 2005 and Katrina Hurricane had the biggest cost of 135 billion dollars (Alper & Anbar, 2008). Provided that permanent solutions are not found about climate change, it will be impossible to overcome the negative effect of it on the economy. The economic facts show that just 1-degree celsius increase in temperature will end in at least 300 billion dollars every year until 2050 and 2 trillion in 2050 (Anderson et al., 2006, p. 9). Therefore, the economic effects of climate change cannot be over emphasized.

THE EFFECT OF CLIMATE CHANGE ON THE SECTOR

The effect of climate change on sectors and management is in varying ways and degrees. However, in this context, the most important and sensitive sectors are agriculture, energy, construction, and tourism because they are carried out directly related to nature, climate conditions and weather events (Pres, 2009).

One of the negatively affected sectors by climate change is the agricultural sector. The agricultural sector is the one of the main sectors on which climate and weather conditions dominance are felt the most (Bazzaz & Sombroek, 1996). The changes in these sources are also effective on agricultural production as they use natural sources because of the sector form. On the other hand, there is a decrease in agricultural production with the effect of harmful herbs and bugs caused by high temperatures. Global warming causes a decrease summer and winter yields of cereal products and this leads to a lack of raw material in sectors such as flour, biscuit. This problem affects the costs. Besides, climate changes also reduce product variety (Özdemir, 2008). Along with this, the changes in rain regime causes an increase in product amount in arid and sub-arid regions (because of increase in the rain); while causing a rise in production amount in some products at middle and high altitudes, it will show its effect in a negative way at lower altitudes. The general effect of climate change on agriculture is expected to be negative because of drought (Nelson et al., 2009, p. 4). Cline (2007) stated in his study that the average land temperature will increase between 4.5-5 degrees Celsius averagely during 2080 and this will cause a decrease in global agriculture fertility by about 16%. Besides, he estimated that developing countries will be affected by the increasing temperature more than developed countries and that the fertility loss will be about 21% in developing countries and will be about 6% in developed countries. Along with this, fertility loses are less when the positive of CO_2 on plants is taken into consideration. In developed countries, climate change fertility will increase about 7.7% when carbon effect and temperature rise are evaluated together. Despite this positive effect of carbon, a decrease in agriculture fertility worldwide and in developing countries will continue (Başoğlu, 2014).

Climate change affects food products. According to (IPCC, 2013), it is possible that price rises can be experienced up to 45% until 2050 (when the effect of CO_2 is considered). The losses in agricultural fertility and production because of climate change will cause a cost rise both in processed food and the sectors related to agricultural sectors. Thus, huge rises in worldwide food costs were experienced after 2007 along with agricultural production which was less than before because of hot and arid (Başoğlu, 2014).

Another sector that can be negatively affected by climate change is tourism. Hot air masses formed because of climate change causes summer tourism to move towards spring and autumn months (IPCC, 2007b, p. 58) and also affects winter tourism negatively as snow melts (IPCC, 2007b, p. 53). For example, the loss of snow thickness in Australia causes 10% income loss and also this loss reaches about 30% when estimated with other economic multiplies and this is equal to about 1.5% of Australia's GNP (Scott et al., 2006, p. 377).

The direct effects of climate change like aridness, floods, storm and rising of sea level are also seen on insurance. The loss of the ice storm which happened in Canada in 1998 on insurance sector was about 1.44 billion dollars can be shown as a concrete example of the effect of global warming on management "The combined Canadian and United States insured loss stands in excess of $1.2 billion U.S. or $1.75 billion Cdn as at October 1, 1998" (Lecomte et al., 1998).

It is not easy to calculate and estimate actual economic cost based on climate change. Besides, the precautions to be taken against climate change, the questions related to what extent these precautions will be effective also makes it hard to determine the economic costs of climate. In spite of these difficulties, taking precaution against climate change is becoming obligatory and it is stated that the cumulative global loss of this situation will be 74 trillion Euros unless the precautions are taken (Dlugolecki & Lafeld, 2005, p. 5).

THE PRECAUTIONS TAKEN AGAINST CLIMATE CHANGE

The long-term effects and causes of climate change can be easily or immediately identified. Some studies have been made to cope with this problem which should be dealt with globally. These studies began with Cross-governmental Climate Change Panel which was founded by the support of the World Meteorology Organization and United Nations Environment Program in 1998. Rio Summit was gathered in 1992 and the United Nations Climate Change Contract (UNFCCC) was signed after that.

Rio Contract that confers responsibilities to countries for reducing greenhouse gas emissions went in effect in 1994 (Saraç, 2010). UNFCCC separated countries into three groups as Appendix 1 countries, countries out of Appendix 1 and Appendix 2 countries (see Table 2; Öztürk et al., 2011).

Although no obligatory aims about limiting greenhouse gas emissions were identified for countries by a contact, some countries were responsible. Appendix 1 countries are members of OECD, in the process of becoming a part of EU and market economy, and these countries are given responsibilities related to limiting greenhouse gas emissions, protecting greenhouse sinks and reporting data. Appendix 2 countries consist of countries which are members of OECD and EU and they are given responsibilities about transferring technologies compatible with the environment to the developing countries and financing them. Countries out of Appendix 1 are consisting of the countries that don't have any responsibilities about subjects such as reducing greenhouse gas or protecting sinks (Öztürk et al., 2012).

That UNFCCC could not identify the numeral aim depending on the time for reducing greenhouse gas emissions and those countries could not form the needed base about countries' emission reduction commitments showed that there was a need for extra-legal regulations for reducing greenhouse gas emissions (Arı, 2010). Kyoto Protocol (KP) was signed at the end of the conference in Kyoto in 1997 to fulfill this drawback and it went in effect in 2015 (at least 55 countries should

Table 2. UNFCCC countries

Appendix 1 Countries			**Appendix 2 Countries**	
Germany	Croatia	Hungary	Germany	Switerland
USA	Holland	Monaco	USA	Italy
EU	Ireland	Norway	EU	Iceland
Australia	Spain	Poland	Australia	Japan
Austria	Sweden	Portugal	Austria	Luxembourg
Belgium	Switzerland	Romania	Belgium	Canada
White Russia	Italy	Russia	England	Norway
Bulgaria	Iceland	Slovakia	Denmark	Portugal
England	Japan	Turkey	Finland	New Zealand
Czech Republic	Latvia	Ukraine	France	Greece
Denmark	Liechtenstein	New Zealand	Holland	
Estonia	Lithuania	Greece	Ireland	
Finland	Luxembourg		Spain	
France	Canada		Sweden	

agree with the protocol, the total emissions of the agreeing countries should be at least 55% of the total emissions of Appendix 1 countries in 1990 for this law to go in effect) (Finance Ministry, 2010). The determination of the greenhouse gases that need to be taken under control (carbon dioxide, methane, diazotmonoxide, hydrophloric carbons, petrofluoridecarbons, and sulfhur hexafluoride) was made and the sectors associated with these and source categories (energy, industrial processes, other solvent product usage, agriculture, and waste sectors and the sub-categories associated with these sectors) were determined. Therefore, the general outline related to which sectors and branches countries that will deal with climate change were formed legally (Şaylan, 2010).

According to this protocol, the behalves (countries in Appendix 1) were predicted to reduce their greenhouse gas emissions between years 2008-2012 period (the first commitment period) below 5% of 1990 levels and in this outline, an Appendix 1 list was formed. (In the content of Appendix B, the countries in the transition process to marketing economy [Bulgaria, Estonia, Romania, Slovakia, Slovenia, Poland, Croatia, Ukraine were given elasticity in basic year election] by accepting 1990 as the basic year) As a result of the negotiations, the parties took the responsibility of reducing greenhouse gas emissions in different ranges in order to reach the general aim. Austria, Belgium, Bulgaria, Czech Republic, Denmark, Estonia, European Commune Finland, France, Germany, Greece, Ireland, Slovakia, Slovenia, Spain, Sweden, Switzerland, Great Britain, United Kingdom, and North Ireland should reduce their emissions 8%, the USA 7%, Canada, Hungary, Japan and Poland 6%, Croatia should reduce its emission 5%; New Zealand, Russia Federation and Ukraine should be the same and that Norway should increase its emission by 1%, Australia should increase its emission 8%, and Iceland should increase its emission 10% are stated legally. Besides, subjects like policy and precautions about market in accordances not fitting the aim of UNFCCC and the application of market means should be removed, the determination of agriculture and transportation policies in a way that will arise environment sensibility, increasing energy fertility, developing edible energy, protecting forest, greenhouse gas like vegetation cover etc., making searching studies for technologic development about the subject are included (Binboğa, 2014, p. 5737).

It is decided that the countries in the Appendix B list should reduce their emission at least by 18% by the year 2020. Consequently, the average temperature increase should be fixed at 2 degrees celsius globally at the end of 2020 by 'Doha Change' which forms the second commitment period of the protocol. Germany, England, France, Denmark, Sweden, and EU Commission guaranteed to transfer 6 billion dollars to developing countries in the content of dealing with climate change until 2015. Russia, The USA, Canada, Japan, and New Zealand didn't take responsibility in the second period of the Kyoto Protocol (Binboğa, 2014, p. 5737).

Table 3. Country classifications in UNFCCC and Kyoto Protocol

Document	Lists	Countries	Responsibilities
UNFCCC	Appendix 1	OECD + EU + PEGSÜ (41 countries) Turkey (with special rights)	Emission Reduce, Historical Responsibility (Industrialized Countries)
	Appendix 2	OECD + EU-15 (24 countries) except Turkey	Technology Transfer and Financial Support
	Out of Appendix 1	Other countries (Chiana, India, Pakistan, Mexico, Brasilia...)	They have no responsibility
Kyoto Protocol	Appendix B	Appendix-1 countries (27 countries) except Turkey and Belarus UNFCCC Appendix-1 list (Turkey and Belarus weren't behalfs of UNFCCC when KP was accepted)	1. Commitment Period: 5%reduce in greenhouse gas emissions according to 1990 level for the 2008-2012 periods. 2. Commitment Period: 18% decrease in greenhouse gas emission according to 1990 level for 2013-2020 periods.

Source: Binboğa (2014)

In the organization of the Kyoto Protocol, flexibility mechanisms are formed to reach the aim of reducing greenhouse gas emission of countries in a cost-effective way. Both fulfilling the attendance of countries to emission aims utmost level and maintaining the share of the benefits and profits between behalves that will be obtained by this process with the least cost are provided by means of the flexibilities that is in the content of these mechanisms (Karakaya, 2008).

The flexibility mechanisms brought in the content of the Kyoto Protocol are the Clean Development Mechanism (CDM), Emission Trade and Joint Implementation (JI). CDM and JI are formed as Mechanism project-based and Emission Trade is formed market-based. Countries that determined the emission reduce aim taking part in Appendix 1 (except for Turkey the countries taking part in UNFCC) and Kyoto Protocol Appendix B can benefit from Joint Implementation and Emission Trade Mechanism. Being the behalf of Kyoto Protocol is the needed prior condition to benefit from these mechanisms. Mechanisms supply important advantages for the behalves who benefit from them. Especially project-based mechanisms present the possibility of foreign capital income and new technology to a great extent in developing countries while supplying cost advantages in developed countries (Karakaya, 2008).

There is a comparison related to project and market based mechanism in Table 4.

Joint Implementation: JI

In Joint Implementation Mechanism that's based on project, it is stated that the projects aiming the reduce of greenhouse gas emission of countries that take part in

Table 4. The comparison of mechanisms

Flexibility Mechanism	Project/Market Based	Investor (Buyer) Country	Host (Seller) Country	Emission Unit
Clean Development Mechanism	Project Based	Appendix-B Countries	Out of Appendix-1 Countries	CER
Joint Implementation	Project Based	Appendix-B Countries	Appendix-B Countries	ERU
Emission Trade	Market Based	Appendix-B Countries	Appendix-B Countries	AAU

Source: Öztürk et al. (2011)

Appendix 1 can be implemented under certain circumstances in other Appendix 1 countries (like distinctive income supply of the country and taking the confirmation of related behalves). In Joint Implementation, host country means the country where the cost of reducing greenhouse emission amount is less than its own country, a country which tries to reduce or bring it to the borders in greenhouse gas emission or in the whole of emission system or just in a part in its own country (Akkaya & Uzar, 2012). Therefore, the investor makes it possible for Appendix 1 to fulfill the projects that will reduce or limit the emission on the part of the host Appendix 1 (Şaylan, 2010). The host country which fulfills emulsion reduce by means of these prepared projects (the country in which the projects are applied and emission reduction is supplied) can get Emission Reduce credit which it can sell to the investing country. The investing country can subtract the credits that it takes from its own total emission reduce aim (Karakaya, 2008).

The most common subjects that are preferred in the content of Joint Implementation are coal gas removal from coal mining (a share of 27%), energy efficiency (a share of 23%), nitrogen removal (a share of 16%), as shown in Figure 3.

Clean Development Mechanism (CDM)

According to the project, Clean Development Mechanism was developed in order to ensure that the countries in Appendix 1 will fulfill their responsibilities of reducing/limiting greenhouse gas emission that countries out of Appendix 1 will fulfill permanent development and contribute to the final aim of UNFCCC (Şaylan, 2010). Clean Development Mechanism which is a project-based mechanism shows the difference between behalves who cooperate in their Joint Implementation Mechanism. If a country which defined the emission aim in the content of Clean Development Mechanism carries out projects for reducing emissions in that country by cooperation with a country out of Appendix 1, then that country gets Certified

Figure 3. Joint implementation project portfolio
Source: Öztürk et al. (2011)

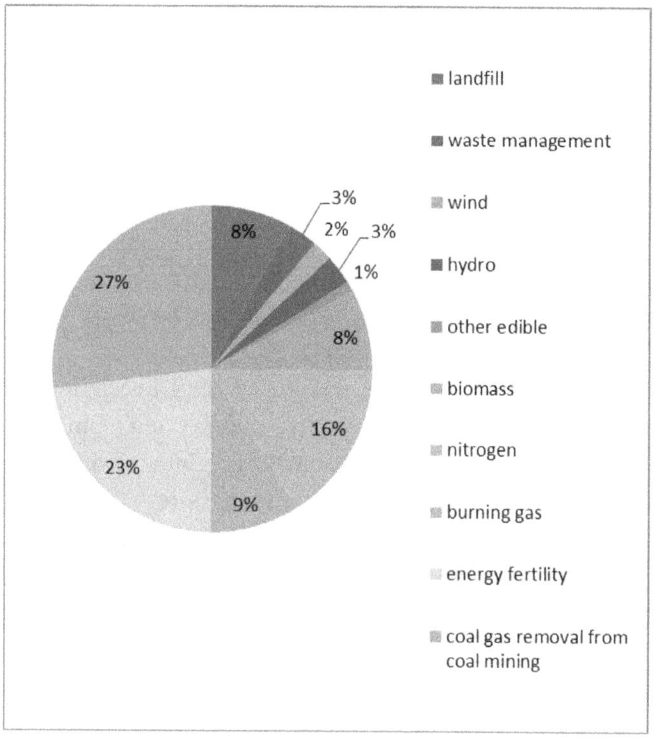

Emission Reductions and that credit amount is reduced from total emission reduce aim (Karakaya & Özçağ, 2003). Thus, while Appendix 1 country has the opportunity to reach its development aim with less cost, less developed country (out of Appendix 1) has the opportunity of benefiting from foreign invention and technology transfer that will fasten them to reach their development aims (Şaylan, 2010).

Clean Development Mechanism that provides long-term benefits which are real, acceptable, and tend to remove the negative effects of climate change by providing the voluntary attendance of behalves and in a way to fulfill extra emission reductions. The behalves need to take place in Kyoto Protocol and form Clean Development Mechanism organizations at the national level to benefit from the Clean Development Mechanism. Besides, this mechanism sets conditions for calculating emission amounts assigned to Appendix 1, a national system from predicting greenhouse gases and to have founded evaluating systems about buying-selling that will be done in the content of national record departments and to have prepared yearly greenhouse gas stocks (Şaylan, 2010).

Figure 4. Clean development mechanism project fields
Source: UNFCCC (2017)

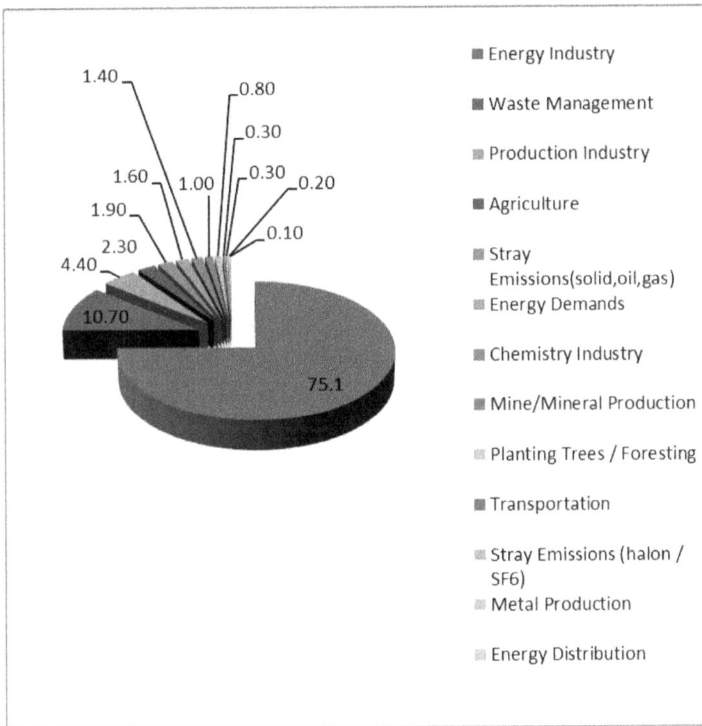

Projects related to energy forms more than half of the Clean Development Mechanism Project. The projects related to solid waste disposes (10.7%) and production industry (4.4%) are other project fields as seen in Figure 4 (UNFCCC, 2010).

Emission Trade

Emission trade envisages the behalves who determined greenhouse gas reduce aim for themselves to do buying-selling with each other in order to maintain the sale they promised (Akkaya & Uzar, 2012). This means that the country which provides more of the promised emission amount has the right to sell this extra reduction in emission to another country. For instance, when it is considered that there are two foundations reducing greenhouse gases to 10 Euros/ton and 25 Euros/ton gradually the second foundation enables the first foundation to make more greenhouse gas reduce use the credits that it gained from the emissions that the first one reduced. Therefore, it fulfills the responsibilities with 10 Euros/ton instead of 25 Euros/ton (with a less cost) (Binboğa, 2014, p. 5740). On the other side, if the emissions are above the adjusted quota, emission permission can be taken from other places. These kinds of systems are called 'cap and trade systems'.

The policies which will be applied to reduce greenhouse gas emission amount will also affect the costs. Emission trade cause declines in the general cost of goods when compared to legal arrangement approach directly. Emission trading presents the business institutions and countries that have high margin cost (at the local level) the facility to buy reduction from companies and countries that have low marginal cost (Akkaya & Uzar, 2012). For instance, consider that A and B firms each have the right of 90,000 tons of emission usage and the yearly emission rate of these forms are 100,000 tons. Each form has to reduce the emission rate of 10,000 tons. When it is accepted that while the cost for 1 ton carbon dioxide emission sale is 15 TL; this cost is 10 TL for firm A and 20 TL for firm B; a firm will prefer sale by means of new technology as it has less cost compared to the market and firm B; firm B will prefer buying carbon from the market. That's because its own cost is more than the market rate. If there weren't emission trade, the same production level for firm A would be 100,000 TL, while it would cost 200,000 TL for firm B. In the existence of emission trade, firm A earns 150,000 TL by selling its extra emissions on the market, firm B spends 150.000 TL by buying 10.000 tons from the market and maintains this with 50.000 TL fewer costs (Akkaya & Uzar, 2012).

CARBON TRADE

Carbon Funding and Carbon Market

Carbon funding is the source which is supplied for a project in order to buy greenhouse gas emission reduces (Binboğa, 2014). When carbon funding is taked about, there is needed to talk about carbon offset as well. A carbon offset is the emission offset operation of greenhouse gas emissions which are formed somewhere done by buying the credits (certificates) which are as a result of reducing or preventing the same amount of greenhouse gas by buying from another place (Tunahan, 2010). As the reducing and limiting of greenhouse gas emissions are targeted in dealing with climate change, an emission reduces activity anywhere in the world supports that aim to happen. As a result of the projects which are carried out in order to prevent or reduce the emissions that will happen in another source by cost-effective methods, carbon offset certificates are got. The companies which cannot reduce emission in its source or prefer reducing it with low cost maintain carbon offset activity by buying carbon offset certificates in order to fulfill their voluntary or obligatory emission reducing targets (Binboğa, 2011).

The Carbon market is the market where carbon certificates are bought and sold. Carbon markets which are market-based financial solutions means in the struggle to deal with climate change and provide the basis for the usage of carbon financing have had a serious growth by the Kyoto Protocol. Emission reduces by these markets has reached equipotent tons with 10.28 billion carbon dioxide at the end of 2011 (ÇOB, 2011).

It is possible to classify carbon markets as obligatory flexibility mechanisms that appear according to international responsibilities and arrangements based on Kyoto Protocol (Clean Development Mechanism, Emission Trade, and Joint Implementation Mechanism) and voluntary carbon market that appear in accordance with their own preferences although the behalves do not have any responsibilities (ÇOB, 2008).

Voluntary Carbon Markets

In the countries which do not make a commitment to greenhouse gas emission reductions as a part of the Kyoto Protocol, voluntary carbon markets are different from obligatory carbon markets. Emission reduce projects that are completely voluntary in voluntary carbon markets and the emission rights got from these projects are again bought voluntarily (Ekinci & Gönençgil, 2015).The organizations who want to be carbon neutral function in voluntary carbon factors by buying carbon certificates in other words, buying certificates that are formed as a result of emission reductions as a part of a standard greenhouse gas emissions based on their activities by calculating carbon footprint in order to reduce and balance these emissions (ÇOB, 2011).

Lastly, in 2014, demand for offsetting has reached 87 billion tons carbon dioxide equipotent (Mt CO_2) by growing %14. Voluntary carbon market size and the changes in average prices for each CO_2 ton are given in Table 5.

The important carbon certificates which are processed in voluntary markets are listed as Verified Carbon Standard (VCS), Gold Standard (GS), American Carbon Registry (ACR) and The Climate Action Reserve (CAR) (Ekinci & Gönençgil, 2015).

Table 5. Voluntary carbon market size and average price compression

	2012	**2013**	**% Change**	**2014**	**% Change (According to 2013)**
Volume	103 Mt	76 Mt	-26%	87 $MtCO_2$ e	+14%
Value	\$523 M	\$379 M	-28%	\$395 M	+4%
Avarage Price	\$5.9/t	\$4.9/t	-16%	\$3.8/ tCO_2 e	-22%

Source: Ekinci and Gönençgil (2015)

Weather Derivations

Businesses cannot control and manage some risks while they can manage some risks easily. One of the risks that businesses have difficulty in managing is weather risks (Özdemir, 2008). It is possible to examine weather risk as catastrophic and non-catastrophic (Corbally & Dang 2002). The first one is related to the losses which weather events like flood, hurricane cause. The second one is the possibility the possibility of being exposed to the financial effects happening as a result of weather events like heat, cold, snow, rain of a business (Clemons, 2002, p. 3). These types of weather risks can affect the financial results of businesses directly or indirectly. Directly effect is generally in the from of decrease in sales volume or increase in additional costs. Especially agriculture, construction, entertainment, transportation businesses are exposed to these type of risks.

Indirect impact correlates with the price and/or number of such contracts they may amortize primary(volumetric) direct exposure (e.g., European Union Allowance (EUA) CO_2 for electric companies) or heighten it (e.g., Renewable Energy Certificates for wind farms), and in most cases refers to the energy sector especially in the energy sector, real weather exposure is more complex and usually contains such variables as volume and price of (1) energy, (2) EUA CO_2 and 'coloured certificates' and (3) resources required in energy production, mainly coal and natural gas. (Pres, 2009, p. 428)

The risks which businesses are exposed to should absolutely be managed in order to reduce these risks. However, the management of these risks is not so easy. The first operation in weather derivatives market that is used in risk management was done in the USA in 1997.The record of the market happened in the winter of 1997-1998 El Nino which was one of the hardest events. This event took a huge place in the American press and many companies decided to protect themselves from seasonal weather forecast risk to reduce weather risk (Alaton et al., 2002). Weather derivations markets have grown rapidly and agreements have started to be processed in over-the-counter market (OTC) as an agreement that was discussed one by one. Businesses could defeat the changes in weather conditions easier by using weather derivations market.

Weather derivations are a new, fascinating security type that makes a payment which is determined beforehand if pre-determined weather events appear. In weather derivations, behalves make payment to each other according to the difference between the fulfilled levels of based weather index and the fixed usage level determined in the agreement (Özdemir, 2008). In these agreements, there are two behalves one of whom protects its business and transfer risks for this reason and the other one takes the relevant risk on for a certain price (Özdemir, 2008). The businesses that do not have profit purpose have the need of avoiding from weather forecast risks in order to make their budget plans in a more healthy way. Whereas, other businesses have (Akkaya, 2011):

- Less change in profit.
- Higher share value if this business is accessible to the public.
- Benefits like reducing bankrupt risk by avoiding from weather forecast risks.

The being affected by weather conditions of businesses in different sectors is also different. This situation is summarized in Table 6 (Akkaya, 2011).

It is difficult to apply standard derivation pricing theory based on arbitrage and market completeness on the weather forecast as it is not the subject of trade and it doesn't have a cost itself (Broody et al., 2002, p. 189).

Swaps based on different weather indexes, bargains for an account and call/put options are used for weather derivations. Some commonly used weather indicators or indexes are hot and cold days, rain and snow. These indexes are summarized in Table 7 (Akkaya, 2011).

Agreements are generally formed on temperature. Basic weather indexes are defined as the degree of hot (Heating Degree day; HDD) and the degree of coldness (Cooling Degree Day; CDD; Cao & Wei, 2004). If the temperature degree of a certain day is shown with (T_i) HDD and CDD indexes are formed as below (Cao et al., 2004).

Table 6.

Sector	Risk Factor	Effect
Energy Producer	Hot	Low sale in warm winter periods
Skiing Centre	Hot	Few customers as a result of little snow
Energy Consumer	Cold	Rise in energy use as a result of extreme cold
Construction Companies	Cold	Delay of projects as a result of extreme cold and avalanche
Municipalities	Cold	Rise in cleaning costs as after extreme snow
Hydro-Electric Plants	Rainfall	Reduce production in a drought period
Funfair Business Rainfall	Rainfall	The reduction of visitor number in extreme rainfall

Table 7.

HDD	Hot degree day
CDD	Cold degree day
EDD	Energetic degree day (HDD+CDD)
GDD	Calming degree day
VDD	Variable degree day
Flood	Rain for square meter
Avalanche	Snow for square meter
Up to Demand	The mixture of the indexes above

HDD_i = maks. (0,65 degrees F - T_i) CDD_i = maks (0, T_i - 65 degrees F)

We see that the number of HDD or CDDs for a specific day is just the number of degrees that the temperature deviates from a reference level. It has become industry standard in the US to set this reference level at 65 Fahrenheit (18.0 degrees Celsius). (Cao & Wei, 2004)

If the measured heat is 13 degrees Celsius, the agreement is defined as a 5 degrees Celsius day because there is a 5 degrees Celsius deviation from the reference price. Besides, as the measured heat isn't permanent within time, there is the need for a certain heat that will be the subject of the agreement to stand for the day. For this, mostly arithmetic average method is used (along with the fact that it has some lacks). Cumulative valves should be taken into consideration for HDD and CDD weather forecast derivations. Therefore, yearly HDD and CDD predictions will change according to the places where the agreement will be 'valid'.

Weather Options

Option agreement is the agreement that gives the buyer the right to buy or sell a good, value that is the subject of the agreement or a financial indicator at a price which is determined on the present day until a certain maturity; in return for the option premium that it will pay; the agreement that gives the seller the responsibility of selling or buying the value that is the subject of the agreement if the buyer uses his right that he has because of the agreement. These agreements are divided into two as buying and selling options depending on the right that it gives to its owner. Buying option gives the buyer the right to buy a certain amount of good value or financial indicator to a certain maturity at the defined price. The expectation of the buyer of buying option (seller) is the rise of underlying asset price in the future (decline). (Reva, 2006). Selling options are the agreements that give the buyer the right to sell a certain amount of food, value or financial indication at a certain price in a certain maturity. Weather options are the option agreements that are arranged on several indexes showing weather conditions. Weather options which aim to avoid from temperature fluctuations form about 70% -80% of the operations in the market. The temperature degrees (HDD) and the Cooling degree indexes used as the base of weather option operations. HDD index winter season measures the average temperature for the summer season. There are lower limit and upper limit (limit and floor price) in weather options (Özdemir, 2008). The parameters below are found in a weather option agreement (Alaton et al., 2002, p. 4).

- The contract type (call or put).
- The contract period.
- The underlying index (HDD or CDD).
- An official weather station from which temperature data are obtained.
- The striking level.
- The maximum payout (if there is any).
- The tick size.

The buyer pays prim to the seller in an HDD buying option at the beginning of the agreement. If the amount of HDD is more than the user level which is determined in the agreement, the seller makes a payment to the buyer at the end of the maturity. The price of the payment is determined according to the usage level and the original cost value (Müller & Grandi, 2000, p. 2). An original cost is equipotent of a degree day in these agreements.

While the owner of buying option takes part in the agreement in order to avoid from the extreme rising level of weather fluctuations like temperature and rain, the buying option seller, stays as the behalf of the agreement thinking that the weather

Table 8. System for temperature options

Option Type	Protection Against	Exercised When	Payout
HDD call	...overly cold winters	HDD>*strike value*	Tick size *(HDD-strike value)
HDD put	...overly warm winters	HDD>*strike value*	Tick size * (strike value- CDD)
CDD call	..overly hot summers	CDD>*strike value*	Tick size * (CDD-strike value)
CDD put	.overly cool summers	CDD<*strike value*	Tick size * (strike value- CDD)

Source: Müller and Grandi (2000, p. 2)

fluctuations won't rise above the determined values and so in order to get the prim income.

In Table 9, an option agreement is prepared by taking the table into consideration (Akkaya, 2011).

Option Type: Buying
Primary Asset: HDD
Performance Value: 3.500
Unit Value: (Tick) 1500 TL
Maximum Payment: 1.500.000 TL
Option Premium: 100.000 TL

When HDD number reaches to 3500 in the period related to the prepared option agreement put into effect and 1500 TL payment will be made for each HDD. Maximum payment cost is 1.500.000 TL for behalves in this agreement.

In the same concept, when the selling option is dealt, an option like below can be obtained in order to avoid from cold weather risk (for example in order to manage the risk that the cancel of flights will cause because of the rise in the cost of airfield care cost of X Airport management in cold weathers)

Option Type: Selling
Primary Asset: HDD

Table 9. Sample HDD and CDD measurement

	HDD Measurement November Month Reference Value 18 degrees Celsius					
	1st day	*2nd day*	*3rd day*	*4th day*	*5th day*	*Total HDD*
Daily Average Temperature	*25°*	*26°*	*23°*	*23°*	*23°*	
Daily HDD	*7*	*8*	*5*	*5*	*5*	*30*
	CDD Measurement December Month Reference Value 18 degrees Celsius					*Total CDD*
	1st day	*2nd day*	*3rd day*	*4th day*	*5th day*	
Daily Average Temperature	*15°*	*15°*	*17°*	*17°*	*16°*	
Daily CDD	*3*	*3*	*1*	*1*	*2*	*10*

Performance Value: 5000 HDD
Unit Value: (Tick) 1000 TL
Maximum Payment: 1.000.000 TL
Option Premium: 100.000 TL

If the expected risk happens, (the air to be extremely cold) the 1.000.000 part of the risk that will be created by the cancellation of flights will be paid by the other side of the agreement. The airport management must consider making a payment of 100.000 TL to pay this agreement (Akkaya, 2011).

In this case, the utility company will buy a CDD put option for the summer half-year (long put). By way of example, the specifics of this option contract will be shown in Table 5. The strike value of 985 CDDs taken as the basis here corresponds to an average temperature calculated over 180 days, of 70.47 celcius F (= (985/180) + 65). If the contract specifications given above are also assumed, the option price of US 335,000 and a tick size of US 15,000 can be used to determine the break-even point X*DD of this option on the basis of the following linear relationship: 15.000 X (985 - X * CCD) - 335.000 - 0 985 - X * CDD =335.000/15000=22.33 X*CDD = 985-22.33=962.66. The break-even point of 962.66 degrees F for this option contract can furthermore be used to calculate a corresponding average temperature of 70.34 degrees F (= (962.66/1 80) + 65) which can be interpreted as follows.

If temperature during the 1 80- If the average temperature is average temperature of 70.47 degrees celcius above 70.47 degrees celcius US dollars 335,000. Based on the calculation above can be formalized as follows:

Payoff= Min (I - OP,TS*Max (O,SV- CDD) - OP)

where CDD = (180 T (t) -65

(L:Limit, TS: Tick Size, SV.Strike Value, OP: Option Price)

If, for example, a total of 800 CDDs is determined over the 180-day period a basis here, the buyer of the above option achieves the following result:

Min (3,000,000-335, 000, 15,000 X Max (0,985-800) -335,000) =15,000 X (985-800)-335,000= 2.444,000 "(Müller& Grandi, 2000: 280-281)

Table 10. Specifics of an exemplary weather option contract

City	State	start	end	deal	Strike value	Tick size in US$	Limit in US$	Price in US$
Cincinnati	*Ohio*	*1/5/99*	*31/10/99*	*CDD put*	*985*	*15.000*	*3 million*	*335.000*

Weather Swaps

Swap are contracts that the behalves change their risks in the period determined beforehand (Alaton et al., 2002). Weather swap is a financial agreement in which the cash flow between behalves can be changed depending on the swap level being studied on and the weather index formed at the end of the agreement maturity.

They are traded without a premium and have a payoff that is linearly dependant on some weather index. Prices are equated in terms of the strike level of the index. Swamps as forwards (which are mostly capped, and so are not strictly linear) are traded OTC for a very wide of locations and indices. Swamps as future (which doesn't have caps) are traded on the Chicago Mercantile Exchange for monthly and seasonal contracts on 21 locations: 15 in the US, 5 in Europe and 1 in Japan. All the exchange-traded swamps are based on Daily temperature, but the daily temperatures are converted into the monthly or seasonal settlement index in different ways in different regions. (Jewson, 2004, p. 1)

A swap agreement arranged on HDD is seen below (Cao & Wei, 2004, p. 1068):

Purpose: The protection of Gas Ltd. Company against winter
Location: New York, La Guardia Airport
Buyer: XYZ Co. (paying fixed rate)
Seller: ABC Co. (paying floating rate)
Accumulation Period: January 1- 31 2002
Tick Size: 5000 dollars per HDD
Fixed Rate: 1000 HDD
Floating Rate: The actual for January, 2002=956 HDD

CONCLUSION

When the industrialization and development process that started in the 18th century and the cost of this process for the physical environment of the earth is compared, whether the result is profit or loss has become one of the most debatable topics today. Along with the fact that telling the numerical result of this cost-benefit analysis is hard. There is a known fact that the bill of this big development and change process is the feedback to human as climate change and global warming. In order to decrease the density in the atmosphere, the greenhouse gas emissions whose density has increased with industrialization and which are human-sourced, several enterprises were attempted and United States Climate Change Environment

Agreement (UNFCCC) was signed in 1992 Kyoto Protocol was formed as a part of this agreement in 1997. In this context, several flexible mechanisms and carbon markets were formed. Climate change which is a global problem, weather derivation subject which managements apply to avoid climate change risk were given place in the study.

REFERENCES

Akkaya, C. (2011). Hava Durumu Türevleri ve İklim Risklerine Karşı Potansiyel Faydaları Üzerine Bir İnceleme. *Girişimcilik ve Kalkınma Dergisi*, *6*(1), 205–220.

Akkaya, G. C., & Uzar, C. (2012). Karbona Dayalı Finansal Gelecek sözleşmeleri ve Fiyat Gelişimi Üzerine Bir İnceleme. *Dumlupınar Üniversitesi, Sosyal Bilimler Dergisi*, *32*(1), 67-80.

Alaton, P., Boualem, D., & Stilberger, D. (2002). On Modelling and Pricing Weather Derivatives. *Applied Mathematical Finance*, *9*(1), 1–20. doi:10.1080/13504860210132897

Alper, D., & Anbar, A. (2008). İklim Değişikliğinin Finansal Hizmet Sektörüne Etkileri. *Elektronik Sosyal Bilimler Dergisi*, *7*(23), 223–253.

Anderson, M., Dobardzic, S., & Gardiner, D. (2006). *Climate Change and Insurance: An Agenda for Action in the United States*. Allianz Group and WWF.

Arı, İ. (2010). *İklim Değişikliği İle Mücadelede Emisyon Ticareti ve Türkiye Uygulaması*. Ankara: Uzmanlık Tezi, Devlet Planlama Teşkilatı.

Bakanlığı, M., Birliğim, A., & Başkanlığı, D. I. D. (2010). *Birleşmiş Milletler iklim Değişikliği İklim Değişikliği Çerçeve Sözleşmesi (BMİDÇS) ve Kyoto Protokolü Bilgi Notu*. Retrieved from www.abmaliye.gov.tr/sites/default/files/BMIDCSveKyotoProtokoluBilgiNotu2010.pdf

Başoğlu, A. (2014). Küresel İklim Değişikliğinin Ekonomik Etkileri. *Sosyal Bilimler Dergisi*, 175-196.

Başoğlu, A., & Telatar, O. M. (2013). İklim Değişikliğinin Etkileri: Tarım Sektörü Üzerine Ekonometrik Bir Uygulama. *Karadeniz Teknik Üniversitesi Sosyal Bilimler Dergisi*, *6*, 7–25.

Bayrak, M. R. (2012). Low Carbon Economy And Financial Sources Of The Kyoto Protocol For Sustainable Development In Turkey. *Journal Of History Culture And Art Research*, *1*(4), 266–279. doi:10.7596/taksad.v1i4.90

Bazzaz, F., & Sombroek, W. (1996). Global climate change and agricultural production. In Direct and Indirect Effects of Changing Hydrological Pedological and Plant Physiological Processes. Wiley/FAO.

Binboğa, G. (2014). Uluslar Arası Karbon Ticareti ve Türkiye. *Journal of Yaşar Universitesi*, *9*(34), 5732–5759.

Brody, D. C., Syroka, J., & Zervos, M. (2002). Dynamical Pricing of Weather Derivative. *Quantitative Finance*, *2*(3), 189–198. doi:10.1088/1469-7688/2/3/302

Cao, M., & Wei, J. (2004). Weather Derivatives Valuations and Market Price of Weather Risk. *Journal of Futures Markets*, *24*(11), 1065–1089. doi:10.1002/fut.20122

Çevre ve Orman Bakanlığı (ÇOB) İklim Değişikliği Dairesi Başkanlığı. (2008). *Kyoto Protokolü Esneklik Mekanizmaları ve Diğer Uluslararası Emisyon Ticareti Sistemleri Özel İhtisas Komisyonu Raporu*. Retrieved from http://iklim.cob.gov.tr/iklim/Files/eKutuphane/KP_OIK_FinalRapor-28%2012%202008.pdf

Çevre ve Orman Bakanlığı (ÇOB) İklim Değişikliği Dairesi Başkanlığı. (2011). *Karbon Piyasalarında Ulusal Deneyim ve Geleceğe Bakış*. Retrieved from.http://iklim.cob.gov.tr/iklim/Files/Karbon%20Piyasalarında%20Ulusal%20Deneyim%20ve%20Geleceğe%20Bakış_2011.pdf

Clemmons, L. (2002). Introduction to weather risk management. In E. Banks (Ed.), *Weather Risk Management: Market, Products and Applications* (pp. 3–12). London: Palgrave.

Cline, W. R. (2007). *Global Warming and Agriculture: Impact Estimates by Country* (1st ed.). Washington, DC: Peterson Institute.

Corbally, M., & Dang, P. H. (2002). Underlying markets and indexes. In *Weather Risk Management: Market, Products and Applications*. London: Palgrave.

Demireli, E., & Hepkorucu, A. (2010). Çevre Finansmanı: Kavramsal Bir Yaklaşımla Karbon Finans Borsası. *Ekonomi Bilimleri Dergisi*, *2*(2), 37–48.

Dlugolecki, A., & Lafeld, S. (2005). *Climate Change & the Financial Sector: An Agenda for Action*. Allianz Group and WWF. Retrieved from http://www.wwf.org.uk/filelibrary/pdf/allianz_rep_0605.pdf

Ekinci, F., & Gönençgil, B. (2015). *Dünya Karbon Emisyon Piyasalarında Türkiye'nin Yeri, 6. Ulusal Hava Kirliliği ve Kontrolü Sempozyumu*.

IPCC. (2007a). *The Physical Science Basis. Contribution of Working Group I to the Fourth Assessment Report of the Intergovernmental Panel on Climate Change*. New York: Cambridge University Press.

IPCC. (2007b). *Impacts, Adaptation and Vulnerability. Contribution of Working Group II to the Fourth Assessment Report of the Intergovernmental Panel on Climate Change*. Cambridge, UK: Cambridge University Press.

IPCC. (2013). *The Physical Science Basis. Working Group I Contribution to the Intergovernmental Panel on Climate Change Fifth Assessment Report*. Stockholm: IPCC.

Jewson, S. (2004). Introduction to weather derivative pricing. *Journal of Alternative Investments*, *7*, 57–64. doi:10.3905/jai.2004.439646

Karakaya, E. (2008). Proje Temelli Esneklik Mekanizmaları: Temiz Kalkınma Mekanizması ve Ortak Yürütme. In Küresel Isınma ve Kyoto Protokolü. İstanbul: Bağlam Yayıncılık.

Karakaya, E., & Özçağ, M. (2003). Türkiye Açısından Kyoto Protokolü'nün Değerlendirilmesi ve Ayrıştırma (Decomposition) Yöntemi ile CO2 Emisyonu Belirleyicilerinin Analizi, 7. ODTÜ Ekonomi Konferansı.

Lecomte, E. L., Pang, A. W., & Russell, J. W. (1998). *Ice storm'98*. Toronto: Institute for Catastrophic Loss Reduction.

Liu, Q., Yu, G., & Liu, J. J. (2009). Solar Radiation as Large-Scale Resource for Energy-Short World. *Energy & Environment*, *20*(3), 319–329. doi:10.1260/095830509788066466

Müller, A., & Grandi, M. (2000). Weather Derivatives: A Risk Management Tool for Weather Sensitive Industries. *The Geneva Papers on Risk and Insurance. Issues and Practice*, *25*(2), 273–287.

Nelson, G. C., Rosegrant, M. W., Koo, J., Robertson, R., Sulser, T., Zhu, T., ... Lee, D. (2009). *Impact on Agriculture and Costs of Adaptation. Food policy report*. Washington, DC: IFPRI. doi:10.2499/0896295354

OECD. (2005). *Catastrophic Risks and Insurance*. Paris: OECD Publishing.

Özdemir, E. (2008). Küresel Isınmanın Etkilerine Karşı Bir Önlem: Hava Türevleri ve Pazarlama Stratejilerinde Yardımcı Olarak Kullanımı. *Gazi Üniversitesi İktisadi ve İdari Bilimler Fakültesi Dergisi*, *10*(1), 141–162.

Öztürk, A., Demirci, U., & Türker, M. F. (2012). İklim Değişikliği ile Mücadelede Karbon Piyasaları ve Türkiye için Bir Değerlendirme. *Ulusal Akdeniz Orman ve Çevre Sempozyumu*, 306-312.

Pres, J. (2009). Measuring noncatastrophic weather risks for businesses. *Geneva Papers Risk Insur.*, *34*(3), 425–439. doi:10.1057/gpp.2009.16

Reva, H. Z. (2006). Borsa Opsiyon Sözleşmeleri. *Prof. Dr. Özer Seliçi'ye Armağan*, 529-558.

Samur, H. (2007). Küresel İklim Değişikliğinin Etkileri ve Uluslararası Alandaki Mücadele Stratejileri. *Uluslararası Küresel İklim Değişikliği ve Çevresel Etkileri Konferansı*, 18-20.

Saraç, M. (2010). Çevre Sorunları ve İskonto Edilmiş Nakit Analizine Dayalı Değerleme Yaklaşımı. *Muhasebe ve Finansman Dergisi*, *45*, 169–179.

Şaylan, İ. B. (2010). *İklim Değişikliği ile Uluslararası Mücadelenin Ekonomik ve Mali Boyutu ve Avrupa Birliği Politikaları. Avrupa Birliği Uzmanlığı Yeterlilik Tezi, Uzmanlık Tezi.* T. C. Maliye Bakanlığı Avrupa Birliği ve Dış İlişkiler Dairesi Başkanlığı.

Scott, D., Mcboyle, G., Minogue, A., & Mills, B. (2006). Climate Change and the Sustainability of Ski-based Tourism in Eastern North America: A Reassessment. *Journal of Sustainable Tourism*, *14*(4), 376–398. doi:10.2167/jost550.0

Tunahan, H. (2010). Küresel iklim değişikliğini azaltmanın bir yolu olarak karbon finansmanı. *Muhasebe ve Finansman Dergisi*, *46*, 199–215.

Türkeş, M. (2012). Türkiye'de Gözlenen ve Öngörülen İklim Değişikliği, Kuraklık ve Çölleşme. *Ankara Üniversitesi Çevrebilimleri Dergisi*, *4*(2), 1–32.

UNEP (United Nations Environment Programme). (2006). *Adaptation and Vulnerability to Climate Change: The Role of the Finance Sector.* CEO Briefing, UNEP Finance Initiative Climate Change Working Group. Retrieved from http://sefi.unep.org/fileadmin/media/sefi/docs/briefings/CEO_Nov06.pdf

UNFCCC. (2010). Retrieved from http://unfccc.int/kyoto_protocol/mechanisms/emissions_trading/items/2731.php

UNFCCC. (2017). Retrieved from http://cdm.unfccc.int/Statistics/Public/index.html/

Yalçın, A. Z. (2010). Sürdürülebilir Kalkınma İçin Düşük Karbon Ekonomisinin Önemi ve Türkiye İçin Bir Değerlendirme. *Balıkesir Üniversitesi Sosyal Bilimler Enstitüsü Dergisi*, *13*, 24.

KEY TERMS AND DEFINITIONS

Carbon Funding: It is the source which is supplied for a project to buy greenhouse gas emission reduction.

Carbon Market: It is the market where carbon certificates are purchased and sold.

Global Warming: The rise in the burning of fossil fuels such as carbon like petrol, natural gas, and coal which causes temperature increase in lower layers of the earth and the atmosphere.

Greenhouse Gas: It is a gas that absorbs and emits radiant energy within the thermal infrared range.

Weather: Derivations: It is a security type that makes a payment which is determined earlier if pre-determined weather events appear.

Weather Options: These are the option agreements that are arranged on several indexes showing weather conditions.

Weather Swamp: It is a financial agreement in which the cash flow between behalves can be changed depending on the swap level being studied on and the weather index formed at the end of the agreement maturity.

Compilation of References

Adams, W. M. (2006). The Future of Sustainability: Re-thinking Environment and Development in the Twenty-first Century. Report of the IUCN renowned thinkers meeting.

Ahsan, K., & Rahman, S. (2017). Green Public Procurement Implementation Challenges in Australian Public Healthcare Sector. *Journal of Cleaner Production*, *152*, 181–197. doi:10.1016/j.jclepro.2017.03.055

Akkaya, G. C., & Uzar, C. (2012). Karbona Dayalı Finansal Gelecek sözleşmeleri ve Fiyat Gelişimi Üzerine Bir İnceleme. *Dumlupınar Üniversitesi, Sosyal Bilimler Dergisi*, *32*(1), 67-80.

Akkaya, C. (2011). Hava Durumu Türevleri ve İklim Risklerine Karşı Potansiyel Faydaları Üzerine Bir İnceleme. *Girişimcilik ve Kalkınma Dergisi*, *6*(1), 205–220.

Aksu, C. (2011). Sürdürülebilir Kalkınma ve Çevre. *Güney Ege Kalkınma Ajansı*, 1.

Alan, Y., & Gaur, V. (2015). *Operational investment and capital structure under asset-based lending*. Johnson School Research Paper Series, Cornell University.

Alaton, P., Boualem, D., & Stilberger, D. (2002). On Modelling and Pricing Weather Derivatives. *Applied Mathematical Finance*, *9*(1), 1–20. doi:10.1080/13504860210132897

Alexander, K. (2016). *Greening banking policy*. Retrieved April 10, 2018, from http://unepinquiry.org/wp-content/uploads/2016/09/10_Greening_Banking_Policy.pdf

Ali, A. N. A., Jainudin, N. A., Tawie, R., & Jugah, I. (2016). Green initiatives in Kota Kinabalu Construction industry. *Procedia: Social and Behavioral Sciences*, *224*, 626–631. doi:10.1016/j.sbspro.2016.05.453

Allen, J. H., & Potiowsky, T. (2008). Portland's Green Building Cluster. *Economic Development Quarterly*, *22*(4), 303–315. doi:10.1177/0891242408325701

Alper, D., & Anbar, A. (2008). İklim Değişikliğinin Finansal Hizmet Sektörüne Etkileri. *Elektronik Sosyal Bilimler Dergisi*, *7*(23), 223–253.

AlSanad, S. (2015). Awareness, drivers, actions, and barriers of sustainable construction in Kuwait. *Procedia Engineering*, *118*, 969–983. doi:10.1016/j.proeng.2015.08.538

Ametepey, O., Aigbavboa, C., & Ansah, K. (2015). Barriers to successful implementation of sustainable construction in the Ghanaian construction industry. *Procedia Manufacturing*, *3*, 1682–1689. doi:10.1016/j.promfg.2015.07.988

An. (2018). Legal Problems and Countermeasures Faced by Internet Finance Supervision in China. *Time Finance, 8*, 55-58.

Andersen, M., & Skjoett-Larsen, T. (2009). Corporate social responsibility in global supply chains. *Supply Chain Management*, *14*(2), 75–86. doi:10.1108/13598540910941948

Anderson, M., Dobardzic, S., & Gardiner, D. (2006). *Climate Change and Insurance: An Agenda for Action in the United States*. Allianz Group and WWF.

Anton, S., & Bostan, I. (2017). The Role of Access to Finance in Explaining Cross-National Variation in Entrepreneurial Activity: A Panel Data Approach. *Sustainability*, *9*(11), 1947. doi:10.3390u9111947

Anwar, S., & Sun, S. (2011). Financial development, foreign investment and economic growth in Malaysia. *Journal of Asian Economics*, *22*(4), 335–342. doi:10.1016/j.asieco.2011.04.001

Apergis, N., & Payne, J. E. (2010a). Renewable energy consumption and growth in Eurasia. *Energy Economics*, *32*(6), 1392–1397. doi:10.1016/j.eneco.2010.06.001

Apergis, N., & Payne, J. E. (2010b). Renewable energy consumption and economic growth: Evidence from a panel of OECD countries. *Energy Policy*, *38*(1), 656–660. doi:10.1016/j.enpol.2009.09.002

Apergis, N., & Payne, J. E. (2011). The renewable energy consumption–growth nexus in Central America. *Applied Energy*, *88*(1), 343–347. doi:10.1016/j.apenergy.2010.07.013

Arı, İ. (2010). *İklim Değişikliği İle Mücadelede Emisyon Ticareti ve Türkiye Uygulaması*. Ankara: Uzmanlık Tezi, Devlet Planlama Teşkilatı.

Artz, K. W., Norman, P. M., Hatfield, D. E., & Cardinal, L. B. (2010). A Longitudinal Study of the Impact of R&D, Patents, and Product Innovation on Firm Performance. *Journal of Product Innovation Management*, *27*(5), 725–740. doi:10.1111/j.1540-5885.2010.00747.x

Association of Corporate Treasurers. (2010). *Supply chain finance: Report of the supply chain finance working group*. Technical Report, ACT.

Ata, S. U. (2013). Sürdürülebilir enerjinin finansmanı [Financing of Sustainable Energy]. In Türkiye'de İklim Değişikliği ve Sürdürülebilir Enerji [Climate Change and Sustainable Energy in Turkey]. İstanbul: ENİVA- Enerji ve İklim Değişikliği Vakfı.

Atkinson, W. (2008). Supply chain finance: The next big opportunity. *Supply Chain Management Review*, *12*(3), 57–60.

Autry, Ch. W., & Griffis, S. (2008). Supply chain capital: The impact of structural and relational linkages on firm execution and innovation. *Journal of Business Logistics*, *29*(1), 157–173. doi:10.1002/j.2158-1592.2008.tb00073.x

Ba, S. S., Yang, C. P., & Yao, S. D. (2018). Review on the green financial research progress in China. *Journal of Financial Development Research*, 3-9.

Babich, V. (2010). Independence of capacity ordering and financial subsidies to risky suppliers. *Manufacturing & Service Operations Management: M & SOM*, *12*(4), 583–607. doi:10.1287/msom.1090.0284

Baird, D. G., & Picker, R. C. (1991). A simple noncooperative bargaining model of corporate reorganizations. *The Journal of Legal Studies*, *20*(2), 311–349. doi:10.1086/467889

Bakanlığı, M., Birliğim, A., & Başkanlığı, D. I. D. (2010). *Birleşmiş Milletler iklim Değişikliği İklim Değişikliği Çerçeve Sözleşmesi (BMİDÇS) ve Kyoto Protokolü Bilgi Notu*. Retrieved from www.abmaliye.gov.tr/sites/default/files/BMIDCSveKyotoProtokoluBilgiNotu2010.pdf

Bakırtaş, İ., & Çetin, M. A. (2016). Yenilenebilir enerji tüketimi ile ekonoik büyüme arasındaki ilişki: G-20 Ülkeleri. *Sosyoekonomi*, *24*(28), 131–145. doi:10.17233e.43089

Ballet, J., Banzin, D., Lioui, A., & Touahri, D. (2007). Green Taxation and Individual Responsibility. *Ecological Economics*, *63*(4), 732–739. doi:10.1016/j.ecolecon.2007.05.005

Ballou, B., Heitger, D. L., Landes, C. E., & Adams, M. (2006). The future of corporate sustainability reporting. *Journal of Accountancy*, *202*(6), 65–74.

Bals, C. (2018). Toward a Supply Chain Finance (SCF) Ecosystem–Proposing a Framework and Agenda for Future Research. *Journal of Purchasing and Supply Management*. doi:10.1016/j.pursup.2018.07.005

Banerjee, S. B. (2008). Corporate Social Responsibility: The Good, the Bad and the Ugly. *Critical Sociology*, *34*(1), 51–79. doi:10.1177/0896920507084623

Bank. (2003). *Internet Dynamics and Expansion of European Financial Markets: Issues from a Behavioral Finance Perspective*. Springer Berlin Heidelberg.

Barde, J. P. (1998). Environmental Taxes in OECD Countries an Overvıew. *Workshop on Environmental Taxes in China and OECD Member Countries*, CCNM/CHINA/EPOC(98)4.

Barnett, M. L. (2007). Stakeholder influence capacity and the variability of financial returns to corporate social responsibility. *Academy of Management Review*, *32*(3), 794–816. doi:10.5465/amr.2007.25275520

Basnet, H. C., & Donou-Adonsou, F. (2016). Internet, consumer spending, and credit card balance: Evidence from US consumers. *Review of Financial Economics*, *30*, 11–22. doi:10.1016/j.rfe.2016.01.002

Başoğlu, A. (2014). Küresel İklim Değişikliğinin Ekonomik Etkileri. *Sosyal Bilimler Dergisi*, 175-196.

Başoğlu, A., & Telatar, O. M. (2013). İklim Değişikliğinin Etkileri: Tarım Sektörü Üzerine Ekonometrik Bir Uygulama. *Karadeniz Teknik Üniversitesi Sosyal Bilimler Dergisi*, *6*, 7–25.

Baştürk, M. F. (2014). Mülkiyet Problemi, Dışsallıklar ve Coasean Çözüm. *Yönetim ve Ekonomi: Celal Bayar Üniversitesi İktisadi ve İdari Bilimler Fakültesi Dergisi*, *21*(1), 143–154.

Batırel, F., Ö. (2002). Büyüme Dostu Vergileme ve Türkiye Uygulaması. *Journal of Life Economics*, *2*(4), 1-8.

Baum, C. F., Schäfer, D., & Talavera, O. (2011). The impact of the financial system's structure on firms' financial constraints. *Journal of International Money and Finance*, *30*(4), 678–691. doi:10.1016/j.jimonfin.2011.02.004

Bayrak, M. R. (2012). Low Carbon Economy And Financial Sources Of The Kyoto Protocol For Sustainable Development In Turkey. *Journal Of History Culture And Art Research*, *1*(4), 266–279. doi:10.7596/taksad.v1i4.90

Bazzaz, F., & Sombroek, W. (1996). Global climate change and agricultural production. In Direct and Indirect Effects of Changing Hydrological Pedological and Plant Physiological Processes. Wiley/FAO.

Bebbington, J., Unerman, J., & O'Dwyer, B. (2014). *Sustainability Accounting and Accountability*. Abingdon, UK: Routledge.

Bebchuk, L. A., & Chang, H. F. (1992). Bargaining and the division of value in corporate reorganization. *Journal of Law Economics and Organization*, *8*(2), 253–279.

Beck, T., & Levine, R. (2002). Industry growth and capital allocation: Does having a market- or bank-based system matter? *Journal of Financial Economics*, *64*(2), 147–180. doi:10.1016/S0304-405X(02)00074-0

Bell, S., & Morse, S. (2008). *Sustainability Indicators: Measuring the immeasurable?* London: Earthscan.

Berle, A. A. (1931). Corporate Powers as Powers in Trust. *Harvard Law Review*, *44*(7), 1049–1074. doi:10.2307/1331341

Bertrand, O. (2009). Effects of foreign acquisitions on R&D activity: Evidence from firm-level data for France. *Research Policy*, *38*(6), 1021–1031. doi:10.1016/j.respol.2009.03.001

Bina, O. (2013). The Green Economy and Sustainable Development: An Uneasy Balance? *Environment and Planning. C, Government & Policy*, *31*(6), 1023–1047. doi:10.1068/c1310j

Binboğa, G. (2014). Uluslar Arası Karbon Ticareti ve Türkiye. *Journal of Yaşar Universitesi*, *9*(34), 5732–5759.

Birge, J. R. (2000). Option methods for incorporating risk into linear capacity planning models. *Manufacturing & Service Operations Management: M & SOM*, *2*(1), 19–31. doi:10.1287/msom.2.1.19.23269

Bitlis, M. (2016). Green bonds. *Escarus Blog*. Retrieved April 15, 2018, from http://www.escarus.com/green-bonds

Blackman, I. D., Holland, C. P., & Westcott, T. (2013). Motorola's global financial supply chain strategy. *Supply Chain Management*, *18*(2), 132–147. doi:10.1108/13598541311318782

Boele, R., Fabig, H., & Wheeler, D. (2001). Shell, Nigeria and the Ogoni. A study in unsustainable development: II. Corporate social responsibility and 'stakeholder management' versus a rights-based approach to sustainable development. *Sustainable Development*, *9*(3), 121–135. doi:10.1002d.168

Bohari, A. A. M., Skitmore, M., Xia, B., & Zhang, X. (2016). Insights into the adoption of green construction in Malaysia: The drivers and challenges. *Environment-Behaviour Proceedings Journal*, *1*(4), 45–53.

Bond, S. (2010). *Best of the Best in Green Design: Drivers and Barriers to Sustainable Development in Australia*. Lincoln University Digital Dissertation.

Booth, C. (2003). Does history matter in strategy? The possibilities and problems of counterfactual analysis. *Management Decision*, *41*(1), 96–104. doi:10.1108/00251740310445545

Booth, L., Ntantamis, C., & Zhou, J. (2015). Financial Constraints, R&D Investment, and the Value of Cash Holdings. *The Quarterly Journal of Finance*, *05*(04), 1550011. doi:10.1142/S2010139215500111

Borck, R., Caliendo, M., & Steiner, V. (2007). Fiscal Competition and the Composition of Public Spending: Theory and Evidence. *Finanz-Archiv*, *63*(2), 264–277. doi:10.1628/001522107X220107

Bougheas, S., Görg, H., & Strobl, E. (2003). Is R & D Financially Constrained? Theory and Evidence from Irish Manufacturing. *Review of Industrial Organization*, *22*(2), 159–174. doi:10.1023/A:1022905102446

Bourdieu, P. (1985). The forms of capital. In J. G. Richardson (Ed.), *Handbook of theory and research for the sociology of education* (pp. 241–258). New York: Greenwood.

Bowen, H. R. (1953). *Social Responsibilities of the Businessman*. New York: Harper.

Boyabath, O., & Toktay, L. B. (2011). Optimal control and hedging of operations in the presence of financial markets. *Management Science*, *57*(12), 2163–2179.

BP. (2018). *BP Statistical Review of World Energy*. Retrieved June 25, 2018, from https://www.bp.com/content/dam/bp/en/corporate/pdf/energy-economics/statistical-review/bp-stats-review-2018-full-report.pdf

Braam, R. R., Moed, H. F., & van Raan, A. F. J. (1991a). Mapping of science by combined co-citation and word analysis, I. Structural aspects. *Journal of the American Society for Information Science*, *422*(4), 233–251. doi:10.1002/(SICI)1097-4571(199105)42:4<233::AID-ASI1>3.0.CO;2-I

Braam, R. R., Moed, H. F., & van Raan, A. F. J. (1991b). Mapping of science by combined co-citation and word analysis, II: Dynamical aspects. *Journal of the American Society for Information Science*, *422*(4), 252–264. doi:10.1002/(SICI)1097-4571(199105)42:4<252::AID-ASI2>3.0.CO;2-G

Broadie, M., Chernov, M., & Sundaresan, S. (2007). Optimal debt and equity values in the presence of Chapter 7 and Chapter 11. *The Journal of Finance*, *62*(3), 1341–1377. doi:10.1111/j.1540-6261.2007.01238.x

Brody, D. C., Syroka, J., & Zervos, M. (2002). Dynamical Pricing of Weather Derivative. *Quantitative Finance*, *2*(3), 189–198. doi:10.1088/1469-7688/2/3/302

Brown, J., Makinson, S., & Magallon, D. (2012). *Financial mechanisms and investment frameworks for renewables in developing countries*. International Renewable Energy Agency (IRENA), Retrieved April 15, 2018, from http://www.irena.org/publications/2013/Jan/Financial-Mechanisms-and-Investment-Frameworks-for-Renewables-in-Developing-Countries

Brown, J. R., Fazzari, S. M., & Petersen, B. C. (2009). Financing Innovation and Growth: Cash Flow, External Equity, and the 1990s R&D Boom. *The Journal of Finance*, *64*(1), 151–185. doi:10.1111/j.1540-6261.2008.01431.x

Brown, J. R., & Petersen, B. C. (2009). Why has the investment-cash flow sensitivity declined so sharply? Rising R&D and equity market developments. *Journal of Banking & Finance*, *33*(5), 971–984. doi:10.1016/j.jbankfin.2008.10.009

Brownsword, R., & Han, S. (2009). Law, innovation and technology: Before we fast forward—a forum for debate. *Law Innovation & Technology*, *1*(1), 1–73. doi:10.1080/17579961.2009.11428364

Brummer, C. (2015). Disruptive technology and securities regulation. *Social Science Electronic Publishing*, *84*(3), 977–1052.

Brunnée, J. (2009). *The Stockholm Declaration and the Structure and Processes of International Environmental Law. In The Future of Ocean Regime-Building* (pp. 39–62). Brill.

Buchner, B. (2018). *Global landscape of renewable energy finance*. International Renewable Energy Agency (IRENA). Retrieved April 15, 2018, from https://www.irena.org//media/Files/IRENA/Agency/Publication/2018/Jan/IRENA_Global_landscape_RE_finance_2018.pdf

Burkart, M., & Ellingsen, T. (2004). In-kind finance: A theory of trade credit. *The American Economic Review*, *94*(3), 569–590. doi:10.1257/0002828041464579

Buys, F., & Hurbissoon, R. (2011). Green buildings: A mauritian built environment stakeholders' perspective. *Acta Struct.*, *18*, 81–101.

Buzacott, J. A., & Zhang, R. Q. (2004). Inventory Management with Asset-Based Financing. *Management Science*, *50*(9), 1274–1292. doi:10.1287/mnsc.1040.0278

Cachon, G. (2004). The allocation of inventory risk in a supply chain: Push, pull, and advance-purchase discount contracts. *Management Science*, *50*(2), 222–238. doi:10.1287/mnsc.1030.0190

Caixin Global. (2017). *Quick Take: JD.com Finance Unit Launches Microlending in Chongqing*. Retrieved October 19, 2017, from https://www.caixinglobal.com/

Cai, Z. (2016). Principle, application and suggestion of blockchain technology. *Software*, *11*, 51–54.

Calabrese, A., Costa, R., Levialdi, N., & Menichini, T. (2016). A fuzzy Analytic Hierarchy Process method to support materiality assessment in sustainability reporting. *Journal of Cleaner Production*, *121*, 248–264. doi:10.1016/j.jclepro.2015.12.005

Caldentey, R., & Haugh, M. B. (2006). Optimal control and hedging of operations in the presence of financial markets. *Mathematics of Operations Research*, *31*(2), 285–304. doi:10.1287/moor.1050.0179

Callon, M., Courtial, J. P., Turner, W. A., & Bauin, S. (1983). From translations to problematic networks – an introduction to co-word analysis. *Social Science Information Sur Les Sciences Sociales*, *22*(2), 191–235. doi:10.1177/053901883022002003

Callon, M., Courtial, J., & Laville, F. (1991). Co-word analysis as a tool for describing the network of interactions between basic and technological research-The case of polymer chemistry. *Scientometrics*, *22*(1), 155–205. doi:10.1007/BF02019280

Caniato, F., Gelsomino, L. M., Perego, A., & Ronchi, S. (2016). Does finance solve the supply chain financing problem? *Supply Chain Management*, *21*(5), 534–549. doi:10.1108/SCM-11-2015-0436

Canpolat, S. (2009). *Çevre Vergileri ve Türkiye Uygulaması. Ankara Üniversitesi Sosyal Bilimler Enstitüsü*. Yayımlanmamış Yüksek Lisans Tezi.

Cao, M., & Wei, J. (2004). Weather Derivatives Valuations and Market Price of Weather Risk. *Journal of Futures Markets*, *24*(11), 1065–1089. doi:10.1002/fut.20122

Carpenter, S. (2009). Do green buildings really save energy? *Building*, *59*(2), 22.

Carroll, A. B. (1979). A three-dimensional conceptual model of corporate performance. *Academy of Management Review*, *4*(4), 497–505. doi:10.5465/amr.1979.4498296

Carroll, A. B. (1991). The pyramid of corporate social responsibility: Toward to moral management of organizational stakeholders. *Business Horizons*, *34*(4), 39–48. doi:10.1016/0007-6813(91)90005-G

Carroll, A. B., & Buchholtz, A. K. (2000). *Business & Society. Ethics and Stakeholder Management* (4th ed.). Cincinnati, OH: South Western College Publishing.

Çelikkaya, A. (2011). Avrupa Birliği Üyesi Ülkelerde Çevre Vergisi Reformları ve Türkiye'deki Durumun Değerlendirilmesi. *Anadolu University Journal of Social Science, 11*(2), 97–120.

Çevre ve Orman Bakanlığı (ÇOB) İklim Değişikliği Dairesi Başkanlığı. (2008). *Kyoto Protokolü Esneklik Mekanizmaları ve Diğer Uluslararası Emisyon Ticareti Sistemleri Özel İhtisas Komisyonu Raporu*. Retrieved from http://iklim.cob.gov.tr/iklim/Files/eKutuphane/KP_OIK_FinalRapor-28%2012%202008.pdf

Çevre ve Orman Bakanlığı (ÇOB) İklim Değişikliği Dairesi Başkanlığı. (2011). *Karbon Piyasalarında Ulusal Deneyim ve Geleceğe Bakış*. Retrieved from.http://iklim.cob.gov.tr/iklim/Files/Karbon%20Piyasalarında%20Ulusal%20Deneyim%20ve%20Geleceğe%20Bakış_2011.pdf

Chen. (2018). Research on the Development Model of Science and Technology Financial Service Industry under Internet Thinking. *Journal of Fujian Institute of Financial Management, 1*, 3-9.

Chen, C. (1999). Visualising semantic spaces and author co-citation networks in digital libraries. *Information Processing & Management, 35*(2), 401–420. doi:10.1016/S0306-4573(98)00068-5

Chen, C. (2006). CiteSpace II: Detecting and Visualizing Emerging Trends and Transient Patterns in Scientific Literature. *Journal of the American Society for Information Science and Technology, 57*(3), 359–377. doi:10.1002/asi.20317

Chen, C. (2017). Science Mapping: A Systematic Review of the Literature. *Journal of Data and Information Science, 2*(2), 1–40. doi:10.1515/jdis-2017-0006

Chen, L., & Zhao, D. (2006). Optical color image encryption by wavelength multiplexing and lensless Fresnel transform holograms. *Optics Express, 14*(19), 8552–8560. doi:10.1364/OE.14.008552 PMID:19529234

Chen, S., Sun, Z., Tang, S., & Wu, D. (2011). Government intervention and investment efficiency: Evidence from China. *Journal of Corporate Finance, 17*(2), 259–271. doi:10.1016/j.jcorpfin.2010.08.004

Chen, X., & Hu, C. (2011). The value of supply chain finance. In *Supply Chain Management-Applications and Simulations*. InTech. doi:10.5772/19208

Chen, Z. (2017). *The transition from traditional banking to mobile internet finance: an organization innovation perspective*. Financial Innovation.

China Daily. (2017). *Supply chain in focus with new approach*. Retrieved October 27, 2017, from http://www.chinadaily.com.cn/

Chod, J. (2016). Inventory, risk shifting, and trade credit. *Management Science, 63*(10), 3207–3225. doi:10.1287/mnsc.2016.2515

Choi, T. M., & Chiu, C. H. (2012). Mean-downside-risk and mean-variance newsvendor models: Implications for sustainable fashion retailing. *International Journal of Production Economics, 135*(2), 552–560. doi:10.1016/j.ijpe.2010.10.004

Chu, C. C., Tsai, S. B., Chen, Y., Li, X., Zhai, Y., Chen, Q., ... Li, B. (2017). An Empirical Study on the Relationship between Investor Protection, Government Behavior, and Financial Development. *Sustainability*, *9*(12), 2199. doi:10.3390u9122199

Chuck, W. F., & Kim, J. T. (2011). Building environmental assessment schemes for rating of IAQ in sustainable buildings. *Indoor and Built Environment*, *20*(1), 5–15. doi:10.1177/1420326X10397780

CIDB. (2009). *Greenhouse gas emission reduction: potentials from buildings*. Construction Industry Development Board (CIDB) discussion document. Retrieved from www.cidb.org.za

Çınar, S., & Yılmazer, M. (2015). Yenilenebilir enerji kaynaklarının belirleyicileri ve ekonomik büyüme ilişkisi: Gelişmekte olan ülkeler örneği. *Dokuz Eylül Üniversitesi İktisadi ve İdari Bilimler Fakültesi Dergisi*, *30*(1), 55–78.

Ciocirlan, C., & Bruce, Y. (2003). The Political Economy of Green Taxation in OECD Countries. *European Journal of Law and Economics*, *15*(3), 203–218. doi:10.1023/A:1023390126187

Clarkson, M. E. (1995). A stakeholder framework for analyzing and evaluating corporate social performance. *Academy of Management Review*, *20*(1), 92–117. doi:10.5465/amr.1995.9503271994

Clemmons, L. (2002). Introduction to weather risk management. In E. Banks (Ed.), *Weather Risk Management: Market, Products and Applications* (pp. 3–12). London: Palgrave.

Clemons. (2000). The Internet and the Future of Financial Services. The Wharton Financial Institutions Center.

Cline, W. R. (2007). *Global Warming and Agriculture: Impact Estimates by Country* (1st ed.). Washington, DC: Peterson Institute.

Coase, R. H. (2013). The Problem of Social Cost. *The Journal of Law & Economics*, *56*(4), 837–877. doi:10.1086/674872

Cochran, P. L. (2007). The evolution of corporate social responsibility. *Business Horizons*, *50*(6), 449–454. doi:10.1016/j.bushor.2007.06.004

Colbert, B. A., & Kurucz, E. C. (2007). Three conceptions of triple bottom line business sustainability and the role for HRM. *People and Strategy*, *30*(1), 21.

Com Score, Inc. (2009). Nine Out of Ten 25-34-Year-Old U.K. Internet Users Visited a Social Networking Site in May 2009; Internet Users Age 55 and Older More Likely to Visit Social Networking Sites than Business & Finance, Technology and Travel. *M2 Presswire*.

Corbally, M., & Dang, P. H. (2002). Underlying markets and indexes. In *Weather Risk Management: Market, Products and Applications*. London: Palgrave.

Cousins, P. D., Handfield, R. B., Lawson, B., & Petersen, K. J. (2006). Creating supply chain relational capital: The impact of formal and informal socialization processes. *Journal of Operations Management*, *24*(6), 851–863. doi:10.1016/j.jom.2005.08.007

Craig, N., & Raman, A. (2013). *Improving store liquidation*. Harvard Business School.

Cull, R., Davis, L. E., Lamoreaux, N. R., & Rosenthal, J. (2006). Historical financing of small- and medium-size enterprises. *Journal of Banking & Finance*, *30*(11), 3017–3042. doi:10.1016/j.jbankfin.2006.05.005

Czarnitzki, D., & Hottenrott, H. (2011). Financial Constraints: Routine Versus Cutting Edge R&D Investment. *Journal of Economics & Management Strategy*, *20*(1), 121–158. doi:10.1111/j.1530-9134.2010.00285.x

Czarnitzki, D., & Hottenrott, H. (2011). R&D Investment and Financing Constraints of Small and Medium-Sized Firm. *Small Business Economics*, *36*(1), 65–83. doi:10.100711187-009-9189-3

D'Avanzo, R., Lewinski, H. V., & Wassenhove, L. N. V. (2003). The link between supply chain and financial performance. *Supply Chain Management Review*, *7*(6), 40–47.

Da Da, W. (2014). On the main mode, evolution and Enlightenment of internet banking in America. *Asia Pacific Economic*, *4*, 70–71.

Da Wang, W. (2014). The development of internet banking in the United States and the comparison of internet finance between China and America -- Research and Reflection Based on the perspective of internet economics. *International Finance Review*, *12*, 47–57.

Dada, M., & Hu, Q. J. (2008). Financing newsvendor inventory. *Operations Research Letters*, *36*(5), 569–573. doi:10.1016/j.orl.2008.06.004

Dai. (2014). Internet Financial authenticity. *Harvard Business Review*, 4.

Daily Telegraph. (2017). *Unilever's Paul Polman on why he didn't get angry when Kraft Heinz came to call, and why he'll still keep talking about sustainability*. Retrieved June 19, 2017, from http://www.telegraph.co.uk/business/2017/04/08/unilevers-paul-polman-didnt-get-angry-kraft-heinz-came-call/

Daly, H. E. (1990). Toward Some Operational Principles of Sustainable Development. *Ecological Economics*, *2*(1), 1–6. doi:10.1016/0921-8009(90)90010-R

Darton, R. C. (2015). Setting a policy for sustainability: the importance of measurement. In J. Klemes (Ed.), *Assessing and Measuring Environmental Impact and Sustainability* (pp. 479–496). Oxford, UK: Butterworth-Heinemann. doi:10.1016/B978-0-12-799968-5.00014-2

Daugbjerg, C., & Svendsen, G. (2001). *Green Taxation in Question: Politics and Economic Efficiency in Environmental Regulation*. Springer. doi:10.1057/9780230595538

Dehesa, M., Druck, P., & Plekhanov, A. (2007). Relative Price Stability, Creditor Rights, and Financial Deepening. *IMF Working Papers*, *7*(139).

Demica. (2014). *A study on the growth of supply chain finance, as evidenced by SCF dedicated job titles at top European bank*. Demica.

Demireli, E., & Hepkorucu, A. (2010). Çevre Finansmanı: Kavramsal Bir Yaklaşımla Karbon Finans Borsası. *Ekonomi Bilimleri Dergisi*, *2*(2), 37–48.

Djokoto, S. D., Dadzie, J., & Ohemeng-Ababio, E. (2014). Barriers to Sustainable Construction in the Ghanaian Construction Industry: Consultants Perspectives. *Journal of Sustainable Development, 14*(1). doi:10.5539/jsd.v7n1p134

Dlugolecki, A., & Lafeld, S. (2005). *Climate Change & the Financial Sector: An Agenda for Action.* Allianz Group and WWF. Retrieved from http://www.wwf.org.uk/filelibrary/pdf/allianz_rep_0605.pdf

Dodd, E. M. Jr. (1932). For whom are corporate managers trustees? *Harvard Law Review, 45*(7), 1145–1163. doi:10.2307/1331697

Dodge Data & Analytics. (2016). *World green building trends: Developing markets accelerate global green growth. Smart Market report.* Design and Construction Intelligence.

Donohue, K. (2000). Efficient supply contracts for fashion goods with forecast updating and two production modes. *Management Science, 46*(11), 1397–1411. doi:10.1287/mnsc.46.11.1397.12088

Downes, R. (2018). *Green Budgeting can Spur Governments to Improve Our Planet's Bottom Line.* Retrieved from http://oecdinsights.org/2018/01/19/green-budgeting-can-spur-governments to-improve-our-planets-bottom-line/

DPT. (1997). *Ulusal Çevre Eylem Planı.* Retrieved from http://okulonceciyiz.biz/upload/ulusal-cevre-eylem-plani-egitim-ve-katilim.pdf

Dumay, J., Guthrie, J., & Farneti, F. (2010). GRI sustainability reporting guidelines for public and third sector organizations: A critical review. *Public Management Review, 12*(4), 531–548. doi:10.1080/14719037.2010.496266

EBRD. (n.d.). *Türkiye Sürdürülebilir Finansman Programı.* Retrieved February 12, 2018, from https://www.ika.org.tr/upload/duyurular/Turkiye-Surdurulebilir-Enerji-Programi-aciklanmistir-526300.pdf

Edmark, K., & Ågren, H. (2008). Identifying strategic interactions in Swedish local income tax policies. *Journal of Urban Economics, 63*(3), 849–857. doi:10.1016/j.jue.2007.06.001

Ehrenfeld, J. R. (2008). *Sustainability by Design.* New Haven, CT: Yale University Press.

Eichholtz, P., Kok, N., & Quigley, J. M. (2010). Doing Well by Doing Good? Green Office Buildings. *The American Economic Review, 100*(5), 2492–2509. doi:10.1257/aer.100.5.2492

Eisenberg, D., Done, R., & Ishida, L. (2002). *Breaking down the barriers: Challenges and solutions to code approval of green building.* Tucson, AZ: Development Center for Appropriate Technology.

Ekinci, F., & Gönençgil, B. (2015). *Dünya Karbon Emisyon Piyasalarında Türkiye'nin Yeri, 6. Ulusal Hava Kirliliği ve Kontrolü Sempozyumu.*

Ekins, P. (1999). European Environmental Taxes and Charges: Recent Experience, Issues and Trends. *Ecological Economics, 31*(1), 39–62. doi:10.1016/S0921-8009(99)00051-8

Elforgani, M. S., & Rahmat, I. (2010). An investigation of factors influencing design team attributes in green buildings. *American Journal of Applied Sciences*, *7*(7), 7. doi:10.3844/ajassp.2010.976.986

Elkington, J. (1997). *Cannibals With Forks: The Triple Bottom Line of 21st Century Business*. Oxford, UK: Capstone.

Elkins, P. (2000). *Economic Growth and Environmental Sustainability: The prospects for green growth*. London: Routledge.

Ellis, K. (2011). *Green Growth Opportunities and Requirements in Egypt*. Eschborn: Deutsche Gesellschaftfür Internationale Zusammenarbeit.

Epstein, M. J., & Buhovac, A. R. (2014). *Making sustainability work: Best practices in managing and measuring corporate social, environmental, and economic impacts*. Oakland, CA: Berrett-Koehler Publishers.

Eroğlu, E., & Serbes, H. (2018). Fiscal Autonomy of Sub-Central Governments in Turkey. In *Financial Sustainability and Intergenerational Equity in Local Governments* (pp. 83–100). IGI Global. doi:10.4018/978-1-5225-3713-7.ch004

Erten, D. (2011) Istanbul: The Challenges for Sustainable Buildings in Emerging Economies. Leverkusen: *UNEP-SBCI Symposium on Sustainable Buildings*.

European Commission. (2012). *Policies to Encourage Sustainable Consumption, Technical Report 2012-061*. Brussels: European Communities.

European Union. (2016). *Regulation (EU) 2016/679 of the European Parliament and of the Council of 27 April 2016 on the protection of natural persons with regard to the processing of personal data and on the free movement of such data, and repealing Directive 95/46/EC (General Data Protection Regulation)*. Retrieved August 13, 2018, from http://eur-lex.europa.eu/legal-content/EN/TXT/?uri=CELEX:32016R0679

Federal Reserve System. (2017). *Consumer and Mobile Finance Services 2016*. Author.

Ferguson, M., DeCroix, G., & Zipkin, P. (2005). Commitment decisions with partial information updating. *Naval Research Logistics*, *52*(8), 780–795. doi:10.1002/nav.20119

Ferhatoğlu, E. (2003). Article. *Avrupa Birliği'nde Ortak Çevre Politikası Çerçevesinde Çevre Vergileri*, *3*, 1–7.

Fernando, J. L. (2003). *Rethinking sustainable development. In The Annals of the American Academy of Political and Social Science*. London: Sage Publications.

Florman, M., Klingler-Vidra, R., & Jacinto Facada, M. (2016). *A critical evaluation of social impact assessment methodologies and a call to measure economic and social impact holistically through the External Rate of Return platform*. LSE Enterprise Working Paper # 1602. London: LSE.

Foley, J. A., Ramankutty, N., Brauman, K. A., Cassidy, E. S., Gerber, J. S., Johnston, M., ... Zaks, D. P. M. (2011). Solutions for a cultivated planet. *Nature*, *478*(7369), 337–342. doi:10.1038/nature10452 PMID:21993620

Forsman-Hugg, S., Katajajuuri, J. M., Riipi, I., Mäkelä, J., Järvelä, K., & Timonen, P. (2013). Key CSR dimension for the food chain. *British Food Journal*, *115*(1), 30–47. doi:10.1108/00070701311289867

Forward-Looking Industry Research Institute. (2015). *Report of market prospective and investment strategy planning on China supply chain finance industry (2015-2020)*. Author.

Foundation Centre. (2017). *Tools and Resources for Assessing Social Impact*. Retrieved April 13, 2017, from http://trasi.foundationcenter.org/browse.php

Fowler, K. M., & Rauch, E. M. (2006). *Sustainable Building Rating Systems Summary, Pacific Northwest National Laboratory*. Richland, WA: PNNL. doi:10.2172/926974

Friedman, M. (1970). The social responsibility of business is to increase its profits. New York: Academic Press.

Fu & Gao. (2018). Research on Legal Risk Prevention of Internet Finance. *Journal of Beijing Institute of Political Science and Law*, *2*, 6-10.

Gale, R., & Barg, S. (Eds.). (2014). *Green Budget Reform: An International Casebook of Leading Practices*. Routledge. doi:10.4324/9781315070636

Gallagher, A. U., & Yuan, F. (2017). Standardizing Sustainable Development: A Comparison of Development Banks in the Americas. *Journal of Environment & Development*, *26*(3), 243–271. doi:10.1177/1070496517720711

Gao, J., & Bansal, P. (2013). Instrumental and Integrative Logics in Business Sustainability. *Journal of Business Ethics*, *112*(2), 241–255. doi:10.100710551-012-1245-2

Garanti Bankası. (2018a). *Garanti Bankası 2017 Entegre Faaliyet Raporu*. Retrieved June 24, 2018, from https://surdurulebilirlik.garanti.com.tr/media/1233/garanti-bankasi-2017-entegre-faaliyet-raporu.pdf

Garanti Bankası. (2018b). Retrieved from https://www.garanti.com.tr/tr

Garriga, E., & Melé, D. (2004). Corporate Social Responsibility Theories: Mapping the Territory. *Journal of Business Ethics*, *53*(1-2), 51–71. doi:10.1023/B:BUSI.0000039399.90587.34

Gelsomino, L. M., de Boer, R., Steeman, M., & Perego, A. (2018). An optimisation strategy for concurrent Supply Chain Finance schemes. *Journal of Purchasing and Supply Management*. doi:10.1016/j.pursup.2018.07.004

Gelsomino, L. M., Mangiaracina, R., Perego, A., & Tumino, A. (2016). Supply chain finance: A literature review. *International Journal of Physical Distribution & Logistics Management*, *46*(4), 348–366. doi:10.1108/IJPDLM-08-2014-0173

Ghazilla, R. A. R., Sakundarini, N., Abdul-Rashid, S. H., Ayub, N. S., Olugu, E. U., & Musa, S. N. (2015). Drivers and barriers analysis for green manufacturing practices in Malaysian SMEs: A preliminary findings. *Procedia CIRP*, *26*, 658–663. doi:10.1016/j.procir.2015.02.085

Giddings, B., Hopwood, B., & O'Brien, G. (2002). Environment, Economy and Society: Fitting Them Together into Sustainable Development. *Sustainable Development*, *10*(4), 187–196. doi:10.1002d.199

Giri, B. C., & Sharma, S. (2017). Optimising an integrated production–inventory system under cash discount and retailer partial trade credit policy. *International Journal of Systems Science: Operations & Logistics*, 1-20.

Global Reporting Initiative (2017b). *The benefits of sustainability reporting*. Author.

Global Reporting Initiative. (2017a). *GRI's History*. Retrieved April 13, 2017, from https://www.globalreporting.org/information/about-gri/gri-history/Pages/GRI%27s%20history.aspx

Global Reporting Initiative/United Nations Global Compact/wbcsd. (2015). *SDG Compass: The guide for business action on the SDGs*. Author.

Global Reporting Initiative/United Nations Global Compact/wbcsd. (2017a). Retrieved April 12, 2017, from http://sdgcompass.org/business-tools/

Global Reporting Initiative/United Nations Global Compact/wbcsd. (2017b). Retrieved April 12, 2017, from http://sdgcompass.org/business-indicators/

Global Sustainability Standards Board. (2017). *Global Sustainability Standard Board*. Retrieved April 13, 2017, from https://www.globalreporting.org/information/about-gri/governance-bodies/Global-Sustainability-Standard-Board/Pages/default.aspx

Goel, P. (2016). *Green Finance: A step towards sustainable financial system*. Abhnav Publications.

Goering, J. (2009). *Sustainable real estate development: The dynamics of market penetration*. Academic Press.

Goldin, I., & Winters, L. A. (1995). *The Economics of Sustainable Development*. Cambridge, UK: Cambridge University Press. doi:10.1017/CBO9780511751905

Gomes, V., Gomes da Silva, M., Lamberts, R., Vespoli, M. T., & Sangoi de Oliveira, M. (n.d.). Sustainable Building in Brazil. *International Initiative for a Sustainable Built Environment.*

Gouzee, N., Mazijn, B., & Billharz, S. (1995). *Indicators of Sustainable Development for Decision-making*. Report on the UNCSD Workshop of Ghent. Brussels: Federal Planning Office of Belgium.

Governance and Accountability Institute. (2016). *81% of S&P 500 companies published sustainability reports in 2015*. Retrieved July 10, 2018 1 from http://www.ga-institute.com/press-releases/article/flash-report-eighty-one-percent-81-of-the-sp-500-index-companies-published-corporate-sustainabi.html

Gray, R., & Milne, M. (2004). Towards reporting on the triple bottom line: mirages, methods and myths. In The triple bottom line: Does it all add up? London: Earthscan.

Gray, R. (2010). Is accounting for sustainability actually accounting for sustainability… and how would we know? An exploration of narratives of organisations and the planet. *Accounting, Organizations and Society*, *35*(1), 47–62. doi:10.1016/j.aos.2009.04.006

Green Building Council South Africa. (2007). Available online: http://www.gbcsa.org.za

Green Finance Research Group of Industrial and Commercial Bank of China. (2017). Research on the construction of green strategic system in commercial banks. *Financial Forum*, (1), 3-16.

Griffith-Jones, S., Ocampo, J. A., & Spratt, S. (2012). *Financing renewable energy in developing countries: Mechanisms and responsibilities*. European Report on Development. Retrieved March 5, 2018, from http://policydialogue.org/files/publications/Financing_Renewable_Energy_in_Developing_Countries.pdf

Grosse-Ruyken, P. T., Wagner, S. M., & Jonke, R. (2011). What is the right cash conversion cycle for your supply chain. *International Journal of Services and Operations Management*, *10*(1), 13–29. doi:10.1504/IJSOM.2011.041987

Guan, R., Zheng, H. T., Hu, J., Fang, Q., & Ren, R. E. (2017). The Higher Carbon Intensity of Loans, the Higher Non-Performing Loan Ratio: The Case of China. *Sustainability*, *9*(4), 667. doi:10.3390u9040667

Gu, D., Li, J., Li, X., & Liang, C. (2017). Visualizing the knowledge structure and evolution of big data research in healthcare informatics. *International Journal of Medical Informatics*, *98*, 22–32. doi:10.1016/j.ijmedinf.2016.11.006 PMID:28034409

Gündüz, O., & Agun, B. H. (2013). Çevre Vergilerinin Yerel Yönetim Düzeyinde Uygulanması: Avrupa Birliği ve Türkiye Uygulaması. *Maliye Finans Yazıları*, *27*(99), 55–79.

Gupta, D. (2008). *Technical note: Financing the newsvendor.* University of Minnesota.

Gupta, D., & Wang, L. (2009). A stochastic inventory model with trade credit. *Manufacturing & Service Operations Management: M & SOM*, *11*(1), 4–18. doi:10.1287/msom.1070.0191

Guthrie, J., & Farneti, F. (2008). GRI sustainability reporting by Australian public sector organizations. *Public Money & Management*, *28*(6), 361–366. doi:10.1111/j.1467-9302.2008.00670.x

Güzel, A. (2001). Sürdürülebilir Kalkınma'da Yerel Yönetimlerin Mali Sorumlulukları. *Çevre ve Sürdürülebilir Kalkınma Paneli*, 2023.

Habitat, U. N. (2011). *Sustainable Building Practices for Low Cost Housing: Implications for Climate Change Mitigation and Adaptation in Developing Countries. Shelter Initiative for Climate Change Mitigation and Adaption.* SICCMA.

Häkkinen, T., & Belloni, K. (2011). Barriers and drivers for sustainable building. *Building Research and Information*, *39*(3), 239–255. doi:10.1080/09613218.2011.561948

Halkbank. (2018a). Retrieved from https://www.halkbank.com.tr/

Halkbank. (2018b). *Sürdürülebilirlik Raporu 2017*. Retrieved June 24, 2018, from https://mediaservice.halkbank.com.tr/media/document/Halkbank/Biz/Surdurulebilirlik/raporlarveetkinlikler/Halkbanksrtr2017.pdf

Halpern, D. (2009). *The Hidden Wealth of Nations*. Cambridge, UK: Polity.

Hamilton, K. (2010). *Scaling up renewable energy in developing countries: Finance and investment perspectives*. Energy, Environment & Resource Governance Programme Paper 02/10. Retrieved March 15, 2018, from http://www.chathamhouse.org/sites/default/files/public/Research/Energy,%20Environment%20and%20Development/0410pp_hamilton.pdf

Han. (2016). Conflict and integration of internet Finance and traditional financial model. *Commercial Economy Research*, *15*, 177-179.

Handl, G. (2012). Declaration of The United Nations Conference on the Human Environment (Stockholm Declaration), 1972 and the Rio Declaration on Environment and Development, 1992. *United Nations Audiovisual Library of International Law, 11*.

Hanh, P. T. H. (2014). *Financial Development, Financial Openness and Trade Openness: New evidence*. FIW Working Paper.

Hanifan, L. J. (1916). The rural school community centre. *The Annals of the American Academy of Political and Social Science*, *67*, 130-138.

Hansen, B. E. (1999). Threshold effects in non-dynamic panels: Estimation, testing, and inference. *Journal of Econometrics*, *93*(2), 345–368. doi:10.1016/S0304-4076(99)00025-1

Han, X. (2018). Legal Regulation of Anonymous Information in the Age of Big Data. *Journal of Dalian University of Technology*, *4*, 64–75. doi:10.100711595-018-1786-z

Harper, J. (2011). *Reputation Under Regulation: The Fair Credit Reporting Act at 40 and Lessons for the Internet Privacy Debate*. Retrieved August 13, 2018, from https://ssrn.com/abstract=2033360

Hasen. (2011). Political Equality, the Internet, and Campaign Finance Regulation. *The Forum*, 6.

Health and Safety Executive. (2017). *How many toilets should a workplace have?* Retrieved July 10, 2018, from http://www.hse.gov.uk/contact/faqs/toilets.htm

He, Q. (1999). Knowledge discovery through co-word analysis. *Library Trends*, *48*(1), 133–159.

Hill, R. P., Stephens, D., & Smith, I. (2003). Corporate social responsibility: An examination of individual firm behaviour. *Business and Society Review*, *108*(3), 339–364. doi:10.1111/1467-8594.00168

Hofmann, E. (2005). Supply chain finance: some conceptual insights. *Beiträge Zu Beschaffung Und Logistik*, 203-214.

Hofmann, E. (2009). Inventory financing in supply chains: A logistics service provider-approach. *International Journal of Physical Distribution & Logistics Management, 39*(9), 716–740. doi:10.1108/09600030911008175

Hofmann, E., & Kotzab, H. (2010). A supply chain-oriented approach of working capital management. *Journal of Business Logistics, 31*(2), 305–330. doi:10.1002/j.2158-1592.2010.tb00154.x

Houser, K. A., & Sanders, D. (2017). The Use of Big Data Analytics by the IRS: Efficient Solutions or the End of Privacy as We Know It? *19 Vand. J. Ent. & Tech., L*, 817.

Hua & Hui. (2015). Internet banking is a new financial instrument or a new financial format. Based on the comparative perspective with the United States. *Asia Pacific Economy, 4*, 31-36.

Hu, F., Liu, W., Tsai, S.-B., Gao, J., Bin, N., & Chen, Q. (2018). An Empirical Study on Visualizing the Intellectual Structure and Hotspots of Big Data Research from a Sustainable Perspective. *Sustainability, 10*(3), 667. doi:10.3390u10030667

Huh, W. T., & Park, K. S. (2013). Impact of transfer pricing methods for tax purposes on supply chain performance under demand uncertainty. *Naval Research Logistics, 60*(4), 269–293. doi:10.1002/nav.21533

Hurley, M., & Adebayo, J. (2016). Credit Scoring in the Era of Big Data. *18 Yale J. L. & Tech., 148*, 150–215.

Hutchins, M. J., & Sutherland, J. W. (2008). An exploration of measures of social sustainability and their application to supply chain decisions. *Journal of Cleaner Production, 16*(15), 1688–1698. doi:10.1016/j.jclepro.2008.06.001

Hwang, B. G., Zehu, L., Wang, Y., & Cheong, X. (2017). Green Building construction projects in Sngapore; Cost premiums & Cost performance. *Project Management Journal, 48*(4), 67–79. doi:10.1177/875697281704800406

Hydes, K. R., & Creech, L. (2010), Reducing mechanical equipment cost: the economics of green design. *Building Research & Information, 1*(1). Available at: http://www.tandfonline.com/loi/rbri20

IDFC. (2014). *Scaling up renewable energy investments*. Retrieved March 15, 2018, from https://www.idfc.org/Downloads/Publications/02_other_idfc-expert_documents/IDFC_Sustainable_Infrastructure_Paper_01-12-14.pdf

IEA. (2016). *Energy policies of IEA countries Turkey 2016 review*. Retrieved January 25, 2018, from https://www.iea.org/publications/freepublications/publication/EnergyPoliciesofIEACountriesTurkey.pdf

Ikelegbe, A. (2005). The economy of conflict in the oil rich Niger Delta region of Nigeria. *Nordic Journal of African Studies, 14*(2), 208–234.

Institute for Human Rights and Business (2015). *State of play – Business and the Sustainable Development Goals: Mind the gap – Challenges for implementation*. Retrieved April 13, 2017, from http://www.ihrb.org/media/images/reports/state_of_play_reportbusiness_and_the_sdgs.pdf

Institute of Development Studies SWUFE. (2015). Environmental and Economic Policy Research Center Research Group of the Ministry of Environmental Protection. Green finance and sustainable development. *Financial Forum*, (10), 30-40.

IntelC. R. R. (2008). Available online: http://www.intel.com/

International Accounting Standards Board (2018). Retrieved July 10, 2018, from https://www.ifrs.org/

International Integrated Reporting Framework. (2013). *The International IR Framework*. Retrieved June 19, 2017, from http://integratedreporting.org/wp-content/uploads/2015/03/13-12-08-THE-INTERNATIONAL-IR-FRAMEWORK-2-1.pdf

International Labour Office. (2017). *Tripartite Declaration of Principles Concerning Multinational Enterprises and Social Policy*. Geneva: International Labour Office.

International Labour Organisation. (1998). *Declaration on Fundamental Principles and Rights at Work*. Retrieved August 10, 2017, from http://blue.lim.ilo.org/cariblex/pdfs/ILO_Declaration_Work.pdf

IPCC. (2007a). *The Physical Science Basis. Contribution of Working Group I to the Fourth Assessment Report of the Intergovernmental Panel on Climate Change*. New York: Cambridge University Press.

IPCC. (2007b). *Impacts, Adaptation and Vulnerability. Contribution of Working Group II to the Fourth Assessment Report of the Intergovernmental Panel on Climate Change*. Cambridge, UK: Cambridge University Press.

IPCC. (2013). *The Physical Science Basis. Working Group I Contribution to the Intergovernmental Panel on Climate Change Fifth Assessment Report*. Stockholm: IPCC.

IRENA. (2014). *REmap 2030: A renewable energy roadmap*. Retrieved January 25, 2018, from http://www.irena.org/-/media/Files/IRENA/Agency/Publication/2014/IRENA_REmap_Report_June_2014.pdf

IRENA. (2016). *Unlocking renewable energy investment: The role of risk mitigation and structured finance*. Retrieved January 25, 2018, from https://www.res4med.org/wp-content/uploads/2017/11/IRENA_Risk_Mitigation_and_Structured_Finance_2016.pdf

ISO. (2017). *ISO 14000: Environmental Management*. Retrieved May 3, 2017, from https://www.iso.org/iso-14001-environmental-management.html

Iyer, A., & Bergen, M. (1997). Quick response in manufacturer–retailer channels. *Management Science*, *43*(4), 559–570. doi:10.1287/mnsc.43.4.559

Jaeger, E. (2014). Facebook Messenger: Eroding User Privacy in order to Collect, Analyze, and Sell Your Personal Information. *31 J. Marshall J. Computer & Info., L*, 393.

JD.com. (2017). *JD.com Announces Fourth Quarter and Full Year 2016 Results*. Retrieved March 2, 2017, from http://corporate.jd.com/

Jefferson, G. H., Huamao, B., Xiaojing, G., & Xiaoyun, Y. (2006). R&D Performance in Chinese industry. *Economics of Innovation and New Technology, 15*(4-5), 345–366. doi:10.1080/10438590500512851

Jewson, S. (2004). Introduction to weather derivative pricing. *Journal of Alternative Investments, 7*, 57–64. doi:10.3905/jai.2004.439646

Jiang & Wu. (2016). Intelligent investment adviser situation and supervision suggestions on the development. *Securities Market Herald, 12*, 4-10.

Jie, H. (2018). The application and legal regulation of blockchain technology and intelligent contracts in the confirmation and transaction of intellectual property rights. *Intellectual Property, 2*, 14–15.

Jing, B., & Seidmann, A. (2014). Finance sourcing in a supply chain. *Decision Support Systems, 58*(1), 15–20. doi:10.1016/j.dss.2013.01.013

Jones, P., Hillier, D., & Comfort, D. (2016). The sustainable development goals and business. International Journal of Sales. *Retailing and Marketing, 5*(2), 38–48.

Joseph, C. (n.d.). *What Are the Benefits of Going Green for a Business?* Available online: http://www.smallbusiness.chron.com/

Joyner, B. E., & Payne, D. (2002). Evolution and implementation: A study of values, business ethics and corporate social responsibility. *Journal of Business Ethics, 41*(4), 297–311. doi:10.1023/A:1021237420663

Jun, X. (2017). The Legal Position of "Privacy" and "Personal Information" in the Network Environment. *Journalism Lover, 02*, 50–53.

Kalamova, M., Kaminker, C., & Johnstone, N. (2011). *Sources of finance, investment policies and plant entry in the renewable energy sector.* OECD Environment Working Papers, No.37. OECD Publishing. doi:10.1787/5kg7068011hb-en

Kalra, R., & Bonner, R. (2012). *Addressing Climate Change with Low-Cost Green Housing*. Washington, DC: World Bank.

Kandır, S. Y., & Yakar, S. (2017). Yenilenebilir enerji yatırımları için yeni bir finansal araç: Yeşil tahviller. *Maliye Dergisi, 172*, 85–110.

Karagöl, E. T., & Kavaz, İ. (2017). *Dünyada ve Türkiye'de yenilenebilir enerji* [Renewable Energy in the World and Turkey]. SETA. Retrieved April 4, 2018, from https://setav.org/assets/uploads/2017/04/YenilenebilirEnerji.pdf

Karagöl, E. T., Kaya, S., & Koç, Y. E. (2016). *2016'da Enerji* [Energy in 2016]. SETA. Retrieved April 4, 2018, from https://www.setav.org/2016da-enerji/

Karakaya, E. (2008). Proje Temelli Esneklik Mekanizmaları: Temiz Kalkınma Mekanizması ve Ortak Yürütme. In Küresel Isınma ve Kyoto Protokolü. İstanbul: Bağlam Yayıncılık.

Karakaya, E., & Özçağ, M. (2003). Türkiye Açısından Kyoto Protokolü'nün Değerlendirilmesi ve Ayrıştırma (Decomposition) Yöntemi ile CO2 Emisyonu Belirleyicilerinin Analizi, 7. ODTÜ Ekonomi Konferansı.

Kargı V., & Cihan Y. (2010). Çevresel Dışsallıklarda Kamu Ekonomisi Çözümleri. *Maliye Dergisi*, *159*, 183-202.

Kates, R. W., Parris, T. M., & Leiserowitz, A. A. (2005). What is Sustainable Development? Goals, Indicators, Values, and Practice. *Environment (Washington DC)*, *47*(3), 8–21.

Kats, G., Alevantis, L., Berman, A., Mills, E., & Perlman, J. (2003). *The costs and financial benefits of green buildings*. A report to California's sustainable building taskforce. Retrieved from http://www.usgbc.org/Docs/News/News477.pdf

Kats, G. (2003). *Green Building Costs and Financial Benefits*. Massachusetts Technology Collaborative.

Kats, G. (2010). *Greening Our Built World: Costs, Benefits, and Strategies*. Washington, DC: Island Press.

Kayapınar, E. Y. (2006). *Ulusal Çevre Stratejisi Eylem Planı*. Çevre ve Orman Bakanlığı ÇED ve Planlama Genel Müdürlüğü, Sunum.

Kaygusuz, K. (2007). Energy for sustainable development: Key issues and challenges. *Energy Sources. Part B, Economics, Planning, and Policy*, *2*(1), 73–83. doi:10.1080/15567240500402560

Kazıcı, S. (1992). *Vergilendirme ve Çevre. Vergi Dünyası*. Aralık.

Kennickell. (1996). *Saving and Financial Planning: Some findings from a Focus Group*. Author.

Kibert, C. J. (2008). Sustainable Construction: Green Building Design and Delivery (3rd ed.). Wiley.

Kılıç, R., & Aslan, V. (2017). Yenilenebilen ve yenilenemeyen enerjinin iktisadi büyüme üzerindeki etkisi: 28 OECD ülkesi üzerine ampirik bir çalışma. *Eskişehir Osmangazi Üniversitesi İİBF Dergisi*, *12*(1), 1–12.

Kim & Just. (2018). Potential Antitrust Risks in the Development and Use of Blockchain. *31 J. Tax'n F. Inst. 5*.

Kim, M. C., Jeong, Y. K., & Song, M. (2014). Investigating the integrated landscape of the intellectual topology of bibliometrics. *Scientometrics*, *101*(1), 309–335. doi:10.100711192-014-1417-1

Kırıcı, M. (2010). *Avrupa Biriliği'nde ve Türkiye'de Çevre ve Ulaştırma Sektör Politikalarının Bütünleştirilmesi ve Uygulamaların Karşılaştırılmalı Olarak İncelenmesi, 5.* Ulusal Çevre Mühendisliği Kongresi.

Klapper, L. (2005). *The role of factoring for financing small and medium enterprises.* The World Bank. doi:10.1596/1813-9450-3593

Klapper, L. F. (2006). The role of factoring for financing small and medium enterprises. *Journal of Banking & Finance, 30*(11), 3111–3130. doi:10.1016/j.jbankfin.2006.05.001

Klassen, R. D., & Vereecke, A. (2012). Social issues in supply chains: Capabilities link responsibility, risk (opportunity), and performance. *International Journal of Production Economics, 140*(1), 103–115. doi:10.1016/j.ijpe.2012.01.021

Kolk, A. (2003). Trends in sustainability reporting by the Fortune Global 250. *Business Strategy and the Environment, 12*(5), 279–291. doi:10.1002/bse.370

Kordana, K. A., & Posner, E. A. (1999). A positive theory of Chapter 11. NYU Law Review, 74(1), 161-178.

Kouvelis, P., & Zhao, W. (2010). The newsvendor problem and price-only contract when bankruptcy costs exist. *Production and Operations Management, 20*(6), 921–946. doi:10.1111/j.1937-5956.2010.01211.x

Kouvelis, P., & Zhao, W. (2012). Financing the newsvendor: Supplier vs. bank, and the structure of optimal trade credit contracts. *Operations Research, 60*(3), 566–580. doi:10.1287/opre.1120.1040

Kouvelis, P., & Zhao, W. (2016). Supply chain contract design under financial constraints and bankruptcy costs. *Management Science, 62*(8), 2341–2357. doi:10.1287/mnsc.2015.2248

Krause, D. R., Handfield, R. B., & Tyler, B. B. (2007). The relationships between supplier development, commitment, social capital accumulation and performance improvement. *Journal of Operations Management, 25*(2), 528–545. doi:10.1016/j.jom.2006.05.007

Kreiser, L. A., Sterling, A. Y., Herrera, P., Milne, J. E., & Ashiabor, H. (Eds.). (2012). *Green Taxation and Environmental Sustainability* (Vol. 12). Edward Elgar Publishing. doi:10.4337/9781781952184

Kumar, A., Kumar, K., Kaushik, N., Sharma, S., & Mishra, S. (2010). Renewable energy in India: Current status and future potentials. *Renewable & Sustainable Energy Reviews, 14*(8), 2434–2442. doi:10.1016/j.rser.2010.04.003

Labuschagne, C., & Brent, A. C. (2008). An industry perspective of the completeness and relevance of a social assessment framework for project and technology management in the manufacturing sector. *Journal of Cleaner Production, 16*(3), 253–262. doi:10.1016/j.jclepro.2006.07.028

Labuschagne, C., Brent, A. C., & Van Erck, R. P. (2005). Assessing the sustainability performances of industries. *Journal of Cleaner Production, 13*(4), 373–385. doi:10.1016/j.jclepro.2003.10.007

Lai, G., Debo, L. G., & Sycara, K. (2009). Sharing inventory risk in supply chain: The implication of financial constraint. *Omega*, *37*(4), 811–825. doi:10.1016/j.omega.2008.06.003

Lai, Y., Lin, F., & Lin, Y. (2015). Factors affecting firm's R&D investment decisions. *Journal of Business Research*, *68*(4), 840–844. doi:10.1016/j.jbusres.2014.11.038

Lamoureux, J. F., & Evans, T. A. (2011). *Supply chain finance: a new means to support the competitiveness and resilience of global value chains*. Working Paper. No. 2179944. Social Science Research Network.

Lam, P., & Law, A. (2018). Financing for renewable energy projects: A decision guide by developmental stages with case studies. *Renewable & Sustainable Energy Reviews*, *90*, 937–944. doi:10.1016/j.rser.2018.03.083

Lan & Chen. (2017). Analysis on the Legal Supervision of Internet Finance under the New Normal——Based on the Perspective of Network Lending. *Chinese Prices, 2*, 49-51.

Lariviere, M. A., & Porteus, E. L. (2001). Selling to the newsvendor: An analysis of price-only contracts. *Manufacturing & Service Operations Management: M & SOM*, *3*(4), 293–305. doi:10.1287/msom.3.4.293.9971

Lau, K.T., Tan, K.T., Lee, A.R., & Mohamed. (2009). A comparative study on the energy policies in Japan and Malaysia in fulfilling their nations' obligations towards the Kyoto Protocol. *Energy Policy*, *37*, 4771–4778. . doi:10.1016/j.enpol.2009.06.034

Lawson, B., Tyler, B. B., & Cousins, P. D. (2008). Antecedents and consequences of social capital on buyer performance improvement. *Journal of Operations Management*, *26*(3), 446–460. doi:10.1016/j.jom.2007.10.001

Leal Filho, W. (2000). Dealing with Misconceptions on the Concept of Sustainability. *International Journal of Sustainability in Higher Education*, *1*(1), 9–19. doi:10.1108/1467630010307066

Lecomte, E. L., Pang, A. W., & Russell, J. W. (1998). *Ice storm'98*. Toronto: Institute for Catastrophic Loss Reduction.

Lee, Y. W., & Stowe, J. D. (1993). Product risk, asymmetric information, and trade credit. *Journal of Financial and Quantitative Analysis*, *28*(2), 285–300. doi:10.2307/2331291

Lei, Q. (2017). The Difficulties and Countermeasures of Internet Financial Law Supervision. *Business and Economic Review*, *01*, 107–109.

Li, H. H. (2017). Analysis of profitability and commonweal relationships of green finance. *Financial Forum*, (5), 3-11.

Li, L., Shubik, M., & Sobel, M. J. (2005). *Control of dividends, capital subscriptions, and physical inventories*. Yale School of Management.

Li, S., & Chen, X. (2018). The role of supply chain finance in third-party logistics industry: a case study from China. *International Journal of Logistics Research and Applications*, 1-18.

Li. (2015). Research on the improvement of credit reporting system under internet financial background. *China North Finance*, *2015*(6), 48-53.

Li, H., Mai, L., Zhang, W., & Tian, X. (2018). Optimizing the Credit Term Decisions in Supply Chain Finance. *Journal of Purchasing and Supply Management*. doi:10.1016/j.pursup.2018.07.006

Lin, B., & Moubarak, M. (2014). Renewable energy consumption – economic growth nexus for China. *Renewable & Sustainable Energy Reviews*, *40*, 111–117. doi:10.1016/j.rser.2014.07.128

Lindlein, P., & Mostert, W. (2005). *Financing renewable energy: Instruments, strategies, practice approaches*. KfW Discussion Paper. Retrieved January 14, 2018, from http://docplayer.net/76204320-Financing-renewable-energy.html

Lin, W. (2015). Research on the application of collection scoring technology in small and micro enterprises of commercial banks in China. *Hainan Finance*, *6*, 33–35.

Liu, Xin, & Guo. (2013). Internet financial development and its impact on traditional financial model. *Economics Trends*, *8*, 73-83.

Liu. (2014). Xia Ling. Enlightenment of American internet financial development path to China. *Southwest Finance*, *6*, 19-21.

Liu, J. Y., Low, S. P., & He, X. (2012). Green practices in the Chinese building industry: Drivers and impediments. *Journal of Technology Management in China*, *7*(1), 50–63. doi:10.1108/17468771211207349

Liu, Q., Yu, G., & Liu, J. J. (2009). Solar Radiation as Large-Scale Resource for Energy-Short World. *Energy & Environment*, *20*(3), 319–329. doi:10.1260/095830509788066466

Liu, W. H., Bai, E., Liu, L. W., & Wei, W. Y. (2017). A Framework of Sustainable Service Supply Chain Management: A Literature Review and Research Agenda. *Sustainability*, *9*(3), 421. doi:10.3390u9030421

Liu, X., & Wei, D. (2014). Application and enlightenment of the big data credit investigation: A case study of American internet finance company - ZestFinance. *Tsinghua Financial Review*, *10*, 93–98.

Liu, X., Zhou, L., & Wu, Y. C. (2015). Supply chain finance in china: Business innovation and theory development. *Sustainability*, *7*(11), 14689–14709. doi:10.3390u71114689

Liu, Z., Yin, Y., Liu, W., & Michael, D. (2015). Visualizing the intellectual structure and evolution of innovation systems research: A bibliometric analysis. *Scientometrics*, *103*(1), 135–158. doi:10.100711192-014-1517-y

Li, Z. (2016). *American Internet Finance Research*. Jilin University.

Li, Z. (2016). Regulation thinking of big data credit investigation: Inspiration from the *Fair Credit Reporting Act*. *Credit Investigation*, *11*, 32–37.

Lodhia, S., & Martin, N. (2014). Corporate sustainability indicators: An Australian mining case study. *Journal of Cleaner Production*, *84*, 107–115. doi:10.1016/j.jclepro.2014.05.050

Love, P. E. D., Niedzweicki, M., Bullen, P. A., & Edwards, D. J. (2012). Achieving the green building council of Australia's world leadership rating in an office building in Perth. *Journal of Construction Engineering and Management*, *138*(5), 652–660. doi:10.1061/(ASCE)CO.1943-7862.0000461

Lu. (2014). Internet financial supervision in the United States and Its Enlightenment to China. *Finance Research in Jilin*, *10*, 27-29.

Lu. (2017). Intelligent adviser: "look at the future". *Expo Financial Chaos (Wealth)*, *2*, 43-46.

Lu. (2017). On the Improvement of China's Internet Financial Market Access Legal System. *Discussion on Modern Economy*, *2*, 88-92.

Lunn, J., Downing, E. & Booth, L. (2015). *The Sustainable Development Goals and the post-2015 Development Agenda*. House of Commons Library Briefing Paper 7291. London: House of Commons.

Luo, W., & Shang, K. (2013). *Managing inventory for entrepreneurial firms with trade credit and payment defaults.* Working paper, IESE Business School.

Luo, Ying, & Yong. (2013). *Internet finance.* China Finance and Economics Press.

Lu, S. F., & Yao, Y. (2009). The Effectiveness of Law, Financial Development, and Economic Growth in an Economy of Financial Repression: Evidence from China. *World Development*, *37*(4), 763–777. doi:10.1016/j.worlddev.2008.07.018

Ma, C. (2015). Construction of green financial system in China. *Financial Forum*, (5), 18-27.

Ma, C. (2016). Development and prospect of green finance in China. *Comparative Economic and Social Systems*, (6), 26-32.

Määttä, K. (2006). *Environmental taxes: an introductory analysis*. Edward Elgar Publishing.

Maggioni, D., & Santangelo, G. D. (2017). Local Environmental Non-Profit Organizations and the Green Investment Strategies of Family Firms. *Ecological Economics*, *138*, 126–138. doi:10.1016/j.ecolecon.2017.03.026

Magnuson, W. J. (2017). *Regulating fintech*. Social Science Electronic Publishing.

Malthus, T. (1798). *An essay on the principle of population as it affects the future improvement of society*. London: J. Johnson.

Margolis, J. D., & Walsh, J. P. (2003). Misery loves companies: Rethinking social initiatives by business. *Administrative Science Quarterly*, *48*(2), 268–305. doi:10.2307/3556659

Markman, G. D., & Krause, D. (2016). Theory Building Surrounding Sustainable Supply Chain Management: Assessing What We Know, Exploring Where to Go. *The Journal of Supply Chain Management*, *52*(2), 3–10. doi:10.1111/jscm.12105

Martinsson, G. (2010). Equity financing and innovation: Is Europe different from the United States? *Journal of Banking & Finance*, *34*(6), 1215–1224. doi:10.1016/j.jbankfin.2009.11.015

Matsumoto, A., Merlone, U., & Szidarovszky, F. (2008). Cartelizing groups in dynamic linear oligopoly with antitrust threshold. *International Game Theory Review*, *10*(04), 399–419. doi:10.1142/S0219198908002011

Matsumoto, A., Merlone, U., & Szidarovszky, F. (2012). Some notes on applying the Herfindahl–Hirschman Index. *Applied Economics Letters*, *19*(2), 181–184. doi:10.1080/13504851.2011.570705

Matthews, L., Power, D., Touboulic, A., & Marques, L. (2016). Building bridges: Toward alternative theory of sustainable supply chain management. *The Journal of Supply Chain Management*, *52*(1), 82–94. doi:10.1111/jscm.12097

McGraw Hill Construction. (2013). *World Green Building Trends*. Bedford, MA: Author.

Meadows, D. H., Meadows, D. L., Randers, J., & Behrens, W. (1972). *The Limits to Growth*. New York: Universe Books.

Medema, S. G. (1994). *Ronald H. Coase*. London: The Macmillan Press.

Meho, L. I., & Yang, K. (2007). Impact of data sources on citation counts and rankings of LIS faculty: Web of science versus Scopus and Google scholar. *Journal of the American Society for Information Science and Technology*, *58*(13), 2105–2125. doi:10.1002/asi.20677

MENR. (2014). *National renewable energy action plan for Turkey*. Retrieved April 24, 2018, from http://www.ebrd.com/documents/comms-and-bis/turkey-national-renewable-energy-action-plan.pdf

MENR. (2018). *National energy efficiency action plan (NEEAP) 2017-2013*. Retrieved May 24, 2018, from http://www.yegm.gov.tr/document/20180102M1_2018_eng.pdf

MIDSEFF. (2018). Retrieved from http://www.midseff.com/

Ministry of Energy and Natural Resources. (n.d.). Retrieved from http://www.enerji.gov.tr/en-US/Pages/International-Negotiations

Ministry of Finance. (n.d.). *General Directorate of Accounting*. Retrieved from www.muhasebat.gov.tr

Ministry of Foreign Affairs (MFA). (n.d.). Retrieved from http://www.mfa.gov.tr/united-nations-framework-convention-on-climate-change-_unfccc_-and-the-kyoto-protocol.en.mfa

Min, K., Stephen, K., & Chen, H. (2008). Developing social identity and social capital for supply chain management. *Journal of Business Logistics*, *29*(1), 283–304. doi:10.1002/j.2158-1592.2008.tb00079.x

Minsky, H. P. (2009). Banking and a fragile financial environment. *Journal of Portfolio Management*, *3*(4), 16–22. doi:10.3905/jpm.1977.408609

Mo. (2014). The financial industry in the internet era. *Development Pattern of Financial Science, 4*, 1-10.

Mohrman, S. A., & Worley, C. G. (2010). The organizational sustainability journey: Introduction to the special issue. *Organizational Dynamics*, *39*(4), 289–294. doi:10.1016/j.orgdyn.2010.07.008

Montabon, F., Pagell, M., & Wu, Z. (2016). Making sustainability sustainable. *The Journal of Supply Chain Management*, *52*(2), 11–27. doi:10.1111/jscm.12103

More, D., & Basu, P. (2013). Challenges of supply chain finance: A detailed study and a hierarchical model based on the experiences of an Indian firm. *Business Process Management Journal*, *19*(4), 624–647. doi:10.1108/BPMJ-09-2012-0093

Moretto, A., Grassi, L., Caniato, F., Giorgino, M., & Ronchi, S. (2018). Supply chain finance: From traditional to supply chain credit rating. *Journal of Purchasing and Supply Management*. doi:10.1016/j.pursup.2018.06.004

Moses, L. B. (2013). How to think about law, regulation and technology: Problems with 'technology' as a regulatory target. *Law Innovation & Technology*, *5*(1), 1–20. doi:10.5235/17579961.5.1.1

Müller, S., Brown, A., & Ölz, S. (2011). *Renewable energy policy considerations for deploying renewables*. Information Paper. IEA. Retrieved April 4, 2018, from https://www.iea.org/publications/freepublications/publication/Renew_Policies.pdf

Müller, A., & Grandi, M. (2000). Weather Derivatives: A Risk Management Tool for Weather Sensitive Industries. *The Geneva Papers on Risk and Insurance. Issues and Practice*, *25*(2), 273–287.

Nahapiet, J., & Ghoshal, S. (1998). Social capital, intellectual capital, and the organizational advantage. *Academy of Management Review*, *23*(2), 242–266. doi:10.5465/amr.1998.533225

Natural Capital Coalition. (2016). *Natural Capital Protocol – Food and Beverage Sector Guide*. Retrieved April 14, 2017, from www.naturalcapitalcoalition.org/protocol

Navonil, M., Nik, B., Simon, J. E. T., & Stelios, S. (2013). Exploring the e-science knowledgebase through co-citation analysis. *Procedia Computer Science*, *19*, 586–593. doi:10.1016/j.procs.2013.06.078

Nelson, G. (2015). *Practical Implications of Sharing Data: A Primer on Data Privacy, Anonymization, and De-Identification*. Retrieved September 25, 2018, from http://support.sas.com/resources/papers/proceedings15/1884-2015.pdf

Nelson, G. C., Rosegrant, M. W., Koo, J., Robertson, R., Sulser, T., Zhu, T., ... Lee, D. (2009). *Impact on Agriculture and Costs of Adaptation. Food policy report*. Washington, DC: IFPRI. doi:10.2499/0896295354

New York Times. (2018). *As China Curbs Borrowing, Growth Shows Signs of Faltering*. Retrieved June 14, 2018, from https://www.nytimes.com/

Newman, M. E. J. (2001). The Structure of Scientific Collaboration Networks. *Proceedings of the National Academy of Sciences of the United States of America*, *98*(2), 404–409. doi:10.1073/pnas.98.2.404 PMID:11149952

Nian, W., Guan, D., & Wang, H. (2016). The challenge of internet finance to modern financial intermediary theory -- Concurrently on the impact on financial democratization. *International Economic Review*, *1*, 71–77.

Nishizawa, T. (2011). Changes in Development Finance in Asia: Trends, Challenges, and Policy Implications. *Asian Economic Policy Review*, *6*(2), 225–244. doi:10.1111/j.1748-3131.2011.01199.x

Nobre, G. C., & Tavares, E. (2017). Scientific literature analysis on big data and internet of things applications on circular economy: A bibliometric study. *Scientometrics*, *111*(1), 463–492. doi:10.100711192-017-2281-6

OECD. (2001). *The Well-Being of Nations: The Role of Human and Social Capital*. Paris: OECD.

OECD. (2003). *Environmentally Sustainable Buildings, Challenges and Policies*. Paris: Organisation for Economic Co-operation and Development.

OECD. (2005). *Catastrophic Risks and Insurance*. Paris: OECD Publishing.

OECD. (2011). *Environmentally Related Taxes in OECD Countries: Issues and Strategies*. OECD Publication Service.

OECD. (2016). *Financing SMEs and Entrepreneurs 2016 (Report)*. Retrieved 2016, from https://www.oecd-ilibrary.org/

OECD. (2017). *Green Growth Indicators*. Retrieved from http://www.oecd.org/greengrowth/green-growth indicators/

OECD/IEA & AFD. (2008). *Promoting Energy Efficiency Investments: Case studies in the residential sector*. Paris: International Energy Agency.

Ofori, G., & Kien, H. L. (2004). Translating Singapore architects' environmental awareness into decision making. *Building Research and Information*, *32*(1), 27–37. doi:10.1080/0961321021013292 8

Olsen, S., & Galimidi, B. (2008). *Catalog of Approaches to Impact Measurement*. Social Venture Technology Group with Support of the Rockefeller Foundation.

Org, Z. (2004). Finance and Growth: Theory and Evidence. *Social Science Electronic Publishing*, *1*(5), 37–40.

Özdemir, B. (2009). Article. *Küresel Kirlenme Sürdürülebilir Ekonomik Büyüme ve Çevre Vergileri Maliye Dergisi*, *157*, 1–36.

Özdemir, E. (2008). Küresel Isınmanın Etkilerine Karşı Bir Önlem: Hava Türevleri ve Pazarlama Stratejilerinde Yardımcı Olarak Kullanımı. *Gazi Üniversitesi İktisadi ve İdari Bilimler Fakültesi Dergisi*, *10*(1), 141–162.

Öz, E., & Kutbay, H. (2016). Ekolojik Vergileme: Seçilmiş Bazı Dünya Ülkeleri ile Türkiye Verilerinin Karşılaştırılması. *Eskişehir Osmangazi Üniversitesi İİBF Dergisi*, *11*(1), 247–272.

Özer, O., Uncu, O., & Wei, W. (2007). Selling to the "newsvendor" with a forecast update: Analysis of a dual purchase contract. *European Journal of Operational Research*, *182*(3), 1150–1176. doi:10.1016/j.ejor.2006.09.057

Öztürk, A., Demirci, U., & Türker, M. F. (2012). İklim Değişikliği ile Mücadelede Karbon Piyasaları ve Türkiye için Bir Değerlendirme. *Ulusal Akdeniz Orman ve Çevre Sempozyumu*, 306-312.

Pallemaets, M. (1997). Stocholm'den Rio'ya Uluslararası Çevre Hukuku: Geleceğe Doğru Geri Adım mı? (trans.) Bülent Duru. *Ankara Üniversitesi SBF Dergisi*, *52*(1), 613–632.

Pedercini, M., Blanco, S. M., & Kopainsky, B. (2011). Application of the malaria management model to the analysis of costs and benefits of DDT versus non-DDT malaria control. *PLoS One*, *6*(11), e27771. doi:10.1371/journal.pone.0027771 PMID:22140467

People's Bank of China Hangzhou Center Branch Office Research Group. (2011). Green finance: International experience, enlightenment and countermeasures. *Monetary Review*, 20-25.

People's Bank of China. (2017). *Announcement of Information Related to Baihang Credit Co. Ltd. (Under Preparation)*. Retrieved August 13, 2018, from http://www.pbc.gov.cn/rmyh/105208/3456248/index.html

People's Bank of China. (2017). *Public Notice on the Relevant Situations of Baixing Credit Information Co., Ltd.* Retrieved September 25, 2018, from http://www.pbc.gov.cn/rmyh/105208/3456248/index.html

Persson, J., & Grönkvist, S. (2015). Drivers for and barriers to low-energy buildings in Sweden. *Journal of Cleaner Production*, *109*, 296–304. doi:10.1016/j.jclepro.2014.09.094

Persson, O. (1994). The intellectual base and research fronts of JASIS 1986–1990. *Journal of the American Society for Information Science*, *45*(1), 31–38. doi:10.1002/(SICI)1097-4571(199401)45:1<31::AID-ASI4>3.0.CO;2-G

Petersen, M. A., & Rajan, R. G. (1997). Trade credit: Theories and evidence. *Review of Financial Studies*, *10*(3), 661–691. doi:10.1093/rfs/10.3.661

Pethokoukis, J. (2015). The time when Elizabeth Warren unexpectedly channelled Milton Friedman. *Business Insider*. Retrieved July 1, 2017, from, http://www.businessinsider.com/when-elizabeth-warren-channeled-milton-friedman-2015-6?IR=T

Peura, H., Yang, S. A., & Lai, G. (2017). Trade credit in competition: A horizontal benefit. *Manufacturing & Service Operations Management: M & SOM*, *19*(2), 263–289. doi:10.1287/msom.2016.0608

Pfohl, H. C., & Gomm, M. (2009). Supply chain finance: optimizing financial flows in supply chains. *Logistics Research*, *1*(3-4), 149-161.

Philibert, C. (2011). *Interactions of policies for renewable energy and climate.* Working Paper. IEA. Retrieved March 10, 2018, from https://www.oecd-ilibrary.org/docserver/5kggc12rmkzq-en.pdf?expires=1527756748&id=id&accname=guest&checksum=E7B1DF8C7058B42939CD1A5A11B1ACC9

Pigou, A. (2017). *The Economics of Welfare*. Routledge. doi:10.4324/9781351304368

Ping & Zou. (2012). Research of internet financial model. *Financial Research*, 12.

Ping, Zou, & Liu. (2014). The necessity and core principles of internet financial supervision. *International Finance Research*, *8*, 3-9.

Pingali, P. L. (2012). Green Revolution: Impacts, limits, and the path ahead. *Proceedings of the National Academy of Sciences of the United States of America*, *109*(31), 12302–12308. doi:10.1073/pnas.0912953109 PMID:22826253

Plott, C. R. (1966). Externalities and Corrective Taxes. *Economica*, *33*(129), 84–87. doi:10.2307/2552274

Porter, M. (2017). *FAQ*. Retrieved July 1, 2018, from http://www.socialprogressimperative.org/faqs/

Porter, M., & Kramer, M. R. (2011). Creating Shared Value: How to Reinvent Capitalism – and Unleash a Wave of Innovation and Growth. *Harvard Business Review*, *89*(1/2), 62–77.

Pres, J. (2009). Measuring noncatastrophic weather risks for businesses. *Geneva Papers Risk Insur.*, *34*(3), 425–439. doi:10.1057/gpp.2009.16

PricewaterhouseCoopers (2015). *Make it Your Business: Engaging with the sustainable development goals*. Retrieved May 10, 2017, from https://www.pwc.com/gx/en/sustainability/SDG/SDG%20Research_FINAL.pdf

Pullman, M. E., Maloni, M. J., & Cater, C. R. (2009). Food for Thought: Social Versus Environmental Sustainability Practices and Performance Outcomes. *The Journal of Supply Chain Management*, *45*(4), 38–54. doi:10.1111/j.1745-493X.2009.03175.x

PYMNTS.com. (2015). *Supply Chain Finance Market Growing Worldwide*. Retrieved April 8, 2015, from https://www.pymnts.com/news/2015/supply-chain-finance-market-growing-worldwide/

Qiang, W., Qing, S., & Ba, J. (2017). Discussion on the application of blockchain in credit investigation industry. *Telecommunications Network Technology*, *5*, 37–41.

Qin, J., Wang, T., & Huang, B. (2016). The Study of Chinese Listed Bank's Efficiency Growth Mode in Internet Finance Era—Based on Full-Combination DEA-PCA Model. *American Journal of Industrial and Business Management*, *06*(11), 11. doi:10.4236/ajibm.2016.611098

Rahdari, A. H., & Rostamy, A. A. A. (2015). Designing a general set of sustainability indicators at the corporate Level. *Journal of Cleaner Production*, *108*, 757–771. doi:10.1016/j.jclepro.2015.05.108

Rajan, R. G., & Zingales, L. (2003). The great reversals: The politics of financial development in the twentieth century. *Journal of Financial Economics*, *69*(1), 5–50. doi:10.1016/S0304-405X(03)00125-9

Raworth, K. (2012). *A safe and just space for humanity: can we live within the doughnut*. Oxford, UK: Oxfam.

Redclift, M. (2005). Sustainable Development (1987–2005): An oxymoron comes of age. *Sustainable Development*, *13*(4), 212–227. doi:10.1002d.281

Rehm, M. & Ade, R. (2013). Construction costs comparison between "green" and conventional office buildings. *Build. Res. Inf.*, *41*, 198–208. http://dx..2013.769145 doi:10.1080/09613218

REN-21. (2016). *Renewables – Global Status Report: 2016*. Retrieved June 4, 2017, from http://www.ren21.net/wp-content/uploads/2016/05/GSR_2016_Full_Report_lowres.pdf

REN-21. (2017). *Renewables – Global Status Report: 2017*. Retrieved April 28, 2018, from http://www.ren21.net/wp-content/uploads/2017/06/17-8399_GSR_2017_Full_Report_0621_Opt.pdf

REN-21. (2018). *Renewables – Global Status Report: 2018*. Retrieved September 28, 2018, from http://www.ren21.net/wp-content/uploads/2018/06/17-8652_GSR2018_FullReport_web_final_.pdf

Reva, H. Z. (2006). Borsa Opsiyon Sözleşmeleri. *Prof. Dr. Özer Seliçi'ye Armağan*, 529-558.

Richard, L., & John, E. (2009). *Urban Construction Project Management. McGraw-Hill.*

Riesa, R., Bileca, M.M.,Gokhanb, N.M., & Needy, K.L. (2006). The Economic Benefits of Green Buildings: A Comprehensive Case Study. *The Engineering Economist: A Journal Devoted to the Problems of Capital Investment*, *51*(3), 259-295.

Rockstrom, Steffen, Noone, Persson, Chapin, III, Lambin, … Foley. (2009). Planetary boundaries: exploring the safe operating space for humanity. *Ecology and Society*, *14*(2), 32.

Rockstrom, J., Steffen, W., Noone, K., Persson, A., Chapin, F. S., Lambin, E. F., ... Foley, J. A. (2009). A safe operating space for humanity. *Nature*, *461*(7263), 472–475. doi:10.1038/461472a PMID:19779433

Rong, W. (2016). Legal regulation of data anonymization. *Communications Technology*, *4*, 38–44.

Rosca, O. (2015a). *EBRD co-finances Turkey's largest geothermal power plant*. Retrieved July 18, 2018, from https://www.ebrd.com/news/2015/ebrd-cofinances-turkeys-largest-geothermal-power-plant-.html

Rosca, O. (2015b). *EBRD supports Turkey's shift to renewable energy*. Retrieved July 18, 2018, from https://www.ebrd.com/news/2015/ebrd-supports-turkeys-shift-to-renewable-energy.html

Sadorsky, P. (2009). Renewable energy consumption and income in emerging economies. *Energy Policy*, *37*(10), 4021–4028. doi:10.1016/j.enpol.2009.05.003

Sahamir, S. R., & Zakaria, R. (2013). Green assessment criteria for public hospital building development in Malaysia. *Procedia Environmental Sciences*, *20*, 106–115. doi:10.1016/j.proenv.2014.03.015

Sajjad, A., Eweje, G., & Tappin, D. (2015). Sustainable Supply Chain Management: Motivators and Barriers. *Business Strategy and the Environment*, *24*(7), 643–655. doi:10.1002/bse.1898

Sakuma, K., & Louche, C. (2008). Socially responsible investment in Japan: Its mechanism and drivers. *Journal of Business Ethics*, *82*(2), 425–448. doi:10.100710551-008-9895-9

Salomon, R. M., & Shaver, J. M. (2005). Learning by Exporting: New Insights from Examining Firm Innovation. *Journal of Economics & Management Strategy*, *14*(2), 431–460. doi:10.1111/j.1530-9134.2005.00047.x

Samari, M., Ghodrati, N., Esmaeilifar, R., Olfat, P., & Shafiei, M. W. M. (2013). The investigation of the barriers in developing green building in Malaysia. *Modern Applied Science*, *7*(2), 1–10. doi:10.5539/mas.v7n2p1

Samur, H. (2007). Küresel İklim Değişikliğinin Etkileri ve Uluslararası Alandaki Mücadele Stratejileri. *Uluslararası Küresel İklim Değişikliği ve Çevresel Etkileri Konferansı*, 18-20.

Sandhu-Rojon, R. (2017). *Selecting indicators for impact evaluation*. New York: UNDP.

Saraç, M. (2010). Çevre Sorunları ve İskonto Edilmiş Nakit Analizine Dayalı Değerleme Yaklaşımı. *Muhasebe ve Finansman Dergisi*, *45*, 169–179.

Şaylan, İ. B. (2010). *İklim Değişikliği ile Uluslararası Mücadelenin Ekonomik ve Mali Boyutu ve Avrupa Birliği Politikaları. Avrupa Birliği Uzmanlığı Yeterlilik Tezi, Uzmanlık Tezi*. T. C. Maliye Bakanlığı Avrupa Birliği ve Dış İlişkiler Dairesi Başkanlığı.

Scalet, S., & Kelly, T. F. (2010). CSR rating agencies: What is their global impact? *Journal of Business Ethics*, *94*(1), 69–88. doi:10.100710551-009-0250-6

Schlegelmilch, K. (1999). *Green Budget Reform in Europe: Countries at the Forefront: With 20 Figures and 142 Tables*. Springer Science & Business Media. doi:10.1007/978-3-642-58637-8

Scott, D., Mcboyle, G., Minogue, A., & Mills, B. (2006). Climate Change and the Sustainability of Ski-based Tourism in Eastern North America: A Reassessment. *Journal of Sustainable Tourism*, *14*(4), 376–398. doi:10.2167/jost550.0

Sebastian, M., & Carlos, L. (2012). *Green Taxes for a Greener Environment*. IDB. Retrieved from http://www.imf.org/external/np/seminars/eng/2012/rio/pdf/smcl.pdf

SEI. (2016). *The Next Wave of Financial Planning*. SEI.

Serageldin, I. (1996). Sustainability as Opportunity and the Problem of Social Capital. *The Brown Journal of World Affairs*, *3*(2), 187–203.

Serwin. (2009). Privacy 3.0 - The Principle of Proportionality. *42 U. Mich. J.L. Reform, 869*.

Setthasakko, W. (2007). Determinants of corporate sustainability: Thai frozen seafood processors. *British Food Journal*, *109*(2), 155–168. doi:10.1108/00070700710725518

Seuring, S., & Müller, M. (2008). From a literature review to a conceptual framework for sustainable supply chain management. *Journal of Cleaner Production*, *16*(15), 1699–1710. doi:10.1016/j.jclepro.2008.04.020

Shen, K. Y. (2017). Compromise between Short-and Long-Term Financial Sustainability: A Hybrid Model for Supporting R&D Decisions. *Sustainability*, *9*(3), 375. doi:10.3390u9030375

Shen, K. Y., Yan, M. R., & Tzeng, G. H. (2017). Exploring R&D Influences on Financial Performance for Business Sustainability Considering Dual Profitability Objectives. *Sustainability*, *9*(11), 1964. doi:10.3390u9111964

Sher, P. J., & Yang, P. Y. (2005). The effects of innovative capabilities and R&D clustering on firm performance: The evidence of Taiwan's semiconductor industry. *Technovation*, *25*(1), 33–43. doi:10.1016/S0166-4972(03)00068-3

Shi, M. (2017). Research on big data credit investigation and the protection of the rights and interests of the personal information subject. *Credit Investigation*, *5*, 38–43.

Shin, M., & Kim, S. (2011). The effects of cash holdings on R&D smoothing of innovative small and medium sized enterprises. *Asian Journal of Technology Innovation*, *19*(2), 169–183. doi:10.1080/19761597.2011.630501

Shi, Q., Zuo, J., & Zillante, G. (2012). Exploring the management of sustainable construction at the programme level e a Chinese case study'. *Construction Management and Economics*, *30*(6), 425–440. doi:10.1080/01446193.2012.683200

Shi, Z., & Huang, H. (2013). Identifying the critical factors for green construction e an empirical study in China. *Habitat International*, *40*(1), 1–8. doi:10.1016/j.habitatint.2013.01.003

Shrestha, P.P & Pushpala, N. (2012). *Green and non-green school buildings*: an empirical comparison of construction cost and schedule. *Constr. Res. Congr.,* 1820–1829. doi:10.1061/9780784412329.183

Shunko, M., Do, H. T., & Tsay, A. A. (2017). Supply chain strategies and international tax arbitrage. *Production and Operations Management*, *26*(2), 231–251. doi:10.1111/poms.12629

Silva, F., & Carreira, C. (2012). Do financial constraints threat the innovation process? Evidence from Portuguese firms. *Economics of Innovation and New Technology*, *21*(8), 701–736. doi:10.1080/10438599.2011.639979

Simsek, H. A., & Simsek, N. (2013). Recent incentives for renewable energy in Turkey. *Energy Policy*, *63*, 521–530. doi:10.1016/j.enpol.2013.08.036

Small, H. (1973). Co-citation in the scientific literature: A new measure of the relationship between two documents. *Journal of the American Society for Information Science*, *24*(4), 265–269. doi:10.1002/asi.4630240406

SME Finance Forum. (2017). *MSME finance gap (Report)*. Retrieved 2017, from https://www.smefinanceforum.org/

Sohn, L. B. (1973). Stockholm Declaration on the Human Environment. *The Harv. Int'l. LJ*, *14*, 423.

Song, H. (2015). *Supply chain finance*. China Renmin University Press. (in Chinese)

Song, H., Yu, K., & Lu, Q. (2018). Financial service providers and banks' role in helping SMEs to access finance. *International Journal of Physical Distribution & Logistics Management*, *48*(1), 69–92. doi:10.1108/IJPDLM-11-2016-0315

Song, Z., Huang, H., Ran, W., & Liu, S. (2016). A Study on the Pricing Model for 3PL of Inventory Financing. *Discrete Dynamics in Nature and Society*.

Soufani, K. (2002). On the determinants of factoring as a financing choice: Evidence from the UK. *Journal of Economics and Business*, *54*(2), 239–252. doi:10.1016/S0148-6195(01)00064-9

Spangenberg, J. H. (2016). The Corporate Human Development Index CHDI: A tool for corporate social sustainability management and reporting. *Journal of Cleaner Production*, *134*, 414–424. doi:10.1016/j.jclepro.2015.12.043

Spitzeck, H., & Hansen, E. G. (2010). Stakeholder governance: How stakeholders influence corporate decision making. *Corporate Governance: The International Journal of Business in Society*, *10*(4), 378-391.

StaropoliC.SteinerM. (2016). *Green Public Procurement*. Retrieved from https://www.webssa.net/files/slides_coursegpp-2017.pdf

State Council Development Research Center Green China Financial System Research Group. (2016). Logic and framework for development of green finance in China. *Financial Forum*, (2), 17-28.

State Council of the People's Republic of China. (2016). *Made in China 2025*. Retrieved August 29, 2016, from http://english.gov.cn/2016special/madeinchina2025/

State Council of the People's Republic of China. (2017). *19th National Congress of the Communist Party of China*. Retrieved October 28, 2017, from http://english.gov.cn/19thcpccongress/

Stefan, A., & Paul, L. (2008). Does It Pay to Be Green? A Systematic Overview. *The Academy of Management Perspectives*, *22*(4), 45–62. doi:10.5465/amp.2008.35590353

Stern, N. H. (2007). *The economics of climate change: the Stern Review*. Cambridge, UK: Cambridge University. doi:10.1017/CBO9780511817434

Stiglitz, J., Sen, A., & Fitoussi, J. P. (2009). *The measurement of economic performance and social progress revisited. Reflections and overview*. Paris: Commission on the Measurement of Economic Performance and Social Progress.

Sudmant, A., Colenbrander, S., Gouldson, A., & Chilundika, N. (2017). Private opportunities, public benefits? The scope for private finance to deliver low-carbon transport systems in Kigali, Rwanda. *Urban Climate*, *20*, 59–74. doi:10.1016/j.uclim.2017.02.011

Sun. (2015). The opportunities and challenges for commercial banks to develop internet financial management. *New Finance, 8*, 36-42.

Sun, G., & Meng, L. (2017). Research on the application of blockchain technology in the field of personal credit investigation - Based on the perspective of digital inclusive finance. *Corporate Finance Research, 1*(15), 121.

Sun, G., Shen, W., & Xing, X. (2013). De-anonymization technology and its application in the big data era. *Communications Technology*, *6*, 52–57.

Tahir, A. C., & Darton, R. C. (2010). The process analysis method of selecting indicators to quantify the sustainability performance of a business operation. *Journal of Cleaner Production, 18*(16-17), 1598–1607. doi:10.1016/j.jclepro.2010.07.012

Tang, C. S., Yang, S. A., & Wu, J. (2018). Sourcing from suppliers with financial constraints and performance risk. *Manufacturing & Service Operations Management: M & SOM*, *20*(1), 70–84. doi:10.1287/msom.2017.0638

Tanrisever, F., Cetinay, H., Reindorp, M., & Fransoo, J. (2012). Value of reverse factoring in multi-stage supply chains. *SSRN*, *2183991*, 28.

Taylor, N., Goodrich, C., Fitzgerald, G., & McClintock, W. (2003). Undertaking longitudinal research. In The international handbook of social impact assessment: Conceptual and methodological advances. Cheltenham: Edward Elgar Publishing.

Taylor, T. (2006). Sale timing in a supply chain: When to sell to the retailer? *Manufacturing & Service Operations Management: M & SOM*, *8*(1), 23–42. doi:10.1287/msom.1050.0089

Templar, S., Cosse, M., Camerinelli, E., & Findlay, C. (2012). *An investigation into current supply chain finance practices in business: a case study approach*. Unpublished paper.

TENVA. (2015). *Turkey's Biggest Geothermal Power Plant "Efeler GPP" Opened*. Retrieved June 11, from http://www.tenva.org/en/turkiyenin-en-buyuk-jeotermal-santrali-efeler-jes-acildi/

The Economist. (2015). *The 169 commandments*. Retrieved June 19, 2017, from http://www.economist.com/news/leaders/21647286-proposed-sustainable-development-goals-would-be-worse-useless-169-commandments

The Guardian. (2010). *Kraft rebuked for broken pledge on Cadbury factory*. Retrieved June 19, 2017, from https://www.theguardian.com/business/2010/may/26/kraft-censured-over-cadbury-takeover-pledge

The Sustainability Consortium. (2016). *Greening Global Supply Chains: From blind spots to hot spots to action*. Author.

The Zero One Research Institute. (2016). *Research Report China personal financial market*. Author.

Tian, X., & Li, Y. (2018). Key factors of People's willingness to pay for green building in a less develop region in China. A pilot research effort in Shaxi province. *International Review for Spatial Planning and Sustainable Development, 6*(3), 78-93.

Tilman, D., Balzer, C., Hill, J., & Befort, B. L. (2011). Global food demand and the sustainable intensification of agriculture. *Proceedings of the National Academy of Sciences of the United States of America, 108*(50), 20260–20264. doi:10.1073/pnas.1116437108 PMID:22106295

Timilsina, G. R., Hochman, G., & Fedets, I. (2016). Understanding energy efficiency barriers in Ukraine: Insights from a survey of commercial and industrial firms. *Energy, 106*, 203–211. doi:10.1016/j.energy.2016.03.009

Timme, S. G., & Williams-Timme, C. (2000). The financial-SCM Connection. *Supply Chain Management Review, 4*(2), 33–40.

Tiwari, S., Cárdenas-Barrón, L. E., Goh, M., & Shaikh, A. A. (2018). Joint pricing and inventory model for deteriorating items with expiration dates and partial backlogging under two-level partial trade credits in supply chain. *International Journal of Production Economics, 200*, 16–36. doi:10.1016/j.ijpe.2018.03.006

Tong, L. (2016). Design of visual Deep Web collection platform based on Hadoop, *Computer. Engineering and Science, 2*, 217–223.

Trainer, T. (2013). Can the world run on renewable energy? A revised negative case. Renewable Energy, 29, 88-104.

TSKB. (2016). *Project Finance, III.* GGDP Roundtable, Reykjavik. Retrieved July 18, 2018, from https://www.esmap.org/sites/esmap.org/files/DocumentLibrary/TSKB_Hepkaya.pdf

TSKB. (2017). *Entegre Rapor 2016.* Retrieved June 24, 2018, from http://www.tskb.com.tr/i/assets/document/pdf/TSKB_Entegre_Rapor_2016.pdf

TSKB. (2018). *Entegre Rapor 2017.* Retrieved June 24, 2018, from http://www.tskb.com.tr/i/assets/document/pdf/TSKB_2017_Entegre_Raporu.pdf

Tunahan, H. (2010). Küresel iklim değişikliğini azaltmanın bir yolu olarak karbon finansmanı. *Muhasebe ve Finansman Dergisi, 46*, 199–215.

Tunca, T. I., & Zhu, W. (2017). Buyer intermediation in supplier finance. *Management Science*, mnsc.2017.2863. doi:10.1287/mnsc.2017.2863

Türkeş, M. (2012). Türkiye'de Gözlenen ve Öngörülen İklim Değişikliği, Kuraklık ve Çölleşme. *Ankara Üniversitesi Çevrebilimleri Dergisi, 4*(2), 1–32.

Türkiye İş Bankası. (2018). Retrieved from https://www.isbank.com.tr/TR/ana-sayfa/Sayfalar/ana-sayfa.aspx

TURSEFF. (2018). Retrieved from http://www.turseff.org/sayfa/facility

Tu, Y., & Wang, X. (2017). Legislative perfection of the protection of the personal credit information in the context of big data. *China Internet*, *5*, 43–53.

Tzschentke, N., Kirk, D., & Lynch, P. (2004). Reasons for going green in serviced accommodation establishments. *International Journal of Contemporary Hospitality Management*, *16*(2), 116–124. doi:10.1108/09596110410520007

UN. (1992). *United Nations Framework Convention on Climate Change*. Retrieved from https://unfccc.int/sites/default/files/conveng.pdf

UN. (2002). National Implementation of Agenda 21: A Summary. *Johannesburg Summit 2012*. Retrieved from http://www.un.org/esa/agenda21/natlinfo/

UN. (2012). Rio Declaration on Environment and Development. *United Nations Conference on Environment and Development,* A/CONF.151/26. Retrieved from http://www.undocuments.net/rio-dec.htm

UNDP. (2013). *Human Development Report 2013*. New York: UN. Retrieved from http://www.unep.org/documents.multilingual/default.asp?documentid=97&articleid=1503

UNEP (United Nations Environment Programme). (2006). *Adaptation and Vulnerability to Climate Change: The Role of the Finance Sector*. CEO Briefing, UNEP Finance Initiative Climate Change Working Group. Retrieved from http://sefi.unep.org/fileadmin/media/sefi/docs/briefings/CEO_Nov06.pdf

UNEP. (2009). *Buildings and climate change—Summary for decision-makers*. Retrieved from http://www.unep.org/ sbci/pdfs/sbci-bccsummary.pd

UNEP. (2009). *Private financing of renewable energy – A guide for policymakers*. Retrieved July 4, 2017, from https://www.chathamhouse.org/sites/default/files/public/Research/Energy%2C%20Environment%20and%20Development/1209_financeguide.pdf

UNEP. (2011). *Global trends in renewable energy investment 2011: Analysis of trends and issues in the financing of renewable energy*. Retrieved June 4, 2017, from http://fs-unep-centre.org/sites/default/files/media/sefi2011finallowres.pdf

UNEP. (2012). *Global trends in renewable energy investment 2012*. Retrieved June 4, 2017, from http://fs-unep-centre.org/sites/default/files/publications/globaltrendsreport2012.pdf

UNEP. (2013). *Global trends in renewable energy investment 2013*. Retrieved June 4, 2017, from http://fs-unep-centre.org/system/files/globaltrendsreportlowres_0.pdf

UNEP. (2014). *Global trends in renewable energy investment 2014*. Retrieved June 4, 2017, from http://fs-unep-centre.org/system/files/globaltrendsreport2014.pdf

UNEP. (2015). *Global trends in renewable energy investment 2015*. Retrieved June 4, 2017, from http://fs-unep-centre.org/sites/default/files/publications/15028nefvisual9mediumres.pdf

UNEP. (2016). *Global trends in renewable energy investment 2016*. Retrieved March 4, 2018, from http://fs-unep-centre.org/sites/default/files/publications/globaltrendsinrenewableenergyinvestment2016lowres_0.pdf

UNEP. (2017). *Global trends in renewable energy investment 2017*. Retrieved March 4, 2017, from http://fs-unep-centre.org/sites/default/files/publications/globaltrendsinrenewableenergyinvestment2017.pdf

UNEP. (2018). *Global trends in renewable energy investment 2018*. Retrieved May 5, 2018, from http://fs-unep-centre.org/sites/default/files/publications/gtr2018v2.pdf

UNFCCC. (2010). Retrieved from http://unfccc.int/kyoto_protocol/mechanisms/emissions_trading/items/2731.php

UNFCCC. (2017). Retrieved from http://cdm.unfccc.int/Statistics/Public/index.html/

United Nations Economic and Social Council. (2016). *Report of the Inter-Agency and Expert Group on Sustainable Development Goal Indicators*. Retrieved June 24, 2017, from https://unstats.un.org/unsd/statcom/47th-session/documents/2016-2-IAEG-SDGs-Rev1-E.pdf

United Nations Environment Programme. (1972). *Declaration of the United Nations Conference on the Human Environment*. New York: United Nations.

United Nations Global Compact / KPMG. (2016). *SDG Industry Matrix: Food, Beverage, Consumer Goods: New Sustainable Development Goals to make our world more prosperous; Inclusive, sustainable, resilient*. Author.

United Nations. (1948). *UN Universal Declaration of Human Rights*. New York: UN General Assembly.

United Nations. (2011). *Guiding Principles on Business and Human Rights: Implementing the United Nations 'Protest, Respect, Remedy' Framework*. New York: United Nations.

United Nations. (2015a). *Sustainable development goals: 17 goals to transform our world*. Retrieved July 9, 2016 from http://www.un.org/sustainabledevelopment/sustainable-development-goals/

United Nations. (2015b). *Transforming Our World: The 2030 Agenda for Sustainable Development*. Retrieved June 9. 2018, from https://sustainabledevelopment.un.org/content/documents/21252030%20Agenda%20for%20Sustainable%20Development%20web.pdf

United Nations. (2015c). *Guiding Principles Reporting Framework with Implementation Guidance*. Retrieved August 10, 2017, from https://www.ungpreporting.org/wp-content/uploads/UNGPReportingFramework_withguidance2017.pdf

United Nations. (2018). *Sustainable Development Goals: 17 goals to transform our world*. Retrieved July 9, 2018, from https://www.un.org/sustainabledevelopment/sustainable-development-goals/

USGBC. (2003). *Building Momentum—National Trends and Prospects for High Performance Green Buildings*. U.S. Green Building Council. Available online: http://www.org/Docs/

Van der Vliet, K., Reindorp, M. J., & Fransoo, J. C. (2015). The price of reverse factoring: Financing rates vs. payment delays. *European Journal of Operational Research*, *242*(3), 842–853. doi:10.1016/j.ejor.2014.10.052

van Wensen, K. V., Broer, W., Klein, J., & Knopf, J. (2011). *The state of play in sustainability reporting in the EU.* Study for the European Commission, by CREM BV and Adelphi Consultant.

Vanclay, F. (2003). International principles for social impact assessment. *Impact Assessment and Project Appraisal*, *21*(1), 5–11. doi:10.3152/147154603781766491

Vancouver Economic Development Commission (VEDC). (2009). *Green Buildings in Vancouver.* Available online: http://www.vancouvereconomic.com/userfiles/file/green-building-profile.pdf

Votaw, D. (1973). Genius becomes rare. In D. Votaw & S. P. Sethi (Eds.), *The Corporate Dilemma: Traditional values versus contemporary problems* (pp. 11–45). Englewood Cliffs, NJ: Prentice Hall.

Walker, P. H., Seuring, P. S., Sarkis, P. J., & Klassen, P. R. (2014). Sustainable operations management: Recent trends and future directions. *International Journal of Operations & Production Management*, *34*(5), IJOPM-12-2013-0557. doi:10.1108/IJOPM-12-2013-0557

Wallart, N. (1999). *The Political Economy of Environmental Taxes. In New Horizons in Environmental Economics*. Cheltenham, UK: Edward Elgar.

Walters, M. (1991). Ecological Unity and Political Fragmentation: The Implications of the Brundlant Report for the Canadian Constitutional Order. *Alberta Law Review*, *29*(2), 420–449.

Wang, H. H., & Liu, N. (2016). Exploration on the long-term sustainable development mechanism of green finance in China. *Taipei Economic Inquiry*, (4), 99-105.

Wang. (2013). Risk challenge of internet banking. *China Finance, 24*, 54-55.

Wang, B. W. (2016). *Crowdfunding and Marketplace Lending - Online Capital Marketplaces as New Asset Classes to Access Funding*. The FinTech Book.

Wang, C., Lu, Y., Huang, C., & Lee, J. (2013). R&D, productivity, and market value: An empirical study from high-technology firms. *Omega*, *41*(1), 143–155. doi:10.1016/j.omega.2011.12.011

Wang, T., Li, X., Liao, P.-C., & Fang, D. (2016). Building energy efficiency for public hospitals and healthcare facilities in China: Barriers and drivers. *Energy*, *103*, 588–597. doi:10.1016/j.energy.2016.03.039

Wang, Y., & Zhi, Q. (2016). The role of green finance in environmental protection: Two aspects of market mechanism and policies. *Proceedings of Applied Energy Symposium and Forum: Low-Carbon Cities and Urban Energy Systems (CUE)*, 104, 311-316. 10.1016/j.egypro.2016.12.053

Waonews. (2018). *Davos Liu Qiangdong dialogue: the orientation of financial support of science and technology of Internet antitrust*. Retrieved January 24, 2018, from https://www.waonews.com/

Wartick, S. L., & Cochran, P. L. (1985). The evolution of the corporate social performance model. *Academy of Management Review*, *10*(4), 758–769. doi:10.5465/amr.1985.4279099

White, H. D., & McCain, K. W. (1998). Visualizing a discipline: An author co-citation analysis of information science 1972–1995. *Journal of the American Society for Information Science*, *49*(4), 327–356.

Wilhelm, M. M., Blome, C., Bhakoo, V., & Paulraj, A. (2016). Sustainability in multi-tier supply chains: Understanding the double agency role of the first-tier supplier. *Journal of Operations Management*, *41*, 42–60. doi:10.1016/j.jom.2015.11.001

Wilner, B. S. (2000). The exploitation of relationships in financial distress: The case of trade credit. *The Journal of Finance*, *55*(1), 153–178. doi:10.1111/0022-1082.00203

World Bank (1999).

World Business Council for Sustainable Development. (2015). *Towards a Social Capital Protocol: A Call for Collaboration: Measuring social impacts and dependencies for better business*. Geneva: WBCSD.

World Business Council for Sustainable Development. (2016). *Delivering on the Sustainable Development Goals: The inclusive business approach*. Geneva: WBCSD.

World Business Council for Sustainable Development. (2017a). *Social Capital Protocol: Making companies that truly value people more successful*. Geneva: WBCSD.

World Business Council for Sustainable Development. (2017b). *Forest Products Sector Guide to the Social Capital Protocol: Measuring Social Impact Along the Forest Products Value Chain. Geneva*: WBCSD.

World Business Council for Sustainable Development. (2017c). *Social and Human Capital Protocol*. Retrieved April 14, 2017, from http://www.wbcsd.org/Clusters/Social-Impact/Social-Capital-Protocol

World Business Council for Sustainable Development. (2017d). *Social Capital Protocol*. Retrieved April 14, 2017, from http://www.wbcsd.org/Clusters/Social-Impact/Social-Capital-Protocol/Resources/Social-Capital-Protocol

World, G. B. C. (2013). *The business case for green building—A review of the costs and benefits for developers, investors and occupants*. Retrieved from http://www.worldgbc.org/files/1513/6608/0674/ Business_Case_For_Green_Building_Report_WEB_2013-04-11.pdf

World, G. B. C. (2014). *Health, wellbeing and productivity in offices—The next chapter for green building*. Retrieved from http://www.worldgbc.org/ files/6314/1152/0821/WorldGBC__Health_Wellbeing__productivity_Full_Report.pdf

Wu, Han, & Han. (n.d.). Internet finance rectification. *Caixin Weekly*, 30-39.

Wu, F., & Chen, X. (2017). Legal Protection of Personal Information in Internet Credit: Taking Sesame Credit as an Example. *Internet Finance*, *9*, 11–16.

Wu, P., Xia, B., & Zhao, X. (2014). The importance of use and end-of-life phases to the life cycle greenhouse gas (GHG) emissions of concrete—A review. *Renewable & Sustainable Energy Reviews*, *37*, 360–369. doi:10.1016/j.rser.2014.04.070

Wuttke, D. A., Blome, C., Foerstl, K., & Henke, M. (2013). Managing the innovation adoption of supply chain finance—Empirical evidence from six European case studies. *Journal of Business Logistics*, *34*(2), 148–166. doi:10.1111/jbl.12016

Wuttke, D. A., Blome, C., & Henke, M. (2013). Focusing the financial flow of supply chains: An empirical investigation of financial supply chain management. *International Journal of Production Economics*, *145*(2), 773–789. doi:10.1016/j.ijpe.2013.05.031

Wu, X. (2015). The Internet Financial Growth Logic. *Finance & Economics*, *02*, 5–15.

Xian, Z., Jiang, Y., & Ying, Y. (2017). Overview of blockchain privacy techniques. *Journal of Information Security Research*, *11*, 981–989.

Xiao, S., & Zhao, S. (2012). Financial development, government ownership of banks and firm innovation. *Journal of International Money and Finance*, *31*(4), 880–906. doi:10.1016/j.jimonfin.2012.01.006

Xinhua News Agency. (2017). *The People's Bank of China: The basic database of financial credit information has collected the information of 926 million natural persons*. Retrieved August 13, 2018, from http://news.xinhuanet.com/fortune/2017-06/20/c_1121179605.htm

Xu, X., & Birge, J. R. (2004). *Joint production and financing decisions: Modeling and analysis*. Northwestern University.

Xu, J., Hsu, V. N., & Niu, B. (2018). The impacts of markets and tax on a multinational firm's procurement strategy in China. *Production and Operations Management*, *27*(2), 251–264. doi:10.1111/poms.12798

Xu, X., & Birge, J. R. (2004). *Joint production and financing decisions: Modeling and analysis*. Ssrn Electronic Journal.

Xu, X., Chen, X., Jia, F., Brown, S., Gong, Y., & Xu, Y. (2018). Supply chain finance: A systematic literature review and bibliometric analysis. *International Journal of Production Economics*, *204*, 160–173. doi:10.1016/j.ijpe.2018.08.003

Yalçın, A. Z. (2010). Sürdürülebilir Kalkınma İçin Düşük Karbon Ekonomisinin Önemi ve Türkiye İçin Bir Değerlendirme. *Balıkesir Üniversitesi Sosyal Bilimler Enstitüsü Dergisi*, *13*, 24.

Yancheng Rural Financial Association Research Group. (2016). Research on the development path of green finance in commercial banks. *Modern Finance*, (6), 46-48.

Yang, S. A., & Birge, J. R. (2009). *How inventory is (should be) financed: Trade credit in supply chains with demand uncertainty and costs of financial distress*. London Business School.

Yang, C. H., & Chen, Y. H. (2012). R&D, productivity, and exports: Plant-level evidence from Indonesia. *Economic Modelling*, *29*(2), 208–216. doi:10.1016/j.econmod.2011.09.006

Yang, F., Shao, C. F., & Chu, M. T. (2015). Analysis of opportunities, challenges and countermeasures for the development of green finance in China. *Ecological Economics*, *31*(11), 85–87.

Yang, K. P., Chiao, Y. C., & Kuo, C. C. (2010). The Relationship Between R&D Investment and Firm Profitability Under a Three-Stage Sigmoid Curve Model: Evidence From an Emerging Economy. *IEEE Transactions on Engineering Management*, *57*(1), 103–117. doi:10.1109/TEM.2009.2023452

Yang, S. A., Birge, J. R., & Parker, R. P. (2015). The Supply Chain Effects of Bankruptcy. *Management Science*, *61*(10), 2320–2338. doi:10.1287/mnsc.2014.2079

Yao, J. (2017). Legal Basis and Norm Reconstruction of De-identification of Personal Information. *Law Review*, *3*, 120–130.

Yao, Y., & Dresner, M. (2008). The inventory value of information sharing, continuous replenishment, and vendor-managed inventory. *Transportation Research Part E, Logistics and Transportation Review*, *44*(3), 361–378. doi:10.1016/j.tre.2006.12.001

Ye, W. (2015). Operational Models and Regulatory Countermeasures of Big Data Credit Information Agencies—Taking Sesame Credit as an Example. *Internet Finance*, *7*, 60–63.

Yi, C. P., Chiang, C., & Peng, Y. (2014). Development status and optimization path of green finance-A case study in Hubei. *Journal of Huazhong Agricultural University*, (4), 112-117.

Yong, W., & Wang, P. (2016). Privacy risks and countermeasures in big data credit investigation. *Studies in Dialectics of Nature*, *7*, 118–122.

Yoon, S. W., & Lee, D. K. (2003). The development of the evaluation model of climate changes and air pollution for sustainability of cities in Korea. *Landscape and Urban Planning*, *63*(3), 145–160. doi:10.1016/S0169-2046(02)00186-X

Yu, C. W. F., & Kim, J. T. (2010). Buildingpathology,investigationofsickbuildings—VOC emissions. *Indoor and Built Environment*, *19*(1), 30–39. doi:10.1177/1420326X09358799

Yudelson, J. (2008). *The Green Building Revolution*. Washington, DC: Island Press.

Yudelson, J. (2009). *Cost of green buildings, Green Building through Integrated Design. McGraw-Hill Professional.*

Yudelson, J. (2010). *Greening Existing Buildings*. McGraw Hill Companies Inc.

Yue & Hao. (2015). Internet finance, technology spillover and total factor productivity of commercial banks. *Financial Research*, *3*, 160-175.

Yüksek, M. (2010). *Sürdürülebilir Kalkınma ve Türkiye'de Çevre Politikaları. Gaziantep Üniversitesi Sosyal Bilimler Enstitüsü*. Yayımlanmamış Yüksek Lisans Tezi.

Yu, L., & Zheng, C. (2017). Research on Deep Web crawler based on Scrapy. *Design Research and Application, 7*, 112.

Yun, Z., Yu, X., & Nan, Z. (2016). A preliminary study on the reliability of social data in personal credit investigation. *Shanghai Finance, 3*, 50–54.

Zerbe, R. O. (1980). The Problem of Social Cost in Retrospect. *Research in Law and Economics, 2*, 83–102.

Zhang & Wu. (2015). Development, risk and Development Forum - internet financial review. *Economic Research, 11*, 183-186.

Zhang, C. (2017). Legal regulation on data anonymization processing. *Journal of Chongqing University of Posts and Telecommunications, 6*, 52–58.

Zhang, D., Wang, J., Lin, Y., Si, Y., Huang, C., Yang, J., ... Li, W. (2017). Present situation and future prospect of renewable energy in China. *Renewable & Sustainable Energy Reviews, 76*, 865–871. doi:10.1016/j.rser.2017.03.023

Zhang, M., Ma, L. J., Su, J., & Zhang, W. (2014). Do Suppliers Applaud Corporate Social Performance? *Journal of Business Ethics, 121*(4), 543–557. doi:10.100710551-013-1735-x

Zhang, S., & He, Y. (2013). Analysis on the development and policy of solar PV power in China. *Renewable & Sustainable Energy Reviews, 21*, 393–401. doi:10.1016/j.rser.2013.01.002

Zhang, Z., & Liu, Y. (2017). Application and Prospect of Blockchain Technology in Credit Investigation Industry. *Credit Investigation, 7*, 47–49.

Zhao. (2017). Discussion on the Legal Supervision of Internet Finance. *Chinese Business Theory, 1*, 44-45.

Zhao, X., Hwang, B. G., & Lee, H. N. (2016). Identifying critical leadership styles of project managers for green building projects. *International Journal of Construction Management, 16*(2), 150–160. doi:10.1080/15623599.2015.1130602

Zheng, X. (2014). Legal Analysis of Internet Finance. *Journal of Xihua University, 6*, 68–75.

Zhou, R. (2017). Research on the legal regulation of blockchain technology. *Journal of Beijing University of Posts and Telecommunications, 3*, 39–43.

Zhu, Q., & Zhang, Q. (2015). Evaluating practices and drivers of corporate social responsibility: The Chinese context. *Journal of Cleaner Production, 100*, 315–324. doi:10.1016/j.jclepro.2015.03.053

Zorlu Energy. (2017). *Enerjimiz gelecek için, Zorlu Enerji Elektrik Üretim Anonim Şirketi 01 Ocak-30 Eylül 2017 Dönemi Faaliyet Raporu*. Retrieved May 5, 2018, from http://console22.zorluenerjigrubu.com/Upload/Document/9.11.2017-ZORENFR0917_YK_Faaliyet_Raporu.pdf

Zuo, J., & Zhao, Z. (2014). Green building research–current status and future agenda: A review. *Renewable and Sustainable Energy Reviews, 30*, 271-281.

About the Contributors

Sang-Bing Tsai is currently the Professor and the Lecture Professor at University of Electronic Science and Technology of China Zhongshan Institute & Civil Aviation University of China. He is both Technology Management and Business Management PhD. He has published many research articles in SCI / SSCI journals, including International Journal of Production Research, International Journal of Web Services Research, Advances in Mechanical Engineering, IEEE Transactions on Systems Man Cybernetics-Systems, Plos One, Environment and Planning B-Planning & Design, Sustainability, Renewable & Sustainable Energy Reviews, etc. His recent research interests in Computer Science, Information Management, Big Data, Sustainability, Green Operation and Applied Mathematics. He has well over 100 published peer-reviewed journal articles. Dr. Tsai is will be the Co-Editor-in-Chief for the Journal of Organizational and End User Computing. He is currently the Associate Editor for Journal of Global Information Management, and Associate Editor for International Journal of R&D Innovation Strategy, and Associate Editor for IEEE ACCESS, as well as serving on the editorial boards of 8 other journals.

* * *

Clinton Aigbavboa is a Professor of Sustainable Human Settlement, and Construction Management in the Faculty of Engineering and the Built Environment, University of Johannesburg, South Africa; with a multidisciplinary research focus on the built environment. Before entering academia, he was involved as quantity surveyor on several infrastructural projects, both in Nigeria and South Africa. He holds a PhD in Engineering Management and has published over 500 research papers in his areas of interest. He has extensive knowledge in practice, research, training and teaching. His research interest are situated in the fields of sustainable human development, with the focus on: sustainable housing regeneration (urban renewal and informal housing), Life Cycle Assessment in the Construction Industry, remanufacturing, leadership in low-income housing, sustainable construction thinking, biomimicry, digitalisation of the construction industry, infrastructure development, construction industry development, construction and engineering management, construction education, construction industry development and research methodological thinking and paradigm, post-occupancy evaluation and green job creation. He is also an author of five research books that were published with Springer Nature and CRC Press. He is currently the editor of the Journal of Construction Project Management and Innovation (accredited by the South Africa Department of Higher Education and Training) and has received national and international recognition in his field of research.

Bei Chen is a researcher at the School of Business, Dalian University of Technology. His research direction is innovation and entrepreneurship, and involves research related to the entrepreneurial ecosystem.

Cheng Chen is currently a Master Degree Candidate at National Taiwan University School of Management. She holds a Master of Laws from Renmin University of China School of Law, China.

Sonal Choudhary is a Lecturer in Sustainable Management at Sheffield University Management School (SUMS). She is also a member of Logistics and Supply Chain Management (LSCM) Research Centre and Centre for Environment Energy and Sustainability (CEES). Prior to joining SUMS, Sonal worked as a Marie Curie Research Fellow in the field of environmental sustainability (Project Sunshine and N-SINK) at the University of Sheffield. She has also worked on a number of other projects funded by DEFRA, European Commission (FP-7), Ministry of Environment and Forest, India, and IPCC. She has published about 25 papers in leading international journals, peer-reviewed conferences and national newspapers. She has also received two best paper awards in international conferences. She acts as a reviewer to many international journals in the area of sustainability, climate change, ecology, environmental economics, operations and supply chain management. She has chaired various international environmental and sustainability conferences.

Min Du is a PhD and teach in the Department of Economic Management in Yingkou Insititute of Technology. She has researched in the field of entrepreneurship and strategy management for 8 years. As a research author, she has published many academic papers. She is also the reviewers of several international journals.

Erdal Eroğlu is an Assistant Professor in the Department of Public Finance in the Faculty of Economics and Administrative Sciences of the Çanakkale Onsekiz Mart University, Turkey. He received his PhD in Public Budgeting and Fiscal Planning from the Institute of Social Sciences, Uludağ University in 2016. His research interests concern public budgeting, the political economy of budget, taxation, public expenditures, public procurement and fiscal transparency.

Meryem Filiz Baştürk is an Associate Professor, PhD and received a graduate degree at Uludag University, from the Department of Economics in 2003. She has worked in the same department since 2005 as a scholar. Filiz Baştürk earned a PhD. within "A Theoretical and Empirical Study on the Efficiency of Monetary Transmission Mechanism" in Turkey in 2012. Her research areas are monetary theory, financial markets, and renewable energy.

Yang Gao is the Professor in School of Bussiness at the Dalian University of Technology in China. He has researched in the field of strategy management and entrepreneurship for 8 years. He has presided over multiple projects at the national level of China. As a research author, he has published many academic papers. He is also the reviewers of several international journals.

Jiye Hu is a professor at the Business School of China University of Political Science and Law. He has published many research articles in SSCI/CSSCI journals. His recent research interests in Legal Economics, Financial Law, and Legal Game Analysis. He had much academic experience and industry experience. He is one of the core members of the China Pension Finance 50 Forum and has published many articles on pension finance, making a significant contribution to this field of research.

Filiz Konuk is in the department of business administration, Sakarya University. Her research interests are financial management, time series, and capital market. She has some articles published in *Journal of Applied Economic Sciences*, *Theoretical and Applied Economics*, *International Journal of Tourism and Hospitality Management*, and *Business and Economics Research Journal*.

Cheng-Yong Liu is currently an associate professor at Beijing Institute of Technology, Zhuhai. He received his Ph.D. from Tsinghua University, China. He was an reward-gainer of the Excellent Ph.D. Dissertation of Tsinghua University. He has published more than 10 journal papers and one book. His research interests include Fintech, Big Data-Based Credit Reference and artificial intelligence.

Zihao Mu's focus is on the combination of business phenomenon and literature, the present research direction is "Cross border distribution channel structure design and coordination under tax planning", try to innovate based on extant literature.

Elizabeth Motunrayo Ojo-Fafore is a Postdoctoral research fellow at the Department of Construction Management and Quantity Surveying, University of Johannesburg, South Africa. She holds a phd in Engineering Management, University of Johannesburg. She works in a private construction company in Nigeria for several years before she proceeds for her Ph.D. Her research areas are in Supply chain management, Sustainability, and Engineering management. She has authored and co-authored articles in peer-reviewed conference proceedings and reputable journal. She has served as a reviewer for peer-reviewed conferences and journals.

Pretty Remaru is currently a postgraduate student at the Department of Construction management and Quantity surveying, Univerity of Johannesburg, South Africa.

Wellington Thwala, Ph.D., is a Professor of Construction Project Management and Masters Programme Coordinator at the Department of Construction Management and Quantity Surveying, University of Johannesburg. Professor Thwala has varied research interests, which include project management, construction health and safety, engineering design management, economic and social infrastructure delivery, operations and production management and business competitive intelligence.

Yu Wang is the Doctor in School of Business at the Dalian University of Technology in China. He has researched in the field of Sustainable Finance for many years. He has presided over multiple projects at the national level of China. As a research author, he has published many academic papers.

John P. Wilson is a researcher and consultant with forty years' experience in education and training including teaching from nursery education to PhD supervision. He also has extensive experience working with a wide variety of international organisations including: armed forces; aviation; civil service; banking; engineering; health care; international development, justice; manufacturing; media; nuclear power generation; national pensions and investment; oil; telecommunications; and transportation.

Wen Yang is a Distinguished Research Fellow and Lecturer at College of Economics of Shenzhen University. He achieved PhD at Peking University in 2013. His paper are published at more than 10 journals including some of China's top journals such as the Economic Research Journal and China Economic Quarterly. He is also the anonymous reviewer of the two journals. His research interests include security investment, RMB internationalization, internet finance and income distribution.

Chi Chien Zhu is a Professor at Business and Law School of Foshan University. He has authored over 10 international journals including but not limited to Academy of internet finance and environment science, His papers are published at Management Science in China, Sustainability and International Journal of Environmental Research and Public Health, Review of Development Economics and Emerging Markets Finance and Trade. He has served on the editorial review board for many international journals. His research interests include internet finance and fintech regulation, law and finance, and education reform of finance in China. Published at Management Science in China, Sustainability and International Journal of Environmental Research and Public Health, Review of Development Economics and Emerging Markets Finance and Trade. He has served on the editorial review board for many international journals. His research interests include internet finance and fintech regulation, law and finance, and education reform of finance in China. He has authored over 10 international journals including but not limited to Academy of internet finance and environment science, His papers are published at Management Science in China, Sustainability and International Journal of Environmental Research and Public Health, Review of Development Economics and Emerging Markets Finance and Trade. He has served on the editorial review board for many international journals. His research interests include internet finance and fintech regulation, law and finance, and education reform of finance in China.

Index

A

Account Receivables Financing 13, 29
Advance Payment Financing 11, 15-17, 19-20, 29

B

Banking Regulatory Commission 68-70, 72
Benefit 9, 12, 113, 122, 221, 246, 263, 269, 272-274, 285, 291, 312, 321, 330, 332
Bibliometrics 84-86, 100, 102
Big Data 22, 24, 39, 148-150, 152, 160, 165, 175, 178, 188, 193-197, 199-204, 207, 209-210, 213
Big Data Credit Investigation Agencies 194, 196-197, 199, 203-204, 213
Big Three 222, 231, 241
Biofuels 222
Biomass and waste-to-energy 223
Blockchain Technology 22, 193-194, 209-210
Bruntland Report 110, 146
Building 3, 63, 99, 111-112, 127, 183, 244-245, 247-252, 254-258, 260, 262-263, 269

C

Carbon Funding 334, 347
Carbon Market 334-335, 347
Climate Change 64, 68, 74, 99, 112, 219, 221, 234-235, 257, 263, 270-271, 279-283, 296, 321-323, 325-327, 329, 332, 334-335, 342-343
Co-citation Analysis 84, 87, 91-92, 96, 102
Construction 4, 22, 24, 64, 67, 69, 77-80, 82, 103, 169, 178, 188, 190, 202, 210, 244-248, 251-252, 255, 257, 260-263, 269, 282, 306, 308, 316, 326, 336
Conventional Building 244-245, 255, 257, 260, 263, 269
Core Enterprises 1-2, 7, 10, 20-21, 23-24, 29, 31-33, 61
Corporate Social Responsibility 68, 99, 113-114, 122, 131, 146
Cost 2, 7-8, 12, 16, 18, 21, 23, 33, 38, 43, 73, 81, 94, 125, 127, 129, 134, 166, 182, 188, 190, 204, 226, 244-245, 248, 251, 254-258, 260-263, 269, 271, 273-276, 287, 296, 321, 325-327, 330-332, 334, 337, 339-340, 342
Co-word Analysis 84, 87, 99, 102
Credit Evaluation 150, 196-197, 199
Credit Information 70, 159, 187-188, 194-197, 201, 209, 213

D

Developing Countries 31, 66, 76, 219-225, 227-228, 232, 236, 241, 280, 325-330
Development Banks 85, 220, 227-228, 232, 235, 242
development tendency 148, 153

E

E-Commerce 5, 31, 33, 35, 39-41, 60, 149, 152, 158, 183
Empirical Study 84-85

Environment 10, 20, 62-67, 69, 71, 75-76, 78-79, 85, 99, 110-111, 120, 122, 125, 132, 146, 148, 154, 166, 170, 174, 197, 219, 222, 246, 248, 252, 262-263, 269, 271, 274-276, 279-285, 287-291, 300, 321, 324, 327-329, 342
environmental financing 63
Environmental Problems 64-65, 67, 71, 219, 229, 236, 271, 274-275, 279-281, 289-290, 296
Environmental Sanitation Tax 285, 289, 291, 296
Externalities 71, 112, 119, 162, 270-271, 273-274, 289, 296

F

Factoring 3, 10-13, 29
financial competition 66, 297-299, 302-303, 308-310, 312, 315
financial efficiency 297-299, 301-303, 308-310, 312, 315-316
Financial Mechanism 75

G

Geothermal Energy 232, 241-242
Global Warming 219, 245, 270-271, 281, 296, 322-327, 342, 347
Green Bonds 74, 76-77, 227-228, 232-233, 242
Green Building 99, 244-252, 254-258, 262-263, 269
green credit 63, 65, 67-69, 71-73, 76-77, 80, 85-86
Green Credit Guideline 68, 72
Green Economy 68, 76-77, 285, 291
Green Finance 34, 62-82, 84-97, 99-100, 102, 148, 166, 244-246, 252, 269, 297
Green financing 69, 86, 244, 246
Green Taxation 270-272, 274, 277, 279, 281, 283, 285, 289-290, 296
Greenhouse 74, 235, 245-246, 250, 280-281, 322-325, 328-335, 342, 347
Greenhouse Gas 74, 235, 245-246, 250, 280-281, 322, 328-335, 342, 347

H

heterogeneity 22, 298-299, 306-307, 309, 314

I

Identification of the Information Subject 213
Information Isolated Island 209, 213
Information Security 181, 193, 209
Internet finance 147-149, 151-154, 156, 158-161, 163-165, 169-170, 173-175, 177-183, 185, 188-190, 193-194
Inventory Financing 11, 15, 17-19, 29

M

MidSEFF (Turkish Mid-Size Sustainable Energy Financing Facility) 242
Millennium Development Goals 108, 111, 128, 134, 146
Minimum Adequacy Principle 213
Motor Vehicle Tax 276, 283-285, 287-289, 296

N

National Energy Efficiency Action Plan (NEEAP 2017-2023) 229, 242
National Renewable Energy Action Plan for Turkey (NREAP) 242
Natural Capital Protocol 107, 120, 146
Negative Externalities 162, 270-271, 273, 296
Newsvendor Retailer 37-38, 60

O

Occupants 246, 249, 252, 257, 263, 269
Online Retailer 33, 37, 39, 53-55, 57, 60

P

Personal Information 194, 196-197, 201-204, 209-210, 213-214

Pull Supply Chain 34, 38, 41-42, 47-48, 55-56, 61
Push Supply Chain 42, 47-48, 56, 61

R

regulation and law 173
Renewable Energy 74, 99, 220-236, 241-242, 252, 271, 281-282, 336
Renewable Energy Financial Instruments 242

S

Small and Medium-Sized Enterprise 32, 54, 61
Social Capital 74-76, 80, 107, 109-110, 112-113, 115, 117-124, 126-127, 130-135, 146, 316
Social Capital Accounting 107, 120, 133, 146
Social Capital Protocol 107, 109-110, 113, 115, 117-121, 126, 130, 133-134, 146
Social Impact Assessment 116-117, 119, 146
social responsibilities 72, 113, 115
Solar Energy 222-224, 234, 242
Special Consumption Tax 283-284, 287, 289, 296
Supply Chain 1-11, 14-15, 17, 20-24, 29-35, 37-42, 47-48, 53-57, 60-61, 107, 109, 113, 115-116, 119, 121, 123-128, 130, 132, 134, 146
Supply Chain Finance 1, 4-5, 20, 29-36, 38-41, 53-57, 61
Supply Chain Management 5, 7-8, 21-22, 55, 109
Sustainability 34, 54, 56, 65, 67, 73-74, 82, 99, 107-113, 115-119, 122, 124-135, 219, 232-233, 255, 274, 280-281, 297
Sustainable Development 62-67, 69, 71, 73, 76, 78, 82, 85, 99, 107-110, 112, 117, 129, 134, 146, 236, 275, 279, 281-283, 290-291, 296, 300
Sustainable Development Goals 107-108, 112, 134, 146
Sustainable Growth 33, 35, 64, 131, 219, 221, 236, 270-272, 274, 277-281, 285, 291, 296

T

The Carbon market 335
threshold panel 309, 314
Trade Credit 9, 13, 29, 36
Traditional Credit Investigation Agencies 194, 196, 214
TurSEFF (Turkey Sustainable Energy Financing Facility) 242

U

United Nations 66, 93, 107-108, 110, 112, 118, 124, 128-129, 134, 146, 246, 327

W

Weather 321, 326, 336-340, 342-343, 347
Weather Derivations 321, 336-337
Weather Options 338-339, 347
Weather Swamp 347
Wind Energy 222-224, 234, 242
World Bank 66, 78, 93-94, 227, 232, 282

www.ingramcontent.com/pod-product-compliance
Lightning Source LLC
LaVergne TN
LVHW080342011026
849161LV00009B/2166